THE FAUST LEGEN

What do men and women desire? For what will they barter their immortal souls? These two questions have haunted Western society, and these persistent queries find their fullest embodiment in the Faust legend. This memorable story, told and retold in novels, prose fiction, and drama, has also profoundly influenced music, art, and cinema. Sara Munson Deats explores its impact, tracing the development of the Faust topos from the seminal works of Marlowe and Goethe to the large number of dramatic and cinematic adaptations which have fascinated audiences and readers throughout the centuries. Her study traces the durability of this legend and its pervasive influence on the literature of the Western world, in which it has been adapted across time, languages, and nations to reflect the concerns of a given era or place. This is the first comparative analysis of the Faust legend in drama and film.

SARA MUNSON DEATS is a Distinguished University Professor Emerita at the University of South Florida. Former President of the Marlowe Society of America, she has published over fifty essays on early modern drama. Her twelve published books include three collections of essays on Christopher Marlowe, co-edited with Robert Logan; a collection of essays on Marlowe's *Doctor Faustus*; and *Sex, Gender, and Desire in the Plays of Christopher Marlowe* (1997), for which she received the Roma Gill Award.

THE FAUST LEGEND

*From Marlowe and Goethe To Contemporary
Drama and Film*

SARA MUNSON DEATS

University of South Florida

CAMBRIDGE
UNIVERSITY PRESS

University Printing House, Cambridge CB2 8BS, United Kingdom

One Liberty Plaza, 20th Floor, New York, NY 10006, USA

477 Williamstown Road, Port Melbourne, VIC 3207, Australia

314–321, 3rd Floor, Plot 3, Splendor Forum, Jasola District Centre,
New Delhi – 110025, India

79 Anson Road, #06–04/06, Singapore 079906

Cambridge University Press is part of the University of Cambridge.

It furthers the University's mission by disseminating knowledge in the pursuit of
education, learning, and research at the highest international levels of excellence.

www.cambridge.org
Information on this title: www.cambridge.org/9781108475853
DOI: 10.1017/9781108614290

First published 2019

Printed and bound in Great Britain by Clays Ltd, Elcograf S.p.A.

A catalogue record for this publication is available from the British Library.

Library of Congress Cataloging-in-Publication Data
NAMES: Deats, Sara Munson, author.
TITLE: The Faust legend : from Marlowe and Goethe to contemporary drama
and film / Sara Munson Deats.
DESCRIPTION: Cambridge ; New York, NY : Cambridge University Press,
2019. | Includes bibliographical references and index.
IDENTIFIERS: LCCN 2019008518 | ISBN 9781108475853 (alk. paper)
SUBJECTS: LCSH: Faust (Legendary character) | European literature – History and criticism.
CLASSIFICATION: LCC PN57.F3 D37 2019 | DDC 809/.93351–dc23
LC record available at https://lccn.loc.gov/2019008518

ISBN 978-1-108-47585-3 Hardback

I gratefully dedicate this book to my mother, Eula Bea Munson, who taught me to overreach

"Ah, but a man's reach should exceed his grasp, Or what's a heaven for?"

Robert Browning
"Andrea del Sarto"

Contents

vii

Illustrations

Acknowledgements

This study is the result of my life-long fascination with the Faust legend. This interest, originally sparked in a graduate seminar offered by my mentor R. W. Dent of UCLA, developed into a dissertation comparing the *English Faustbook* to Christopher Marlowe's *Doctor Faustus*, and this fire continued to burn brightly throughout the years as I taught and wrote about Marlowe and participated actively in the Marlowe Society of America. In the early 1990s my colleague Flora Zbar invited me to give a plenary address comparing the treatment of the Faust legend in Marlowe and Goethe at an interdisciplinary conference at the University of South Florida. Discovering Goethe's *Faust* was a monumental event in my scholarly life; to paraphrase John Keats, I felt like a watcher of the skies when a new planet swims within her ken, and my interest in the Faust legend ignited anew. At that time, I conceived a plan someday to write a book analyzing the various treatments of the Faust legend in drama and film. Twenty-five years later I submitted my manuscript to Cambridge University Press.

Completing this study did not take a village, perhaps, but this book certainly benefited markedly from the support and assistance of many friends, colleagues, and institutions. First, I am grateful for all the aid I have received in locating not easily available information on the many plays, films, and productions discussed in this study. Special thanks must go to Nils Frischknecht and Martina Maria Sam for the insights they provided me personally on the premiere production of Goethe's complete *Faust* at the Goetheanum and also on subsequent productions of Goethe's complete play at the same venue. Also, my deepest appreciation goes to the library staff at the University of South Florida, which worked tirelessly to seek out information on the often obscure texts and criticism that I analyze in this volume.

In addition, I am deeply indebted to the friends and colleagues – David Bevington, Sheila Diecidue, Lagretta Lenker, Robert Logan, and Katherine

Wyly – who labored over my manuscript and offered many valuable insights and suggestions that have greatly improved the effectiveness of this study. I also owe thanks to Ann Basso who helped me locate and select the illustrations that I have used in this book. I would like also to express my gratitude to my two readers at Cambridge University Press, whose perceptive evaluations sent me back to my word processor for yet another revision.

Many thanks as well to my helpful and co-operative editors at Cambridge University Press – Jane Bowbrick, Kate Brett, and Eidith Burrett – who graciously answered my multitudinous questions and skillfully guided me through the circuitous route from acceptance to publication. In addition, I will forever be obligated to my super conscientious research assistant Robin Rogers, who formatted my notes, indefatigably proofread my manuscript, and prepared my Bibliography and Index.

And most of all, I wish to thank my husband, Gordon Deats, who throughout the long writing of this book offered nurture, critique, and frequently just the right word. His constant support for this and many other of my scholarly endeavors has energized and sustained me throughout my scholarly career.

Abbreviations

DF   Christopher Marlowe. *Doctor Faustus: The A- and B-Texts (1604, 1616)*, ed. David Bevington and Eric Rasmussen. Manchester University Press, 1993. (All quotations of the play are from the A-text unless otherwise stated.)

EFB   John Henry Jones (ed.). *The English Faust Book: A Critical Edition Based on the Text of 1592*. Cambridge University Press, 1994.

F-AH   Johann Wolfgang von Goethe. *Faust: A Tragedy*, trans. Walter Arndt, ed. Cyrus Hamlin. 2nd edn. New York: W. W. Norton, 2001 (1st edn. 1976).

FI-L   Johann Wolfgang von Goethe. *Faust. Part One*, trans. David Luke. Oxford University Press, 2008 (1st edn. 1987).

F2-L   *Faust. Part Two*, trans. David Luke. Oxford University Press, 1998 (1st edn. 1984).

F-P   Johann Wolfgang von Goethe, *Faust, Part I & II*, ed. and trans. Charles E. Passage. Indianapolis: Bobbs-Merrill, 1965.

GFB   *German Faustbook*

SFT   Philip Mason Palmer and Robert Pattison More. *The Sources of the Faust Tradition: From Simon Magus to Lessing*. New York: Octagon, 1966.

SOED   *The Shorter Oxford English Dictionary*, rev. and ed. C. T. Onions. Oxford: Clarendon Press, 1968.

Prologue

What do men and women most desire? For what would they be willing to barter their immortal souls? These two questions have haunted society for centuries, and these eternal queries find their fullest embodiment in the Faust legend.

The literature of the Western world has been dominated by a few pervasive myths that have obsessed human consciousness for hundreds of years. A number of these immediately rush to mind: the Cinderella fantasy (perhaps the formative myth of our Western civilization); the biblical story of David and Goliath; the folk tale of Jack the Giant Killer or St. George and the dragon; the narrative of King Arthur, the Round Table, and the Holy Grail. My study focuses on another of the seminal legends that define Western culture: the magical Faust story. This hardy legend found its roots in the marshy soil of medieval folklore, budded in the Renaissance, blossomed in nineteenth-century drama and opera, and flowered in twen-tieth- and twenty-first-century drama, opera, novel, and cinema.

This memorable story has been told and retold in novels, prose fiction, and drama by such distinguished prose writers as Washington Irving, Ivan Turgenev, Mikhail Bulgakov, and Thomas Mann, and such eminent play-wrights/writers as Christopher Marlowe, Gotthold Ephraim Lessing, Johann Wolfgang von Goethe, George Sand, W. B. Yeats, A. V. Lunacharski, Frank Wedekind, Michel de Ghelderode, Dorothy Sayers, Paul Valéry, Lawrence Durrell, Václav Havel, David Mamet, and David Davalos, as well as such lesser-known playwrights as Arthur Davidson Ficke.

Moreover, the Faust legend has had a profound influence on music, art, and cinema, as well as literature. This pervasive legend has inspired songs by Ludwig van Beethoven, Franz Schubert, and Modest Mussorgsky; orchestral and choral works by Robert Schumann, Richard Wagner, and Felix Mendelssohn; symphonies by Franz Liszt and Gustav Mahler; and operas by Hector Berlioz, Charles Gounod, Arrigo Boito, Ferruccio Busoni, Sergei Prokofiev, and Igor Stravinsky. Indeed the list of Faust's musical adapters reads like a "Who's Who" of the musical world. In addition, the legend has been vividly illustrated by painters, including Rembrandt van Rijn, Eugène Delacroix, Salvador Dalí, and Max Beckmann. Finally, this archetypical tale has provided the theme for numerous films, dating from the days of the silent screen until contemporary times.[1]

Since to discuss all of the incarnations of the Faust legend in Western literature would require several volumes rather than one, my study will, reluctantly, limit its exploration to the influence of the Faust narrative on drama and film – eschewing all musical compositions and prose adaptations – and, even here, limitations of space and time require a most selective treatment.

Of course, this legend has remained popular throughout the centuries primarily because it recounts a spellbinding story: a man, striving for transcendence of human limitations, pursues the forbidden secrets of the occult and sells his soul to the Devil in return for some desirable goal – power, knowledge, wealth, fame, or youth. I use the term "man" advisedly here since the Faust figure is traditionally male, and all of the Faust avatars treated in this study with the exception of Yeats's Countess Cathleen and Wedekind's Franziska are male.

However, despite the fascination of the Faust narrative, my study contends that the durability of this legend and its pervasive influence on the literature of the Western world also derives from its adaptability to the mores of many different epochs and countries. Indeed, I argue, the Faust legend has served throughout the years as a kind of Rorschach test, in which the narrative assumes different shapes depending on the perspective of the author who adapts it and the customs and values of the period in which it is written, with the meaning of the legend shifting to reflect the zeitgeist of a given era or place. Thus the Faust avatar's desideratum – the goal for which the hero sells his soul – often reflects the values of a specific society, even as the character of the Devil evolves to represent a particular culture's concept of evil.

Chapter 1: The Background of the Faust Legend

Assuming that one cannot fully appreciate the later permutations of this archetypical tale without some knowledge of the legend's history of origin, I begin my examination by delving into the fertile loam of medieval folklore to search for the roots of the Faust story. The Magus legend provides the deepest of these roots, since many of the stories later told about Faust appeared earlier in the accounts of charismatic conjurors such as Simon Magus, St. Cyprian, and Theophilus, all of whom have been cited as possible forerunners of Faust. The medieval biblical cycle plays, focusing on the theme of temptation and fall and featuring malicious Devils and presumptuous Antichrists, supply another important root. Finally, the medieval morality plays, with their Everyman figures, cunning Vice tempters, and *psychomachiae* between good and evil, furnish a significant radical source for this literary mandrake.

Having canvassed the literary influences on the Faust legend, this chapter undertakes a search for the historical Faust. Although the background of this itinerant sorcerer has been much debated, scholars agree that there existed a man called Johann Faustus, whose surname means "auspicious," perhaps a Latin cognomen granted the magician in recognition of his magical exploits.[2] In 1587, the numerous accounts of this widely traveled, rather shady miracle worker were compiled by an unknown author and published by a devout Protestant named Johann Spies as the *Historia von D. Johann Fausten,* popularly known as the *German Faustbook.* Unfortunately, there exists no contemporary English translation of the *German Faustbook;* however, sometime between 1587 and 1592 a mysterious figure, identified only as P. F. Gent (Gentleman), adapted this text into English, and this English version, popularly referred to as the *English Faustbook,* has been widely accepted by scholars as the source for Christopher Marlowe's great tragedy, *Doctor Faustus.* Because of its literary significance, I will base my discussion on this English version. Fortunately, however, John Henry Jones, editor of the version of the *English Faustbook* on which I base my analysis, has translated large portions of the German original into English, and, relying on this translation, I compare the *German* and *English Faustbooks,* delineating how each contributes its own vision to the Faust legend.

The *Faustbooks* introduce the basic formula that will pervade many of the subsequent dramatic versions of the legend: the two dominant figures, the protagonist Faust (or Faustus) and his demonic antagonist and tempter Mephostophiles,[3] the first time in folklore or scripture that this name had been associated with the Devil; the contract inscribed in blood, echoing the legend of Theophilus; the female seductress distracting Faustus from repentance and leading him to damnation; and the degeneration of the protagonist, although not all of Faust's later avatars suffer the damnation inflicted on the protagonists of both *Faustbooks.*

Chapter 2: Marlowe's *Doctor Faustus*

Both the *German* and the *English Faustbooks* represent a paradoxical blending of soaring aspiration and groveling lust, of grandiose dreams and ignoble desires, of rollicking humor and tragic despair. In the second chapter of this book, I demonstrate the influence of the *English Faustbook* on Marlowe's tragedy, showing how Marlowe retained the hybrid structure of his source (part tragedy, part jest book) and the mutilated form of its hero (part titan, part buffoon). If anything, Marlowe, an insatiable dramatic innovator, exacerbated the paradoxical quality of the original text, creating one of the most problematic plays and oxymoronic heroes in all of literature.

Few works of literature have occasioned such vehement debate as Marlowe's *Doctor Faustus*. Commentators adopting a heroic interpretation of the tragedy see the play as a celebration of Faustus, the humanist hero of Renaissance individualism, who barters his soul in return for all the things the Renaissance privileged: knowledge, beauty, power. Conversely, Christian apologists read the play as a religiously orthodox drama condemning Faustus as a damned sinner. After seeking to guide the reader through the labyrinth of critical controversy surrounding the tragedy, I conclude that the play validates both the Christian and humanist readings, depicting a hero whom we can simultaneously admire and censure, sympathize with and deplore. The presence of contradictory perspectives evoking markedly divergent responses to the multifaceted hero suggests that in *Doctor Faustus* Marlowe penned an interrogative drama that brilliantly argues on both sides of the question.

In this play, his most often read and most frequently performed drama, Marlowe also anticipates Shakespeare, not only by scripting one of the first interrogative dramas in English literature but also by creating the first fully developed, internalized tragic hero to tread the English stage. This chapter also demonstrates how Marlowe's play codifies the basic characteristics of the Faust narrative that will pervade many of the subsequent dramatic versions of the legend: the Devil as tempter, the blood-inscribed contract, the femme fatale luring Faust to his damnation, and the downward trajectory of the protagonist. Moreover, Marlowe's balancing of contradictory perspectives – especially the heroic and ironic interpretations of his hero – will influence Goethe's *Faust* and many of the subsequent dramatizations of the Faust legend.

Chapter 3: Goethe's *Faust*

The third chapter of the book begins by tracing the debasement of the Faust legend in the seventeenth and eighteenth centuries, when the Faust story continued to be dramatized not only in truncated revivals of

Marlowe's play but in folk dramas and puppet shows throughout England, Germany, and the rest of Europe. Increasingly, these plays stressed the comic shenanigans that had accreted around the Faust tradition, finally degenerating into degrading *commedia dell'arte* treatments of this once-tragic story, in which Marlowe's suffering overreacher declined into a pathetic Harlequin.

The remainder of the chapter discusses Johann Wolfgang von Goethe's recuperation of Faust in his monumental two-part drama, with Part I appearing in 1808 and Part II published in 1833 after Goethe's death. I base the majority of my analysis on the translation of Parts I and II by David Luke although I also make frequent reference to the alternative translations by Walter Arndt and Charles E. Passage. Goethe transforms Marlowe's ambiguous hero – part heroic overreacher, part folksy buffoon – and his great but equivocal play – part searing tragedy, part comic morality – into a magnificent drama that fits no category, a phantasmagoric epic with a biblical play frame, a fully tragic hero, and a surprise happy ending. Chapter 3 compares Goethe's master-piece to Marlowe's tragedy and demonstrates how each play mirrors the zeitgeist of its own historical period as well as the vision of its creator. Marlowe's play reflects a society torn between allegiances to traditional pieties and the emerging secular discourse. Over a hundred years later when Goethe wrote his version of this venerable legend, the emerging discourse had become the dominant one, and Goethe's vision of Faust celebrates this dominant discourse – secular, empirical, humanist, and individualist.

However, no matter how different the ethos animating these two versions of the Faust story, Goethe's drama continues the innovations introduced by Marlowe, creating one of the great interrogative dramas of all time. As with Marlowe's tragedy, Goethe offers two contrary readings of his hero and his quest, raising the following question. Is the play ultimately a celebration of its aspiring hero who before his death denies the use of magic, achieves his desideratum, dies triumphant and in a state of grace, and is ultimately redeemed? Or does Faust's striving, even at the denouement of the play, result only in failure and frustration, leaving a trail of broken bodies and shattered lives in its wake? After seeking to guide the reader through the mountain of scholarship on the drama, I conclude that, as with Marlowe's play, Goethe's masterpiece validates both the celebratory and ironic readings, balancing both interpretations with stunning equipoise as it convincingly argues on both sides of the question.

Goethe's *Faust* also redefines good and evil for the Enlightenment and Romantic periods. In the "Prologue in Heaven," God identifies virtue with activity and striving, evil with inactivity and inertia. After Goethe's great cosmic drama, ceaseless striving and indefatigable aspiration became forever associated with the Faustian spirit.

Chapter 4: Post-Goethe Dramatic Versions of the Faust Legend

The two centuries following Goethe's publication of the two parts of *Faust* witnessed a proliferation of dramas (some intended for the stage, some not) based on the Faust legend. As I began this project, I was surprised at the number of plays inspired by this ubiquitous legend, representing the United States, Britain, and a cross-section of European countries. Indeed, it appears that sometime in their lives many established writers have had a yen to write a Faust play. This seems true whether the author is a playwright like Frank Wedekind, Michel de Ghelderode, David Mamet, or David Davalos, or a novelist like George Sand or Lawrence Durrell, or a mystery-story writer like Dorothy Sayers, or a poet like W. B. Yeats, Arthur Davison Ficke, or Paul Valéry, or a political polemist like A. V. Lunacharski or Václav Havel. I thus realized that I must set strict guidelines in my selection of plays lest I drown in a plethora of theatrical scripts.

First, this chapter is devoted to adaptations of the Faust story, not to dramatizations of the two seminal Faust plays, Marlowe's *Doctor Faustus* and Goethe's *Faust*. In defining "adaptations" I follow Linda Hutcheon who considers adaptations to be a subgenre of "intertextuality"; according to Hutcheon, "we experience adaptation (as adaptations) as palimpsests through our memories of other works that resonate through reception with variation."[4] Hutcheon further praises the "adaptive facility" as "the ability to repeat without copying, to embed difference in similarity, to be at once both self and Other."[5] In my opinion, all of the works analyzed in this chapter serve as palimpsests to previous versions of the Faust legend, and many of these adaptations also display the fluidity between self and Other celebrated by Hutcheon. Julie Sanders, in her indispensable guide *Adaptation and Appropriation*, develops this definition to observe that "we associate adaptation with reinterpretations of established, canonical texts in new generic contexts or perhaps with relocations of the source text's cultural or temporal setting." Moreover, "an adaptation most often signals a relationship with an informing source text either through its title or more embedded references."[6]

In discussing the various post-Goethe dramas channeling the Faust legend, I have also tried to discriminate between "adaptations" and "appropriations." Within Shakespeare studies there exists a rich matrix of criticism devoted to defining these terms and discriminating between adaptation and appropriation, with some critics associating appropriation with a kind of "seizing" or "thievery," usually for political motives.[7] However, for my purposes, I will adopt the distinction offered by Sanders, who explains that "appropriation frequently effects a more decisive journey away from the informing text into a wholly new cultural product and domain," displaying a greater distance from the so-called source than adaptation, along with a possible shift in media.[8] Following this criterion, I would identify Yeats's significant contribution, *The Countess Cathleen*, and Wedekind's provocative play, *Franziska*, as appropriations rather than adaptations, since neither of these dramas, although providing a palimpsest for the most salient features of the Faust legend, contains any explicit reference to the Faust narrative. Similarly, Sand's *A Woman's Version of the Faust Legend: The Seven Strings of the Lyre*, although including a character named Mephistopheles and making oblique references to the Faust story, nevertheless departs markedly from the traditional scenario of the Faust legend. Finally, Davalos's *Wittenberg*, although foregrounding a protagonist named Doctor Faustus, nevertheless features no tempter and contains no explicit reference to the diabolical contract. But, then, the action of this play occurs in the halcyon days before Doctor Faustus's fatal conjuring of Mephistopheles and serves as a kind of prequel to Marlowe's tragedy, foreshadowing much of the action of this seminal drama. Thus, I consider these four plays sufficiently removed from the original source to constitute appropriations rather than adaptations. All of the adaptations analyzed in this chapter contain explicit references to the Faust narrative, featuring a character named Faust, or a derivative thereof, and including his antagonist Mephistopheles, or his surrogate, among the dramatis personae, while making some reference to the diabolical contract. The substitutes for Mephistopheles include Veit Kunz in Wedekind's *Franziska*, Nicholas Satan in Ficke's *Mr. Faust*, Diamotoruscant in Ghelderode's *The Death of Doctor Faustus: A Tragedy for the Music Hall*, Fistula in Havel's *Temptation*, and Magus in Mamet's *Faustus*. In addition, I have excluded plays that claim parentage from the Faust legend, either through title or dramatis personae, but which actually bear only a tenuous relationship to the Faust tradition; these include Tommaso

Landolfi's *Faust 67*, Edgar Brau's *Fausto*, and two unfinished fragments, Paul Valéry's *The Only One or the Curse of the Cosmos* and John Evelyn's *A Tragedy of Faustus*.

Despite their obvious relevance to the Faust narrative, many of the selected plays adapted for a contemporary audience eschew as anachronisms some of the most salient characteristics of the Faust formula as established in the *Faustbooks* and Marlowe's tragedy: the overreaching hero, the demonic tempter, the blood-inscribed contract, the female seductress, the degeneration of the Faust figure, and even the supernatural architecture. It is important to note here that the Faust tradition as inherited from Goethe often varies markedly from that associated with Marlowe. Although both conventions feature an aspiring hero, the Goethean format stresses the diabolical wager rather than the blood-signed contract, the redemptive female rather than the femme fatale, the amelioration rather than the degeneration of the hero – although this final point has been much debated – and, of course, the ultimate salvation of the Faust figure instead of his damnation. Nevertheless, notwithstanding their frequent departures from the traditional Faustian blueprint, the selected plays all vividly illustrate the central thesis of this study, demonstrating the manner in which playwrights have adapted the Faust legend to reflect the ethos of their own particular historical period.

In yet another way these adaptations/appropriations differ from their progenitors: although the seminal dramas of the Faust legend, Marlowe's *Doctor Faustus* and Goethe's *Faust*, have inspired abundant scholarly commentary, the criticism on post-Goethe dramatic adaptations/appropriations of the legend is comparatively sparse. I am hopeful that this book will generate interest in these little-known but always intriguing dramas.

In Chapter 4, I shall discuss the following adaptations and appropriations: George Sand, *A Woman's Version of the Faust Legend: The Seven Strings of the Lyre* (written in French, 1838); W. B. Yeats, *The Countess Cathleen* (written in English, 1892–1913); A. V. Lunacharski, *Faust and the City* (written in Russian, 1908–16); Frank Wedekind, *Franziska* (written in German, 1911); Arthur Davison Ficke, *Mr. Faust* (written in English, 1913–22); Michel de Ghelderode, *The Death of Doctor Faustus: A Tragedy for the Music Hall* (written in French, 1925); Dorothy Sayers, *The Devil to Pay* (written in English, 1939); Paul Valéry, *My Faust* (written in French, 1940); Lawrence Durrell, *An Irish Faustus* (written in English, 1963); Václav Havel, *Temptation* (written in Czech, 1985); David Mamet, *Faustus* (written in English, 2003); and David Davalos, *Wittenberg* (written in English, 2008).

Chapter 5: Cinematic Fausts

The fifth chapter of the book traces the fortunes of Faust as he thrived in both European and British movies while also migrating to America, continuing to mesmerize audiences in the cinema as he had earlier charmed them in the theater. Or perhaps it is the devilish Prince of Darkness with his many aliases (Mephistopheles, Mr. Scratch, Applegate, and Henry O. Tophet, to note only a few) who is the real star of this long-running hit. There have been numerous cinematic adaptations and appropriations of the Faust legend in multiple different languages; thus I have had to be extremely limited in the selection of films to treat in this chapter. Because of the abundance of films from which to choose, I have selected to analyze only those that adhere most closely to the traditional formula as established by the *Faustbooks* and both Marlowe's *Doctor Faustus* and Goethe's *Faust*, although following this blueprint has meant the exclusion of a number of provocative films: *The Picture of Dorian Gray, The Cabin in the Sky, The Devil and Max Devlin,* and *The Devil's Advocate,* to mention only a few.

Moreover, in my analysis of cinematic treatments of the Faust legend, as in my discussion of dramatic recreations of the Faust story, I have tried to distinguish between adaptations and appropriations. Again, applying the definition offered by Sanders, I define adaptations as films that make explicit reference to the Faust legend, featuring a character named Faust and a Mephistophelian figure. I define appropriations as films that have a greater distance from their source and thus are not explicitly based on the Faust legend and usually make no explicit reference to either Faust or Mephistopheles, but that nevertheless contain most of the characteristics of the traditional Faustian format and provide palimpsests for the earlier Faust narratives.

I begin this chapter with an analysis of the only cinematic adaptation of Marlowe's *Doctor Faustus* of which I am aware, the Nevill Coghill/Richard Burton version, produced in 1967. Because the Coghill/Burton film departs markedly from Marlowe's script, I consider it an adaptation rather than a dramatization of Marlowe's drama. I then treat the following foreign film adaptations of the Faust narrative: F. W. Murnau's silent film *Faust* (German, 1926), René Clair's, *The Beauty of the Devil* (French, 1952), Jan Švankmajer's *Faust* (Czech, 1994), and, the most recent film to be explicated in this study, Alexander Sokurov's *Faust* (Russian, 2011). I shall also analyze the following British and American cinematic appropriations of the Faust narrative: *The Devil and Daniel Webster* (1941), *Alias Nick Beal* (1949), *Damn Yankees* (1958), *Bedazzled* (1967), *Oh, God! You Devil* (1984), *Crossroads* (1986), *Angel Heart* (1987), and a remake of *Bedazzled* (2000).

All of the foreign films I consider – and a majority of those I exclude – make explicit reference to the Faust legend, featuring the dramatis personae associated with this narrative and deriving their provenance primarily from Goethe's drama. Conversely, only one of the English-language films that I analyze, the Coghill/Burton adaptation of Marlowe's *Doctor Faustus*, overtly identifies with the Faust narrative, even though all of these English-language films exhibit most of the salient characteristics of the legend as identified above. This marked disparity between European and British/American Faust films may be due to the durable influence of Goethe's *Faust* on the European cinema. Conversely, although all of the English-language films analyzed in this chapter show the influence of Marlowe and Goethe, the primary inspiration, at least for the American Faust films, is neither Marlowe's *Doctor Faustus* nor Goethe's *Faust*, but that icon of American Faust films, *The Devil and Daniel Webster*, and the blockbuster musical hit, *Damn Yankees*.

Epilogue

The Epilogue of the book will summarize both the unifying characteristics and the marked differences to be found in the many dramatic and cinematic adaptations/appropriations of the Faust legend. In the Epilogue, I will also speculate on the reason for the legend's durability and its continuing relevance to our contemporary society.

CHAPTER I

The Background of the Faust Legend

The Magus Legend

I shall begin my exploration by searching medieval lore for the source of the Faust legend. Many of the stories told about Faust appear in the accounts of earlier charismatic conjurors such as Simon Magus, St. Cyprian, and Theophilus, all of whom have been cited as possible forerunners of Faust. The stories surrounding these magicians are typical Magus Legends: tales centering on some individual, invariably a male, who has achieved a reputation as a conjuror and whose multiple magical feats are recounted with great zest and wonder. According to King James, the word *magus* derives from Persia and refers to "a contemplator or Interpreter of Divine and heavenly sciences"[1]; however, the term soon came to describe any ancient magician, astrologer, or sorcerer.[2]

Simon Magus, a famous first-century CE sorcerer who bewitched the people of Samaria with his miraculous exploits, first appears in the Acts of the Apostles (8:9–24). After his conversion to Christianity, Simon marveled at the ability of Peter and John to grant the gift of the Holy Spirit by the laying on of hands and offered the two disciples money, beseeching: "Give me this power also, that on whomsoever I lay the hands he may receive the Holy Ghost." But Peter indignantly rejected this offer, berating him: "Your money perish with you, because you think that the gift of God may be obtained with money" (Acts 8:19–20).[3] The New Testament account never answers the question of whether Simon ever received the gift of the Holy Ghost; however, as noted by Philip Mason Palmer and Robert Patterson More, through this act "the unfortunate sorcerer has gained undying notoriety by lending his name to one of the great vices of the Church – simony."[4]

In addition to this brief scriptural reference, legendary material accreted around the figure of Simon Magus from the beginning of Christianity into the Middle Ages. According to legend, Simon, a sorcerer living in the first century CE, trained in Greek literature and desirous of glory, boasted that his power exceeded even that of Christ, thus providing an early archetype of the hubristic overreacher. He mimicked the role of Christ, establishing himself as a leader with many disciples, purportedly performing all kinds of miraculous feats, including raising the dead and flying through the air. He chose as his consort a beautiful woman named Luna, whom he later reinvented as an incarnation of Sophia (Wisdom) and Helen of Troy. Many stories circulated around this mysterious figure, stressing either his puissance or his guile, but none so completely captured the medieval imagination as the competition between Simon and Peter in Rome. According to this narrative, a rivalry developed in Rome between the converts of Simon and those of Peter, some proclaiming Simon a true magician and Peter a charlatan and vice versa. Hearing of this controversy, Nero, who had adopted Simon as a protégé, convened a contest between the two rival miracle-workers. The first test required the two competitors to duplicate Christ's most stunning miracle: the raising of the dead. Both attempted to revive a young man who had recently died, but despite Simon's incantations the body remained immovable, whereas Peter, praying to the Lord Christ of Nazareth crucified, successfully resurrected the young man. Nero then commanded Simon to fulfill his boast that he could fly to heaven. Mounting the lofty tower constructed in the Campus Martius, his head crowned with laurels, Simon stretched forth his arms and began to fly, amazing Nero and all the assembled dignitaries. Then in the name of his Savior Jesus Christ, Peter commanded the angels of Satan who bore Simon aloft to let him go, and Simon (like Icarus before him) plummeted to earth and perished.[5]

This virtuoso sorcerer – who blasphemed God and Christ and sought to be their equal in power, who navigated the heavens in a fiery chariot, who commanded devils and through their potency performed spectacular feats before the Pope at Rome or before the Emperor, who conjured phantoms of historical figures during festive meals, who transformed a horse into hay, who selected the fair Helen of Troy to be his consort, who achieved fame for his discussions of demonology and cosmology, who attempted to fly too high and fell to an ignominious death – obviously contributed to the rich matrix of myth that has accreted around the figure of the historical Faust.[6]

St. Cyprian represents another important predecessor of Faust. St. Cyprian, whose provenance derives not from scripture but from Church tradition, purportedly lived in the second century CE, was consecrated by his parents to the Devil at the age of seven, and became a doyen in the Greek mysteries of Apollo, Mithras, Demeter, and Dionysus. As a young man, he studied in Egypt and later among the Chaldeans before coming to Antioch and through his studies became a master of demonology and performed many supernatural exploits. A rich friend employed Cyprian to use his magical powers to win for him the love of the holy virgin Justina, whom he wished to make his wife. So the magician conjured the Devil and instructed him to seduce the innocent Christian maiden. However, when the conjured demon proved powerless before the holiness of Justina, Cyprian realized the vacuity and impotence of his demonic power and converted to Christianity. Later he became a bishop and established the saintly Justina as an abbess supervising many other holy virgins in a nunnery. According to one of the many stories circulating around these two holy figures, the fame of Cyprian and Justina spread far and wide, and the earl of the country sought to counteract their celebrated faith by forcing them to sacrifice to the Roman gods. When they refused, the two believers were cast into a burning caldron full of wax, pitch, and grease, from which they miraculously emerged unscathed, only to be beheaded and their bodies thrown to the dogs. Later, their bodies were reassembled and they were buried in Rome in the year 280 CE.[7]

However, the story of Theophilus of Adana, according to *The Golden Legend* dating from 537 CE, remained the most popular of all of the Magus legends, perhaps because this legend introduced two significant features into the tradition: the diabolical blood pact and the merciful intervention of the Virgin Mary. According to this legend, Theophilus, initially a godly man and vicar of a church in Adana, in his extreme humility refused the offered position of bishop and because of this refusal was removed from his post as vicar. Angered at his unfair treatment by the Church, this formerly humble man became obsessed with jealousy and a desire for worldly glory and in his rage and frustration sought out a Jew, a practitioner of diabolical arts, who conjured the Devil. By command of the Devil, Theophilus then "denied God and his Mother, and renounced his Christian profession, and wrote an obligation with his blood, and sealed it with his ring, and delivered it to the devil ..."[8] Later the bishop reinstated Theophilus as vicar of the church and, having received much respect and preferment, Theophilus experienced genuine penitence for his apostasy, praying to the Blessed Virgin for forgiveness. Although he had earlier denied both the Virgin Mary and her Son, the blessed Virgin appeared to him in a vision, rebuking him for his heresy and commanding him to forsake the Devil and confess Jesus Christ to be the Son of God, which he did with great fervor.

After many days of prayer and supplication, the vicar awoke one morning and discovered the bond of apostasy he had signed miraculously returned to him and lying upon his breast. Theophilus died a few days later, having been redeemed through the intercession of the Virgin Mary.[9]

Since the blood pact does not appear in some of the earliest accounts of this legend, scholars suspect that this important element of the story became a part of the Theophilus narrative in the thirteenth century[10] and may have served as the source for the contract in the *German Faustbook*. Nevertheless, validating direct influence proves notoriously difficult, and according to John Bakeless, the practice of making a blood compact with the Devil to obtain superhuman power boasts a venerable ancestry, originating in Jewish traditions before the time of Christ. Conversely, Henry Ansgar Kelly locates the prototype of the diabolical pact in Satan's temptation of Jesus when he promises the Messiah all the kingdoms of the world in return for his worship of the Devil.[11] Elizabeth M. Butler speculates that the notion of the formal bond with Satan "crept into legend" with the tale of a certain Proterius, who sold his soul to marry his master's pious daughter and was "delivered from the consequences of such a pact by St. Basil" in the fourth century.[12] Significantly, this may be the first example of a man selling his soul for love and also the first example of a human *deus ex machina* intervening to save the damned from his fate, a motif that will dominate contemporary cinematic versions of the Faust legend.

According to Beatrice Daw Brown, other elements of the Theophilus story might also have influenced the development of the eclectic Faust legend. These include the scenes of revelry with the Devil in a castle, Faustus's many disputations with the Evil One, and the pious old neighbor's exhortations to Faustus to repent.[13] Thus, although the denouements of the two legends diverge, Brown speculates that the story of Theophilus "was grafted upon the main stem of the Simon-Faustus narrative theme – the bold magician punished."[14]

Although all three of these stories date back to the early Middle Ages, legendary material continued to accrete around these almost mythical figures throughout the centuries, anticipating and perhaps even contributing to the production of the Faust legend. In one aspect, however, the careers of two of these three magicians differ markedly from that of their more famous descendant, Johannes Faustus. Given its multiple versions, the manner of the death of Simon Magus and his possible salvation remain problematic; however, both St. Cyprian and Theophilus ultimately accepted Christ and were redeemed, whereas Faustus, at least in the original story, continued in his reprobate course until his death and presumed damnation.

The Biblical and Morality Plays

If the Magus Legend provided one source for the Faust legend, the medieval drama, particularly the biblical cycle plays and the moralities, furnished another inspiration for this haunting narrative. The biblical cycle plays emerged in fourteenth- and fifteenth-century England as vibrant proletarian theater. Clerics usually authored these short verse plays, always based, however loosely, on scripture or Church tradition. Linked into long cycles that often took three days to perform, usually presented as part of the Feast of Corpus Christi by the medieval trade guilds, these dramas chronicle the Christian history of the world from the Creation to the Last Judgment. Despite the homiletic qualities of these dramas, their primary goal was to celebrate the awesome mysteries of the Christian faith – the incarnation and resurrection – rather than to instruct the audience in the rudimentary ethics of Christian life.

Conversely, the moralities, or "moral plays" as they were called at the time, provide a sermon rather than a celebration. The moralities can be defined as a type of drama,[15] flourishing in the fifteenth century, "characterized primarily by the use of allegory to convey a moral lesson about religious or civil conduct, presented through the medium of abstractions or representative social characters."[16] Abstractions like the World, Justice, and Mercy; qualities like Beauty, Strength, and Five Wits; representative social figures like Kindred and Cousin; and sometimes supernatural figures like God and the Devil people these dramas. The protagonists of these moralities – invariably male – bear such names as Mankind, Everyman, or Homo Genus to signify that they represent the entire human race. The typical plot focuses on the allegorical conflict between good and evil for the spiritual allegiance of this mankind figure. Mankind's chief tempter, commonly called the Vice but often sporting colorful names like Folly, Mischief, Backbiter, or Ambidexter, attempts to lure the hero from the straight and narrow road of virtue to the primrose path of sin and dalliance, while the representatives of virtue, bearing such names as Wisdom, Knowledge of God, Good Counsel, Mercy, or Good Deeds, urge the Everyman hero to adhere faithfully to the dictates of the Bible and the Church. The entire drama occurs within the human psyche, which becomes a battleground on which good and evil battle for ascendancy. According to David Bevington:

This story of spiritual conflict, named the "Psychomachia" after an allegorical work of the fourth century by Prudentius, was the basis of nearly every morality play in the English drama. Its emphasis became increasingly secular in the mid-sixteenth century, preaching lessons of civil rather than religious conduct; in the later moralities, representative social types often outnumbered the more abstract personifications . . . of the earlier moralities.[17]

Dorothy Castle adds another level of conflict, suggesting that a number of the moralities, primarily *Mankind*, are constructed around the element of "game." Thus for Castle, the "typical struggle between Good and Evil that characterizes morality plays" is "depicted in *Mankind* as a game between God and the Devil with Mankind's soul going to the winner."[18] Although this portrayal of the typical morality *psychomachia* as "a diabolical game to win man's soul," to employ Castle's vivid phrase, does not seem relevant to the *Faustbooks* and Marlowe's *Doctor Faustus*, arguably the wager between God and Mephistopheles in Goethe's *Faust* suggests a type of game, and this metaphor of *psychomachia* as deadly game resonates through a number of cinematic adaptations and appropriations of the Faust legend, particularly Murnau's *Faust, Bedazzled*, and *Oh, God! You Devil*.

A distinctive characteristic of medieval plays, both the biblical cycle plays and the moralities, is the treatment of evil. Whether originally a ruse to introduce comedy into the sublimity of the religious drama or a serious attempt to banish vice by laughing it away, the blending of the humorous with the homiletic in the presentation of evil emerges as a distinguishing feature of the medieval drama. Murray Roston suggests that as the medieval drama developed from the liturgical plays to the biblical cycles, certain groups of characters of lesser sanctity became available for comic elaboration and realism. The first and most obvious group of characters accessible for more lively dramatization were the enemies of Christ, the goats of the New Testament narrative – Herod, Pilate, Judas, and, most significantly, the Devil – since even the most priggish cleric would hardly disapprove of treating these evil characters irreverently. Roston describes how before a performance of the biblical cycle plays, "the unholy trinity" – composed of Herod, Pilate, and the Devil – often "served the useful purpose of quieting the crowd, sometimes by running among the bystanders and striking them over the head with inflated bladders, while the more sacred characters kept their distance from the mob."[19] However, Roston also insists that we should not exaggerate the comedy of evil, agreeing with L. W. Cushman that these plays rarely treated the Devil as a purely comic figure, despite his braggadocio, since "his didactic function and his participation in the central New Testament scenes precluded frivolity." [20] However, subordinate demons, such as Titivillus in the Townley *Last Judgment*, were often subjected to boisterous levity, and Naught in *Mankind* may well have originally worn the costume of the fool to stress his vacuity. [21]

Critics have actively debated the purpose of this raucous humor. Although most scholars agree that the Devils and Vices cavorting throughout the medieval drama combine the malignant, the irreverent, and the humorous, the purpose of this singular conflation has aroused considerable controversy. One of the major questions concerning the medieval drama remains: do the Devils function as exuberant subverters of a hegemonic social order or as threats to the community social fabric to be conquered by laughter? On the one hand, E. K. Chambers suggests that the Devil's or Vice's heretical parodies might be a subversive device inherited from pagan festivals whereby anti-establishmentarian clerics undermined the repressive authority of the Church. If so, the audience would be expected to secretly cheer for the Devil or Vice in his irreverent tomfoolery. Conversely, O. B. Hardison and John D. Cox insist that the fusion of the comic with the diabolical operated, as in satire, as a means of diminishing the demonic, literally laughing it away. V. A. Kolve supports this reading, insisting that the biblical cycle plays never show a tendency to mock, blaspheme, or ridicule the sacred characters of the story, reserving their laughter – often a vulgar guffaw – for the evil figures, primarily the grotesque, obscene enemy of humankind, the Devil. [22] Cox further demonstrates that the medieval drama invariably identifies the Devil and his cohorts with powerful, socially privileged individuals, particularly the courtier, not with the commoners; [23] thus it would be unlikely that the proletarian audience would empathize, even unconsciously, with this ally of the oppressor.

Although the solution to this knotty controversy transcends the focus of this book, it is sufficient to note that this melding of the malevolent with the comic so characteristic of the medieval drama remains one of the near constants of the Faust narrative, continuing from the menacing yet sometimes humorous Mephostophiles in the *Faustbooks* (I have preserved the spelling of Faustus's demon familiar as it appears in the *Faustbooks*), through Marlowe's disjunctive tragic/comic Devil, to Goethe's urbane but antic demon, to the many baleful yet risible diabolic tempters in nineteenth-, twentieth-, and twenty-first-century dramatic and cinematic recreations of the Faust narrative. Sometimes the comic dominates (*The Beauty of the Devil, Damn Yankees, Bedazzled, Oh, God! You Devil*), sometimes the terrifying (Murnau's *Faust, Alias Nick Beal, Angel Heart*), but the

most effective tempters (like Mr. Scratch in *The Devil and Daniel Webster*)
retain this hallmark of the medieval drama, the comically depraved Devil.
Moreover, in all the multiple dramatic adaptations of the Faust legend
I have explored, I can think of none in which the Devil consistently
operates as a subversive mouthpiece for the author.

In addition to the Devil, the biblical cycle plays introduced a fascinating
character who serves as a forerunner of both Faustus and his antagonist
Mephistopheles. This intriguing figure, the Antichrist, referred to by name
only briefly in the scriptures – 1 John 2:18, 22; 2 John 7 – although
frequently associated with "the beast" in Revelation 13 and 17, occupies
an important position in the theology of the Middle Ages. As his name
implies, the Antichrist represents the antagonist of Christ, the false
Messiah. Mentioned frequently in sermons of the period, the Antichrist
appears in only one of the biblical cycles, the Chester mystery cycle.[24]
Here, the Antichrist boasts that he is the true Messiah, defaming Jesus as
a charlatan who has bamboozled the people with his bogus magic
(23:9–16), echoing Simon Magus as he seeks to recruit his own apostles
by bragging of his power to perform all the miracles attributed to Jesus,
including the raising of the dead (23:77–105). Ultimately, like Simon
Magus before him, the Antichrist is unmasked as a mountebank. Indeed,
instead of rising from the dead as he earlier has pretended to do, he is slain
by the Angel Michael and carried down to hell from whence he came.
Although the protagonists of the *Faustbooks* never presume to godlike
power, Christopher Marlowe's Doctor Faustus, like both the Antichrist
and Simon Magus, yearns to perform the miracles of Christ, "to make man
to live eternally? / Or, being dead, raise them to life again" (DF, 1.1.24–25),
indeed, to "gain a deity" (DF, 1.1.65). [25]

Paradoxically, the Antichrist also foreshadows Mephistopheles as well as
Faustus. In seeking to seduce the kings of the world, in the biblical play *The
Coming of the Antichrist* the Antichrist bribes them with "rived riches, land,
and fee" (abundant riches, land, and reward; 23:49–54), even as
Mephistopheles offers Marlowe's Faustus gold and rich apparel after he
signs the demonic contract. Many subsequent tempters throughout the
dramas and films based on the Faust legend will mimic the Antichrist by
enticing their victims with gold, lands, and other rewards.

In the moralities, the Vice usually replaces the Devil or Antichrist as the
symbol for evil. The Vice differs from the Devil and the Antichrist in
significant ways. As Bernard Spivack insists, a medieval audience would
view the Devil and the Antichrist as historical figures whereas the Vice is
clearly an abstraction.[26] Moreover, the Devil in the biblical cycles is

a comparatively humorless figure, who provoked laughter from the audience primarily by his fantastic appearance and gross obscenities rather than by his wit.[27] Similarly, although the braggadocio of the Antichrist renders him ridiculous, he remains a frightening rather than a comic figure. On the other hand, the morality Vice is a ribald rogue, a "homiletic showman, intriguer extraordinary, and master of dramatic ceremonies."[28] Even more than his diabolical predecessor, he presents a conniving manipulator who delights in chicanery for its own sake, while also frequently masquerading as the virtue antithetical to his particular vice. Displaying a singular intimacy with the audience, the Vice usually introduces and anatomizes himself on his first entrance.[29] The Vice frequently acts the role of antic trickster and stand-up comic; people may have applauded him because, although they disapproved of his machinations, he made them laugh, but as with the Devil in the biblical cycles, the audience is probably invited to laugh *at* the Vice not *with* him. Lastly, the Devil, the Vice, and the other evil figures often serve as devices through which the unknown authors of the plays satirize the social injustices of the period, but, again, evidence suggests that the Devils and Vices are generally the targets of the satire not the agents of it.

The view of evil as comic may seem somewhat bizarre, even naïve, to the weary veterans of a century and a half marked by genocidal war after genocidal war. Yet this perspective undergirds satiric dramas from the biblical cycle plays and moralities to the modern Theatre of the Absurd. I should add, however, that although often humorous, the Devil or Vice is also horrific, and the levity of his antics in no way diminishes the terror he inspires. As Clifford Davidson stresses when describing the Devil figure in the morality *Mankind:* Titivillus "has all the exaggerated traits of the devil who is at once the butt of laughter and yet a creature to be feared: he is comic, and yet he is indicative of evil forces which must be respected in spite of his absurdity."[30] The majority of people in the medieval and Renaissance periods believed in the Devil as a real presence – ubiquitous, baleful, wily, lurking behind every wheat field, awaiting the chance to ensnare the unwary and lure them to their doom. Perhaps the comic treatment of humanity's great adversary provided a way of coping with the anxiety this figure evoked.

Many of the dramatic renderings of the Faust legend, from Marlowe through Goethe to most of the modern plays and films treated in this study, bear the imprint of the medieval drama. The biblical cycle plays, as well as the scriptures on which they are based, bequeathed the theme of Temptation and Fall; the moralities added the centrality of human choice and the *psychomachia* between dichotomous value systems. But the richest legacy from both dramatic modes remains the diabolical tempter, an ingenious commingling of the comic and the sinister, who continues to dominate contemporary theatrical and cinematic versions of this legend even as he dominated the morality stages 600 years ago.

The Historical Faust

Having canvassed the literary sources of the Faust legend, I will undertake a search for the historical Faust. This brings us to the vexing question: did a historical personage named Johannes Faustus really exist? Like the majority of humanity's myths, the Faust legend appears to have had some basis in fact although the actual identity of the historical Faust is much disputed. Records suggest that a Georgius of Helmstadt enrolled at the University of Heidelberg in 1483 and on March 1, 1487 graduated as a magister (at this time, a liberal arts equivalent to a doctorate in theology, medicine, or law), and some scholars, including Frank Baron, link this Georgius of Helmstadt to the historical miracle-worker designated as Faustus or Faust. However, this view has been actively contested, particularly by Ian Watt, who identifies Faust with a wandering magician in Germany who went under the name of George and traveled around the country performing magical tricks for financial reward. Watt posits that this itinerant sorcerer may have had "a smattering of learning; he may even have been to university, but there is no extant evidence of his having taken any degree."[31] Provocatively, historical records also show that a Johannes Faust ex Simern matriculated at the University of Heidelberg in 1508; however, since a notorious conjuror called Faustus Junior or the younger Faustus appears in contemporary documents as early as 1507, these matriculation dates seem too late to correlate with the Faust of legend. Most scholars agree that whatever the identity of the historical magus, his name was not originally Faustus; rather, as noted above, "Faustus," meaning "auspicious," may have been a Latin cognomen granted the magus in recognition of his magical exploits.[32]

Apparently between 1507 and 1540, many references to a wonder-worker bearing a number of different names – Faust or Faustus, Georgius Faustus, George Faust, Jorg Faustus, Georgius Sabellicus – appear in contemporaneous letters and diaries. Baron insists that the name John or Johannes does not occur at all in the earliest sources and becomes linked with the famous magician for the first time some twenty-five years after his death, and a canvas of the earlier references to this legendary figure supports this assertion. Johannes Manlius, a pupil of Melanchthon, one of Luther's most significant followers, compiled many of the diverse episodes surrounding the figure of Faustus into a long series of exempla, and according to Baron, Manlius was the first person to associate the figure of Faustus with the name Johannes in a written document.[33] The confusion of names may have resulted from a careless error when Manlius transcribed Melanchthon's lectures or may have derived from Melanchthon himself. Conversely, some scholars argue for two conjurors bearing the appellation Faustus, identifying Johannes as the older and more respectable and Georgius as the younger and more notorious.[34]

However, despite the multiple names, the original documents appear to limn a single figure: a widely traveled, well-educated, rather shady miracle-worker, journeying with a black dog or a black horse as his familiar, who was also a braggart, a vagabond, and something of a mountebank. Although we have little detailed information concerning the lineaments of the historical Faustus, artists have, throughout the ages, speculated on his appearance. For one such imaginary creation, see Figure 1.1, which appeared in the frontispiece of the 1896 edition of Christopher Marlowe's *The Tragical History of Doctor Faustus*. Apparently, this itinerant scholar/ magician had already become notorious by 1507, for Abbot Johannes Tritheim of Würzburg, writing to mathematician and Court astrologer Johannes Virdung, censures a Georgius Sabellicus as "a vagabond, a babbler and a rogue," "not a philosopher but a fool with an overabundance of rashness," who, like Simon Magus before him, boasted that "the miracles of Christ the Saviour were not so wonderful, that he himself could do all the things which Christ had done, so often and whenever he wished."[35] Moreover, Sabellicus, taking the position of a schoolmaster in Kreuznach, Germany, performed "the most dastardly kind of lewdness with the boys and when discovered, he avoided by flight the punishment that awaited him."[36]

In the years 1507 to 1540 accounts of this disreputable figure proliferated throughout Germany. A letter written in 1513, from Conrad Mutianus Rufus to Heinrich Urbanus, dismisses a Georgius Faustus as a mere braggart and fool, although the ignorant marvel at him.[37] On the other hand, a comment from the account book of the bishop of Bamberg in 1519–20 dignifies Faustus as a philosopher who made the bishop a horoscope or prognostication.[38] An entry from the records of the city of Ingolstadt in 1528 notes that the city fathers commanded a Dr. George Faust of Heidelberg to leave the city and "spend his penny elsewhere."[39] Another entry, this time from the records of the city council of

Figure 1.1 Doctor Faustus. Frontispiece to *The Tragical History of Doctor Faustus* by
Christopher Marlowe, published in 1897. This drawing presumably represents
a portrait of the historical Johannes Faustus. Photograph by Universal History
Archive/Universal Images Group/Getty Images.

Nuremberg in 1532, defames a Doctor Faust as "the great sodomite and
necromancer."[40] Still another letter, in this case from Joachim
Camerarius to Daniel Stibar in 1536, accuses a man named Faustus of
puffing up Camerarius's friend Stibar with "silly superstitions" and
"juggler's tricks."[41] Augustin Lercheimer, a professor of Greek at
Heidelberg University, further condemns Faustus as "a parasite, drun-
kard, and gourmand," who "supported himself by his quackery."[42]
According to other records, a Georgius Faustus of Helmstadt boasted
to be the commander of the order of the Knights of St. John at a place
called Hallestein in 1528,[43] and Dr. Faustus, the famous necromancer,
accurately prophesied the bishop of Münster's investment in that city in
1535.[44] The *Table Talk of Martin Luther*, edited by Johannes Aurifaber in
1566, also makes reference to a Faustus, who purportedly called himself
the Devil's brother-in-law.[45] Other documents narrate the exploits of

a conjuror named Faustus, ranging from the hubristic – seeking, like Simon Magus, to fly to heaven, and, like Simon Magus, "dashed to the ground and almost killed"[46] – to the puerile – playing practical jokes on unfortunate monks who failed to offer him their vintage wine[47] – to the grotesque – devouring another magician whole.[48] Finally, several accounts describe the death of this sorcerer, with his neck broken or twisted, his face turned completely to his back, the traditional death of a wizard or witch dating back at least to Dante's *Inferno*.[49]

The abundant references to this fascinating figure from multiple sources lead me to the inescapable conclusion that a historical person bearing the title Faustus did actually exist.

Contemporary evidence of the activities of this historical figure ceases about 1540, and the development of the legend probably dates from this time. Significantly, Luther in his *Table Talk* (written around 1537) is the first person to associate Faustus with the Devil, an idea expanded by his follower Philip Melanchthon (1549–60), although this became a commonplace in the years after Faustus's demise, thanks to the polemics of fervent Protestants, such as Johannes Wier and Augustin Lercheimer.[50] Originally, according to Baron, folkloric sources depict Faustus as primarily an astrologer and thaumaturge. Baron locates the denigration of Faustus and his association with the Devil-pact and witchcraft in the Protestant polemics of Luther and Melanchthon. Ian Watt goes even further, insisting unequivocally that "it was the Luther counter-movement that eventually transformed the historical George Faust into the legendary figure of myth, by inventing his pact with the devil and his terrible end."[51] Conversely, Michael H. Keefer postulates that the Faustus legend arose as a form of "ideological assassination" against the Hermetic-Cabalistic tradition associated with such luminaries as Marsilio Ficino, Giovanni Pico, and Cornelius Agrippa.[52] However that may be, as Palmer and More observe, after his death Faustus, presumably one individual despite the variations in nomenclature, became "the lodestone about which gathered in time a mass of superstition which in turn is the deposit of centuries," including tales associated not only with Simon Magus, St. Cyprian, and Theophilus, but also with the Antichrist, Solomon, Virgil, Merlin, Roger Bacon, Robert the Devil, Zyto, Albertus Magnus, Hermes Trismegistus, and Cornelius Agrippa.[53] These many narratives endowed Faustus with a unique mythic allure, through the alchemy of myth-making transforming this distinctly disreputable figure into the archetypal symbol of humanity's anxieties and aspirations, its follies and its impossible dreams.

The Faustbooks

During the latter decades of the sixteenth century, oral and occasionally written accounts of Faustus's magical exploits circulated throughout Europe. H. G. Haile maintains that the first collection of Faust tales was probably compiled by a man named Wolf Wambach in the university town of Erfurt. However, as with the elusive *Ur-Hamlet*, since we have only oral reports of this collage, we can only speculate on its contents. The oldest surviving collection of Faustus anecdotes consists of four tales assembled sometime in the 1570s by a Christoph Rosshirt, a teacher at the Sebaldus school of Nuremberg. This collection features a number of outlandish jests that, slightly modified, found their way into the *German* and *English Faustbooks*: Faustus's leg jerked off by an irate Jewish debt collector who then flees in terror; fat swine, conjured from bundles of straw and sold cheap, which dissolve back into straw when driven over water; boisterous peasants charmed into dumbness by the annoyed magician.[54]

Of much greater significance is the Wolfenbüttel Manuscript, the oldest extant version of the material that would first be compiled into the *German Faustbook* and then later into its English translation. Haile maintains that this manuscript derives from a much-expanded version of a still earlier, now lost, *Faustbook*. According to Haile, the common ancestor of the Wolfenbüttel Manuscript and the *German Faustbook* appeared sometime before 1580, the work of a forgotten novelist who sought only to produce a piece of light entertainment, "exciting in that it dealt with abominations, sophisticated in that the blasphemous hero was presented not entirely unsympathetically, serious only to the extent that it did justify itself by demonstrating that Faust went to Hell for the same reasons that all good Catholics were going there ..."[55]

Haile and William Rose further posit that this little novel underwent considerable amplification at the hands of prolix scribes, who included the kingdoms of hell copied from an old Latin–German, German–Latin dictionary, as well as geographical descriptions of the arch-conjuror's travels lifted verbatim from Hartmann Schedel's *Nürnberger Chronik*. Similarly, they assert, these scribes mechanically copied from the Latin–German, German–Latin dictionary of the Swiss humanist Dasypodius the list of game, fish, and wine with which Faustus entertains his guests in the enchanted castle of Anholt, even maintaining its alphabetical order.[56] Unfortunately, just as we do not have the original lost *Faustbook*, we do not have the supplemented copy either. However, a very conscientious copy of this copy, transcribed sometime in the mid-1580s, still resides in the

Duke August Library in Wolfenbüttel, and Haile has translated a slightly condensed version of this manuscript into English.[57]

It was not long before an enterprising publisher realized the commercial possibilities of the legend; that man's name was Johann Spies, and in the year 1587 a press at Frankfurt am Main produced the first coherent printed biography of the life and death of this itinerant magician, titled *Historia von D. Johann Fausten.* However, although critical consensus agrees on Spies as the publisher of this very popular book, the actual author of the work remains unknown. Haile posits that the unknown author based his *Faustbook* on the same expanded version employed by the scribe of the Wolfenbüttel Manuscript, deleted a couple of the more salacious chapters and insolent remarks, added a few pious morals and numerous Christian admonitions, and thus sought to impose upon the amorphous form of the original lost manuscript a moral coherence and religious didacticism. The author's efforts evidently proved enormously successful, for before the end of the year this little volume had appeared in four reprints, a new original edition, and a further edition containing eight new chapters;[58] indeed, Spies had produced one of the biggest money-makers of the century. Most commentators agree that Spies's *German Faustbook* of 1587 (henceforth referred to as the GFB) and the Wolfenbüttel Manuscript are variants of the same (now lost) expanded text, which is, therefore, the linear ancestor not only of the GFB, but also of both the *English Faustbook* and Christopher Marlowe's *Doctor Faustus.* Some scholars speculate that blatant contradictions appearing in both the GFB and the Wolfenbüttel Manuscript suggest that both works derived from multiple, now lost, manuscripts, but since none of these manuscripts is now extant, this must remain mere speculation.[59]

What kind of book is this first printed version of the Faust legend? Almost all commentators agree on the pervasive Protestantism of the GFB. Butler finds the inspiration behind the biographical (as distinguished from the anecdotal) portions of the book "so Lutheran that one almost seems to hear the clarion tones of the great Reformer proclaiming his disastrous conviction that the whole of human life is entangled beyond disentangling in the wiles and snares of the devil."[60] Rose also identifies the vivid reality of hell and the Devil and the blatant anti-clericalism animating the GFB as characteristically Lutheran, even designating Faustus as the "great counterpart of Luther."[61]

Eugen Wolff adopts a contrary position. While not denying the patent anti-clericalism of certain passages in the GFB, he rejects these passages as interpolations imposed upon the original manuscript by the unknown

Protestant author of the GFB. Far from judging the original, now lost *Faustbook* a Lutheran document, Wolff interprets it as a decidedly Catholic parody of Luther. As Wolff points out, two of the most trenchant anti-clerical taunts in the GFB do not appear in the Wolfenbüttel Manuscript and thus may have been added by the polemical Spies. The first of these occurs during the "marriage proposal" episode, in which Mephostophiles denies Faustus a wife on the grounds that marriage is a sacred institution ordained by God. In the GFB, Faustus scornfully retorts that the clergy do not marry, an obvious taunt at the celibacy of nuns and priests, a passage absent from the Wolfenbüttel Manuscript. The other anti-clerical jibe, present in the GFB and missing from the Wolfenbüttel Manuscript, concerns Faustus's mocking reference during his tour of Europe to the Devil in the church of St. Ursula with 11,000 virgins; the use of the term *Temple* (church) in the Wolfenbüttel Manuscript instead of the term *Teufel* (Devil) in the GFB totally erases any element of anti-clerical satire from this episode.[62] However, the appearance in both the Wolfenbüttel Manuscript and the GFB of other anti-clerical slurs undermines Wolff's argument. These include Faustus's mocking description of the Pope and his court – "these pigs at Rome are fattened and all ready to roast and cook" – and his parodic ascension at Constantinople in the vestments of a Pope. Wolff rejects both of these satiric episodes as interpolations by some unknown copyist of the manuscript, but as we have no extant version of any pre-Wolfenbüttel document, Wolff's theory must remain mere conjecture.[63] Ultimately, although the anti-clerical bias looms larger in the GFB than in the Wolfenbüttel Manuscript, I conclude that the focus on salvation by faith rather than works, the scornful treatment of the priest-hood, and the obsession with a burning hell and the malignant power of the Devil all identify the GFB as a distinctively Protestant document.

Sometime between 1588 and 1592, the GFB was adapted into English by a figure almost as shadowy as the book's eponymous hero, an author known to posterity only by the cipher P. F. Gent (Gentleman). Although the identity of the mysterious P. F. may never be established beyond the shadow of a doubt, in his Introduction to his edition, John Henry Jones makes an excellent case for a man named Paul Fairfax as the author of the popular jest book/cautionary tale. Whatever the identity of its author, commentators almost universally accept this adaptation, titled *The Historie of the Damnable Life and Deserved Death of Doctor John Faustus* and popularly known as the *English Faustbook* (henceforth referred to as the EFB), as the source for Christopher Marlowe's *Doctor Faustus*.[64] P. F., in his free-wheeling, sometimes grossly inaccurate but always sprightly and frequently eloquent rendering into English of Spies's biography, expanded, condensed, diverged, and interpolated at will, and some of these modifications help to identify the EFB rather than the German original as the source for Marlowe's drama. However, the majority of P. F.'s many modifications are stylistic rather than substantial, and in terms of genre, ideology, structure, and content the two *Faustbooks* remain very similar. Thus, because of its literary significance, my discussion of the *Faustbooks* will focus on P. F.'s translation, currently the only comprehensive version available to English-language readers, although a number of contemporary scholars have translated portions of the GFB into English.[65]

The date of the EFB has occasioned considerable controversy, especially because the publication of Marlowe's accepted source would have relevance to the much-debated composition of the playwright's monumental tragedy. Since I will treat this issue in greater detail in Chapter 2, at this time, I would simply like to suggest that although scholars have traditionally accepted 1592 as the probable date for the first publication of the EFB, there is considerable evidence of an earlier printing, perhaps in 1588, which would correspond with the critically preferred date for the composition of Marlowe's *Doctor Faustus*.[66]

An anomaly in the literary world, the EFB, like the GFB on which it is based, reveals a profound ambivalence of tone between the jovial exuberance of the middle episodes and the deep religious fervor of the first and last sections. Despite the author's emphasis on the heinousness of Faustus's sin, the magician emerges from his multifarious shenanigans as far more a mischievous prankster than a blasphemous apostate. Although the authors of both *Faustbooks* undoubtedly condemn their heroes, I agree with Rose that P. F. "frequently tones down the German author's denunciation of Faust's wicked ways, and emphasizes the fantasies and cogitations rather than the presumption and arrogance of the sorcerer." John Henry Jones concurs, observing that "In the German, the accent is upon pride, arrogant presumption and wantonness . . . Whereas in the EFB it is on 'speculation' (44f, 74), 'devilish cogitation' (169), and a contempt for a pious vocation (46f, 233f, 553f) . . ."[67] Certainly, his buoyant, often racy narrative style and frequent use of the term "merry jest" suggest that P. F., like much of his reading public, probably shared some of the prurient delight that, following the GFB author, he often pontifically condemns. I propose that this marked disjunction of tone, which P. F. adopted from the German original, derives from the multiple lost sources of the GFB or perhaps from the book's mixed ancestry: part passionate religious tract, part rollicking jest book.

The EFB divides into three sections. Part I, composed of sixteen chapters and almost one half of the book, treats Faustus's early life: his disillusion with the disciplines of theology, medicine, and mathematics; his conjuring of Mephostophiles; the execution of the diabolical pact; and Faustus's endless musings on occult and para-theological matters, such as the fall of Lucifer, the nature of hell, and the reality of salvation and damnation. Here, as in the GFB, we encounter the insatiable speculator of Faustian lore. Part II, composed of twelve chapters and approximately one-fourth of the work, relates Faustus's peregrinations and his meditations on the natural rather than the supernatural, although the inclusion in this section of Faustus's question, "Tell me how and after what sort God made the world and all the creatures in them, and why man was made in the image of God?" (116), combining as it does ruminations on both first and second causes, partially obscures this pattern. In this section, Faustus is presented as the indefatigable tourist as well as the insatiable speculator. Like his peripatetic counterpart in the GFB, the hero of the EFB journeys through the universe in a fiery chariot, makes a mock trip to hell, glimpses Paradise, and visits the two great enemy fortresses of Protestantism – the seat of Catholicism and the seat of Islam – where he makes sport of Protestantism's two arch-enemies, the Pope and the Sultan. The latter part of this section is devoted to Faustus's learned discourses on comets, falling stars, thunder, etc. Part III, consisting of thirty-four chapters (some of these quite short) and a little over one-fourth of the book, follows the pattern of degeneration characteristic of the German original as it shifts from speculation to clowning to tragedy. This section first recounts Faustus's multifarious "merry conceits" – a gallimaufry of episodes, including Faustus's entertainments at the courts of potentates and the infantile pranks he plays on sleepy knights, greedy Jews, gullible horse-coursers and swineherds, rowdy students, and misanthropic peasants – before concluding with his "miserable and lamentable end" (176).

The most dramatic section of the book remains the first sixteen chapters, which narrate the story of the insatiable speculator who, "taking to him the wings of an eagle, thought to fly over the whole world and to know the secrets of heaven and earth" (93), an image of presumption recalling both Icarus and Simon Magus. Although well versed in the Holy Scriptures, in his obsession with forbidden knowledge, Faustus rejects divinity, first studying astrology and mathematics, then medicine, and finding all of these disciplines unsatisfying, finally turning to necromancy. Seeking out adepts in the Chaldean, Persian, Hebrew, Arabian, and Greek mysteries, Faustus learns the art of incantation, conjures the Devil, and makes a blood pact with Mephostophiles in return for knowledge of earth, heaven, and hell.

This first section stresses aspiration for illicit knowledge as the *summum bonum* for which Faustus barters his soul, although this motivation is not immediately apparent in Faustus's first confrontation with the conjured Spirit, in which he asks only that his "Spirit" will be his servant and will bring him whatsoever he commands and "tell him nothing but that which is true" (95). However, the Spirit declines to make a commitment at this time, seeking permission from a higher power, and thus departs, promising to return on the following day. When the "Spirit" returns on the second day, Faustus designates an entirely new set of demands, stressing his desire to be a "spirit" and have Mephostophiles as his servant, always at his command. Surprisingly, in this second confrontation with his infernal familiar, Faustus makes no reference to knowledge although he insists that Mephostophiles must bring him anything he demands. At any rate, the "Spirit" immediately accepts these articles, which bear little reference to his previous propositions and unaccountably contain no reference to knowledge. As scholars speculate, the contradiction between these two very different specifications probably results from two very different sources for the GFB.[68] However, when he finally composes the contract, Faustus clearly delineates his desideratum, this time stressing that he will pledge both his body and soul to the Devil if, in return, Mephostophiles shall "learn me and fulfil my desire in all things" (98). Moreover, the desire to probe, to speculate, to search beyond what can be discovered in the learned disciplines of humanity epitomizes Faustus's actions throughout much of the EFB.

Faustus signs the contract but he has not yet been irrevocably damned; thus the task of preventing his repentance falls to Mephostophiles, who, as Jones points out, adopts a two-pronged strategy. On the one hand, the Spirit inundates Faustus with a generous allowance and all kinds of good things – sumptuous clothing, delectable food, vintage wine, expensive plate (all, of course, stolen from the rich) – so that he "may habituate himself to luxury." On the other hand, he must be "brought to despair of salvation by the disputations which Mephostophiles cunningly engineers to this purpose." However, these two strategies seem to work at cross purposes, perhaps again the result of multiple contradictory sources. Drowned in luxury, Faustus "continued thus in his epicurish life day and night, and believed not that there was a God, hell, or devil" (101), although, as Jones remarks, it appears "curious not to believe in a being one has just made a deal with." [69] If luxury blinds Faustus to metaphysical reality, his disputations with his Spirit achieve the opposite result, vividly clarifying the actuality of God, hell, and the Devil, and would, one might suppose, serve as cautionary narratives encouraging repentance rather than despair.

Before fulfilling his insatiable curiosity, Faustus makes another foray into the hedonist life and learns for the first time the limitations of his contract. Not content with rich delicacies and rare wines, Faustus's restless libido leads him to desire a wife; reversing St. Paul, since he is already destined to burn, he decides that he should marry in order to have available sex. But he discovers immediately that certain things are forbidden to him, in this case marriage since "wedlock is a chief institution ordained of God" (101). When the rebellious Faustus protests against his demon familiar's failure to keep his promise, Mephostophiles resorts to the modus operandi he will employ throughout the book to control his luckless victim – the carrot and the stick. Faustus's insubordination immediately evokes the stick: a circle of fire and a Devil so horrible and malformed that Faustus cannot look upon him. Having totally quelled the mutinous magician, Mephostophiles then proffers him the carrot, not the wife that he has demanded but any woman in the city whom he might lecherously desire to be his bedfellow, and Faustus enthusiastically embraces these surrogates, whether succubae or human females (103).

But before Faustus, disappointed with the limited knowledge granted him by Mephostophiles, surrenders himself to debauchery and practical jokes, his curiosity concerning the infernal arcane must be satisfied. His questions begin simply enough as he inquires about the nature of spirits, with probable reference to devils. In answer to his query, Mephostophiles launches into a long admonitory account of how Lucifer, the most radiant and beloved of God's angels, rebelled against his Creator, leading to his fall and that of his followers. The Spirit continues with a graphic account of Lucifer's machinations against humanity, concluding with a ghastly, blood-curdling description of hell – worthy of Dante – as a "filthy, sulphurish [sic], fiery, stinking mist or fog," a place of inconceivable and endless torment (104, 110), and this lurid depiction of hell considerably dampens Faustus's enthusiasm for his contract. However, although Mephostophiles insists that the damned can never escape from this perpetual torment and that Faustus ranks among the lost, a couple of verbal slips reveal the Spirit's belief that not only Faustus, but also the condemned spirits that fell with Lucifer may – perhaps – eventually be saved. In a shockingly unorthodox statement, Mephostophiles longingly declares that "he [Lucifer] and we all have a hope [of salvation]," although he immediately reaffirms his conviction that this yearning is "to small avail"

(111). Later, the much subdued magician inquires plaintively: "if thou wert a man in manner and form as I am, what wouldest thou do to please both God and man?" In a moment of rare compassion – the only humanizing instance for Mephostophiles in the entire narrative – the Spirit replies wistfully: "would I humble myself unto his Majesty, endeavouring in all that I could to keep His commandments, praise Him, glorify Him, that I might continue in His favour, so were I sure to enjoy the eternal joy and felicity of His kingdom" (112). Then immediately realizing his slip, Mephostophiles reiterates that this option is no longer available to Faustus, further dashing the sorcerer's hope of salvation.

The graphic descriptions of hell, the most powerful and vivid in the book, almost succeed in catalyzing Faustus's repentance, but, as the EFB author reiterates, despair overwhelms Faustus (112). Moreover, following the pattern established earlier in the marriage sequence, after applying the stick – the horrendous depiction of hell – Mephostophiles offers the carrot: "or if by chance he had any good motion, straightways the devil would thrust him a fair lady into his chamber, which fell to kissing and dalliance with him, through which means he threw his godly motions to the wind, going forward still in his wicked practices to the utter ruin both of his body and soul" (112). But even as Faustus fails to repent, the EFB author frequently reminds the reader that if Faustus had been able to achieve faith, even if he had been compelled by the contract to yield up his body, his soul would nevertheless have been saved (106).

These significant chapters affirm a number of doctrinal issues crucial to both the EFB and the GFB. First, salvation continues to be always possible for Faustus, an assurance unwittingly implied by Mephostophiles and explicitly acknowledged in the pious asides of both the EFB and GFB authors, thereby refuting the Calvinist doctrine of predestination. Second, the EFB makes reference to the theory, endorsed by the influential third-century Church father Origen Adamantius but rejected by Church orthodoxy, that eventually all rational beings – human, angelic, and demonic – would be saved.[70] Third, faith remains the most vital ingredient in salvation, thus supporting Luther's famous assertion that Christians are "justified by faith" (Romans 5:1). According to this doctrine, no matter how nefarious the deeds of the sinner, he or she can always be saved by faith in Christ, a faith that deplorably Faustus can never attain. Lastly, these chapters also identify despair – the conviction that one's transgressions, like those of Cain and Judas, are too great to be forgiven – as Faustus's mortal sin (108).

Departing from Faustus's speculations about salvation and damnation, Part II demonstrates the magus's curiosity about all aspects of the natural world as revealed in the numerous discourses between Faustus and Mephostophiles on a myriad of subjects. Of the twelve chapters composing this section, the majority are devoted to Faustus's pursuit of information about heaven, hell, and earth, as he quizzes his Spirit concerning almanacs and horoscopes, astrology, the stars, comets, thunder, and the nature of the heavens. These chapters depict the insatiable speculator with a vengeance! Some of the Spirit's answers appear true, given the limited astronomical knowledge of the period; others are confused or patently false. Moreover, Faustus, not content with unsatisfactory explanations, desires to experience heaven, Paradise, and hell first-hand. Mephostophiles does transport Faustus around the heavens, if not on the wings of an eagle at least in a dragon-drawn chariot, although, following a previously established pattern of substitutes and surrogates, Mephostophiles offers the magician a bogus vision rather than the genuine experience of hell (Chapter 20). After journeying around the heavens and taking a mock trip into hell, Faustus visits the two religious capitals of the world, Rome and Constantinople. In Rome, an invisible Faustus indulges in playing vacuous practical jokes on the Pope – while also stealing food, wine, and goblets. In Constantinople, Faustus assumes first the form of Mahomet in order to sexually enjoy the entire harem of the Turkish Emperor and, later, the shape of a Pope in his ersatz ascension to heaven. Both episodes irreverently parody figures most revered by Protestantism's two *bêtes noirs*: Catholicism and Islam (Chapter 22). Foreshadowing Part III, these two (Chapters 21 and 22) focus on licentiousness and hijinks rather than scientific inquiry.

Moving from scientific and pseudo-scientific queries to practical jokes, Part III narrates the inane antics on which Faustus squanders his dearly purchased magical power. Dissatisfied with the paltry pabulum granted him by Mephostophiles and despairing of salvation, Faustus surrenders to luxuriousness and foolish pranks as a balm to assuage his disappointment and divert him from despair. However, Faustus may also be motivated by more pragmatic concerns as he exploits his magical powers for financial rewards, performing theatrical feats for generous patrons and swindling vulnerable gulls for monetary gain.

Amid this hodgepodge of comic episodes, scholars have discerned a nebulous pattern of degeneration, and, arguably, Faustus does decline socially and ethically as the narrative progresses, although strangely irrelevant episodes sometimes obscure this downward trajectory. Certainly, Faustus does descend hierarchically. He begins his shenanigans at the top, duping first the Pope and then the Turkish Emperor. Faustus then acts as impresario to the Emperor of all Christendom, orchestrating a pageant in which appear the forms of Alexander and his Paramour, thereby winning a princely honorarium from the grateful Emperor. Significantly, Faustus explains to the Emperor that since he cannot resurrect the actual bodies of the Emperor's famous ancestors, he will raise spirits to assume their forms; thus Faustus here takes the role not of the necromancer but of the theatrical director, although the Emperor seems pleased with the substitution (Chapter 29). During this same encounter with the Emperor, Faustus mischievously puts antlers on the head of a sleeping knight, arousing much mirth at the knight's expense (Chapter 30) and motivating two unsuccessful attempts at revenge by the ridiculed nobleman (Chapters 31 and 32). The pattern of social demotion continues as Faustus moves from impresario at the Emperor's court to entertainer at the Duchy of Anhalt, providing diversion and nourishment (grapes, pears, and apples out of season) for the pregnant Duchess, while also erecting a magnificent castle for the Duke and Duchess, thereby exciting wonderment, and, we assume, a generous handout from the Duke (Chapters 39 and 40). Melanchthon recounts how a John Faust of Knutlingen also conjured grapes in winter. Interspersed between the episode at the Emperor's court and that at the castle of the Duke of Anhalt are a series of absurd escapades derived directly from the tales edited by Christoph Rosshirt, although probably finding their origin in earlier folk tales of magic. These include sequences in which Faustus hoodwinks a credulous Jewish usurer by giving him a mock leg as collateral for a loan (Chapter 33); deceives first a horse-courser and later a swineherd by selling them horses and swine, respectively, that dissolve into straw when driven over water (Chapters 34 and 38); eats a load of hay (Chapter 35); and magically mutes first a group of contentious students and later a crowd of drunken clowns (Chapters 36 and 37). Certainly, these puerile tricks represent both a social and ethical demotion. However, this downward spiral remains somewhat obscured because interwoven with these low-life antics are adventures in which Faustus interacts with upper-class friends to promote positive outcomes, usually receiving a sumptuous gift in return. He helps three friends attend a royal wedding (Chapter 32); he unites two lovers in a happy marriage (Chapter 50); and, amid winter snow, he magically conjures a beautiful garden to charm his friends at Christmas (Chapter 51). Throughout Part III, Faustus also presides over numerous bacchanals of feasting and drinking with his friends and students (Chapters 41, 42, 43, and 44), climaxing in an episode in which the magician conjures a spirit in the form of Helen of Troy, the most beautiful woman in history, for the gratification of some of his students (Chapter 45).

Faustus continues to decline ethically as the narrative progresses. In the earlier sections of the EFB, Faustus's sins, although frivolous and foolish, remain largely innocuous. However, the later section includes two incidents in which Faustus, for the first time, engages in genuinely wicked behavior: in one, Faustus commits murder; in the second, he seeks to harm a solicitous old neighbor who attempts to lead him to repentance. In the first episode, Faustus becomes inflamed with envy when he encounters a group of Jugglers (sorcerers) performing "miracles" whereby they are first beheaded and then after having their beards washed and chopped by barbers their heads are reconnected to their shoulders. Considering himself the "only Cock in the devil's basket" (164), Faustus intervenes and arranges so that the head of one magician cannot be reconnected and the sorcerer dies unshriven (Chapter 47). In the later sequence, a devout old neighbor, concerned with the welfare of the students flocking to Faustus's quarters and also with the magician's soul, confronts Faustus in his rooms, urging him to repent his nefarious apostasy and turn to God. In opposition to the Spirit who continually insists that Faustus can never be saved, the kindly old neighbor urges the ubiquity of God's grace and the ever-present opportunity for redemption, a guarantee supported by the author's many exhortatory asides and by the assurances of Faustus's students in the final chapter. Much moved by the old man's appeal, Faustus desires to repent and revoke his promise to the Devil. At that moment, however, Mephostophiles applies the stick, seizing Faustus by his head and threatening to kill him immediately if he considers penitence; moreover, in punishment for his perfidy, Mephostophiles demands that Faustus make a second pact with the Devil. So the terrified Faustus agrees and his chance for redemption slips away. Angry and frustrated at his inability to repent, Faustus projects his rage onto the old man and commands his Spirit to slay the kindly neighbor who sought to redeem him. Yet echoing the demon's failure to seduce the saintly Justina in the legend of St. Cyprian, Mephostophiles proves powerless against the old man's faith. This episode in Part III marks the nadir in Faustus's descent into depravity, as he seeks to return evil for good (Chapter 48).

Having succumbed to envy and wrath, Faustus returns to lechery. Seeking to alleviate his despair with the pleasures of the flesh, he first enjoys the sexual favors of the seven most beautiful women in the world, probably succubae assuming the shapes of the desired ladies, although the EFB remains noncommittal on this issue (Chapter 53). Later he takes Helen of Troy as his concubine (Chapter 55), although, of course, his paramour is no more the spirit of the real Helen than Luna, the consort of Simon

Magus, was the spirit of the fabled Grecian queen. Given his explanation to the Emperor, Faustus must be aware of the diabolical nature of Helen; nevertheless, he comes to love her so much that "he could not be one hour from her . . . she had so stolen away his heart" (Chapter 55). Moreover, the succubus bears him a child called Justus Faustus, who disappears with his mother after Faustus's demise.

This center section of the EFB, following the GFB, presents a potpourri of familiar stories associated with previous magi, both elevated and debased. Faustus's magical nights with the entire harem of the Turkish Emperor might recall Solomon's 700 wives and 300 concubines. The conjuring of Alexander and his consort provides an excellent exemplum of legend-grafting since myth associated Simon Magus with raising historical personages at feasts before rulers. [71] A number of zany escapades, such as horning the sleeping knight, selling fat swine and a horse that melt into bundles of straw when driven over water, muting both raucous peasants and unruly students, and allowing an irate creditor to pull off the magician's leg, might derive from anecdotes associated with the escapades of Zyto, a fourteenth-century Bohemian sorcerer, who, like so many magus figures, was associated with a miscellany of magical feats and antic jests. Also, like Albertus Magnus, Faustus conjures a glorious garden in the dead of winter; like the tenth-century sorcerer and Pope, Gerbert/Pope Sylvester II, Faustus erects a dazzlingly beautiful palace; and the odious piece of Jew-baiting, in which Faust saws off his leg and gives it to a Jewish creditor as collateral for a debt, derives from a story told about a sorcerer in 1274.[72] In addition, the trick whereby Faustus "beheads" a rival sorcerer resonates with many ancient myths of decapitation and resurrection, including a sham beheading and regeneration by Simon Magus, with the difference that in the EFB episode, there is no rebirth.[73] Finally, like Simon Magus, Faustus first raises a spirit in the likeness of Helen of Troy at the request of a group of students and later couples with this spirit. As Erich Kahler points out, the raising of Helen belonged among the commonplaces of magical lore: not only did Simon Magus claim to have resurrected and cohabited with the fair Helen of Greece, but a "sorcerer in the 'Historia' of Hans Sachs, the Nuremberg shoemaker, also produced Helen of Troy for the edification and amusement of the Emperor Maximilian."[74]

The last chapter of the book (Chapter 63) rehabilitates Faustus somewhat. Faustus throws a farewell party, a parodic Last Supper, inviting many of the beloved brethren and students with whom he has feasted and caroused throughout his twenty-four-year career, and his friends' obvious respect and fondness for him help to ameliorate his character. At this feast,

Faustus confesses his contract with the Devil to the amazement of all his comrades, who "wondered greatly thereat, that he was so blinded, for knavery, conjuration and suchlike foolish things, to give his body and soul unto the devil" (179). His friends chide him for his secrecy, insisting that had they known of his apostasy they might have helped bring him to repentance, suggesting that even now, it might not be too late. However, although his friends and students urge the desperate magician to pray, the EFB denies the tormented sorcerer even this last slim hope of salvation, describing how Faustus tried to pray but could not: "but even as Cain he also said his sins were greater than God was able to forgive" (179). Thus, after they have prayed for him, his companions weep and depart, leaving Faustus to face his doom alone. Next day, Faustus's friends, who had not slept a wink that night, encounter a horrific scene: a parlor splashed with blood, fragments of brain, teeth, and eyes, and dismembered limbs, but the book makes no reference to the fate of Faustus's immortal soul. The final chapter concludes with a solemn, cautionary coda, warning all readers to heed the frightful and horrible example of Faustus's contract and death.

To summarize, the EFB, following the GFB, creates a multifaceted hero: part insatiable quester after forbidden knowledge, part lecher, part infantile prankster, and part convivial drinking partner, hale-fellow-well-met, and likable joker. Moreover, despite the EFB's consistent refrain of sanctimonious censure, Faustus emerges as a strangely sympathetic hero, primarily because of the vast gap between the relative puerility of his sins and the enormity of his punishment – at least to a contemporary and even, I suspect, to many a sixteenth-century reader. Thus, although the author, through edifying asides, insists throughout that repentance is always possible, the book depicts the portrait of a removed and inscrutable Deity.

The EFB follows the GFB so closely that any salient differences between the two texts deserve consideration. Jones concludes that the majority of P. F.'s changes from the German original are stylistic.[75] However, Jones also convincingly argues that in two substantive areas the English translation diverges markedly from the German original. First, P. F. depicts Mephostophiles as more dominating and frightening than the GFB Spirit, elevating him to the status of a prince, the ruler of all the circuit from Septentrio to the Meridian. Second, P. F. alters his source to present his Devil as more malicious than his GFB counterpart. The episode in which Faustus questions his Spirit concerning the creation of the world offers an example of the increased malevolence of P. F.'s Mephostophiles. In the GFB, when asked to describe the creation of the world, the imperturbable Spirit blatantly lies, stating that God did not create the world or mankind but that both have existed since eternity. Faustus remembers the story of Genesis and remains unconvinced, but, subdued, he does not cavil. In the following chapter, Faustus receives a state visit from the whole infernal hierarchy in their true bestial shapes, but this visit apparently bears no relationship to Faustus's earlier inquiry, nor is this diabolical masquerade intended to punish or intimidate. The EFB treats the analogous episode (Chapter 19) very differently. Mephostophiles not only refuses to answer Faustus's query, stating, "I am not bound unto thee in such respects as concerns the hurt of our kingdome" (116), but when the stubborn knowledge-seeker perseveres, the angry Spirit threatens to tear the intransigent necromancer into a thousand pieces. Immediately after, the greatest Devil in hell appears, accompanied by his hideous and diabolical company in various bestial shapes, and this infernal visitation functions as both a warning and a punishment for the insubordination implicit in Faustus's question.[76] I suggest that by stressing Mephostophiles's role as a bully, P. F. renders his hero more sympathetic.

P. F. makes another significant alteration to his source that expands Faustus's gratifications from the contract. After refusing to grant Faustus a wife, the Spirit of the GFB promises him "if thou canst not live chastely, then will I lead to thy bed any day or night whatever woman thou seest in the city or elsewhere," while making it plain to the reader that all of these women are succubae. Conversely, the EFB remains silent on the actual nature of these willing sexual partners. William Empson insists that the women Mephostophiles procures for Faustus in recompense for his lack of a wife or to detract him from pious thoughts are all real in the EFB, whereas in the German text they are explicitly devils or succubae. Jones agrees and expands this difference in the two texts to include the seven most beautiful women with whom Faustus cohabits.[77] However, I have problems with the arguments of both Empson and Jones. I contend that given the emphasis in the jest book on both the ubiquity of free will and the limitations of the Devil's power, it appears highly unlikely that the Devil could coerce these beautiful women to sexual activities against their wills. Thus although the GFB makes explicit the diabolic identity of these women, the EFB remains ambiguous on this issue, thereby creating an atmosphere of uncertainty that will influence subsequent recreations of the Faust legend.

Despite these many changes, the EFB maintains the central theology of the German original. In addition, both *Faustbooks* support the thesis of this study, the conviction that the Faust legend in each of its permutations mirrors the ethos of the period in which it was written. Thus, both the GFB and the EFB, in their fascination with the Devil, hell, and witchcraft, their anti-clerical bias, and their elevation of faith over works, reflect the militant Protestantism of the time and place as well as the obsession with witchcraft sweeping Europe and England in the sixteenth century.

When compared to the illustrious magi of mythic lore – Zoroaster, Pythagoras, Apollonius of Tyana, Virgil, Merlin, Roger Bacon – the *historical* Faust ranks low on the thaumaturgic totem pole.[78] However, the *legendary* Faust has soared above his cohorts in magic to become practically a household word, while many of his fellow magi have receded into obscurity. The fame of Faust, I argue, derives in no small part from the intervention of a brash young sixteenth-century genius, as arrogant and aspiring as Faust himself, whose mighty poetic incantation released the magician from the confines of the antic *Faustbooks* and set him on his path to immortality. That playwright's name was Christopher Marlowe.

CHAPTER 2

Marlowe's Doctor Faustus

Introduction

Critical consensus identifies Christopher Marlowe's *Doctor Faustus*, written in either 1588 or 1592, as the first great tragedy in the English language, a powerful drama that ushered in thirty years of unparalleled creativity on the English stage. However, Marlowe's most often read and most frequently performed play offers the ultimate scholarly conundrum. For over 400 years, the play has been surrounded by conjecture; indeed, second only to Shakespeare's *Hamlet, Doctor Faustus* may be the most controversial drama ever written. Almost every aspect of the play has been questioned: the date has been disputed; the authorship of the comic sections has been challenged; the correct text has been contested; and the meaning of the play has been vigorously debated. This chapter seeks to guide students and scholars of Marlowe through this labyrinth of critical controversy and to aid them in gaining a fuller appreciation of the originality and profundity of this memorable work.

Date

Did *Doctor Faustus* first appear on the London stage in 1588, immediately following Marlowe's triumphant theatrical debut with *Tamburlaine, Part I* and *Part II*, or does the play represent Marlowe's crowning dramatic achievement, composed sometime in 1592–93, shortly before his tragic and untimely death? Critical opinion on this issue has long been divided, with the majority of critics favoring the earlier date. Critics supporting an early date cite the possible allusions to *Doctor Faustus* in both dramatic and nondramatic literature predating 1592: *Friar Bacon and Friar Bungay* (1588), *The Taming of the Shrew* (1588–93?), *A Looking Glass for London and England* (1591), *A Knack to Know a Knave* (1592), and the anonymous "A ballad of the life and deathe of Doctor Faustus the great Cunngerer" (Stationers' Register, 1589). But, as Bruce Brandt sensibly points out, "conclusions based on dramatic allusions are complicated by textual problems, dating problems and questions of who borrowed from whom."[1] More significant is William Prynne's ominous 1633 reference to

> the visible apparition of the devil on the stage of the Belsavage playhouse, in Queen Elizabeth's days, to the great amazement both of the actors and spectators, while they were there playing the History of Faustus . . .

Since the Belsavage Playhouse was in use only until 1588–89, if accepted as valid this statement offers convincing evidence for an early performance of a drama about *Doctor Faustus*, most probably Marlowe's play.[2]

The case for the later date of 1592–93 rests on one important piece of evidence. Among the many questions surrounding Marlowe's enigmatic play, one certainty emerges: almost all scholars agree upon Marlowe's source for his drama, the *English Faustbook* authored by P. F. Gent, and the earliest extant edition of this jest book was not published until 1592. Scholars favoring an earlier date suggest that Marlowe must have read the *English Faustbook* in some previous version: some interpret the statement on the title page of the 1592 edition that describes the book as "newly imprinted, and in convenient places imperfect matter amended" as alluding to an earlier edition; others speculate that Marlowe may have read P. F.'s jest book in manuscript. Finally, an Oxford inventory of books published in 1587 makes reference to what is probably an early English version of the *English Faustbook*.[3] However, all of these assumptions, although persuasive, fail to prove the point; thus, the problem of dating, like so many of the issues surrounding this problematic play, remains an unresolved ambiguity.

Text

Perhaps the most vexing controversy concerns the valid text of the play, which exists in two very different versions, both printed after Marlowe's death: the A-text published in 1604 and the B-text published in 1616. The B-text, by far the longer of the two, contains a number of largely comic episodes and 676 additional lines not found in the A-text. For decades the argument over the textual authenticity of these two very different versions has engaged Marlowe scholars, with critical consensus oscillating back and forth between the original preference for the A-text, the later defense of the B-text, and the current re-endorsement of the A-text. Supporters of the

B-text have dismissed the terser A-version as a memorial reconstruction or a truncated adaptation for a touring company, while advocates of the A-text have rejected the additional lines in the B-version as the additions for which Philip Henslowe, an Elizabethan theatrical entrepreneur and part-owner of the Rose Theater, paid William Birde and Samuel Rowley in 1602. Because of the very different ideologies informing each version, Michael J. Warren and Leah S. Marcus have concluded that the two texts should be treated as separate plays, and a number of editors now include both versions in their editions.[4] Following current critical consensus, with which I agree, I shall assume that the A-text most closely represents Marlowe's vision of the play, and all quotations from *Doctor Faustus* in this volume will be from the A-text unless otherwise noted.[5]

Authorship

Much less worrisome is the question of authorship since the majority of critics, including myself, concur that *Doctor Faustus* represents a collaborative effort. Most commentators award Marlowe the eloquent, stirring scenes bracketing the tragedy, while relegating to the collaborator the majority of Faustus's comic antics in Acts 3 and 4 as well as the hijinks of the clowns in the farcical sub-plot. An anonymous wit once quipped that the tragedy has a beginning, a muddle, and an end, and critics have tended to attribute the "muddle" to Marlowe's collaborator. However, the comic sections have also mustered defenders who argue for a careful thematic counterpoint between the comic and tragic episodes of the drama. W. W. Greg insists that Marlowe planned the whole and that his collaborators carried out his plan according to his instructions.[6] Focusing primarily on the B-text, G. K. Hunter demonstrates a carefully structured trajectory of social and professional descent operating throughout the comic sections in Acts 3 and 4.[7] Similarly privileging the B-text, Robert Ornstein reveals how the farcical capers of the clowns burlesque Faustus's grandiose aspirations.[8] And even Johann Wolfgang von Goethe famously exclaimed of the entire play: "How greatly is it all planned!"[9]

Scholarly consensus offers less unanimity on the identity of Marlowe's collaborator or collaborators. The leading candidates are Samuel Rowley and/or William Birde, both reimbursed by Philip Henslowe for later additions to the play, a transaction recorded in *Henslowe's Diary.* Another popular nominee is Thomas Nashe, putative collaborator with Marlowe on *Dido, Queene of Carthage.* Finally, Bevington and Rasmussen propose Henry Porter as a likely candidate, since Porter was a contemporary of Marlowe at Cambridge and a dramatist for the Admiral's Men at the time.[10] But the identity of Marlowe's collaborator(s) remains another of the many unsolved mysteries haunting the play.

The Source

Chapter 1 of this study enumerates the changes that P. F. makes in his translation of the GFB into English. Significantly, Marlowe adapts all of these alterations, and these and other minor modifications to the GFB help to identify the EFB, not the GFB, which Marlowe might well have read in the original German, as the source for the drama. As John D. Jump observes, P. F. augments the account of Faustus's travels to Rome to include references to Virgil's tomb, Saint Mark's Cathedral, and the Tiber, all of which are unmistakably echoed in Marlowe's play. Jump further marshals an impressive array of other evidence to identify the EFB as Marlowe's source:

> The articles of Faustus' compact with Lucifer as given in scene v of the play agree with P. F.'s version in that the fourth of them is a conflation of the fourth and fifth articles of the German original; whereas the German author makes Faustus blow in the Pope's face, the playwright in scene ix follows P. F. in making him smite the Pope in the face; and in the same scene the playwright takes over from P.F. the addition to the Pope's curse of "Bel, Booke, and Candle."[11]

Therefore, despite the many other ambiguities surrounding Marlowe's tragedy, few scholars would deny the EFB as the unquestionable source for the play.

Performance History

William Prynne's reference to the appearance of the Devil on the stage of the Belsavage Theatre has led most theater historians to identify 1588 or 1589 as the date of the first performance of *Doctor Faustus*. However, the first documented performance, referred to in *Henslowe's Diary*, did not take place until September 30, 1594 at the Rose Theatre, and many subsequent, highly remunerative performances attest to the play's success. Henslowe records seven stagings in each of the following years, 1594, 1595, and 1596, as well as a revival in 1597. Other references imply that the play was enacted numerous times between 1597 and 1603, and Henslowe's commissioning in 1604 of additions to the play bears witness to the drama's popularity and to the public's demand for more rousing comedy and more spectacular demonic pranks. The play, probably including the additions, was also performed in Graz (Austria) and in Dresden in 1608 and 1626, respectively, and was still being staged a year or so before the closing of the theaters in 1642. As Bevington concludes: "Not many other plays of the English Renaissance can touch that record."[12] However, tastes change, and Restoration adaptations of the play trivialized Marlowe's great drama, expanding the play's buffoonery and all but eliminating the woe and wonder of its tragic elements, with the result that *Doctor Faustus,* the first great tragedy in the English language, disappeared entirely from the English stage until 1885, when it was revived at London's Lyceum Theatre. The play was staged several times during the late nineteenth and early twentieth centuries and by the 1940s and 1950s had become an established feature of the classical repertory. Since that time, *Doctor Faustus* has been continually performed throughout the English-speaking world, and these many productions establish it as Marlowe's most frequently performed drama.

The Play

In *The Tudor Play of Mind,* Joel Altman situates the problematic dramas of the early modern theater within the convention of arguing on both sides of the question. Altman describes the interrogative plays so popular at this period as constructed from a series of statements and counterstatements, both equally valid, in which thesis evokes antithesis, yet without resolving synthesis. These plays ask questions rather than providing answers and deliberately arouse mixed reactions in their audiences.[13] Although all of Marlowe's plays have traditionally evoked contradictory responses, none has provoked the heated debate generated by *Doctor Faustus.* Establishing the polarities of this response are Una Ellis-Fermor and George Santayana, at one extreme, and Leo Kirschbaum, at the other. Ellis-Fermor and Santayana, the prototypic heroic expositors of the play, identify *Doctor Faustus* as "the most nearly Satanic tragedy that can be found," and Faustus as "a martyr to everything that the Renaissance prized – power, curious knowledge, enterprise, wealth, and beauty." Conversely, Kirschbaum, a leading Christian interpreter, insists: "there is no more obvious Christian document in all Elizabethan drama than *Doctor Faustus,*" dismissing Faustus as "a wretched creature who for lower values gives up higher values . . ."[14] Even though the majority of commentators today assume less hyperbolic stances, Faustus still arouses widely disparate reactions in audiences and critics alike, ranging from breathless admiration for the magician's aspiring mind and eloquent verse to utter contempt for his inane tricks. These widely divergent responses suggest that in *Doctor Faustus* Marlowe has penned an interrogative drama that brilliantly argues on both sides of the question. Indeed, Robert Logan has identified Marlowe's deliberate use of ambiguity as his definitive aesthetic characteristic and the source of his greatest influence on Shakespeare.[15]

Much of the interrogative tenor of Marlowe's play derives from its accepted source, since Marlowe retains the hybrid form of the EFB and the bifurcated figure of its hero. If anything, this insatiable dramatic innovator exacerbates the paradoxical quality of his source, creating one of the most problematic plays and most oxymoronic heroes in all of literature. In adapting the jest book magus to the pattern of a tragic hero, Marlowe pours out the riches of his mighty line to stress his hero's titanic qualities while, at the same time, accentuating the magician's self deceit in order to create a psychologically credible portrait of the tormented magician. This simultaneous elevation and deflation permeates Marlowe's tragedy, particularly in its treatment of Faustus's motivation, his temptation, his rewards, and his tragic failure to repent.

A Christian Reading of the Play

A comparison between play and source reveals a number of modifications that support a Christian reading of the play.[16] First, let us consider the much debated crux of Faustus's motivation. What drive impels the eminent Divine to reject discursive knowledge for the occult science of magic? Is it desire for worldly pleasure, forbidden knowledge, godlike power, or a combination of all three? As discussed in the previous chapter, the *Faustbooks* offer two primary incentives for Faustus's fatal contract: a voracious curiosity for arcane knowledge and an itch for sensual pleasure. In his dramatic adaptation Marlowe surpasses his source in deeply probing his hero's motivation, during the first two acts of the play allowing Faustus consistently to rhapsodize on his dreams.

Throughout these rhapsodies, the magus stresses his desire for wealth, fame, and, most centrally, power. In his opening ecstatic reverie, immediately following the rejection of divinity for "heavenly necromancy," Marlowe's magician, like his fellow hedonist in the EFB, grants pleasure ('profit and delight') priority, but immediately expands this pleasure to include power, both metaphysical and political:

All things that move between the quiet poles
Shall be at my command. Emperors and Kings
Are but obeyed in their several provinces,
Nor can they raise the wind or rend the clouds;
But his dominion that exceeds in this
Stretcheth as far as doth the mind of man.
A sound magician is a mighty god.
Here, Faustus, try thy brains to gain a deity. (1.1.58–65)

Conversely, the sorcerer of the EFB never presumes to control nature; although he desires to have the powers of a spirit – certainly a less ambitious violation of hierarchy – he never aspires to be a god!

Following the departure of the Good and Evil Angels, Marlowe's Faustus again revels in visions of glory and wealth. The thrilling exuberance of this passage should not obscure the basic materialism underlying his longing for "gold," "pearls," and "princely delicates." In his earlier soliloquy, Faustus had surprisingly made no mention of the quest for forbidden knowledge so central to both *Faustbooks*. Now, for the first time, Faustus reveals not only the innate human desire for resolution of ambiguities, but also a curiosity – like his predecessors in both *Faustbooks* – concerning esoteric lore, in this case, knowledge of "strange philosophy" and "the secrets of all foreign kings" (1.1.88–89). However, the concluding ten lines of the soliloquy (90–99) shift the emphasis from wealth, fame, and knowledge to catalogue the desperate enterprises Faustus hopes to undertake with his newly acquired power. These represent a remarkable pastiche of subversive fantasies whereby Faustus desires to turn all hierarchies topsy-turvy: Faustus would disrupt natural law, altering the geography of Europe by making swift Rhine circle fair Wittenberg; he would violate political hierarchy, dethroning hereditary monarchs and reigning "sole king" of all the provinces; and he would upset social privilege, transgressing the sumptuary laws and clothing the public-school students in the silk normally reserved for the aristocracy. These sumptuary laws specifically reserve silk garments for gentlemen and ladies, usually those with revenues of at least 20 pounds a year. A. W. Ward notes that "Silk was considered a reprehensive luxury in persons not belonging to the upper or wealthier classes" and "Simplicity of apparel was enjoined in both English and German Universities" and, presumably, in the public schools as well. [17] Thus, while partisan Protestants might applaud Faustus's patriotic aspirations to wall Protestant Germany with brass and chase the Catholic Prince of Parma from the land (an enterprise that the armies of Elizabeth had not been able to accomplish), and the students in the audience would surely cheer the prospect of finer apparel, more traditional spectators might recognize the presumption inherent in this hymn to soaring ambition and social upheaval.

Faustus's desire for wealth and fame dominates the succeeding dialogue with Valdes and Cornelius as the two tempters fervently anticipate treasure (1.1.132–34, 146–50), fame (119–22, 143–45), and control over spirits (123–25) as rewards for Faustus's incantations, but the only knowledge mentioned is the occult skill necessary for acquiring this wealth, fame, and power. Although the presence here of human tempters, as in Shakespeare's *Macbeth*, serves to partially mitigate Faustus's responsibility for his downfall, Faustus himself locates his decision to conjure the Devil not in the enticements of Valdes and Cornelius but in his own fantasy, "That will receive no object, for my head / But ruminates on necromantic skill" (1.1.106–07).

In his first confrontation with Mephistopheles, Faustus continues to express his yearning for wealth, pleasure, and, especially, power. Faustus particularly specifies control over Mephistopheles, who will be at his command, bringing him whatever he desires (see Figure 2.1). Then in ten lines of soaring rhetoric, Faustus, like Tamburlaine before him, elevates the "sweet fruition of an earthly crown" (*Tam.* 1, 2.7.29) over "knowledge infinite," envisioning himself not as a sage but as "great emperor of the world" (DF, 1.3.106), a political ambition completely absent from the EFB. By introducing this new ingredient into Faustus's aspiration, Marlowe renders Faustus's later encounter with the Emperor (4.1) trenchantly ironic, counterbalancing Faustus's grandiose boast, "The Emperor shall not live but by my leave" (1.3.112) with the magician's later subservience to this same monarch in Act 4 (4.1.13–18).

But where is the "insatiable Speculator" of traditional criticism, the Renaissance martyr to humanity's search for knowledge? I would argue that this curious quester after knowledge still lurks within the persona of Marlowe's hero, although he occupies a less dominant position than in the EFB counterpart. Nevertheless, Marlowe's sorcerer does retain vestiges of the keen curiosity of the EFB original. Like his predecessor, immediately after signing the contract, Marlowe's Faustus queries Mephistopheles concerning the metaphysics of hell, although, unlike the EFB magician, he declines to accept the hard realities of his discovery. Furthermore, Marlowe's necromancer shows an avid interest in astronomical lore, asking probing questions concerning the heavenly bodies. Seeking knowledge of first as well as secondary causes, Marlowe's Faustus boldly demands to know, "Tell me who made the world" (2.3.66), and, like his EFB

Figure 2.1 Woodcut of Faustus conjuring Mephistopheles. Title page to Christopher Marlowe's *The Tragical History of the Life and Death of Doctor Faustus*, 1631 edition. Photograph by Culture Club/Hulton Archive/Getty Images.

counterpart, suffers bullying by devils for his presumption. Significantly, twice Mephistopheles refuses to grant Faustus's desires – first, he denies him a wife, secondly, knowledge of creation – and, on both occasions, devils (Mephistopheles and Lucifer, respectively) divert Faustus from thoughts of rebellion with books of occult knowledge (2.1.162–68; 2.3.171–73). Later, Marlowe's Faustus travels the universe in a dragon-drawn chariot "to know the secrets of astronomy" (Chorus 3.2), as does his EFB analogue. Although consonant with the play's consistent minimizing of intellectual satisfaction, for either thematic or theatrical reasons, Marlowe's tragedy condenses the five chapters in the source exhibiting Faustus's astronomical expertise to four lines of choral comment in the A-text (Chorus 4.8–11) with no reference at all in the B-text.

Finally, critics, like Santayana and Ellis-Fermor, who interpret Faustus as a martyr to the Renaissance love of beauty as well as knowledge, might cite the harmonies of Homer and Amphion (2.3.24–30), as well as the beauty of Helen (5.1.91–110), as compensations for Faustus's disappointing contract. Nevertheless, Faustus, like the audience, should be aware that these shadows are really spirits, probably devils, assuming the roles of the fabled figures, not the shades of the mythic personages themselves. Most commentators agree that in the play the term "spirit" generally refers to "devil," making the diabolical nature of these classical impersonators highly probable.

Of course, Faustus, the supreme overreacher, wants it all: power, wealth, fame, pleasure, and knowledge. Nevertheless, a Christian reading would insist that the quest for forbidden knowledge emerges as a more prominent feature of the EFB than of Marlowe's tragedy. According to this perspective, the desire for power is revealed as Faustus's *hamartia*, and the necromancer, in this instance following Simon Magus more closely than his EFB counterpart, seeks knowledge primarily as an appurtenance to power and pleasure or as a means of obtaining them. By shifting the emphasis from the sin of Prometheus to that of Lucifer, Marlowe ironically undercuts his hero's grandiose ambitions, largely invalidating the heroic view of Faustus as a martyr to the Renaissance search for knowledge.

The Christian interpretation of Faustus's motivation supports the thesis of this book, which contends that the aspirations of Faust figures almost invariably reflect the value systems of the societies that produce them. Thus, Marlowe's *Doctor Faustus*, probably written in 1588, the very year that the stalwart English defeated the mighty Spanish Armada, radiates with the heady intoxication with power so characteristic of this period. In the 1580s, England became more actively involved with both European politics and the exploration of the New World. In 1580, Sir Francis Drake dropped anchor in Southampton after a three-year voyage in which he circumnavigated the globe, returning with a ship loaded with treasure. In 1587, England embarked on two military interventions: one in the Low Countries to aid their rebellion against Spain; the other in France to assist Navarre against the Guise. This was also a time of tremendous tension between the militant strategies of the court hawks – the Earl of Leicester, Sir Walter Raleigh, Sir Francis Drake – and the more cautious policies of Elizabeth and her councilors. However, despite Elizabeth's more prudent polities, war fever was in the air, and Marlowe's Faustus expresses the desire for political dominance motivating both the belligerent court leaders and the combative populace. [18]

According to Christian commentators, Marlowe also modifies his source to suggest willful self-deceit as a determinant in Faustus's damnation. This perversion of reason by passion finds a brief analogue in the EFB, but this occurs later than in the play and remains undeveloped. Initially, the EFB magician is not deceived concerning the reality of damnation and vainly seeks to obtain his requests of the devil without the loss of his soul (96). However, a change occurs after his second parley with the infernal Spirit, and Faustus's mind becomes so inflamed with greed that "he forgot his soul and promised Mephostophiles to hold all things as he had mentioned them; he thought the devil was not so black as they use to paint him, nor hell so hot as people say, etc." (97). After the contract and his enjoyment of its many fruits – fine wines, delicious food, rich apparel – Faustus's reason becomes so clouded that he doubts the existence of the very Spirit with whom he has so recently made a bargain:

> Doctor Faustus continued thus in his epicurish life day and night, and believed not that there was a God, hell, or devil: he thought that the body and soul died together, and had quite forgotten divinity or the immortality of the soul but stood in his damnable heresy day and night. (101)

This brief reference perhaps provided the inspiration for Marlowe's complex treatment of the perversion of reason by desire.

In the EFB, only after the infernal covenant does Faustus become completely deluded; in Marlowe's tragedy, at least according to Christian readers, Faustus manifests this delusion in his opening soliloquy, a masterly exemplum of reason pandering will. The opening scene of the play discovers the eminent divine in his study surveying his career opportunities in an attempt to "settle his studies." Systematically, he investigates the various vocations in which he claims to be an adept, the four great professions of the early modern period – philosophy, medicine, law, and divinity. Faustus's canvass of his professional opportunities, particularly his consideration of medicine and rejection of divinity, may have been suggested by a passage from the EFB, which describes how after he received his degree, Faustus fell into deep cogitations and "sometime he would throw the scriptures from him as though he had no care of his former profession" (92). In addition, "he could not abide to be called doctor of divinity but waxed a worldly man and named himself an astrologian, and a mathematician: and for a shadow, sometimes a physician, and did great cures, namely with herbs, roots, waters, drinks, receipts and clysters" (93). From these two brief allusions, Marlowe may have crafted Faustus's memorable opening soliloquy. For an early modern audience, the soliloquy provided a vehicle for a character to express his or her inner thoughts; thus information presented in soliloquy can be considered reliable or at least representative of the truth as the speaker perceives it, and no character on the early modern stage deliberately lies in soliloquy, although he or she may be mistaken or even self-deceived. I submit that Faustus's complex opening address – anticipating Iago's "motive hunting of a motiveless malignity," to quote Coleridge's memorable phrase – constitutes the first time on the early modern stage that a character rationalizes in soliloquy.

This rationalization permeates Faustus's rejection of the four great professions of the early modern period in favor of necromancy. From one perspective, this refutation of traditional learning for magic can be seen as the archetypical choice of empirical over discursive knowledge, since empirical science at this time was often associated with magic, and many of the leading scientists of the medieval and early modern periods – Roger Bacon, Cornelius Agrippa, Paracelsus, John Dee – were considered white magicians. Nevertheless a Christian reading would insist that despite his fascination with astronomy and astral travel, Faustus's primary motivation remains power, not empirical knowledge of the world. Moreover, in his dismissal of discursive knowledge, Faustus's specious rationale implies that the limitation lies not in these studies but in himself, and that his refutation of these possible careers provides a convenient rationalization for his future conduct. First, Faustus considers and then discards philosophy:

> Sweet *Analytics*, 'tis thou hast ravished me!
> [*He reads*] *Bene disserere est finis logices.*
> Is to dispute well logic's chiefest end?   (1.1.6–8)

As a number of scholars have recognized, in his opening soliloquy, Faustus consistently misquotes learned authorities, often out of context, twisting their meanings to justify his desires. For example, in eschewing philosophy, Faustus cites Ramus, although appearing to read from Aristotle's *Analytics*; moreover, the cited passage from Ramus actually suggests that the end of logic is not to win arguments, as Faustus seems to conclude, but to discover truth:

> Man ought to study dialectic in order to dispute well, because it proclaims to us the *truth of all argument* and as a consequence the falsehood, whether the truth be necessary, as in science, or, as in opinion, contingent, that is to say, capable both of *being and non being* (emphasis mine).[19]

Reinforcing Ramus, Pierre de La Primaudaye in *The French Academie*, a popular book with which Marlowe might have been familiar, comments on "what men ought chiefly to level at," observing that the "art" of philosophy is "to find out and to know the truth both of divine and human things." [20] Rejecting Analytics, Faustus also bids "*On kai me on*" ("being and non-being") farewell (1.1.12). R. W. Dent speculates that the term "*On kai me on*" may derive from the Ramus quotation adduced above since it appears rarely in the writings of the ancients; conversely, John D. Jump identifies it as a transliteration of a phrase found, not in Aristotle, but in the sophist Gorgias. [21] Whatever the origin of this phrase, Faustus's denial of a discipline that deals with such crucial issues as "being and non-being" on the grounds that this discipline is limited to debate remains highly questionable, and the perceptive members of the audience might infer that the inadequacy resides in Faustus's own egocentric perspective rather than in the nature of logic itself.

Faustus next turns to medicine and continues to misquote his sources, attributing the line "*ubi desinit philosophus, ibi incipit medicus*" ("where the philosopher leaves off, there the physician begins," 1.1.13) to Galen, although, according to Jump, this sentence is freely adapted from Aristotle's *De sensu*. [22] Congruent with his earlier confusion of values, Faustus contemplates physic (the art or science of healing diseases) not primarily as a method of conquering illness but as a means of garnering wealth and posthumous fame, and he eschews it because, like logic, it does not offer him the superhuman power and eternal renown for which he yearns (1.1.14–26). The lines 24–26, "Wouldst thou make man to live eternally? / Or, being dead, raise them to life again? / Then this profession were to be esteemed," contain an allusion to Christ, who, according to Christian doctrine, possesses these exact powers. This passage reaffirms Faustus's desire for godhead, a pinnacle to which the EFB Faustus never aspires, although both the Antichrist from the biblical cycle plays and Simon Magus claimed to possess the powers of Christ, including the power to raise the dead.

In his evaluation of law, Faustus further reveals his powers of rationalization, dismissing law as dealing only with "paltry legacies" and "external trash," a discipline too "servile" for Marlowe's overreacher (1.1.27–36). Many a sixteenth-century audience member, as well as a contemporary one, might applaud Faustus's debunking of legal pettifoggery, but Faustus should also remember that law deals not only with the minutiae of "petty legacies" but with such critical issues as guilt and innocence, crime and punishment – in a word, with justice. Moreover, Faustus rejects law because, like philosophy and medicine, it does not offer him the "world of profit and delight" for which he yearns.

After repudiating philosophy, medicine, and law, Faustus turns to divinity, at this time considered the Queen of the Sciences, and his earlier misquotations prepare the audience for his notorious fallacious syllogism. The syllogism consists of linking together two biblical verses, "The reward of sin is death" (Romans 6:23) and "If we say that we have no sin, / We deceive ourselves, and there's no truth in us" (1 John 1:8), to draw the conclusion, "Why then belike we must sin, / And so consequently die. / Ay, we must die an everlasting death" (1.1.39–48). In a sense, orthodox Christianity of the period affirmed that the sin of Adam and Eve had doomed humanity to die an everlasting death, while also acknowledging that this same humanity had been ransomed by the sacrifice of the atonement. Thus, although a kind of logic informs Faustus's syllogism, this logic depends on ignoring the promise of commutation contained in the second half of each scripture that nullifies the condemnation of the first half.

How can we explain the obvious sophistry of Faustus's logic? How could so eminent a theologian as Doctor Faustus fail to recall the ameliorating complement of each of these two verses? Both verses, as part of the Book of Common Prayer, would have been familiar to even an occasional church-goer, but particularly the passage from John, one of the *Thirty-Nine Articles of the Church of England* and a passage authorized for both Morning and Evening Prayer. As Tom Rutter points out, this passage is also cited in full in the popular *Homily on the Misery of Mankind*. Moreover, the passage from Romans appeared in the service for the seventh Sunday after Trinity, was often quoted in the Homilies, and constituted a favorite subject for biblical exegesis. [23] Given the extreme familiarity of these two passages, the caveat: "the reward of sin is death," would surely have automatically recalled for the audience its mitigating complement: "but the gift of God *is* eternal life, through Jesus Christ our Lord" (Romans 6:23). Moreover, the assertion: "If we say that we have no sin, we deceive ourselves, and truth is not in us," would have similarly evoked the promise of Christ's mercy: "If we acknowledge our sins, he is faithful and just, to forgive us our sins, and to cleanse us from all unrighteousness" (1 John 1:8–9). [24] It seems unthinkable that so learned a scholar as Doctor Faustus should fail to remember two such well-known verses of scripture. Perhaps Faustus unconsciously suppresses the second half of each scripture because believing himself irrevocably damned the promise that each contains has for him no real relevance, or because the recognition of this promise would interfere with the course of action on which he has already determined. [25] Or is Marlowe, the theatrical showman, deliberately teasing his audience by introducing a fascinating ambiguity, an ambiguity that will pervade the play and later become his signature?

Reinforcing the assumption that a biblically indoctrinated sixteenth-century audience would have recognized the fallacy of Faustus's logic, scholars have argued that not only the two verses but also Faustus's very syllogism was a commonplace of the period. Paul Kocher discovered a refutation of a similar syllogism in *The Dialogue between the Christian Knight and Satan* by Thomas Becon, and Susan Snyder located a parallel syllogism in the writings of Martin Luther: "He [the Devil] can fashion the strangest syllogisms, 'You have sinned; God is wrathful toward sinners; therefore despair.'" After reaching this philosophical cul-de-sac, Luther gives advice that Faustus might well have heeded: "Here it is necessary to proceed from the Law to the Gospel and lay hold of the article of the forgiveness of sin."[26] Given the familiarity of both the biblical verses and perhaps even of Faustus's syllogism, Marlowe might reasonably expect the majority of his audience to immediately recognize the sophistry of Faustus's logic and grasp the implications of his failure to dispute well.

Faustus's rationalizations about hell further reflect his self-delusion. Having convinced himself that damnation is ineluctable, he seeks to define it in palatable terms. Damnation initially terrifies him not at all; he judges hell a fable (2.1.130) and confounds it in Elysium (1.3.61). When confronted with undeniable evidence to the contrary – Mephistopheles come from hell to seize his "glorious" soul – he employs casuistic reasoning to convince himself that Mephistopheles cannot be in hell, completely ignoring the definition of terms that would invalidate his logic (2.1.130–42), as he ignores anything that might impede his headlong career toward power and pleasure.

Similarly, Marlowe's protagonist dismisses all of the Devil's warnings. First, he ignores the account of Lucifer's fall by aspiring pride, presented as a kind of "mirror for magistrates" in which he may view his own image and possible fate (1.3.64–74), since Lucifer clearly exemplifies the same prideful overreaching that characterizes Faustus. The Lucifer analogue, although introduced at similar points in both play and source, receives very different treatment in the two versions (cf. EFB, 95; DF, 1.3.64–74). In the EFB, the Spirit acknowledges but minimizes Lucifer's sin, while accentuating Lucifer's glamour and puissance; only after the contract does he grant Faustus a fuller chronicle of Lucifer's physical and social descent. Conversely, in the parallel scene in Marlowe's play, Mephistopheles accentuates Lucifer's pride and insolence and his power and eminence are minimized.

Second, although the EFB demon gives an orthodox report of Lucifer's rebellion, before the compact he withholds any reference to the suffering of

the fallen angels, whereas Marlowe's fiend graphically depicts the torment
of the damned even before the compact. Incredibly, Marlowe's Faustus
fails to heed Mephistopheles's passionate exhortation to "leave these frivolous demands" (1.3.83) and remains unmoved by the demon's poignant
description of the psychological pain of hell (1.3.78–84), so much more
sophisticated than the crude version of a physical hell depicted in the EFB,
but no less terrible:

> Why, this is hell, nor am I out of it.
> Think'st thou that I, who saw the face of God,
> And tasted the eternal joys of heaven,
> Am not tormented with ten thousand hells
> In being deprived of everlasting bliss?
> O, Faustus, leave these frivolous demands,
> Which strike a terror to my fainting soul!   (1.3.78–84)

The unfortunate necromancer of the EFB receives no such cautionary
advice and his Spirit presents no portrait of damnation before the signing
of the bond, although after the contract Mephistopheles describes hell with
lurid particularity. Here, Marlowe surprisingly reverses the traditional roles
of tempter and tempted. The tempter of both *Faustbooks*, like the morality
Vice and any savvy salesman, minimizes the liabilities and maximizes the
advantages of his product until he has his victim's name on the dotted line,
while the vacillating conjuror seeks the best bargain possible. Conversely,
in Marlowe's drama, Mephistopheles frequently speaks the truth and, in
this instance, even urges his "client" to abstain from purchasing his product
at such an exorbitant price, while Marlowe's Faustus himself plays the
Devil's Advocate. Therefore, according to a Christian reading, Marlowe
consistently alters his source to highlight Faustus's responsibility for his
damnation and to ironically undermine his hero's aspiring mind.

A Christian interpretation would also point out that Marlowe modifies
his source to stress the oxymoronic quality not only of his hero but also of
his villain, thus allowing the Devil himself to speak for Christian values. In
the early scenes of the play, Mephistopheles portrays a tormented Devil
unlike any demon who had ever trod the medieval or Renaissance stages or
appeared in either poetry or prose, thereby anticipating Milton's suffering
Satan. Mephistopheles's plangent warning cited above establishes him as
an individual not only capable of pitying Faustus but also of poignantly
experiencing the pain of separation from God – in short, a potentially
tragic figure. Yet after the contract, the demon sheds his tragic mask and
dons his morality play visor, becoming the comic, conniving, gloating

figure of the moralities and the *Faustbooks*. Although no other treatment of the Faust legend will ever capture the complexity and fascination of Marlowe's Mephistopheles, Marlowe's anguished demon will reappear in several contemporary theatrical and cinematic treatments of the Faust story.

Christian exegetes have further argued that the refusal of Marlowe's Faustus until the end of the play to acknowledge the vacuity of his bargain further diminishes his stature. The sorcerer's intransigence echoes that of his EFB analogue, but again Marlowe enhances the irony by highlighting the vast disparity between desire and achievement and Faustus's delusion in clinging to so empty a commitment.

From his initial encounter with his demon familiar, Marlowe's Faustus shows an inability to distinguish between mastery and servitude. In light of subsequent events, Faustus's boast, "How pliant is this Mephistopheles, / Full of obedience and humility!" (1.3.30–31), becomes bitingly ironic. This confusion of slavery with dominance finds slight correspondence in the EFB where Faustus's magic has some, although limited, efficacy and the conjuror initially constrains his Spirit against his will (94). In Marlowe's play, however, Mephistopheles disallows Faustus even this satisfaction, immediately informing him that not magical coercion but moral corruption called the Spirit from the vasty deep (1.3.46–55).

Not only does Faustus's magical power prove mainly chimerical, but the eagerly anticipated rewards of the compact also remain largely illusory. Ironically, despite some exciting adventures traveling the universe in a dragon-drawn cart and glimpsing the starry heavens, Marlowe's magician achieves few of the conditions for which he barters his soul. In enumerating the first three articles of the bond, Marlowe adheres closely to his source (cf. EFB, 96; DF, 2.1.97–112). The first article states that "Faustus may be a spirit in form and substance," the second that "Mephostophiles shall be his servant, and at his command," and the third that "Mephostophiles shall do for him and bring him whatsoever." In both source and play, the first condition is honored more in the breach than the observance. In both Marlowe's tragedy and his source, the term "spirit" usually designates a "devil," although I interpret this condition not as a request to become a devil but as a demand for the powers associated with a spirit, the transcendence of time and space. In "The Damnation of Faustus," Greg contends, with impressive textual evidence, that throughout the play the term "spirit" is applied in a very special sense to denote "devil." While agreeing with Greg that in the play the term "spirit" almost always denotes "devil," T. W. Craik supports my reading, taking issue with Greg on this particular passage by asserting that the definition of certain terms varies in different contexts of the play.[27] Paradoxically, although the necromancers of both source and play receive the ultimate punishment of an infernal spirit – damnation – neither achieves the powers associated with spirits, although this limitation emerges more powerfully in Marlowe's play than in its source. The EFB Faustus often appears to perform miracles without the aid of Mephostophiles, becoming invisible in the court of the Turkish Emperor and ascending to heaven in the form of the Pope, whereas if Marlowe's magician wishes to travel through space or become invisible, he can only do so through the agency of his Spirit.

The second proposition, although blatantly violated in both drama and source, is treated differently in the two accounts, and this treatment reflects the two versions' contrasting images of hell as places of physical or psychological torment. In both versions, instead of attaining domination over spirits, the sorcerer is demonically manipulated; however, Marlowe's tragedy presents this control as largely psychological, whereas the EFB necromancer suffers ghastly physical torments. Three comparisons illustrate this critical distinction. In Act 2, scene 2, Marlowe's Devil distracts his victim from thoughts of connubial bliss by diversions and promises of sensual indulgence. The infernal masquerade and offering of courtesans innumerable find their origin in the EFB (101–03), but, in the source, the Devil seeks to terrify, not delight, and the discipline of pain precedes the palliative of pleasure. Similarly, Faustus's interrogation concerning God and creation evokes considerably milder punishment in the drama. The appearance of the infernal trinity doubtless terrifies Marlowe's magician, but Faustus's immediate recantation evokes instantaneous reward. Conversely, the hapless EFB necromancer is first frozen and then cowed by a grotesque parade of fiends who intend to horrify, not, like Marlowe's Masque of the Seven Deadly Sins, to amuse, and only after being totally quelled with terror is Faustus granted the balm of infernal music (116–19). Finally, in the scene with the kindly old neighbor, the magician of the source endures harrowing corporal punishment while the mere threat of physical violence quells Marlowe's Faustus, causing him to recant and propose a renewal of his bond. Also, in the source, the Spirit demands the second contract which Marlowe's browbeaten sorcerer freely offers to Mephistopheles (cf. EFB, 165–67; DF, 5.1.70–73).

What is the significance of Marlowe's noteworthy modification of his source? I agree with Douglas Cole that consonant with the philosophical description of hell, which finds no correspondence in the source,

Marlowe's tragedy minimizes physical punishment, accentuating the psychological nature of both Faustus's sin and his suffering.[28] The A-text, unlike the EFB, includes no description of a physical hell or reference to the fragments of Faustus's dismembered body discovered at the play's denouement, although the B-text retains from the source both the graphic depiction of a fire and brimstone hell and a vivid account of the students' discovery of Faustus's mangled limbs. [29] Additionally, in all of the cited instances, punitive threats prove sufficient to control Marlowe's protagonist, rendering physical coercion unnecessary. The A-text of the play thus alters its source to stress the degeneration inherent in any covenant with Satan and the ironic hiatus between Faustus's anticipated dominance and his actual servility.

Marlowe's ironic method becomes even more obvious in his treatment of the third article of the bond. Both source and play stress the degree to which Mephistopheles contravenes the third article – "that Mephistopheles shall do for him and bring him whatsoever." In direct violation of this condition, Marlowe's Mephistopheles refuses two of the magician's first three dramatized requests. Faustus's first request, concerning knowledge of hell, the Spirit answers with disturbing candor, but he denies Faustus's second demand, that he should have a wife, on the grounds that "marriage is a ceremonial toy," perhaps a reference to marriage as a ceremony of the Church. Instead the demon offers Faustus surrogates, in this case, not only courtesans but any female of his choice, although the nature of these willing women remains unclear – are they human females seduced by the devil or diabolical simulacra? In the source, Faustus later enjoys many more sensual rewards – gratifications omitted from Marlowe's play – thus diminishing the irony of the Spirit's initial refusal. These include not only diabolical lovers but also the entire harem of the Great Turk, presumably real women, and the seven most beautiful women in the world, perhaps also actual females.[30] Similarly, Marlowe's Mephistopheles answers Faustus's third dramatized request concerning questions on astronomy and creation evasively, and scholars have actively disagreed on the accuracy of Mephistopheles's dissertation on astronomy in Marlowe's play.[31] Nevertheless, however reliable or unreliable the fiend's data on secondary causes, his astronomical lecture proves unsatisfying because it withholds knowledge of the First Cause. On the analogous occasion in the EFB, although Mephostophiles refuses to answer Faustus's question (116), earlier he grants the inquisitive magician the account of Creation that he is later refused (104). Therefore, by skillfully compressing his material and juxtaposing two scenes of frustration – one sensual, in which Mephistopheles denies Faustus a wife, the other intellectual, in which the demon refuses the necromancer knowledge of creation – and diversion – in both cases, Mephistopheles distracts Faustus with substitutes – Marlowe accentuates the reversal of expectation adumbrated but not fully articulated in the source.

In summary, Marlowe magnifies Faustus's ambitions – the magician aspires to gain a Deity, to be great emperor of the world, and to reign sole king of all the provinces – while limiting his gratifications. Through this strategy, Marlowe foregrounds the disparity between Faustus's boundless aspirations and his limited rewards. I agree with Helen Gardner that "knowledge and felicity he [Faustus] has exchanged for shadows, and for power he gets slavery."[32]

Christian interpreters further stress the deleterious effects of the contract by clarifying the pattern of degeneration foreshadowed but not clearly defined in the source. According to G. K. Hunter's schema, Marlowe's play traces Faustus's descent through human activities, associates, and adversaries. The play initially presents Faustus as a type of polymath, a doyen in the four most prestigious professions of the early modern period. Having rejected these disciplines and embarked on his perilous journey into necromancy, Faustus requests knowledge of astronomy as his reward, thereby partially vindicating him as a knowledge seeker. However, he soon discovers that Mephistopheles, unable to discuss first causes, can provide only the rudimentary knowledge already available to Faustus and even to his assistant Wagner. Frustrated in his effort to discover astronomical truth, Faustus declines from heaven to earth, devoting himself to cosmography, or what we would today call geography, indulging in something equivalent to the Grand Tour as he visits the capitals of Europe. In Rome, Faustus progresses downward from cosmography to politics, since his activities in the papal court, although primarily reduced to slapstick antics, also tangentially involve politics, at least in the B-text, if not in the A.[33] In the Emperor's court, he descends to the role of entertainer, conjuring shadowy proxies of Alexander and his Paramour for the pleasure of the Emperor Charles. Faustus's status further deteriorates in the court of the Duke of Vanholt, where he performs the function of an errand boy, a kind of greengrocer, to adapt Gardner's arresting phrase, sending Mephistopheles around the world to fetch grapes out of season for the pregnant Duchess. Ultimately, he degenerates into comic antics with the horse-courser, although the A-text omits the jejune escapades with carters and clowns present in the B-text and in the EFB. At the same time that his field of activity decreases, Faustus suffers a social demotion as he descends from the court of the Pope, to that of the Emperor, to that of the Duke, and the social status of his adversaries diminishes from the gluttonous Vicar of Christ, to a jesting knight, to a gullible horse-courser. Although Faustus's professional and social decline receives more careful delineation in the B-text than in the A-text, the downward spiral informs both versions, and this consistent debasement accentuates the degenerative effects of the contract.[34]

In addition, as Christian exegetes assert and Robert Ornstein carefully delineates, the play includes a farcical sub-plot that, in true Elizabethan fashion, burlesques the main plot, therefore diminishing Faustus's achievements. Like Faustus with Mephistopheles, Wagner seeks to engage Robin to be his servant. Like Faustus, the clowns Robin and Dick procure a book of magic and conjure Mephistopheles. Like Faustus, who steals a goblet from the Pope, the clowns purloin a cup from the Vintner. Finally, like Faustus, who longs first for a wife and later for the fabled Helen of Troy as his paramour, the clowns lust after the kitchen maid Nan Spit. The clowns' ability to mimic Faustus's magic demeans the sorcerer's thaumaturgy, and their affinity with the magician trivializes the learned Doctor's heroic aspiration. In the center comic sections of the play, we are encouraged to laugh with Faustus as he hoodwinks the Pope, knights, and horse-coursers, but the parodic sub-plot, which finds no correspondence in the source, invites us to laugh *at* Faustus, not *with* him. In this manner, the farcical sub-plot combines with the downward trajectory of the comic episodes to stress the tragic falling off of Faustus and the degree to which his overreach exceeds his grasp.[35]

And yet, critics have consistently asked, why does Faustus continue with his unsatisfactory bargain? Does Faustus's obduracy in damnation result from self-delusion, despair, or simple necessity? This leads us to the central crux of the play: the problem of repentance. What is the exact nature of Faustus's bondage? Is repentance really possible within the universe of the play? On this issue, critics have heatedly disagreed ever since Una Ellis-Fermor first asserted that "implicit in Marlowe's premise is the predestination of man to destruction by some determinate power capable of purpose and intention," a power that she defines as sadistic. Harry Levin endorses Ellis-Fermor, insisting that *Doctor Faustus* presents damnation as "man's unmitigated lot." Nicholas Brooke, although not denying that repentance remains possible, sees it as degrading and "sinful," a view supported by Irving Ribner, who, although acknowledging the possibility of repentance, judges it demeaning, as it would mean the rejection of all those admirable humanist aspirations that led Faustus to make his bargain in the first place.[36]

Christian exegetes, like Leo Kirschbaum, Lily Bess Campbell, Joseph Westlund, and Douglas Cole, among others, read the play differently, insisting that repentance is ubiquitously possible and laudable.[37] However, not all Christian interpreters agree that repentance remains available until the end of the play. For James Smith, Faustus's signing of the contract ensures his damnation. For Greg and Roma Gill, Faustus's copulation with the succubus Helen, whereby he commits the unpardonable sin of demoniality, defined as intercourse with a demon, dooms him eternally. Seeking to refute this reading, T. W. Craik insists that in the play "spirit" does not invariably denote "devil" and thus Faustus does not intentionally fornicate with a demon, a view that I support. Finally, Nicolas Kiessling persuasively explains that at this time demoniality was not considered a mortal sin beyond absolution; the only unforgiveable crime was the sin against the Holy Ghost, the habitual refusal of the grace of God that finally rendered the sinner incapable of repentance. [38] However, even if one agrees with Kiessling, the centrality of Helen in the play should not be minimized, for her appearance in Marlowe's drama, much more than in either of the *Faustbooks*, stresses the role of woman as temptress that has become an important feature of the Faust legend.

Another group of critics, while not rejecting the Christian framework of the play (as would the heroic school), identifies this framework as primarily Calvinist in spirit. According to this interpretation, the tragedy depicts Faustus as the archetype of the Calvinist reprobate. Scholars who hold this view include Ariel Sachs, who sees Faustus as "a martyr to Augustinian and Calvinist predestination," and Wilbur Sanders and John Stachniewski, both of whom interpret the theology of the play as primarily Calvinist. Playing a variation of this theme, A. D. Nuttall asserts that the suspense of the play derives from the uncertainty concerning Faustus's state as reprobate or elect, as audiences "would be on the edges of their seats waiting to learn whether Faustus would *prove to have been* damned from eternity or not . . . Instead of 'Will he or will he not repent?' we have 'Can he or can he not repent?'" Significantly, all of the commentators defending the Calvinist ethos of the play rely on a conflated version of *Doctor Faustus*, which includes the key passages in the B-text excluded from the A-text. Thus, while refuting the view that the play undermines the very Christianity that it ostensibly supports, these critics, following the heroic school, see Faustus as predestined to damnation by an inscrutable Deity.[39] Again, a comparison between tragedy and chapbook may help to illumine, if not resolve, this controversy.

Because of the many differences in the fictional and dramatic forms, treatment of moral issues in these two genres must naturally differ considerably. The EFB, although containing elements of the jest book, remains essentially a didactic moral treatise. In both of the *Faustbooks*, the authors can intrude directly to guide the reader's response, and in many of the edifying asides, among them the coda concluding Chapter 13, the author of the EFB does just that, denying the binding force of the compact, while reminding the reader that although Faustus had made a promise to Satan, "through true repentance sinners come again to the favor of God" (106). Later, one of the most sophisticated passages in the EFB incorporates this concept into a dramatic context, expressing it ironically through the mouth of Satan's emissary:

> "but tell me Mephostophiles, wouldst thou be in my case as I am now?" "Yea," said the spirit (and with that fetched a great sigh), "for yet would I so humble myself that I would win favour with God." "Then," said Doctor Faustus, "it were time enough for me if I amended." "True," said Mephostophiles, "if it were not for thy great sins, which are so odious and detestable in the sight of God, that it is too late for thee . . ." (113)

Despite Mephostophiles's immediate recantation, the speech confirms the demon's own belief in the availability of grace, even for Faustus. In the wistful piety of this speech, do we perhaps find the inspiration for the passionate lamentation of Marlowe's demon over his own damnation (1.3.78–84)? Except for this one careless slip, however, the EFB Mephostophiles, as the agent of "the father of lies," consistently rejects the possibility of salvation, while the author continually assures us of Faustus's ability to repent (for other homiletic asides, see 106, 108).

A Christian reading would insist that in adapting his source to the dramatic medium and in transforming a didactic moral treatise into a complex, psychological study of self-deception, Marlowe not only maintains the moral focus of his source, but even makes salient additions to reinforce this focus. Among his additions, Marlowe adapts two characters from the moralities tradition to explore the problem of repentance – the Good and Evil Angels. These figures probably derive from the early morality *The Castle of Perseverance*, although Marlowe may not have known this play directly, or perhaps from *Piers Plowman*, in which they also appear. In Marlowe's tragedy, they serve multiple functions. First, in genuine morality play fashion, they may represent the conflicting forces operating within Faustus – his Christian belief that repentance remains always possible versus his conviction, perhaps derived from Calvinist theories of predestination, that he is irrevocably damned. Modern productions of the play, adopting this interpretation, rarely stage the two angels as individual personae, usually treating them as externalizations of Faustus's inner conflict. Secondly, however, the widespread belief at this time in attendant angels might have led an early modern audience to accept these two debating figures as representing ontological alternatives (Christian or Diabolical) external to Faustus.

Regarding the second function noted above, the belief in two attendant angels, one good, one evil, although certainly not ex cathedra, seems to have been popularly accepted. One of the original proponents of this doctrine, Origen Adamantius, a patristic figure who lived in the second century CE, drawing his inspiration from the *Shepherd of Hermes* and the pseudepigraphous *Epistle of Barnabas*, describes the operations of these two attendant angels in terms that closely parallel their dramatic function in *Doctor Faustus*: "each individual is attended by two angels; that whenever good thoughts arise in our hearts, they are suggested by the good angel; but when of a contrary kind, they are the instigation of the evil angel." [40] Moreover, this doctrine receives the imprimatur of no less orthodox a Christian apologist than Primaudaye, who asserts: "good and ill spirits have great means, and such as we cannot comprehend, whereby they move the imagination and fantasy of men." [41] Similarly, the *Malleus Maleficarum* of Heinrich Kramer and James Sprenger, first published in German in 1487 but later translated into English and widely distributed throughout Europe, describes the manner by which good and evil angels directly influence the thoughts of humans:

> Therefore it seems that the evil will of the devil is the cause of evil will in man . . . just as a good Angel cleaves to good, so does a bad Angel to evil; but the former leads man into goodness, therefore the latter leads him into evil. [42]

Not surprisingly, John Calvin, with his belief in election and reprobation, appears less convinced, since within his system the presence of good and evil angels would be a waste of valuable resources since the salvation or damnation of individuals had already been preordained by God. Calvin states:

> But whether to every of the faithful be several Angels assigned for their defense, I dare not certainly affirm . . . the common people do imagine that there are appointed to every one two angels . . . a good angel and a bad. But it is not worth while, curiously to search for that which does not much concern us to know. [43]

This issue, like so many in this problematic play, has traditionally evoked considerable controversy among Marlowe scholars. The majority of commentators, like most contemporary directors of the play, accept the two angels as totally subjective. According to M. C. Bradbrook, they are "not tutelary spirits, but projections of Faustus' own contrary impulses." Similarly, Greg characterizes the Good and Evil Angels as impersonations of the two sides of Faustus's human nature, and Levin, following Greg, interprets the two angels as materializations of Faustus's inner conflict. Conversely, E. E. Stoll defends the substantiality of the angels and Robert Hunter West insists: "whenever in Elizabethan drama daemonic figures appear in the body of a play ... it is proper to conceive them as essential according to the dictates of pneumatology, rather than as metaphorical," a view also affirmed by Campbell. In light of the general belief in attendant angels in early modern England, I favor the compromise view endorsed by James Smith, who attributes a dual significance to the two angels, interpreting them as simultaneously supernatural beings and externalizations of Faustus's mind.[44]

I would like to suggest a third alternative: the two angels, at least in their debates about repentance, might thematically embody the competing ideologies of the play, particularly the theologies of Catholicism and moderate Protestantism, on the one hand, which appear to confirm the omnipresent availability of grace and thus of salvation for all, and those of Calvinism, on the other, which endorse double predestination, whereby some individuals are elected for salvation, others preordained to reprobation.

However we interpret the two angels, their disputes stress the importance of choice and of Faustus's responsibility for his damnation; indeed, one might argue that the debates between the two angels would be theologically and theatrically superfluous if Faustus were predestined to damnation by the unfathomable Deity of the heroic school. Nevertheless, we should remember that in the dialogue between the two angels, the play grants both perspectives equal time. Thus, one could argue that both angels are right and both are wrong; it is too late, and yet not too late, in this most interrogative of Marlowe's dramas.

Christian exegetes contend that the Old Man constitutes another device Marlowe employs to stress the ubiquitous possibility of repentance. Marlowe adapts the sequence with the Old Man almost verbatim from the EFB, and, in both play and source, the pious Old Man functions, morality play fashion, as a counterbalance to Mephistopheles. Like Mercy in *Mankind,* he assures Faustus of God's ever available grace even to the most debased of sinners, while Mephistopheles, like Titivillus in the same morality play, insists that Mercy has abandoned Faustus.[45] Moreover, Marlowe's Old Man, far more specifically than his counterpart in the EFB, addresses the theological issues debated at the time. Christian belief, whether Catholic, moderate Protestant, or Calvinist, has traditionally affirmed that no free act leading to salvation can be performed unless initiated, sustained, and brought to completion by the merciful gift of God's grace (John 15:5, 2 Corinthians 3:5). Humans cannot, of course, repent unless they have Christian faith, yet Christians considered faith also a gift of God, and inasmuch as Pauline and Johannine faith involves an act of will, God works in humans, in both their will and their deed (Philippians 2:13). Catholics and most moderate Protestants have traditionally affirmed the availability of grace to all, for, as 2 Peter 3:9 declares: God "would have no man to perish, but would all men to come to repentance." St. Thomas Aquinas, one of the most revered theologians of the Catholic Church, supports this view, asserting that faith is contingent on grace, while simultaneously affirming the freedom of human beings to accept or reject God's gift. Richard Hooker, an extremely influential Anglican divine, also endorses this position, asserting that God makes the grace necessary for salvation available to all.[46] Calvinists, however, believed that God offers the grace necessary for salvation to some and withholds it from others. In the first instance, individuals have some free will since they can accept or reject God's proffered gift; in the second instance, however, free will is obviated, since this saving grace remains available only to those whom God in His inscrutable wisdom has selected for salvation.

Significantly, in Marlowe's tragedy, in the image of the angel hovering over Faustus's head with the precious vial, the Old Man affirms the availability of *prevenient* grace, thus pronouncing in terms that Marlowe's audience would have understood that Faustus is not predestined to reprobation. Theologians of this period made a distinction between universal and salvific grace. They further divided salvific grace into *prevenient* grace that acts upon the sinner before repentance, *converting* grace that effects conversion, and *co-operant* or indwelling grace that sanctifies. The "precious grace" offered to Faustus appears to be the *prevenient* grace that would enable Faustus to overcome despair and repent. Therefore, if we believe the Old Man, we must accept that grace and thus salvation remain available to Faustus, at least until the exit of the kindly old neighbor, and perhaps even until the final scene of the play.

Advocates of a Christian reading also stress Mephistopheles's consistent monitoring of Faustus's behavior to prevent him from repenting. Throughout both source and play, the infernal Spirit works overtime, wielding both carrot and stick to divert and intimidate his recruit from penance. This constant supervision would be totally unnecessary were Faustus irrevocably damned.

Heroic interpreters often comment on the absence of God from the universe of the play, a claustrophobic world peopled with devils. In answer to this objection, a Christian reading might reply that even though Protestant theology endorsed the concept of the *deus absconditus*, maintaining that the age of miracles was over and that God now worked through his human followers (such as the Old Man), not through divine intervention, Marlowe amplifies suggestions from his source and even adds additional episodes to remind us of the "gift of God" so persistently ignored by both Faustus and his humanist defenders. According to this reading, two of God's miraculous interventions occur during the critical contract scene (2.1). In this moment of spiritual crisis, the grace of God penetrates the web of delusion in which Faustus has enveloped himself, first congealing his blood, then inscribing on his arm the brief yet eloquent warning, *Homo fuge* ('man flee'). Ironically, Faustus dismisses this one evidence of divine reality in a mass of deception – the long desired "miracle" – as a hallucination and refuses to accept this ocular proof of divine mercy, exclaiming, "My senses are deceived; here's nothing writ" (2.1.79). Even when Faustus finally acknowledges the stigmatic script on his arm, he shows no awareness of the supernatural grace causing this heavenly caveat, lamenting: "Whether should I fly? / If unto God, he'll throw thee down to hell" (77–78). The treatment of the analogous episode in the EFB is terse and undramatic. The subheading of Chapter 6, "How Doctor Faustus set his blood in a saucer on warm ashes and writ as followeth," probably suggested the congealing of Faustus's blood, and the warning, *Homo fuge*, does appear in the source, but without elaboration. From this exiguous treatment in the EFB Marlowe has evolved a dramatic and ironic scene, which, according to Christian exegetes, affirms the presence of God's grace even in Faustus's moment of denial.

Biblical allusion positions Faustus as a parody of Christ. As Richard Waswo suggests, Faustus's bloodletting in the contract scene provides a "hideous parody . . . of the expiatory suffering of Christ which Faustus here rejects," a parody punctuated by Faustus's blasphemous line, *consummatum est*. Nuttall notes another possible similarity between Faustus and Christ: not only did both offer a blood sacrifice, but Christ on the cross, like Faustus, "was paying a debt, had made a pact with the Devil." Although there is no evidence that Marlowe was familiar with the play *Mankind*, there are many similarities between his tragedy and this popular morality, including the parodying of Christ's last words. In *Mankind*, one of the Vice-lieutenants, Nought, parrots Christ's final words on the cross, "*In manus tuas*"(line 516) and another, Nowadays, echoes the first words Christ spoke to Mary Magdalene after his resurrection, "*noli me tangere*" (line 512).[47]

Later, in the final scene of the play when all seems lost, Marlowe has introduced another reminder of Christ's redemptive sacrifice, a vision of Christ's blood streaming in the firmament, although this reference could be read metaphorically, not literally. The imagery of blood links the two miracles: in the first miracle, blood congeals; in the second, it flows. No corresponding allusion to Christ's blood occurs in the final scene of the EFB; Faustus appears doomed after his rejection of the Old Man and the author offers no ameliorating hope of eleventh-hour salvation. Debatably, through the image of the ensanguined heavens, Marlowe mitigates the EFB portrait of a stern, unyielding Deity, reminding the audience of God's infinite mercy. According to a Christian reading, this latter miracle, like the former ones, would be both dramatically and theologically gratuitous if Faustus were indeed predestined to damnation.

In summary, this analysis reveals several crucial changes that Marlowe has made in his source that can be adduced to support a Christian reading of the play. First, the shift in emphasis from a yearning for forbidden knowledge to a desire for power radically alters the nature of the magician's transgressions. Moreover, by magnifying its hero's aspirations and sharply curtailing his achievements, the play highlights the disparity between the omnipotence of Faustus's dreams and the impotence of his rewards, thus stressing the unsatisfactory nature of his bargain. The exclusion of extraneous elements from the source further clarifies Faustus's progressive demotion from eminent academician, to astrologer, to court entertainer, to greengrocer, to jester. Furthermore, by accentuating the elements of self-deception and rationalization, hinted at but not developed in the source, Marlowe adds psychological credibility to Faustus's irrational determination, while simultaneously reversing the roles of tempter and tempted to stress Faustus's responsibility for his damnation. In addition, the introduction of emblematic characters from the morality tradition (Good and Evil Angels, the Old Man as a Mercy figure) further reinforces the centrality of human choice, while the expansion of the one brief miracle in the source into two in the play reminds the audience of God's promised mercy, which Faustus continually denies. Finally, Marlowe's play adds a farcical sub-plot that parodies and deflates the necromancer's achievements, thus markedly diminishing his heroic stature. Comparing play and source thus suggests that despite the allegedly heterodox opinions of its author, *Doctor Faustus* may paradoxically be the most orthodox of Marlowe's dramas. But, of course, this is only one side of the question.

A Heroic Reading of the Play

Challenging this impressive array of evidence, exponents of a heroic reading offer several quotations from the text that arguably undermine the
drama's affirmations of free will and personal responsibility, as well as
identifying a pervasive pattern of visual irony that destabilizes the ostensible Christian orthodoxy verbally endorsed in the text. [48]

Let us first consider the verbal challenges to a Christian reading of the
play. The first of these quotations, describing Faustus's hubris, appears in
the Chorus preceding Act 1:

> Till, swoll'n with cunning of a self-conceit,
> His waxen wings did mount above his reach,
> And melting heavens *conspired* his overthrow.
>
> (Prologue, 20–22; emphasis mine)

Although the Chorus didactically identifies Icarian pride as the cause of
Faustus's fall, the reference to the "melting heaven *conspiring*" the hero's
overthrow seems to imply the presence of a malignant Deity predestining
Faustus to reprobation, particularly since, at this time as today, the term
"conspire" denoted "to plot, devise, or contrive." [49]

The second crucial quotation occurs only in the B-Text in Act 5 when the
desperate necromancer, facing an eternity in hell, turns in rage to
Mephistopheles, accusing the demon of masterminding his fall and damnation (B-text: 5.2.95–96). Throughout the play, Faustus holds Mephistopheles
culpable for his damnation, and Christian apologists have focused on this
tendency to blame others as an evasion of personal responsibility. In his final
soliloquy, for example, Faustus shifts the blame for his damnation to the stars,
his parents, and Lucifer, in addition to Mephistopheles. However, in this
instance, the demon proudly accepts his guilt, bragging, Vice-like, that he
constrained Faustus to compose his fatal fallacious syllogism:

> I do confess it, Faustus, and rejoice.
> 'Twas I that, when thou wert i'the way to heaven,
> Dammed up thy passage. When thou took'st the book
> To view the Scriptures, then I turned the leaves
> And led thine eye.   (97–101)

Mephistopheles's gloating boast supports John D. Cox's reading of the
Faustus–Mephistopheles relationship in the play whereby Cox denies the
disjunctive Mephistopheles of the Christian interpreters, contending that
Mephistopheles's portrait of an arrogant, rebellious Lucifer and his warning, "Faustus, leave these frivolous demands," operate as a kind of reverse

psychology to goad the arrogant, rebellious Faustus into making the contract.[50]

In addition, heroic interpreters might adduce the didactic speeches of both angels at the play's conclusion, which confirm Faustus's inexorable damnation (5.2.104–37), pointing out that these diatribes call into question the omnipresent possibility of repentance asserted by many Christian advocates and thus their affirmation of a merciful God presiding over the play. Certainly, these vitriolic speeches with their gruesome images of a physical hell strongly undermine any concept of a benevolent providence ruling the universe of *Doctor Faustus* and support the view that God, at least the benevolent God of Christianity "who looks with tenderness on his erring children," is absent from the play.[51]

Heroic advocates, most notably Max Bluestone, have also identified a pattern of visual ironies operating throughout the tragedy by which dialogue says one thing and *mis-en-scène* implies something very different. For example, the diabolical figures looming over the conjuration scene (B-text: 1.3.: *Thunder. Enter Lucifer and four Devils [above]* ...) suggest a world controlled by evil – even before Faustus has penned his blood contract. Similarly, in Faustus's last agonized soliloquy, as the tormented necromancer seeks desperately to pray, the stage tableau of the infernal trinity – Lucifer, Beelzebub, and Mephistopheles – ominously dominating the sequence *from above*, negates any hope of redemption (B-text: 5.2). In an earlier climactic scene, in response to Faustus's desperate cry *de profundis*: "Ah, Christ, my Saviour, / Seek to save distressed Faustus' soul" (A-text: 2.3.82–83; cf. B-text: 2.3.83–84, which reads, "Help to save distressed Faustus' soul!"), not Christ, but a menacing Lucifer appears in what Bluestone posits as a "spectacular challenge" to orthodoxy. According to heroic commentators, therefore, the ironic use of theatrical tableau operates throughout the play to suggest the stark absence of God and Christ in a menacing universe ruled by diabolical forces. Critics of this persuasion thus contend that the contrary signals embedded within the play create an ideological disjunction that implicitly subverts the orthodoxy explicitly endorsed in the drama.[52]

However, the visual imagery of the infernal trinity presiding from above in both the third and last scenes of the play, as well as the grisly final speeches of the two angels, Mephistopheles's boast that he influenced Faustus to devise the fallacious syllogism, the depiction of a burning hell, and the reference to Faustus's mangled limbs are all absent from the A-text, although the troubling reference to "the conspiring heavens" and the disturbing materialization of Lucifer in answer to Faustus's prayer do appear in both versions. Given the marked differences in the two texts, advocates of a Christian reading might rebut that since the strongest anti-Christian statements in the play and the incongruity between explicit verbal statement and implicit visual tableaux do not occur in the A-text, the apparent ambiguity of the drama results primarily from textual difference rather than ideological contrariety. In light of the evidence cited above, Joseph Westlund and Leah Marcus suggest that the A- and B-texts constitute two very different plays, one that affirms Faustus's free will and upholds the availability of repentance (the A-text) and one that interrogates Faustus's volition and presents him as a victim of an infernal plot (the B-text).[53] Although I find both of their arguments compelling, I would insist that ambiguity permeates both versions of the play.

An Alternative Reading of the Play

Notably, in both texts, whether or not God has preordained him to reprobation, Faustus apparently *believes* that He has. Here I would suggest another opposition operating throughout the play, in addition to the much debated conflict between the Christian and heroic interpretations: the tension in the play between two diverse Protestant theologies – moderate Protestant and Calvinist. As noted above, Catholics and most moderate Protestants asserted that the godly grace necessary for salvation was available to everyone no matter how sinful, although, of course, the individual could always reject the proffered grace. Conversely, Calvinists insisted that from the beginning of time God had divided all humankind into two camps, predestining the elect to salvation and the reprobate to damnation, and that both the prevenient grace leading to repentance and the converting grace necessary for salvation were accessible only to the elect. As Kristen Poole wryly observes: "Elizabethan theology was, then, a messy affair," [54] and this confusion is particularly evident in the Anglican attitude toward Calvinist double predestination. On the one hand, Article 17 of *The Thirty-Nine Articles of the Church of England* clearly endorses the predestination of the elect to salvation:

> Predestination to life is the everlasting purpose of God, whereby (before the foundations of the world were laid) he hath constantly decreed by his counsel secret to us, to deliver from the curse and damnation, those whom he hath chosen in Christ out of mankind, and to bring them by Christ to everlasting salvation ...

However, Article 17 makes no explicit mention of the predestination of the reprobate to damnation.[55] Moreover, Richard Hooker further muddies the waters by asserting that the grace necessary for salvation is available to all:

> This may suffice touching outward grace, whereby God invites the whole world to receive wisdom and has opened the gates of his visible Church unto all, thereby testifying his will and purpose to have all saved, if the let were not in themselves ... For seeing the natural will of God desires to impart unto all creatures all goodness ... his desire is, that all men were capable of inward grace, because without grace there is no salvation.[56]

I propose that the profound ambivalence toward Calvinist double predestination revealed in Marlowe's *Doctor Faustus* reflects the ambivalent response toward this doctrine permeating the religious community at this time. Moreover, Marlowe has brilliantly transformed this contradictory, even "messy" theology, into a fascinating theatrical paradox.

Yet, whatever the Anglican view of Calvinist double predestination, from the beginning of the play Faustus seems persuaded that he is among the reprobate, preordained to damnation, as he queries: "*Che serà, serà,* / What will be, shall be?" (1.1.49–50). Much later, echoing the emotional turmoil of the EFB necromancer, Marlowe's Faustus falls more deeply into despair and becomes increasingly convinced that his offence can never be pardoned; indeed, he asserts: "The serpent that tempted Eve may be saved, but not Faustus" (5.2.15–16). This certainty of damnation, perhaps present from the beginning of both texts of the play, may be the reason he fails to recall the mitigating complement of each of the biblical verses comprising his fatal syllogism; he may not feel that these promises of God's grace bear any relevance *to him* as reprobate. This may also be the reason he always listens to his Evil Angel and ignores the counsel of his Good Angel. Finally, this may be the reason he cannot repent, even when the Old Man assures him of the availability of prevenient grace, and his fearfulness in response to Mephostopheles's threats may derive from his lack of faith in God's grace *for him*, even as the courage of the Old Man springs from his assurance of salvation. This conviction of reprobation may thus be the force that "holds him [Faustus] down" and ultimately prevents his leap of faith. Yet whether that conviction of reprobation is valid, we never know for certain.

As appropriate to an interrogative drama, the play consistently presents both sides of the question. Thus, countering Faustus's certainty of damnation, the Old Man endorses the moderate Protestant belief in the ubiquity of God's grace. Moreover, the two angels often represent these conflicting doctrinal positions, their crisp stichomythia establishing the perimeters of the moderate Protestant and Calvinist dichotomy:

> GOOD ANGEL Faustus, repent, yet God will pity thee.
> EVIL ANGEL Thou art a spirit. God cannot pity thee.
> FAUSTUS Who buzzeth in mine ears I am a spirit?
> Be I a devil, yet God may pity me;
> Ay, God will pity me if I repent.
> EVIL ANGEL Ay, but Faustus never shall repent.
> [*Exeunt* ANGELS]
> FAUSTUS My heart's so hardened I cannot repent. (2.3.12–18)

Faustus's use of the passive tense and the association of this phrase with Exodus 4:21, in which God affirms to Moses that He would harden the heart of Pharaoh, has led critics of the heroic school to conclude that God is initiating the process of spiritual petrifaction Faustus here identifies. Indeed, Calvinists insisted that sometimes God did harden the hearts of the reprobate in just the manner here described; as Paul states in Romans 9:18: "Therefore he [God] hath mercy on whom he will, & whom he will, he hardeneth." Calvin affirms God's origination of this hardening process as follows: "But nothing can be desired to be more plainly spoken, than where he so oft pronounces, that he blinds the eyes of men, and strikes them with giddiness ... and hardens their hearts."[57] However, as Kocher asserts, other Protestants as well as Catholics would interpret this phrase differently. For this group, the statement, "My heart is hardened," could depict the consequence of habitually refusing God's grace until God at last withdraws His salvific gift, leaving the individual in his or her naturally corrupt and obdurate condition.[58] Developing the tension between the Anglican and Calvinist theologies discussed above, I offer a third reading: Faustus's lament may be the cry of a tormented individual who has accepted the Calvinist theory of predestination and believes he is irrevocably damned. Thus, the phrase "hardened heart" remains tantalizingly ambiguous: Faustus may be hardening his own heart by his repeated rejections of God's proffered grace; God may be hardening Faustus's heart as He did the heart of Pharaoh; or Faustus, accepting himself as reprobate, may only *believe* God is hardening his heart. This latter reading presents Faustus not as a victim of an unfathomable Deity who has selected him for reprobation but as a casualty of an insidious theology that has perverted his reason and led him to assume that because of his rebellious nature, he belongs among the reprobate. If so, the play may be an interrogation not of Christianity in general, as many heroic interpreters insist, but specifically of Calvinist predestination.

The theological ambiguity in the play has invited multiple diverse interpretations. Pauline Honderich offers an enlightening discussion of the tension in *Doctor Faustus* between Anglican and Calvinist theologies, although she judges the Calvinist position much more dominant in the play than I do, perhaps because she makes no distinction between the A- and B-texts. Differing from Honderich, Poole presents the doctrinal opposition as Catholic and Calvinist rather than Anglican and Calvinist. Moreover, as with Honderich, in her otherwise most informative article, Poole fails to distinguish between the treatments of these different theological positions in the two different texts. Nuttall offers a third paradigm, positing a clash in the play between Hermetic optimism and Calvinist pessimism. Assuming entirely different perspectives, Clifford Davidson and Angus Fletcher stress the influence of Lutheran theology on the play, while Barbara Parker, equating magic with Catholicism, interprets the entire drama as an indictment of the Catholic Church.[59]

As always in this most problematic of Marlowe's plays, the different doctrinal perspectives balance precariously and are never resolved, accentuating the dramatic effectiveness of paradox. Moreover, regardless of whether we interpret Faustus as the victim of a sadistic God or of an invidious theology or of his own stubborn desire for forbidden power, wealth, and knowledge, for centuries, audiences and critics have identified with him as a sympathetic hero. Ultimately, then, the heroic expositors of the play must rely primarily on something far less tangible than visual tableau or explicit statement, offering instead the sense of affinity with which audiences have traditionally responded to Faustus, the fallible human being desperately seeking freedom from human limitation, or, as William Empson limns him: the "demigod rogue," "the ideal drinking companion, the great fixer, who can break taboos for you and get away with it." [60] Marlowe's Faustus, like his EFB counterpart, appears most sympathetic in the final scene of the play. At his "Last Supper," surrounded by loving scholars who offer not only to pray for him but even to stay with him throughout his final ordeal, the quavering magician displays gallantry even in the valley of the shadow, urging his students to retire and not hazard their souls for his sake.

In part, our sympathy for Faustus derives not only from his convivial, ebullient personality but also from the interiority that Marlowe has granted his hero, for, as Logan observes, "It may well be that Marlowe's single most important characterological gift to Shakespeare was his interiorization of character in *Doctor Faustus*."[61] To achieve this interiority, Marlowe has vastly complicated the problem of Faustus's repentance, thereby creating an internalized human being who invites audience empathy. In the *Faustbooks*, repentance is always possible and laudable but despair and fear of punishment from devils prevent the tortured necromancer from achieving this desired goal. However, dramatizing Faustus's vertiginous vacillations between repentance and despair, Marlowe's tragedy poses many questions concerning Faustus's fatal failure to repent. Is repentance really possible within the world of the play? Is Faustus predestined to reprobation by a stringent Calvinist ideology, or does he only believe he is preordained to damnation? Do coercing devils thwart Faustus's attempts to repent, or is it his lack of faith that holds him down? Does Mephistopheles manipulate Faustus with the carrot and stick of alluring rewards and frightful punishments? Is Faustus's repentance impeded by his despair? Or perhaps Faustus cannot achieve genuine penitence simply because he cannot accept responsibility for his fate, always the first necessary step to repentance? Like Hamlet, another famously questioning hero, Faustus does not know why yet he has this thing to do – in this case, repent – and thus readers, audiences, and critics have debated the issue for over 400 years.[62]

Faustus's interiority appears most prominently in his opening and closing soliloquies, for Marlowe brackets his play with two of the most complex and internalized soliloquies in the early modern drama. In the first of these soliloquies, as discussed above, Faustus quotes Aristotle, Galen, and scripture out of context in order to rationalize his desire for power and his eagerness to embrace magic as a means of attaining it; he may also be convinced of his damnation and thus rationalizes in order to enjoy the fruits of his inevitable destiny. In his final soliloquy, in genuine tragic fashion, the anguished magician is wrenched between contrary beliefs, affirming the availability of God's saving grace ("See, see where Christ's blood streams in the firmament! / One drop would save my soul, half a drop. Ah, my Christ!" 5.2.78–79), while denying he can be saved ("The devil will come, and Faustus must be damned," 76). Striving vainly to understand why he cannot repent, Faustus first blames the devils he believes impede his leap of faith and rend his heart (77–80), then the stars whose influence has allotted death and hell (89–90), then the parents that engendered him (113), and, finally, for one brief enlightened moment, himself: "No, Faustus, curse thyself" (114). However, the onus of this responsibility proves too great to bear and he immediately transfers the guilt to Lucifer: "Curse Lucifer, / That hath deprived thee of the joys of heaven" (114–15). In his final soliloquy, therefore, Faustus incorporates within his psyche the Good and Evil Angels, emblems throughout the play of the warring elements of his soul, to create what I assert is the first fully interiorized character in the early modern drama, thereby foreshadowing Hamlet's famed inwardness.

The play also invites sympathy for its hero by highlighting the vast disparity between the puerility of his sins and the enormity of his punishment. In the EFB, amid all his japes and tomfoolery, Faustus performs two genuinely wicked acts: he murders a rival sorcerer (164–65) and he commands Mephostophiles to kill the pious old neighbor as punishment for his efforts to save Faustus's soul (168). Marlowe has omitted the murder of the competing magician and has rendered the ultimate fate of the Old Man ambiguous. If we believe that the Old Man escapes unscathed, indeed that Faustus's one truly deplorable act is ineffectual, then we might argue that Faustus fritters away his twenty-four years of power on inane jests and seriously harms no one. Yes, he commits most of the seven deadly sins – he shows pride in his desire to gain a Deity and also in his despair, the other side of the coin of pride; he demonstrates avarice in his aspiration for wealth; he displays gluttony in his many feasts and carousings; he indulges in lechery with Helen; he exhibits spiritual sloth, *acedia*, in his failure to repent; finally, he surrenders to wrath in his attempted vengeance against the Old Man. In addition, as Christian commentators have frequently pointed out, for a Protestant audience, Faustus has committed the unpardonable sin, the sin against the Holy Ghost, the refusal to repent, a refusal deriving from his failure to believe "wholly and passionately in the mercy of God."[63] Yet, compared to Tamburlaine who puts entire cities to the sword and murders his own son, Titus Andronicus who kills two of his own children, Hamlet who causes the death of six people, Macbeth who metaphorically wades up to his waist in blood and literally slaughters mothers and children, Faustus's sins, except for his shameful response to the Old Man, seem vacuous rather than heinous.

Furthermore, just as he stresses the puerility of Faustus's sins, at least of his actual deeds, Marlowe accentuates the atrocity of his punishment, as Faustus pleads for some end to his agony:

> If thou wilt not have mercy on my soul,
> Yet for Christ's sake, whose blood hath ransomed me,
> Impose some end to my incessant pain,
> Let Faustus live in hell a thousand years,
> A hundred thousand, and at last be saved.
> O, no end is limited to damned souls.   (5.2.99–104)

Faustus's lament at an eternity of damnation reverberates with a controversy within the Christian Church as venerable as Origen, one of the most influential of the Church fathers, a controversy of which Marlowe, as a student of divinity at Cambridge, would doubtless have been aware. Unable to reconcile the belief in a merciful God with perpetual torment, Origen insisted that eventually all, even Satan, would be saved, since all were created by God (a possibility intriguingly hinted at in the EFB, III). Henry Ansgar Kelly points out that this "universalist theory" may have its origin in the writings of Paul, in which the Apostle jubilantly celebrates the final conversions of all created beings – in the heavens above, the earth below, and the waters under the earth – to the worship of Jesus Christ (Philippians 2:10–11; Colossians 1:16–20). Many others in the early Church endorsed Origen's views, so eloquently expressed by the seventh-century monk Isaac: "It is not [the way of] the compassionate Maker to create rational beings in order to deliver them over to unending affliction."[64] Nevertheless, the early Church, in the business of recruiting souls, predictably rejected this enlightened explanation, which would divest them of their trump card: control of everlasting salvation or damnation. Later, the Church partially solved this ethical dilemma by inventing Purgatory and reserving hell for only the most depraved sinners and heaven for only the most beatific believers. However, when Protestants obliterated Purgatory, which had become notoriously tainted with simony, the controversy over Origen's "universalist theory" re-emerged. In response to the hellfire and brimstone theology of Martin Luther and John Wycliffe, and also to the Augustinian (and Calvinist) view that God works in us both good and evil, the humanist Desiderius Erasmus vociferously objected: "Who will be able to bring himself to love God with all his heart when he created hell seething with eternal torments in order to punish his own misdeeds in his victims as though he took delight in human torments."[65] I suggest that in his last agonized soliloquy, Faustus foregrounds this particularly pitiless aspect of Calvinist/Lutheran Protestantism and wins audience allegiance through the failure of his punishment to fit his crimes.

Two recent books offer new readings to support this audience identification with Faustus. Patrick Cheney gives a novel twist to the heroic reading, interpreting the tragedy as an affirmation of artistic freedom in the face of a restrictive religious orthodoxy. By merging Faustus the magician with Marlowe the playwright, Cheney interprets the play as the "author's affirmation of his own artistic power to be free from Orthodox Christian forces dangerously afoot in the universe."[66] Conversely, adopting a feminist perspective, Alison Findlay contends that female audience members, like Faustus bullied by patriarchal authority figures and denied desired knowledge, would have identified with the unfortunate magician.[67]

Although I find both of these readings plausible, I suspect that the empathy, pity, and terror that audiences and readers have traditionally experienced when confronting the tragedy derive from two other elements, in addition to those cited above. First Faustus expresses *all* of our desires, our secret yearnings for more power over our lives, for wealth, for fame, and, yes, for knowledge. Angus Fletcher contends that, despite ourselves, we empathize with Faustus's rebellion, insisting that it is "less his specific desire for knowledge, or riches, or power that makes Faustus appealing than his need to see past his humanness, to find the peace of mind that lurks always in the beyond." [68]

Second, Faustus conveys these very human yearnings in some of the most glorious language ever heard on the English stage. Jane K. Brown astutely observes: "Since the great poetry in the play is all in the mouth of Faustus, it is hard not to sympathize with him as the figure in the play who articulates and embodies the poetic ideals of Marlowe and his great contemporaries."[69] Moreover, Bevington speaks for many spectators when he asserts: "Can we fail to sympathize with the artist who finds philosophy, law, medicine, and theology odious and harsh in comparison with the ravishing prospect of Lapland giants or of young women who display 'more beauty in their airy brows / Than in the white breasts of the Queen of Love?'" (1.1. 130–31).[70] When Faustus utters one of the most ecstatic and justly famous passages in English drama, "Was this the face that launched a thousand ships / And burnt the topless towers of Ilium? / Sweet Helen, make me immortal with a kiss" (5.1.91–93), few in the audience will stop to speculate that the answer should be: "No, Helen is really a succubus who will suck forth Faustus's soul and lead him to damnation." Transported by the poetic splendor of the language, surely few in any audience will pause to consider this eventuality. For Faustus, like many another Marlovian overreacher, pits the magnificent word against the ignoble deed. Those listening with a sensitized ear to Faustus's mellifluous lines while turning a blind eye to his foolish escapades will adopt a heroic reading, against all textual evidence to the contrary. Alternatively, those turning a deaf ear to some of the most soaring poetry of the early modern theater and seeing only the often trivial action on the stage, will judge Faustus not only fatally flawed but something of a fool, as well. Spectators able both to hear and see simultaneously, and to perceive both the swan and the crow of Marlowe's perspective painting,[71] will probably achieve the fullest experience of Marlowe's tragedy, which simultaneously dazzles and disenchants as it both celebrates and deflates magic and the imagination.[72]

Conclusion

Incorporating as it does so many of the theological and aesthetic conflicts of its time, *Doctor Faustus* is very much a play for its own age; however, it is also a play for all time. In many ways, *Doctor Faustus* represents a defining moment in the history of human thought, translating the Faust legend into a sophisticated tragedy that would survive long after history had relegated the *Faustbooks* to dusty libraries and dry footnotes, a tragedy that would, either directly or indirectly, inspire Goethe and through him innumerable operas, plays, and films. Moreover, Marlowe's introduction of simultaneous celebratory and ironic perspectives toward his hero and his problematizing of the theological structure of the legend would profoundly influence Goethe and the majority of post-Goethe theatrical and cinematic adaptations and appropriations of the Faust narrative.

Furthermore, I assert that *Doctor Faustus* occupies a pivotal position in the development of the English drama. Scholars have long credited Marlowe with introducing into the drama a flexible and dynamic verse through which emotion could be communicated and character created. I would add that in *Doctor Faustus*, Marlowe not only creates the first wholly internalized protagonist on the English stage, but also scripts the first dialogical drama that fully inscribes the multiplicity and indecidability of human experience, thereby anticipating, and perhaps even precipitating, the greater achievements of Shakespeare and the early modern theater. On many levels, therefore, reading or viewing *Doctor Faustus* allows us to participate in the creation of the English drama.

CHAPTER 3

Goethe's Faust

From Hero to Harlequin

Despite the scanty available records of early modern productions in England, such records as do exist suggest that Christopher Marlowe's *Doctor Faustus* was probably a big hit. However, tastes change from epoch to epoch, and the mélange of comedy and tragedy constituting Marlowe's *Doctor Faustus* began to lose credibility in the Restoration era. To judge from the comments of contemporaries, the Restoration adaptations of the play expanded the rambunctious comedy and demonic pyrotechnics of the B-text of *Doctor Faustus*, drowning the tragic nuances of the original in trivial farce and hocus-pocus. In 1688, Charles Mountfort, who played Mephistopheles in Thomas Betterton's *Faustus* in 1675, mounted a farcical version titled *The Life and Death of Doctor Faustus: Made into a Farce*, which further mutilated Marlowe's play by excising much of the tragic matter and attaching sizeable portions of slapstick performed by the traditional *commedia dell' arte* figures Harlequin and Scaramouche.

Mountfort's treatment of the comic and tragic portions of *Doctor Faustus* exemplifies the fate of Marlowe's play in both England and Germany throughout the late seventeenth and eighteenth centuries.[1] Mountfort retains the bare bones of Marlowe's plot, but the soaring poetry, philosophical questioning, and psychological complexity – the play's glory and originality – ended up on the cutting-room floor. Conversely, amplifying the trend evident in the B-version of Marlowe's tragedy, Mountfort's travesty preserves much of Faustus's tomfoolery and greatly expands the farcical episodes with the clowns, now played by *commedia dell' arte* characters instead of Wagner, Robin, Rafe, or Dick.

The treatment of the Helen episode epitomizes Mountfort's strategy of condensation and trivialization. According to some commentators, in

Marlowe's play this climactic moment represents the turning point for Faustus, who, transfixed by Helen's beauty, becomes fatally distracted from thoughts of repentance. Others laud Faustus's confrontation with Helen as containing some of the most glorious poetry on the early modern stage. Mountfort, deaf to the theological import, the tragic relevance, and the rhetorical splendor of the scene, diminishes it into the following laconic exchange. When the Devil offers Faustus courtesans innumerable in lieu of the desired wife, Faustus responds:

FAUSTUS Then, Mephistopheles, let me behold the Famous Helen, who was the Occasion of great Troy's Destruction.
MEPHISTOPHELES Faustus, thou shalt.
   [Waves his wand; enters]
FAUSTUS O Mephistopheles! What would I give to gain a Kiss from off those Lovely Lips.
MEPHISTOPHELES Faustus, thou mayst.
   [He kisses her.]
FAUSTUS My Soul is fled; come Helen, come, give me my Soul again; she's gone.
   [He goes to kiss her again, and she sinks.]
MEPHISTOPHELES Women are shy, you know, at the first Sight. ²

Much of the remaining action centers on the slapstick antics of Scaramouche and Harlequin, who, burlesquing Faustus's magic, summons Mephistopheles from Constantinople while travestying Faustus's desire for food, wine, and a comely wench. Later, in a particularly ridiculous episode, Harlequin steals the money and bread that Scaramouche is distributing to the poor and pretends to fall into despair and hang himself, thereby reducing Faustus's wrenching despair and contemplated suicide to absurdity. Segued between the farcical capers of the clowns, Faustus does briefly return, playing tricks on the Horse-Courser, devouring the Carter's entire bale of hay, and horning Benvolio in the Emperor's court, but even Faustus's fleeting encounter with the Old Man is almost immediately interrupted by the raging Horse-Courser and Carter. The Old Man re-emerges in the penultimate scene of the play as he and a single student constitute Faustus's sole comforters. After a few flaccid remonstrations, they depart, leaving the smug Mephistopheles, the lamenting Good Angel, and the gloating Bad Angel to deliver their valedictory addresses. The penultimate scene also retains the tattered remains of Faustus's riveting last soliloquy, omitting its lacerating conflict between belief and doubt, hope and despair, acceptance and rejection of responsibility; the mangled text thus ironically reflects Faustus's mangled limbs later viewed by the two mourners. Finally, hell's mouth opens and Faustus sinks through a trapdoor to his doom. However, all of this remains tongue-in-cheek, and in the last scene, as Christa Knellwolf King notes, all of Faustus's amputated limbs unite and perform a danse macabre, a parody of both the jig concluding most comedies and the cautionary tale associated with the Faust legend.[3] One is also reminded of the reference in the Old Testament to the dry bones coming together, bone on bone (Ezekiel 37:5–8).

Mountfort's "adulterate beast," to use David Bevington's apt adaptation from *Hamlet*, [4] inspired several other monstrosities, including two panto-mimes, John Rich's *The Necromancer: or Harlequin Doctor Faustus* (1723) and John Thurmond's *Harlequin Dr. Faustus* (1724). Indeed, the Faust harlequinades took London by storm in the early eighteenth century, much to the disgust of Alexander Pope, who ridiculed these hybrid horrors in *The Dunciad*. King contends that in their parodic treatment of Faust and his lethal bargain, these harlequinades reduce to absurdity the entire Faust enterprise, not only the aspiring hero but also his condign doom.[5] At any rate, as Bevington observes: "Under the weight of this trivialization, Marlowe's play disappeared entirely from the London stage until 1885."[6]

These English Faustus harlequinades strongly influenced the German puppet plays. Even as playwrights in England first adulterated and then virtually obliterated Marlowe's tragedy, the play began to suffer a similar mutilation in Germany, the home of the Faust legend, in the late sixteenth and early seventeenth centuries. Marlowe's *Doctor Faustus* returned to Germany with troupes of touring actors called the English Comedians, who performed the play first in English and then in limited German adaptations. Later, local companies assumed the production of these plays, staged in still shorter and more maimed versions, and these finally evolved into farcical puppet plays.

Although no copies of the corrupt German versions of Marlowe's play survive, from indirect information about performances, from theater pro-grams, and from the puppet plays based on these German adaptations, we can safely assume that these productions, like the similar stagings in England, highlighted the comic and spectacular aspects of the play, largely neglecting its transcendent poetry or philosophical depth. This indirect evidence reveals that these plays spotlighted the role of the roistering clown – often called Harlekin, Hans Worst, Caspar, or Crispin – expanded the scenes of demonic magic, and presented a formulaic plot of recurring episodes, many of them not found in either the *Faustbooks* or Marlowe's play.[7] Elements apparently retained from Marlowe's tragedy in both the German adaptations and the puppet plays include the following: the rejection of divinity for the study of necromancy; the conjuring of

Mephistopheles; the blood contract; the raising of the classical dead to entertain the Emperor; tricks played on individuals in the Emperor's court; an old man who vainly exhorts the magician to repent; and the sorcerer's final damnation as he is carried off to a sulfurous hell. Supplementary episodes not present in either Marlowe's play or the *Faustbooks* include an introductory Prologue in Hell, which often substitutes Pluto for Satan; Faust's attempts to conjure the swiftest devil to be his servant; the infernal contract transported to Faust by a raven; and the tormenting of Faust before his abduction to hell. [8]

Philip Mason Palmer and Robert Pattison More posit that even though the audiences of the Enlightenment began to reject the superstition and mummery associated with these corrupt German versions of Marlowe's tragedy, the popularity of the puppet plays continued throughout the seventeenth and eighteenth centuries. They date the last production of the old Faust play as 1770 and the first puppet performance as 1746, commenting that the audience appeal of the puppet shows persisted into the nineteenth century.[9]

Scholars postulate that Goethe probably first encountered the Faust legend through these peripatetic puppet plays, although he may also have read the 1587 *German Faustbook* first published in his hometown, Frankfurt am Main, and may even have attended a production of the Germanized *Doctor Faustus*. In a diary note of June 11, 1818, Goethe first acknowledges reading Marlowe's play in translation; later an entry in H. Crabb Robinson's diary dated August 2, 1829 records Goethe's famous response to Marlowe's tragedy: "How greatly it was all planned!" What Goethe thought of the play's execution, we do not know, although he did state that "Now we know that Shakespeare did not stand alone."[10] However, although scholarly consensus agrees that Goethe did not read Marlowe's play in translation until 1818, ten years after the publication of *Faust, Part I*, even without encountering *Doctor Faustus* first-hand, he would certainly have been aware of the central elements of Marlowe's tragedy from the farcical puppet plays and even perhaps from the corrupt Germanized versions, particularly the depiction of Faust as an "overreacher whose energies and aspirations were compounded of both sublimity and depravity; the story of a supremely active self whose activity tended to descend into episodic triviality."[11] Conversely, departing from critical consensus, Otto Heller cites parallels in Marlowe's and Goethe's dramas not found in the puppet shows to argue that Goethe may well have encountered Marlowe's play before his diary entry in 1818. [12]

From Harlequin to Hero: Goethe's *Faust*

Date

As Paul Bishop comments: "The history of the composition of [Johann Wolfgang von Goethe's] *Faust* is of such complexity that it deserves a book in its own right, and has in fact inspired several."[13] Since these issues have been so fully examined elsewhere, I will not reiterate them here, except to observe that, according to critical consensus, *Faust, Part I* was completed in 1806 and published in its present form in 1808, although scholars insist that portions of it, called the *Urfaust*, were begun as early as 1773 and completed around 1776. *Faust, Part II* was not finished until 1831, shortly before Goethe's death, and not published until after his demise. *Faust, Parts I and II*, thus represents the product of almost sixty years of contemplation and composition.[14]

Goethe spent almost sixty years writing Faust, and these years, from 1773–1831, spanned the Enlightenment through the Romantic period, an era that witnessed an epistemic shift from supernatural to natural, God to humanity, system to individual, religious to secular. Jane K. Brown contends that *Faust* embodies the conflicts of this sixty-year period, particularly Goethe's attempt to reconcile the Romantic dialectic between subject (self, spirit) and object (the material world, nature).[15] *Faust* is thus the archetypical epic of the struggles and aspirations of modern man (I use "man" advisedly here, since the aspiring hero of the Faust legend is almost always associated specifically with the masculine gender).

Performance History

According to Hans Schulte, Goethe believed that his massive epic drama – a monumental work three times the length of *Hamlet*, constituting two five-act plays – was unstageable in its entirety, and for many years the theatrical world agreed with him.[16] Even *Faust, Part I* intimidated directors and did not receive its first full-length production in Germany until 1829 at the Brunswick Court Theatre, more than twenty years after the play's publication, and two years after its premiere presentations first in Paris and then in London. After this, Part I continued to be produced in Germany and Europe but always with an abridged script. Not until 1876, almost twenty years after the premier performance of *Faust, Part I*, did Otto Devrient attempt the production of both Part I and Part II, presented in Weimar, Germany, on successive evenings. Later, the great theatrical director Max Reinhardt staged memorable productions of Part I in 1909 and Part II in 1911.[17] Then in 1938, the world premiere of the unabridged version of Goethe's *Faust, Part I* and *Part II* – all 12,111 lines – was performed in Dornach, Switzerland at the Goetheanum, a most unconventional building, designed by Rudolf Steiner, the founder of anthroposophy, and named after Goethe. The production was directed by Marie Steiner, and Martina Maria Sam, a specialist on the stagings of *Faust* at the Goetheanum, speculates that the premiere probably ran around twenty-four hours. Performed by a combination of actors and choruses while stressing the metaphysical aspects of the drama, the Goetheanum *Faust*, from all accounts, was enthusiastically received. Productions of the complete *Faust* have continued to be performed in a similar fashion at the Goetheanum approximately every five years to this very day, although, in contemporary productions, the twenty-four-hour marathon has been shortened to a mere eighteen hours.[18] In 2000 Peter Stein, one of Germany's most celebrated directors and himself something of an aspiring Faust, also undertook to stage Goethe's epic play, totally uncut, in Hanover, Germany. The production took thirteen hours to perform. Stein gave the audience at the Hanover Expo 2000 Compound the choice between a three-day weekend Faust marathon – Friday evening, Saturday all day and evening, Sunday morning – or six sessions staged on consecutive nights.[19] Although some critics caviled at Stein's fidelity to the text and what they viewed as his rather old-fashioned directorial techniques, others recounted an exhilarating, unforgettable experience. Dirk Pilz describes the experience: "The length of the performance, the abundance of tableaux and scenes, of moods and reflection taxed and even overtaxed the audience's capacity. Stein's production of *Faust* was like Faust himself: it challenged by overtaxing." Even today, Peter Stein's production and the productions at the Goetheanum "hold the distinction of being the only productions in history to have performed Goethe's complete tragedy as a unified whole."[20]

Goethe's Adaptation of the Faust Legend

In his great dramatic epic, Goethe made many significant modifications in the Faust legend, the most memorable being the salvation of the erring hero. However, although Goethe is the first artist to redeem Faust from the flames of hell, his work of salvation had been attempted earlier in 1759 by Gotthold Ephraim Lessing, who proposed a German drama based on the Faust legend in his "Seventeenth Letter on Literature," an unfinished play

with which Goethe was doubtless familiar.[21] Although the intended conclusion of the play remains largely speculative, reports suggest that the play
planned to affirm Faust's passion for truth as the cause not of his damnation but of his redemption, "for divinity did not give man the most noble
of drives in order to make him unhappy." [22]

Let us consider Goethe's adaptation of the Faust legend to the zeitgeists
of both the Enlightenment and the Romantic periods of German culture.
In comparing Goethe's and Marlowe's treatments of the legend, one
should remember that whereas the twenty-four-year-old Marlowe probably penned his tragedy in about six months, Goethe composed his vast
poetic drama over a period of almost sixty years (1773–1831), and the
changes in the hero may well reflect Goethe's own maturing and expanding
vision of the world.

Goethe transforms both the ambiguous hero of Marlowe – part aspiring
overreacher, part folksy buffoon – and his great but equivocal play – part
searing tragedy, part comic morality – into a magnificent drama that fits no
category, a phantasmagoric epic with a biblical frame, numerous fantastic
masques and pageants, an aspiring hero, and a surprise happy ending. The
diverse manner in which Marlowe's and Goethe's dramas adapt material
from the medieval and classical traditions serves as an index to the differences in tone and ethos characterizing each play. Marlowe's tragedy
commingles elements from the morality tradition with classical *de casibus*
tragedy. These include a morality frame Prologue and Epilogue, implicat-
ing both the "conspiring heavens" and the sin of hubris in Faustus's fatal
fall; the ubiquitous emblematic figures – the Seven Deadly Sins, the Good
and Evil Angels, the Old Man, and Helen; a Devil alternately assuming the
roles of tragic figure and morality tempter; and the raucous comic montage
of the center section with evil presented primarily as absurd rather than
vicious. Additionally, the play presents an internalized tragic hero whose
catastrophic fate arouses pity, terror, and a sense of waste.

Conversely, Goethe's *Faust* adopts a frame from both the Bible and the
biblical cycle plays, opening, as do most biblical cycles, with God in heaven,
and concluding, again in appropriate biblical play fashion, with the redemption of the blessed. The Prologue of *Faust* makes clear that God, unlike the
"conspiring heavens" in Marlowe's tragedy, is rooting for Faust, even as
Jehovah is rooting for Job in the biblical model for the scene. This
Prologue thus adumbrates Faust's ultimate salvation, a reversal of expectation
also foreshadowed by the Easter chorus praising Christ's resurrection that
saves Faust from suicide in the opening scene, as well as by the later angelic
affirmation of Gretchen's redemption that concludes *Faust, Part I*. However,

the seraphic voice proclaiming the salvation of Gretchen at the end of Part I, and the choruses announcing the redemption of Faust at the denouement of Part II find a provenance not only in the biblical cycle plays but also in the moralities, which frequently end with the salvation of the often unworthy hero. Moreover, the final battle between good and evil concluding Part II, in which the angels conquer the devils by pelting them with roses that burn like flames, also recalls the battle between the Seven Deadly Sins and the Seven Cardinal Virtues in the early morality play, *The Castle of Perseverance*, in which virtue conquers vice in a fusillade of flowers. Although there is no evidence that Goethe was familiar with this play, the similarities are striking. Lastly, the comic treatment at the denouement of both Goethe's Mephistopheles – wounded with the flame-like roses while lusting after the provocative derrieres of the effeminate boy cupids – and the ridiculous Fat and Lean Devils echoes both the antic beating of Satan in the biblical cycle plays and the frequently humorous exits of the Vice in the moralities, even as the farcical Walpurgis Night mimics the ribald buffoonery of the Vice comedy of the morality play.

However, the etiology of *Faust* is far more complex and various than this brief summary suggests, as this towering dramatic masterpiece reveals a multitude of influences reflecting the prodigious reading that contributed to Goethe's own unique vision of the legend. According to some commentators, Goethe's striving hero, like Marlowe's overreacher, conforms to the traditional rubric of the tragic hero: an admirable individual with one tragic flaw, who makes monumental decisions, errs knowingly or accidentally, learns and grows through suffering, and dies more enlightened than he lived. Whether or not we agree that Faust fits this pattern (an issue to be examined below), classical tragedy, particularly the drama of Euripides, certainly influenced Goethe and provided the structure and verse form for sections of the Helena episode.

In addition, a number of scholars have noted the important influence of Dante on the teleology of the drama. Jaroslav Pelikan interprets the central trajectory of the play as a pilgrimage in which the pilgrim Faust matures as he follows the path traversed by Dante, moving from "the world through hell to heaven." Franziska Schöfsler develops the analogy, maintaining that at the eschatological denouement of the drama "Faust rises through the spheres of Heaven, just as Dante ascends through the various angelic hierarchies," and the spirit of Gretchen leads the immortal part of Faust into the presence of the Holy Virgin, here called the Mater Gloriosa, even as Beatrice guided Dante through the levels of heaven to the Divine.[23] Moreover, Faust, like Dante before him, is redeemed through the intercession of "Eternal Womanhood,"[24] or the "Eternal Feminine" as it is sometimes translated.

As expected, the influence of Shakespeare is pervasive and a number of scholars have identified salient allusions to Shakespeare as well as Marlowe in Goethe's masterpiece. E. M. Butler discusses the parallel between the half-demented Gretchen in the dungeon, singing a "gruesome ballad of guilt, cruelty, and infanticide," and the mad Ophelia crooning her folk ditty of illicit love. Cyrus Hamlin associates the three gray crones who haunt Faust in Act 5 of Part II with the three witches in *Macbeth*. David Luke comments not only on the similarities between the crazed Gretchen and the equally mad Ophelia but also on those between the belligerent Valentine and the quarrelsome Mercutio. Echoing Mercutio, Valentine challenges Faust: "Who are you serenading here? / Damned rat catcher" (3699), and Faust's flight after killing Valentine parallels Romeo's banishment after slaying Tybalt. Finally, Brown posits multiple analogies to Shakespeare: not only Gretchen's mimicry of Ophelia's mad songs, but also allusions to *A Midsummer Night's Dream* in the "Walpurgis Night" episode and parallels between Goethe's magus Faust and Shakespeare's magus Prospero, who, like Faust, primarily employs his thaumaturgy for trickery and, like Faust, ultimately renounces his magic, but only after he has achieved his goals. [25]

Several scholars have also suggested that *Paradise Lost*, another poem centrally concerned with the relationship between good, evil, and free will, provided an inspiration for the "Prologue in Heaven." This influence can be seen in God's reference to the necessary intermingling of good and evil, as revealed in His provocative line, "Man errs till he ceases to strive" (317), thereby establishing an ineluctable link between aspiration and error.

As Alfred Hoelzel explains, the correspondence between Goethe and Schiller documents Goethe's reading of *Paradise Lost* by 1799, probably before he had composed the "Prologue in Heaven," and "Persuasive evidence of Milton's influence emanates from the text itself, particularly from the poem's view of evil as ultimately culminating in good."[26]

Finally, Ritchie Robertson identifies a panoply of literary influences on Goethe's drama, ranging from the Bible, Lucan, Virgil, and Dante to *The Arabian Nights*, the Indian play *Sakuntala*, and other oriental works. [27] Goethe's *Faust* is thus a literary mosaic rather than a hybrid, combining elements of classical tragedy and epic, the *Faustbooks*, both the biblical cycle plays and the moralities, Dante, Marlowe, Shakespeare, and Milton, as well as other masterpieces of both Western and Eastern civilizations.

Goethe follows the structure of the medieval biblical plays by bracketing his drama with both a Prologue and an Epilogue in heaven; actually, he inserts three Prologues – "Dedication," "Prelude on the Stage," and "Prologue in Heaven" – all of which comment on the pervasive theme of the mundane versus the transcendent, the pragmatic versus the ideal. The "Prologue in Heaven" also evokes the Book of Job, the first book of the Hebrew Bible in which Satan appears. The Book of Job presents Satan not as a fallen spirit but as a being with the same status as the other "sons of God," a member of God's divine council, with his name, which in Hebrew means "the Adversary," identifying him not as an antagonist of God but rather as a God-sanctioned opponent of human beings.[28] Mephistopheles appears to play a similar role in Goethe's "Prologue in Heaven," and the wager between God and the Devil prefigures that between Faust and Mephistopheles. Moreover, the "Prologue in Heaven" delineates a value system very different from that underlying Marlowe's *Faustus*. In Marlowe's tragedy, the pendulum swings between faith and despair, whereas Goethe's Prologue equates virtue with energy, drive, and activity; vice with sloth, quiescence, and inactivity. Martin Swales maintains that Goethe's poetic drama establishes Faust not only as a particularized individual but as the "all-important test case in a philosophical wager about the nature and value of human being in the world."[29]

The opening scene of the drama, titled "Night," also departs from all antecedent versions of the Faust legend by having its hero conjure not the Devil but the Earth Spirit (see Figure 3.1). In both *Doctor Faustus* and Goethe's *Faust*, the play proper opens with the eponymous hero discovered in his study contemplating the four great disciplines of the medieval university – philosophy, law, medicine, and theology – and repudiating them all as unfulfilling. According to Heller, Faust's survey of the learned disciplines finds no correspondence in the puppet plays, much less in the *German Faustbook*; thus Heller contends that the striking similarity between the opening scenarios in the dramas by Marlowe and Goethe offers salient evidence, refuting received opinion, that Goethe must have read Marlowe's tragedy before he wrote Part I of *Faust*.[30] Although I find Heller's observations highly provocative, in the absence of strong verbal parallels in the two scenes, his argument remains only speculation.

A comparison of the memorable soliloquies of Marlowe's and Goethe's heroes, in many ways so similar, in other crucial aspects so different, highlights the disparate orientations of the two discontented savants. Whereas Faustus's rejection of discursive knowledge appears to be a rationalization, Faust seems genuinely disillusioned with the vacuity of

Figure 3.1 Goethe's *Faust*. "Faust at Work," after a painting by Rembrandt.
Photograph by Culture Club/Hulton Archive/Getty Images.

erudition. He declares that he has learned nothing of importance, nothing
that can help human beings achieve self-awareness or excellence (364–73).
Moreover, unlike the conjuror of the *Faustbooks* who wishes to satisfy his
curiosity and lust or the more hubristic hero of Marlowe's tragedy who

aspires to cosmic command, Goethe's Faust seems genuinely to desire not so much knowledge – certainly not academic learning, which he eschews as sterile and empty – as experience of the meaning of life, an experience that can be found not in books but only in the individual's participation in nature and the world. However, despite the disparity in their goals, Faust, like his Elizabethan predecessor, judges the traditional academic disciplines wearisome and stultifying. Therefore, like Marlowe's Faustus, he turns to magic, selecting empirical over discursive knowledge, since the medieval and early modern periods often associated empirical knowledge, including science, with the occult. The opening soliloquy of Goethe's Faust thus epitomizes the epistemic shift from the medieval/Renaissance privileging of discursive knowledge to the empiricism dominating the eighteenth and nineteenth centuries.

Nevertheless, unlike Marlowe's Faustus, who rejects discursive knowledge for black magic, Faust initially experiments with natural or white magic, counterbalancing the power of nature with the "mouldering bones" and "reek and rot" of academic tomes (416–17), thereby revealing the strong influence of eighteenth-century nature poetry, [31] which presented Nature as the fount of truth. Faust then contemplates two signs: the visual sign of the macrocosm, which he rejects as a mere representation, and a verbal sign whereby he conjures the Earth Spirit. However, although Faust boldly claims equality with this Spirit ('It is I, Faust! you and I are the same!' 500), the Spirit adamantly spurns him and vanishes. Throughout this section, Goethe satirizes academic and scientific studies as tedious, barren, and inane, juxtaposing them with the ecstasy of direct experience of the natural world. Faust's servant cum research assistant Wagner represents the shrunken soul of the academic pedant content to grub for worms in dry and sterile learning, who does not realize he knows nothing, as he hubristically states: "Already I know much, I must know all the rest" (601).

Goethe's Faust, unlike Marlowe's hero, experiences despair and contemplates suicide before not after his contract with the Devil. After Wagner departs, Faust's inability to escape the suffocating constraints of humanity drives him to deep depression, and he contemplates suicide as a release from the "stifling prison-hole" (399) in which he feels incarcerated. However, as Faust raises the poisoned chalice to his lips, the voices of the Easter chorus re-enacting Christ's resurrection cause him to pause, and he remembers the faith of his childhood. Also, according to Hamlin, Goethe juxtaposes the visitation of the Earth Spirit, catalyst to despair and death, with the Easter chorus, catalyst to rebirth and renewal, counterpoising the poisoned cup of death with the Eucharistic cup of rebirth. Moreover, the songs of the Easter chorus presage not only Gretchen's salvation but also Faust's redemption at the end of the drama.[32] I further suggest that the description of Christ's resurrection from the tomb's prison also adumbrates Faust's resurrection from the musty, claustrophobic academic tomb in which he has been stifled.

Although Goethe has delayed Mephistopheles's appearance through three Prologues and two scenes, all readers familiar with the Faust legend eagerly anticipate the first confrontation between Faust and the Devil, and even the innovative Goethe cannot postpone this fateful meeting too long. However, even here Goethe deviates from the familiar formula. In the *Faustbooks* and Marlowe's tragedy, Mephistopheles, although certainly a powerful spirit, is clearly subordinate to Lucifer in the demonic hierarchy; conversely, Goethe's "Prologue in Heaven" establishes him as God's primary adversary, a role reinforced throughout the drama by the frequent identification of Mephistopheles with Satan. Moreover, in all previous versions of the story, Faust conjures the Devil; in Goethe's drama, seeking to win his wager with God, Mephistopheles pursues Faust, initially in the form of a black poodle, recalling the ubiquitous black dog rumored to have accompanied the historic Faust on his peregrinations. When he finally reveals himself, Mephistopheles identifies himself as "the spirit of perpetual negation!" (1338); he also characterizes himself as "Part of that Power which would / Do evil constantly, and constantly does good" (1335–36), although arguably, the Spirit constantly does evil, at least until the end of the drama.

Goethe's magnetic but ambitious devil has fascinated scholars and artists for centuries (for my favorite illustration of Goethe's Mephistopheles, see Figure 3.2). Scholars have defined this spirit of denial differently. According to Brown, following the Neoplatonic dialectic of spirit and world, Mephistopheles represents the world – physical matter unordered by spirit; he is also the purveyor of illusions, as in Marlowe's play, since, in both versions of the Faust legend, all of Mephistopheles's magic involves illusory manipulation of the natural world. Charles E. Passage interprets Mephistopheles as the spirit of evil as Goethe understood evil and as God defines it in the "Prologue in Heaven": "the sum total of non-doing: laziness, procrastination, indifference, self-indulgence, cynicism, idle mockery, frivolity." In this reading, "Faust is the representative of mankind, and, as such, wills positively *to do*; Mephistopheles, the Spirit of Negation, wills *not to do*." Jeffrey Burton Russell also sees Mephistopheles as the essence of nihilism: "the spirit of chaos and disorder in the natural world, he also promotes disorder in society by disrupting justice." However, Osman Durrani stresses the necessity of the Devil in the scheme

Figure 3.2 Mephistopheles's "Prologue in the Sky" from Goethe's *Faust*.
Photograph by Historical Picture Archive/Corbis Historical/Getty Images.

of things, defining the purpose of Mephistopheles as "a stimulant that prevents human creativity from atrophying." Peter-André Alt merges these different conceptions, presenting Goethe's Mephisto as an "intellectual Proteus," "combining heterogeneous qualities into a conflicting unity: the comic and the tragic, the cynical and the ironical, the sarcastic and the melancholy, acuity and cold lust." Assuming a somewhat different

perspective, Dieter Borchmeyer relates Mephistopheles to the mythologi-
cal "trickster" – figures like the Greek deity Hermes, the Roman deity
Mercury, or the Norse god Loki – as an example of demonic laughter.[33]
I would add that in the "Prologue in Heaven," as throughout Goethe's
drama, Mephistopheles also assumes the function of the comic Vice: God
identifies him as an "ironic scold"; in the Emperor's court he plays the role
of the jester; yet, beneath his comic masque lurks a consistent cynicism and
malevolence toward all humanity. Certainly, Goethe's Devil displays none
of the internal conflict of Marlowe's disjunctive fiend or even the brief
moment of poignant humanity revealed by the demon of the *Faustbooks*.
I find Goethe's Mephistopheles, witty and urbane yet cynical, cold, and
bereft of compassion, to be among the most genuinely evil Devils in the
entire rogues' gallery of Faust tempters.

   The first encounter between the magus and the Devil is presented very
differently in the dramas of Marlowe and Goethe. Faust's attempts to
translate the Bible, not his magical conjurations with a necromantic book,
effect the transformation of Mephistopheles from the black poodle who
pursues him into his study into a university student dressed in traveling
robes. Faust's reformulation of the Bible "re-enacts one of the great cultural
achievements of Germany, Luther's translation of the Bible."[34] Pondering
the opening words of the Book of John, Faust muses:

> "In the beginning was the Word": why, now
> I'm stuck already! I must change that; how?
> Is then "the word" so great and high a thing?
> There is some other rendering,
> Which with the spirit's guidance I must find.
> We read: "In the beginning was the Mind."
> Before you write this first phrase, think again;
> Good sense eludes the overhasty pen.
> Does "mind" set worlds on their creative course?
> It means: "In the beginning was the Force."
> So it should be – but as I write this too,
> Some instinct warns me that it will not do.
> The spirit speaks! I see how it must read,
> And boldly write: "In the beginning was the Deed!"   (1224–37)

In his translation of John, a ritual often employed in white magic and in
exorcisms, [35] Faust first rejects language, the Word, as represented by
academic learning or discursive knowledge, as he has earlier eschewed all
"word peddling" (385), seeking to substitute the Mind, the power that
formulates the Word. But even this is not sufficient; he wishes to transcend

mere mind and participate in the power animating the world, thus progressing to Force. However, this also proves unsatisfying: ultimately, he seeks action in the world or "Deeds" as the ultimate good, as he will later affirm in his final monologue in Part II: "Only that man earns freedom, / Who must reconquer both in constant daily strife" (11575–6). This eternal striving has come to be recognized as the mantra of the Faustian spirit.

Surprisingly, given the traditional association of the Faust figure with the quest for knowledge, neither Marlowe's Faustus nor Goethe's Faust is primarily motivated by a desire for knowledge as we normally define it, as information about this world or the other, although Marlowe's Faustus does show considerable curiosity about these issues. However, as I have argued earlier, the desideratum of Marlowe's Faustus remains power, and he pursues knowledge primarily as a strategy to achieve power, pleasure, wealth, and fame. Faust, on the other hand, seeks a particular kind of knowledge – not information, certainly not discursive knowledge – but experience of the world in all its aspects, physical, emotional, and intellectual, with the goal of achieving understanding of the self and of God. Marlowe's hero yearns to transcend nature and "gain a deity"; conversely, Goethe's Faust displays a fierce passion not to transcend nature but to understand its inmost secrets:

> Let us plunge into the rush of things,
> Of time and all its happenings!
> And then let pleasure and distress,
> Disappointment and success,
> Succeed each other as they will;
> Man cannot act if he is standing still.   (1754–59)

However, as Faust has earlier explained, he possesses two souls that war within his breast for rule: one longs for the world, one struggles to transcend it; one seeks immersion in the self, one strives to escape from the self. I agree with Brown that in his initial conflict with the Devil Faust generally speaks for the positive, idealistic view of human capabilities, Mephistopheles for the negative, worldlier view; Faust represents the soul that strives for higher regions, Mephistopheles the one that clings to the dust of the earth. Like the two angels in Marlowe's play, these two perspectives – worldliness and transcendence – reside within Faust as well as external to him, and Faust's long and arduous pilgrim's progress becomes an attempt to reconcile the warring elements within his soul. Durrani supports Brown by identifying the Devil as an alter ego to the philosopher, "whose latent amoral and selfish desires he embodies." Hellmut Ammerlahn develops this reading, presenting Mephistopheles as Faust's doppelgänger, who not only "exhibits aspects of Faust's destructive tendencies," but also "acts as a positive facilitator for Faust's endeavors." [36] This view of the fiendish familiar as Faust's dark doppelgänger – a view I find most persuasive – will be echoed in a number of the post-Goethe Faust dramas discussed in this study.

One of Goethe's most striking alterations in the Faust legend relates to the blood-inscribed contract. Departing from all previous versions of the legend, Goethe has his hero and the Devil conclude not a contract but a wager, mirroring the Job-like bet finalized in heaven between God and the Devil. Although Faust does sign "something" with a drop of blood, Goethe leaves the nature of this document unexplained, even as Faust jests at the mummery of the blood-inscribed pact. Significantly, however, Mephistopheles does mention the diabolical contract on two additional occasions. The first occurs in Act 2 of Part II when, returning the entranced Faust to his study, the Devil espies the pen Faust used to sign his bargain with a drop of dried blood still inside the quill (6575–79). Later, after Faust's death (Part II, Act 5), Mephistopheles triumphantly gloats: "The body's down, the spirit I'll soon fix, / I'll show him his own blood-scribed document" (11612–13). According to the wager between the two, Mephistopheles will have Faust's soul if ever the Devil can lull Faust into complacency, thereby blunting his divine discontent and ceaseless striving. Although neither of the parties mentions the portentous word "soul" at this time, after Faust's death, when Mephistopheles comes to claim his victim, he does remark: "Yet souls come hard these days, their friends invent / Loopholes, and try to play the Devil tricks" (11614–15).

In this bargain, Goethe also deviates from all previous renditions of the Faust legend in which Mephistopheles offers his services to the Faust figure for a limited period of time, usually twenty-four years. Conversely, Goethe's Faust has all the time in the world; time will stop for him as long as he does not stop but seeks new forms of action. As Faust affirms:

> If ever I lie down in sloth and base inaction,
> Then let that moment be my end!
> If by your false cajolery
> You lull me into self-sufficiency,
> If any pleasure you can give
> Deludes me, let me cease to live! . . .
> If ever to the moment I shall say:
> Beautiful moment, do not pass away!

Then you may forge your chains to bind me.
Then I will put my life behind me,
Then let them hear my death-knell toll,
Then from your labours you'll be free,
The clock may stop, the clock-hands fall,
And time come to an end for me!   (Part II, 1692–97, 1699–1706)

Faustus believes that Mephistopheles, the master of illusion, can never offer him anything lasting because no illusion can be permanent; indeed, until the very end of the drama he rejects everything he experiences as ephemeral. He will, of course, prove to be mistaken. Gretchen's love, as the entire drama demonstrates, is permanent and survives even death and salvation.

Another significant difference between the treatment of the bargain in Marlowe and Goethe relates to the fulfillment of the heroes' aspirations. Marlowe alters his source, making his hero's desires more grandiose and his achievements more limited, thereby stressing the degree to which his hero's overreach exceeds his grasp. Conversely, although Goethe's Faust initially requests no rewards except to experience fully both the joy and suffering of life, he receives many of the gratifications denied to Marlowe's hero. Of central importance to both aspirers is erotic pleasure. After signing the fatal contract in blood, Marlowe's Faustus, who initially says little about sensual delights, immediately experiences libidinous yearnings and selects marriage as the most convenient way to satisfy these sexual desires. But the Devil adamantly rejects Faustus's request for a wife. Since Mephistopheles obviously cannot provide this boon, he scoffs at marriage and tries to divert Faustus with courtesans and other beautiful women, all probably succubae assuming the roles of the tempting females. Conversely, Goethe again departs from all tradition by magically rejuvenating his aging hero in the Witch's Kitchen, granting him not only youth but a revitalized libido. As the cynical Mephistopheles quips: "With that elixir coursing through him / Soon any woman will be Helen [of Troy] to him" (Part I, 2603–04). After Faust's rejuvenation, Mephistopheles assists the magus in the seduction of the innocent Gretchen, although, as all lovers of German literature and opera know, the romance ends in terrible suffering and tragedy. Later, following the formula of the *Faustbooks* and Simon Magus before them, both Marlowe's and Goethe's magicians desire and achieve the love of Helen of Troy, or at least of her simulacrum. But whereas Marlowe's play debases Helen, identifying her as a succubus conjured by Mephistopheles to "suck forth" his victim's soul and distract him from repentance, Goethe's drama exalts Helen as the phantom of the storied temptress, the ideal symbol of art and beauty, who elevates Faust instead of damning him.[37]

In the treatment of Gretchen and Helen, Goethe not only grants his hero more fulfilling erotic experiences than Marlowe allows Faustus, but also idealizes the feminine principle generally denigrated in previous treatments of the Faust legend. Marilyn French's delineation of the masculine and feminine principles as identified by Western society since the time of Pythagoras offers a valuable gloss on the treatment of feminine and masculine values in these two dramatizations of the Faust legend. According to French, society has traditionally associated the masculine principle with power-in-the-world, the celebration of individuality, and the conquest of nature; conversely, the in-law feminine principle privileges love over power, community over the individual, and union with nature over its domination, and, at this time, was also linked with the Christian virtues of piety, patience, peacefulness, and pity. [38] As I have argued elsewhere, at the conclusion of Marlowe's *Doctor Faustus*, the feminine values have been rejected in all their manifestations. All the women, even the female supernumeraries (the Duchess of Vanholt, the Hostess) and the infernal female impersonators (the Devil Wife, Alexander's Paramour, and Helen) have been exiled from the play world. Moreover, the embodiments of the in-law feminine principle – the Good Angel, the nurturing neighbor, and the caring students – have all departed. In contrast to the banishment of the feminine concluding Marlowe's tragedy, Goethe's drama ends in an explosion of baroque imagery celebrating Gretchen, the Mater gloriosa, and the feminine principle.[39]

Finally, the two dramatizations of the Faust legend treat their heroes' dynastic ambitions very differently. The boast of Faustus, "The emperor shall not live but by my leave," unfulfilled in Marlowe's play, is ironically realized in Goethe's epic, in which in Part II, Act 4, Faust and Mephistopheles with their spectral army and their bully-boys from hell rescue the incompetent Emperor from his rivals and re-establish him on his throne. Moreover, unlike Marlowe's magician, who futilely yearns to be "great king of all the provinces," in Part II, Act 5, Goethe's Faust gains suzerainty over his own kingdom, magically reclaimed from the sea. Thus, Goethe's superman gains the worldly power to which Marlowe's superman manqué only fruitlessly aspires.

If in the Gretchen tragedy Goethe totally departs from the Faust tradition enshrined in the *Faustbooks* and Marlowe's play, in a number of the other episodes he returns to the legendary pattern, while transmuting it into something highly original. Like Marlowe's Faustus, Goethe's Faust wins the love of the shade (or at least semblance) of Helen of Troy, raises spirits to entertain the Emperor, and employs spectral forces to overcome his opponents (in Faust's case, the rival Emperor rather than the jeering knight). However, a comparison of these episodes reveals the differences rather than the similarities in the two treatments of the Faust narrative.

In almost every aspect *Faust* deviates from the format codified in the *Faustbooks*, Marlowe's play, and all the multiple interpretations of the legend in comic adaptations and puppet shows. First, Goethe changes his hero's name from the Georgius of history, the Johannes of the *Faustbooks*, and the John of Marlowe's tragedy to Heinrich. Moreover, unlike the traditional dabbler in magic, Faust does not conjure the Devil; unlike the traditional quester, Faust makes a Job-like wager instead of a contract; unlike the traditional magus, Faustus gains many concrete awards from his wager and never degenerates into absurdity; and, most significantly, unlike the traditional apostate, Faust is ultimately redeemed. However, in one central way, Goethe's poetic drama maintains, indeed magnifies, one of the defining characteristics of the legend: like Marlowe, he endows his hero with an insatiable aspiring soul. Moreover, after Goethe's great cosmic drama, the term "Faustian" has for all time become associated with ceaseless striving toward impossible goals. But how are we to evaluate this ceaseless striving? Ah, as Hamlet would say, there's the rub, and the primary source of the continuing debate over the ethos and meaning of Goethe's *Faust* – as well as much of the fascination that the play continues to hold for critics, readers, and spectators alike.

Alternative Readings of Goethe's Faust

As noted in Chapter 2, few works of literature have aroused such heated critical controversy as Marlowe's *Doctor Faustus*. One of those few is Goethe's *Faust*. Although controversy has raged around the completed drama since its publication in 1832, the normative and popular reading of Goethe's play, which, according to Hoelzel, continues to this day, interprets the drama as a celebration of its aspiring hero, who before his death discovers the *summum bonum* of existence, dies triumphant, and is ultimately redeemed. This celebratory reading of the drama dates from Heinrich Düntzer (1850–51), the herald of a school of critics dubbed "Perfektibilisten," who tout the work as the crowning achievement of German literature and its hero as a paragon of humanity.[40] Interpreting the drama as an allegory of the human condition in the modern age, throughout the last century and a half, various ideological movements

have sought to appropriate this vast cosmic drama to their political agen-
das. The National Socialists construed Faust's incessant striving as
a glorification of Aryan culture, with Faust functioning as a symbol of
"German man," "endowed with a civilizing mission of an inexorable, fatal
clarity." Marxist critics interpreted Faust's final apotheosis, his vision of
a utopian world of free men in a free land working together in a collective
spirit, as anticipating a great classless socialist republic. Bourgeois commentators stressed the promise of a dedicated, enterprising community,
and other scholars discovered the locus of Goethe's striving Faust in the
Puritan ethic, particularly Calvinist theology. Freudian, Jungian, and
feminist exegetes have scoured *Faust, Part II* to find support for their
various ideologies.[41]

Moreover, a number of explicators, approaching the characters from an
allegorical rather than a political or psychological perspective, insist that
throughout the drama the aspiring Faust grows and matures, moving from
the bourgeoisie to the beau monde, from the Play of Society to the Theatre
of the World. Passage traces Faust's pilgrim's progress through varied
human experiences, including Love (Part I) to Prime Minister/Court
Poet (Part II, Act 1) to Science and Pedagogy (Act 2) to Art (Act 3), to
Generalship (Act 4) to Empire-Building (Act 5), with these wide-ranging
experiences presented as part of Faust's education in the meaning of life.
Marshall Berman posits a slightly different evolution: "he [Faust] first
emerges as The Dreamer, then, through Mephisto's mediation, transforms
himself into The Lover, and finally, long after the tragedy of love is over, he
will reach his life's climax as The Developer": "He expands the horizon of
his being from private to public life, from intimacy to activism, from
communion to organization." Heller concurs, praising Faust's "perfect
execution of unmatched poetic tasks," which "invests Goethe's world
poem with a grandeur beside which even the magnificent accomplishments
of his sole worthy predecessor [Marlowe's *Doctor Faustus*] dwindle to the
proportions of miniature." Although contemporary critics have taken
a more temperate approach to the work, heroic interpreters, like Berman,
can still affirm that in the last act of the play, Goethe presents "the
modernization of the material world as a sublime spiritual achievement,"
with Faust as "the developer" presented as the "archetypical modern hero."
Stuart Atkins's summary epitomizes this positive reading of Faust's pilgrim's progress as an education through suffering: Faust moves from the
libertine, dedicated to self-centered striving toward erotic satisfaction, to
the artist, seeking to synthesize classical beauty and medieval/Renaissance
romantic love with German literature, to the empire-builder, dedicated to

reclaiming the land from the sea and envisioning a society unfettered by the past. According to this positive interpretation, the poem proclaims: "Man is redeemed by insight, not by achievement, and only through consciously directed activity, wise or foolish, successful or unsuccessful, can this insight be gained."[42]

Since World War II, scholars have attempted a more moderate and, in my opinion, a more accurate reading of the work, but the intense political exploitation of the text since the 1870s has left an ambivalence about the drama more profound than that which greeted the work's first appearance. Twentieth- and twenty-first-century critics, more alert than their nineteenth-century forebears to the ironies of the work, have tended to view the drama pessimistically. Although, unlike his Elizabethan prototype and his predecessors in the corrupt German Faust dramas and puppet plays, Goethe's hero never descends into absurdity, expositors observe that his striving inevitably results in failure, frustration, and devastation: the dishonor and death of his beloved Gretchen, the poisoning of her mother, the slaying of her brother, the death of their child, and, later, the murder of the hospitable and pious Baucis and Philemon. In addition, many commentators remain mystified with the "Helena" sequence masterminded by Mephistopheles, which seems a diversion from Faust's principal endeavor, an escape from human life rather than an immersion in it.

However, Faust's reclamation project has aroused the most vociferous debate. In Act 4 of Part II, after Mephistopheles has virtually won the war for the Emperor, Faust asks only for a strip of water where virtually no land exists; he could easily have been "great emperor of the world," but Goethe's hero is not tempted. Hamlin explains: "Faust wants to begin from nothing, imposing human culture on nature by defeating it through the power of his will." Some commentators see this determination as an aspect of Faust's ever-upward striving; others interpret it as the epitome of hubris and a sign of his degeneration. As Hamlin comments, earlier Faust had sought unity with the eternal feminine; now he rejects the feminine principle for masculine conquest and rule. Hans Rudolf Vaget also endorses this ironic perspective, totally rejecting socialist or Marxist readings of Faust's reclamation project while stressing the empire-builder's affinity with feudalism. Moreover, he proclaims Faust's dying speech "the most politically exploited lines in all German literature," rebuking celebratory readings of the drama while asserting that only "a self-deluded *Faust* scholarship intoxicated by the heady dogma of the perfectibility and progress of the Faustian spirit could find anything admirable or elevating in Faust's dying vision."[43]

Thus, as with Marlowe's tragedy, Goethe's drama has throughout the years evoked wildly disparate interpretations. In the discussion below, I shall offer a reading of this interrogative play that seeks to incorporate both the celebratory and ironic interpretations of Goethe's great dramatic epic.

A Reading of Faust

Faust, rejuvenated by Mephistopheles and harassed with a revitalized youthful libido, falls in lust with the beautiful fifteen-year-old virgin Margarete, or Gretchen as she is called throughout the drama, and demands that Mephistopheles bring her to his bed within seven hours. Originally, lust seems to be the rejuvenated savant's primary motivation and, like Don Juan, he feels no moral qualms about seducing an innocent virgin. After persuading Faust that seductions of this type take time, Mephistopheles aids Faust's courtship by stealing jewels from buried treasures with which to tempt the naïve, penurious young woman, but ultimately Gretchen becomes enchanted with Faust's personality and his vast learning, not with his monetary gifts. Later, clandestinely visiting Gretchen's poor but tidy little room, Faust begins to perceive Gretchen as a human being as well as a sex object and to idealize her as an emblem of innocence. The text associates her with order and purity, the characteristics of the spirit as opposed to the flesh. Moreover, the text presents Gretchen as the opposite of Mephistopheles; both will make Faustus strive, Gretchen by pulling him from above, Mephistopheles by pricking him from behind. Faust idolizes Gretchen, yet at the same time, he defiles her purity and destroys her. He thus blends both the idealistic lover and the unscrupulous Don Juan; by uniting Faust with Don Juan, Goethe merges two of the most pervasive "masculine" legends of our Western society.

However, Faust, unlike Don Juan, has his moments of compunction. Faust's psychological conflict occurs in the scene titled "A Forest Cavern." Here, presumably enlightened by love, Faust at last achieves the oneness with nature and through nature with all humankind that he so futilely sought to discover in sterile books and discursive learning. But Faust also realizes that he is about to sacrifice this fellowship with all humankind to feed the desires of his ego.[44] Faust recognizes that he cannot marry Gretchen, cannot imprison his restless, striving spirit within the cozy domestic confines of her little world. He thus fights against the rampaging passion that he knows will annihilate his vulnerable beloved (3345–61). In the midst of Faust's soul struggle, a smirking Mephistopheles appears, informing Faust that his love is pining for him; and although Faust demeans Mephistopheles as a "pimp" and a "serpent," he yields to his Spirit's goading manipulation. Lust conquers love, and Faust departs from the solace of nurturing nature to enter the arena of tragedy.

The Gretchen tragedy [45] dramatizes a saga of callousness and egotism resulting in four deaths, all unwittingly caused by Faust. The first, the death of Gretchen's mother, results from the poisoned drink that Faust through the agency of Mephistopheles gives to Gretchen's mother thinking it is a sleeping potion. This is followed by the manslaughter of Valentine, Gretchen's hot-headed brother, orchestrated by Mephistopheles and committed by Faust in self-defense. Finally, the death of Gretchen's child and the execution of the distraught mother for infanticide committed in a moment of madness are both the direct consequence of Faust's seduction and abandonment of the unfortunate young woman. Faust was forced to flee because of his slaying of Gretchen's brother Valentine, but his careless and irresponsible disregard of Gretchen for months – and it must have been months because he seems totally unaware of her pregnancy – remains unforgivable. From one point of view, therefore, we must judge Faust as either a feckless lover or an unscrupulous cad unworthy of all the suffering he causes.

Of course, the drama partially exonerates Faust, stressing his manipulation by Mephistopheles who arranges the poisoning of Gretchen's mother, stage-manages the slaying of Valentine, spirits Faust away, and distracts his victim from thoughts of Gretchen with the lurid bawdry of the Walpurgis Night.[46] When Faust learns of Gretchen's disgrace, infanticide, and imprisonment, he turns on Mephistopheles in fury, yet his own derelict disregard for his beloved for months renders him equally culpable. Like Marlowe's hero, Faust always blames his demonic enabler, even though, again like Marlowe's Faustus, he is himself at least partially responsible for all of his problems. Faust's determined attempt to save Gretchen partially absolves him; however, as Brown observes, by the Dungeon scene, Faust has probably ceased to love Gretchen. She represents to him the ephemeral pleasure of the world that Mephistopheles can offer, and he is not yet ready to settle for any of these transitory joys. Yet, had he but realized it, Gretchen embodies the one constant in the vertiginous world of *Faust*, a love that survives disgrace, death, and even salvation, and that, to quote Hamlin, "proves to be a redemptive force, which is finally stronger than the devil's wager with Faust."[47] Ultimately, whether because she believes that Faust no longer loves her or because she feels ethically compelled to face the punishment for her infanticide, Gretchen refuses to escape with Faust.

With the dawn threatening and the demonic steeds chafing with fear of the rising sun, Mephistopheles drags away the passive, unprotesting Faust, as an angelic voice proclaims Gretchen's redemption (4611). Thus, Faust and his diabolical mentor desert the abused, half-demented young woman to her cruel and unjust penalty, and throughout the centuries critics and readers have responded ambivalently to Faust's craven abandonment of his beloved.

The ambivalence aroused by the tragic denouement of Part I is exacerbated throughout Part II. The text contains no reference to the passage of time, so the reader/spectator has no conception of how many days, weeks, or months pass between Gretchen's execution and the beginning of Part II, which finds Faust lying in a "Beautiful Landscape," a place of healing and rebirth, where the beauty of nature assuages Faust's guilt and anguish. However, although the singer Ariel alludes to "the noble elfin fashion" that soothes and heals the wearied heart's "fierce conflict" (Part II, 4622–23), neither the spirits nor Faust make any specific reference to the lacerating tragedy surrounding the death of Gretchen. Indeed, the name Gretchen is never explicitly mentioned in Part II until the denouement when Gretchen appears in the guise of a penitent who, like Beatrice with Dante, will guide Faust to the higher realms.

Although most readers/spectators of *Faust* find the Gretchen tragedy enthralling and affecting and the conclusion of Part II suspenseful and elevating, the middle section of *Faust*, primarily Acts 1–4 of Part II, offers a challenge similar to that encountered by the audiences of Marlowe's tragedy. Nevertheless, Part II has enlisted many eloquent defenders. Of course, Parts I and II represent very different dramatic modes, even as Marlowe combines diverse aesthetics in his Faust drama. The Gretchen story depicts realistic characters in a world of linear time, enacting a poignantly moving domestic tragedy. Part II adopts an emblematic, timeless mode in which Faust signifies not so much a psychologically rounded individual as a representative of the German people or even of all humanity in its ceaseless striving, and Helena becomes an emblem of classical beauty and art.[48] Like most commentators, I interpret Faust's arduous quest for Helena in primarily positive terms. I find most convincing Hamlin's scenario whereby Faust evolves from the human lover in Part I to the embodiment of "the Germanic or Romantic spirit of infinite striving" in Part II, and the mating of Romantic Love (Faust) with Classical Beauty (Helena) produces Euphorion (the Byronic spirit of "modern" poetry). Brown expands this reading, maintaining: "Faust seeking Helen among the classical ghosts personifies the modern European mind, and more specifically the German mind, seeking possession of the classical tradition for itself." Helena's meeting and marrying Faust and the birth of their son Euphorion symbolize "literary forms moving through history from antiquity to the Middle Ages to the death of Byron in 1824."[49]

The Helena sequence both adheres to and varies the traditional Faust formula. Following in the footsteps of his predecessors, Goethe's hero travels to the court of the Emperor to raise the semblances of the classical dead for the entertainment of the monarch. Like many Devils before him, Mephistopheles protests that he cannot evoke the actual shades of the long deceased; however, Faust, not content with incubi and succubae playing the roles of classical figures, demands the real thing. In response Mephistopheles sends Faust on a weird journey into the "Place of the Mothers," an uncanny realm without precedent in the traditional Faust narrative, where he must retrieve a phallic key and tripod with which to evoke the dead. Freudians have had a heyday with this mysterious episode with all the mothers, keys, and tripods, and Jungians have enjoyed analyzing Faust's descent into his collective unconscious in search of maternal archetypes.[50] Like Orpheus, Faust descends into Hades, whereupon he locates the key and the tripod, raises the shades (or semblances) of Helena and Paris, and falls into a cataleptic trance at the sight of Helena's dazzling beauty.

This introduces the most bizarre phantasmagoria in the entire poem, and perhaps in world literature: "The Classical Walpurgis Night," which inverts the German/medieval "Walpurgis Night" of Part I. Goethe peoples his German pageant not only with the demons and witches of medieval lore but with satirical portraits of military men, literary figures, and sycophantic ministers of state, probably lampoons of Goethe's contemporaries.[51] Conversely, he populates the classical pageant with a panoply of fantastic figures from classical myth: griffins, sirens, sphinxes, centaurs, and Greek deities. The German festival distracts Faust and leads him away from Gretchen, thereby contributing to her incarceration and execution. The classical festival leads Faust to Helena, culminating in his epic descent into hell to rescue her shade and his allegorical wooing and winning of the fabled beauty.

However we interpret the fantastic Helena episode, it contains a virtuoso contrast of poetic styles, a kind of self-reflexive comment on the nature of poetry itself. In the scene "In Front of the Palace of Menelaus in Sparta," as appropriate to the classical setting, Goethe adopts the complex versification and structure of Greek tragedy, particularly the style of Euripides: "The heroine and her chorus of captive

Trojan women outside the palace, her expository monologue in iambic trimeters, the chorus answering with lyric odes in triadic form, a foreboding of doom, a monstrous prophetic figure confronting the heroine and the chorus, single-line altercations ('stichomythia')." [52] After Mephistopheles rescues Helena from the vengeance of Menelaus and transports her to Faust, the scene shifts to a Gothic palace, where Faust addresses Helena in the blank verse of Marlovian, Shakespearean, and Germanic tragedy. Again, as appropriate to the milieu, Faust assumes the lexicon of the courtly lover, and Helena graciously adapts her speech to Faust's parlance, in both imagery and verse form. Then Faust's watchman Lynceus kneels and troubadour-like praises Helen in rhyme, which she has never heard before since Greek poetry derives its structure solely from its metricality. Faust proceeds to woo Helena, who is enchanted with the new melodic sounds, by teaching her how to rhyme, and the episode in which Helena completes each of the rhymes in Faust's series of couplets offers the most delightful interlude in the entire play. Robertson observes that this engaging scene "unites not only Helena and Faust, Classicism and Romanticism, but also East and West," pointing out that the "story of rhyme being invented to express the harmony of two lovers is an Eastern one, which Goethe found in the works of the Orientalist Joseph von Hammer-Purgstall." [53] Maintaining his stunning merging of language with setting, Goethe transforms the scene from the Gothic castle to Arcadia, a type of bucolic paradise celebrated in both classical and medieval periods, with the pastoral language again mirroring the milieu. Here Faust "magnificently evokes the idealized Arcadia where he now proposes to settle with Helen," creating what Luke praises as "the greatest piece of pastoral poetry in German literature." [54]

Faust displays a new maturation in his courtship of Helena in Acts 2 and 3. Earlier Faust had seized Gretchen without comprehending her or the full import of his actions; now in the wooing of Helena, Faust enacts a mature lover very different from the lustful youth who mindlessly seduced Gretchen. With the aid of Mephistopheles, Faust spends Acts 2 and 3 creating an intricate series of settings – mythic, historic, aesthetic, and poetic – in which Helena can be comprehended in all of her aspects without violating her autonomy. Thus, a much gentler Faust emerges in Acts 2 and 3, and Faust's ultimate loss of Helena bears none of the anguish of his severance from Gretchen in Part I, [55] although, sadly, Faust loses both of his children.

Throughout much of Part II, readers have no concept of the passage of days, weeks, or months in this timeless allegorical world. However, the

Chorus informs the readers that Faust and Helena have married and produced a son named Euphorion. As Goethe makes clear in a letter to his friend Eckermann, Euphorion represents the personification of poetry, the appropriate offspring of the union of Romantic Love and Classical Beauty.[56] This episode finds its provenance in the ancient Greek myth in which the gods allowed Helen to return from the dead to couple with the dead Achilles and produce a son named Euphorion.[57] The Arcadian episode concludes with the death of Euphorion, who, against all the warnings of his parents, attempts to fly and crashes to his death.

Like the courtship and marriage of Faust and Helena, this catastrophic demise has been read on multiple levels. As Goethe's letter to Eckermann on July 5, 1827 explains: Euphorion represents not only Romantic poetry but also Lord Byron, the Faustian rebel who defied the spirit of his age, enchanted the world with the magic of his verse, overreached, and died young, and whose death marked the passing of the entire Romantic move-ment, if not the collapse of the European poetic tradition.[58] On a more encompassing level, Euphorion, the spirit who aspires to fly to the sun and plunges to his death, epitomizes the Faust figure. Although Faust in none of his incarnations attempts flight, according to legend the prefigurative Faust-archetype Simon Magus died in exactly the same manner as Euphorion, and the opening of *Doctor Faustus* associates Marlowe's hero with the ill-fated, high-flying Icarus. Brown argues that Euphorion embo-dies Faust's two combating souls: one of Euphorion's souls clings to the pleasures of this world, attempting to seize and ravish one of the chorus girls who turns to fire, even as Faust grasps and destroys Gretchen; the other soul strives to transcend this world in its endeavor to fly.[59] Thus, Euphorion embodies both the admirable and destructive instincts of the Faust figure. After Euphorion's death, the phantom of the grieving Helena literally "gives up the ghost," melting in Faust's arms as she presumably joins her son in Hades, leaving only her veil and robe behind. This veil then dissolves into a cloud that transports Faust from Greece to Germany and deposits him on the jagged precipice of a high mountain.

The ambivalence toward Faust permeating the entire drama reaches its climax in the later acts of Part II. Many of the decisive moments of the play occur in settings of thrilling natural beauty, and Faust's movement to the "High Mountains," which opens Act 4, signals a change in perspective while introducing one of the most controversial episodes in the drama. In this scene, Faust outlines his final endeavor as he moves from Lover (Part I) to Artist (Part II, Acts 2–3) to Empire-Builder (Part II, Acts 4–5), and nothing in the drama has excited such fervent debate as Faust's final enterprise, his desire to subdue the mighty ocean to his will and build his own empire on the land reclaimed from the sea. As noted above, advocates of a heroic reading have celebrated Faust's developmental project as his greatest achievement, and numerous radical ideologies have appropriated Faust the "Empire-Builder" to their causes. Many heroic exponents also associate Faust's magic with science and interpret his conquest of the sea as an affirmation of modern technology.[60] Conversely, ironic commentators view Faust's rejection of the feminine principle and embrace of the masculine ethos as a sign of his degeneration.

According to ironic expositors, the scene "High Mountains" dramatizes Faust's choice of the masculine over the feminine ethos. The clouds, representing the feminine principle, dissolve, leaving Faust with the phallic peaks and the macho Mephistopheles. The text explicitly associates one cloud with Helena ("I see it! It is like Juno, Leda, Helena; / With what majestic charm it hovers in my sight!" Part II, 10050–51), the other with Faust's unnamed first love Gretchen ("Does joy delude, or do I see / That first, that long-lost, dearest treasure of my youth?" 10058–59). In this reading, the vanishing clouds symbolize the banishment of the feminine principle from the world of the play, and the foreboding mountains represent the masculine principle that will dominate the action until the denouement. In the dialogue between Mephistopheles and Faust, the two debate Faust's last great exploit. The Devil wishes Faust to intervene in the economics of the modern world, exploiting them for his own profit. Conversely, Faust desires to tame the forces of the ocean with dikes and dams in order to create a space on which he will construct his brave new world, a utopia to be built and ruled by him. Ever since Faust's vision of feminine beauty in "A Witch's Kitchen," through the end of Part II, Act 3, the goal of Faust's striving has been a union with the feminine, first Gretchen, later Helena, both episodes ending in loss. At the beginning of Act 4, the emphasis shifts to the masculine realms of politics, war, and technology, and the feminine principle remains absent until the end of Act 5. Hamlin interprets this world, inhabited by Faust but controlled by Mephistopheles, as a parallel to Goethe's own society, asserting that Goethe regarded negatively the development of modern Western industrial society as represented in Faust's use of technology to tame nature.[61] Yet this is only one reading of a complex and ambiguous play.

Ironic exegetes would insist that Faust's attitude toward nature also changes. Earlier he had venerated the Earth Spirit and this reverence for nature permeates the early scenes of the drama. In "A Forest Cavern," enlightened by love, Faust experiences unity with all created nature and thus with all humankind. Later, after his disastrous seduction of Gretchen, the guilt-ridden lover achieves healing through his communion with a benign nature. Now, in "High Mountains," Faust rejects the feminine desire for union with nature and asserts the masculine drive for absolute dominance of nature (note the military metaphors used by Faust to describe his undertaking). Moreover, water has long been associated with the feminine principle; Faust's war against the sea could thus be seen as epitomizing the rejection of the feminine principle and the glorification of the masculine ethic enacted on the rugged pinnacle of the high mountain.

According to ironic explicators, Faust's reclamation project also involves extremely dubious ethical behavior. At Mephistopheles's insistence, in order to receive as a reward the coastline covered by water, Faust agrees to employ demonic forces to support the incompetent Emperor in his war against his opponents. But why, after saving the Empire, does Faust ask only for a small strip of water when he could well have been Great Emperor of the World? Some critics suggest that Faust has no interest in governing a modern metropolis, fraught with economic problems and the constant danger of insurrection; instead, he prefers to create his own ideal state built to his specifications and ruled solely by him. From this ironic perspective, instead of the reformer of feudalism and creator of a new socialist state optimistically envisioned by Marxist supporters, Faust becomes the autocrat, motivated by a desire for absolute power. Far from representing the antithesis to feudalism that many commentators claim, in supporting the ineffectual Emperor instead of the justified Rival-Emperor, Faust endorses the old order in his quest for power, rank, and land. And, finally, instead of advocating a new socialist utopia of free men in a free land, Faust adopts the role of the modern capitalist, passionately committed to his own ownership. Reading the play through this ironic lens, in the last act of the drama Faust, the modern individualist, becomes the "landowner and imperialist entrepreneur," aided by the infernal trinity of "war and trade and piracy" (11188), and as the capitalist and entrepreneur, he becomes the expression of Goethe's own pessimism about the modern age of industrialism. Exponents of this ironic perspective further agree that absolute suzerainty remains Faust's goal and that the generous, idealistic, philanthropic Faust of traditional scholarship remains primarily a wish-fulfillment or a projection of idealistic critics.[62]

In the view of ironic advocates, the Baucis and Philemon episode reveals Faust's desire to own and control everything at any price. After many years, Faust achieves his goal of building an empire to his own specifications; only Baucis and Philemon stand in his way with their small hut and the old church they are unwilling to relinquish to Faust's technological juggernaut. The classical names of this old couple should remind the readers of the virtuous peasants, symbols of hospitality and piety, who succored Jupiter and Mercury on their visit to earth, and, in return, like Noah and his wife, were saved from the devastating flood that killed most of humankind. Because Faust delegates the implementation of his plans to the malevolent Mephistopheles, the virtuous old couple, as well as the Wayfarer, are killed by the Devil and his demonic thugs, the three Mighty Men, instead of being transplanted to the pleasant farm that Faust has provided for them. In this instance, as in the Gretchen episode, Faust's impatience to seize what he covets without thought of others and his reliance on Mephistopheles with his "might makes right" credo to fulfill his desires lead to the death of the innocent. On hearing of the murder of Baucis and Philemon, Faust protests, "And this you claim to have done for me? / I said exchange, not robbery!" (11370–71). Yet, at least according to this ironic reading, his own career under the stewardship of Mephistopheles has been one long spree of robbery. He seduced Gretchen with purloined treasure; he stole Helena from the sojourn of the dead to be his wife; he gained his sea-drenched lands through a war won with trickery; and he amassed treasure through piracy.

Endorsing this ironic perspective, Hamlin posits that in the last four acts of the drama, Mephistopheles gains complete control over the action: "Despite the motives and designs of Faust, it is the devil who provides the means and measures for action within this world."[63] I agree that Mephistopheles acts as stage manager for many events in both Part I and Part II – but certainly not all; significantly, Faust takes the initiative in his descent into hell to retrieve Helena and in his determination to construct a city on the land reclaimed from the sea. Critics supporting an ironic reading of the play argue that the majority of the work on Faust's last venture has been accomplished by Mephistopheles and some of it has been "as black as night." Moreover, it has not caused Faust a single drop of sweat, although Baucis suggests that it has cost others "rivers of blood." A leading spokesperson for this ironic reading, Butler argues that rather than maturing and developing, as many critics insist, at the end of the play, "Corrupted by great possessions and power, Faust is now a much more ruthless person than the young ruffian who stabbed Valentine to death and then abandoned Gretchen for the witches on the Brocken."[64]

And yet, many other commentators throughout the centuries have persuasively celebrated Faust's last enterprise as a crowning example of human achievement whereby Faust escapes from his narrow prison of egotism and endeavors to fulfill his highest human ideal of selfless devotion to others' welfare. Berman speaks eloquently for this interpretation:

> He [Faust] has opened up a vibrant and dynamic new social system, a system oriented toward free activity, high productivity, long-distance trade, and cosmopolitan commerce, abundance for all; he has cultivated a class of free and enterprising workers who love their new world, who will risk their lives for it, who are willing to pit their communal strength and spirit against all threat.

Moreover, in direct contradistinction to Hamlin and the ironic critics, Berman, echoing the view of many socialist critics, insists: "Goethe assigns Mephisto only the most peripheral role in this project."[65]

How can a single literary work evoke such disparate responses from intelligent critics? The play *Faust* suggests that Goethe felt deeply ambivalent about humankind's modernization, and the ambivalence embedded within the text of Part II perhaps expresses his own conflicting feelings. Moreover, like Marlowe, he seems acutely aware of the contrariety of the human condition and the necessity of literature to express this complexity. Goethe thus incorporates this contrariety into his dramatic masterpiece and crafts a profoundly ambiguous drama that has fascinated readers and audiences for centuries.

This marked ambivalence toward Faust and his final venture informs two of Faust's crucial, much debated speeches in Act 5, and our final evaluation of Faust and the success or failure of his quest depends on how we interpret these two soliloquies.

The first of these passages occurs at midnight, always the witching hour for Faust figures, immediately after the bedeviled overreacher has received news of the deaths of Baucis and Philemon. Besieged by four gray crones, Want, Debt (Guilt), Care, and Need – reminiscent of the three weird sisters in *Macbeth* – Faust, for the first time in the drama, considers rejecting magic and his wager with Mephistopheles:

> I have not broken through to freedom yet.
> I must clear magic from my path, forget
> All magic conjurations – for then I
> Would be confronting Nature all alone:
> Man's life worth while, man standing on his own!
>
> (Part II, 11403–07)

Heroic advocates of the drama interpret this speech as Faust's moment of *anagnorisis* when the flawed hero, like Shakespeare's Prospero, at last rejects magic, as none of his legendary predecessors had been able to do. From this perspective, Faust realizes that all of his misdeeds and misfortunes derive

from his dependence on magic and that in renouncing thaumaturgy and
demonstrating his unwillingness to use magical incantations to defend
himself, he makes himself vulnerable to all the disabilities of age. These
infirmities immediately descend on him in the person of Care and in the
form of blindness – throughout Western literature, from Sophocles to
Shakespeare, an emblem of spiritual enlightenment. Moreover, because
Faust surrenders the fruits of his unholy alliance with Mephistopheles
before he dies, he achieves a state in which divine grace can operate and
thus is saved. Heroic exponents contend that in his rejection of magic and
acceptance of responsibility, Faust achieves the heroic stature so often
associated with the Faustian spirit.[66]

Conversely, ironic interpreters of this speech assert that Faust, like all of
his predecessors, only *wishes* that he could reject magic; his resolution is
formulated in the subjunctive, as a statement contrary to fact. I would add
that Faust never uses the indicative, never stating, like Marlowe's Faustus
or Shakespeare's Prospero, that he *will* burn or drown his books, only –
using the conditional – wishing that he *could* liberate himself from spells
and magic, realizing that only then would he be free. Moreover, according
to ironic commentators, Faust clearly intends to continue relying on the
aid of Mephistopheles in building his utopia.[67] Nevertheless, it must be
admitted that here – at last – Faust becomes aware that to achieve his
ultimate goal, he must eschew the use of magic.

But does he eschew it? That is the crux of the debate and the source of
the ambiguity permeating Faust's pivotal *anagnorisis* speech.

Even more tantalizing – and debatable – is Faust's final soliloquy. Since the
celebratory or ironic readings of *Faust* focus primarily on his last ambitious
venture, our response to him and to his ceaseless striving turns on our reading
of his valedictory speech, perhaps the most ambiguous lines in the play:

> Only that man earns freedom, merits life,
> Who must reconquer both in constant daily strife.
> In such a place, by danger still surrounded,
> Youth, manhood, age, their brave new world have founded.
> I long to see the multitude, and stand
> With a free people on a free land!
> Then to the moment, I might say:
> Beautiful moment, do not pass away!
> Till many ages shall have passed
> This record of my earthly life shall last.
> And in anticipation of such bliss
> What moment could give me greater joy than this?   (Part II, 11575–86)

How do we interpret this passage? Do we accept the critical view that dominated nineteenth- and early twentieth-century criticism, affirming that in his final speech Faust at last discovers the *summum bonum* of existence and thus that his life concludes triumphantly? Do we agree with heroic exponents that in this speech Goethe presents "the modernization of the material world as a sublime spiritual achievement," whereby Faust, "in his activity as 'the developer' who puts the world on a new path, is an archetypal modern hero"? Do we see this speech as Faust's final apotheosis, his vision of a world of free men in a free land working together in a communal spirit to establish a utopian state, thus anticipating a great classless socialist republic, as many commentators have maintained? Or do we follow ironic critics and judge Faust's speech "the most politically exploited lines in all of German literature," as simply another vision of "new ways to own and control more land"? Or do we endorse the view that Faust's final project represents Goethe's pessimistic attitude toward modern technology and industrialization? [68]

Hoelzel offers a persuasive compromise between these two divergent readings, speculating that Goethe provides "a double conclusion: one for Faust and one for the reader." From the perspective of Faust, who having rejected magic believes that his heroic endeavor will be achieved not through occult manipulations but through the ceaseless activity of free men working in concert toward a common goal, this speech expresses ecstatic fulfillment. For Faust, then, his final speech celebrates "his ultimate victory in his struggle with life." However, from the readers' or spectators' perspective, this climactic scene is fraught with irony because they know that the sounds of excavation that inspire the blind Faust come not from the spades of free men in a free land striving in communal spirit to finish Faust's last ambitious endeavor but from the demonic Lemurs digging Faust's grave.[69] Additionally, the drama implies that after Faust's death, the hero's last bold enterprise will be totally in the hands of the foreman Mephistopheles, the spirit not of freedom and aspiration but of slavery and denial. Therefore, from the point of view of the reader/spectator, even Faust's greatest moment of affirmation becomes only an illusion. Many critics, including myself, would agree with Butler that the "tragic irony of this scene has still to find its equal in the literature of the world."[70]

This speech raises another question: does Mephistopheles win the wager after all? Some commentators insist that here, at last, Faust rapturously entreats time to have a stop, for the beautiful moment not to pass away; thus, Mephistopheles technically wins the wager, although Faust achieves salvation anyway as an affirmation of his striving spirit. Others point out that here, as earlier in his desire to reject magic, Faust uses the subjunctive rather than the indicative: he seems to be saying that *if* his dream of a free people striving together to build his utopia comes to pass, then he *might* entreat the beautiful minute to stay. Both Luke and Walter Arndt translate the verb as *might* (11581), Passage as *could* (11581).[71] Yet, whether we read the line as *might* or *could*, I would contend that the statement is anticipatory, not actual, and thus technically Mephistopheles has not won the wager. Moreover, Faust's last affirmation remains a celebration of striving, not an acceptance of contentment: "Only that man earns freedom, merits life, / Who must reconquer both in daily strife" (11575–76). However, Mephistopheles, who never comprehends Faust or his desires, does not grasp the conditional quality of Faust's last euphoric utterance. Believing that he has won the wager and gloating in a parody of Christ's last words on the cross – recalling the blasphemous utterance of Marlowe's Faustus in the contract scene, *consummatum est* – Mephistopheles proclaims, in the translations of Luke and Arndt, "All is fulfilled" (11595), or in Passage's translation, "All is finished" (11595).[72] Here, Mephistopheles, the spirit of nihilism, attempts to reduce all of Faust's striving to nothingness.

Despite the ironies surrounding Faust's life and his death, despite the suffering and death caused by his prodigious striving, in the end, unlike any of his predecessors, Goethe's aspiring protagonist is redeemed in an explosion of baroque Catholic spectacle, combining influences of the medieval biblical plays and moralities, Renaissance paintings of the Last Judgment, and the eschatology of Dante's *Divine Comedy*. Indeed, if Marlowe's *Doctor Faustus* reveals the strong influence of Lutheran/ Calvinist Protestantism, the conclusion of *Faust* displays Goethe's sympathy with the spirit of Counter-Reformation Catholicism.

In light of the baroque panorama of the denouement, is *Faust* a tragedy or ultimately a divine comedy? Some critics see the denouement as an apotheosis of the hero, who despite a lifetime of erring is ultimately redeemed because he remains true to himself, and thus the drama becomes a type of divine comedy. However, most commentators insist that the drama is a tragedy as its title, *Faust: a Tragedy*, suggests, the saga of an exceptional human being plagued by at least one tragic failing (be it egotism, reliance on magic rather than his own abilities, inability to reconcile the warring elements of his psyche, or impatient seizing without comprehending), who errs and causes much suffering, who may or may not achieve a tragic *anagnorisis*, but who dies heroically (although perhaps misguidedly), affirming the aspiration that has guided his life. I would contend that, like Marlowe's *Doctor Faustus*, Goethe's *Faust* is also an interrogative drama that argues on both sides of the question and balances multiple perspectives with stunning equipoise.[73]

In lines that Goethe affirmed as containing "the key to Faust's redemption,"[74] the Angels assert:

> The noble spirit saved alive
> Has foiled the Devil's will!
> *He who strives on and lives to strive*
> *Can earn redemption still.*
> And now that love itself looks down
> To favour him with grace,
> The blessed host with songs may crown
> Him welcome to this place. (Part II, 11934–41)

In translating line 11937, Luke and Passage employ *can*, Arndt uses *may*; both suggest the conditional. From these lines, it appears that ceaseless striving itself is not enough; it must be blended with the redemptive power of love, although whether Eros or agape remains ambiguous. Ellis Dye defines Faust as "a man propelled by love and longing," who "owes his redemption not to his proud, lonely striving, but to Divine Love," commenting that, "In *Faust*, love is a *female* donation, embodied in the Mater gloriosa and the transfigured Margarete, who intercedes on Faust's behalf."[75] I would add that these final lines also suggest that humanity can only find redemption through the merging of masculine aspiration and feminine love. Significantly, to the negation of Mephistopheles's the "Eternal-Void" (11603), the realm of nothingness to which the Devil longs to return, in the penultimate line of the drama Goethe counterbalances "Eternal Womanhood" (12110), sometimes translated as the "Eternal Feminine."[76] This force draws Faust upward into the transcendent sphere, and the Epilogue, reinforcing the primacy of the feminine, transforms the masculine Deity of the Prologue into a *dea ex machine*.

Conclusion

The divergence in the fortunes of Marlowe's and Goethe's Faust archetypes reflects the differences between the two ages in which they were created. Marlowe penned his play at a time of enormous philosophical and theological conflict. Although balancing these contradictory discourses with amazing agility, Marlowe's tragedy ultimately withdraws from the threatening celebration of untrammeled individualism and emerging scientific inquiry to embrace a paradoxical and problematic orthodoxy. Over two hundred years later when Goethe completed his drama, the emerging discourse – secular, humanist, empiricist, individualist – had become the dominant one, and society was engaged in confronting different philosophical and political conflicts. By shifting his protagonist's motivation from will to power to desire for experience of the world (the ultimate empirical knowledge), Goethe establishes Faust as a hero, however flawed, of both the Enlightenment and the Romantic period. In the zeitgeist of these eras, the aspiring mind had to be vindicated, and Goethe achieves this problematic justification by reinterpreting the meaning of salvation. Yet even this salvation remains vitiated by uncertainty and ambiguity.

Faust thus constitutes the ultimate paradox. It dramatizes the heroic epic of an aspiring mind in which all the hero's endeavors culminate in frustration, disappointment, and death. It presents the apotheosis of an idealistic overreacher who consistently strives to do good and invariably causes evil, thereby inverting the stated trajectory of Mephistopheles. It offers a celebration of humanism, bracketed with a biblical Prologue and a morality play denouement, beginning in heaven with God and concluding with the salvation of its culpable hero. It depicts the tragedy of a less than ideal lover, whose salvation is made possible only through the sacrifice of two women – Gretchen and Helena – and who in the eschatological conclusion of the play achieves redemption only by the intervention of Eternal Womanhood. *Faust* also consists of a kind of dramatic "stew" (F-AH, 100), to quote the Director in "Prelude in the Theater," or a "ragout" (F-AH, 106), to cite the Poet, which commingles the traditions of Western civilization: Christian and humanist, classical and Romantic, aesthetic and scientific. *Faust* is thus a puzzle enclosed in an enigma encircled by a conundrum. It reigns as the definitive interrogative drama.

CHAPTER 4

Post-Goethe Dramatic Versions of the Faust Legend

This chapter will be devoted to discussing dramas – some written for production on the stage, some obviously closet dramas – based on the Faust legend. In distinguishing between adaptations and appropriations of this legend, I follow the definitions of Linda Hutcheon and Julie Sanders as outlined in the Prologue. Adhering to these definitions, I treat as adaptations plays that explicitly acknowledge their debt to the Faust legend, either through their title or their dramatis personae, and that feature a character named Faust, a tempter, either Mephistopheles or his surrogate, and allusions to the most salient elements of the Faust narrative, particularly the diabolical contract. Conversely, appropriations are based more loosely on the Faust topos, and although they should also serve as a palimpsest to the Faust narrative, these works do not necessarily include Faustus and/or Mephistopheles among their dramatis personae. According to these criteria, I judge the majority of the plays analyzed to be adaptations, with only four categorized as appropriations: *A Woman's Version of the Faust Legend: The Seven Strings of the Lyre*, which does not list Faust among its cast of characters and which deviates markedly from the traditional Faust scenario; *The Countess Cathleen* and *Franziska*, both of which contain no explicit allusion to the Faust legend although including most of its significant narrative elements; and *Wittenberg*, a kind of prequel to *Doctor Faustus*, which features the eminent polymath as its leading character but makes no explicit reference to Mephistopheles or to the diabolical pact.

A Woman's Version of the Faust Legend: The Seven Strings of the Lyre

According to many commentators, an appropriation commandeers a literary work for political purposes, [1] although I do not consider this a necessary component of the definition. However, one could argue that George Sand enacts just this type of appropriation in her adaptation of

Goethe's *Faust* for her own feminist agenda in *A Woman's Version of the Faust Legend: The Seven Strings of the Lyre* (henceforth referred to as *Seven Strings of the Lyre*). According to this reading, in *Seven Strings of the Lyre*, Sand focuses on the tension between "feminine" and "masculine" values, which, following Hamlin,[2] I find operating in *Faust, Part II*. Sand expands this tension into a conflict between heart and head, the power of poetry and music (symbolized by the Spirit of the Lyre) pitted against rational logic (represented by the philosopher Albertus), in short, into an opposition between "feminine" and "masculine" values as identified by Mary Vetterling-Braggin, Hélène Cixous, and other feminists as operating in Western society since the time of Pythagoras. In *"Femininity," "Masculinity," and "Androgyny,"* Vetterling-Braggin discusses Western society's arbitrary division of all human experience into "feminine" and "masculine" principles – active/passive, culture/nature, reason/passion, competition/co-operation, etc. – with the patriarchy traditionally privileging the first term in each hierarchical binary.[3] Although most liberated women and men today reject these arbitrary binaries as socially constructed or non-existent, these concepts have influenced Western writers throughout the centuries and, I would contend, inform George Sand's *Seven Strings of the Lyre*. Moreover, Sand anticipates many modern feminists by privileging the "feminine" principles over the "masculine" ones. George A. Kennedy also suggests that Sand's juxtaposition in the play of two kinds of knowledge, the poetic knowledge represented by Helen and the scientific knowledge associated with Albertus, presages the "two cultures" identified by C. P. Snow and F. R. Leavis. Kennedy further applies Alice A. Jardine's theory of gynesis, whereby technology and time are associated with the male and space and nature with the female, to Sand's play, observing that the male characters "take a positive view of historical progress and technology," whereas "Helen seems to live and think in space outside of history and with an acute sense of human suffering."[4] Although Kennedy makes no reference to Sand's Romanticism, I would argue that the ethos of the Romantic period, in reaction to the rationalism of the Enlightenment, also privileged the "feminine" values of emotion over reason, and poetry/music over logic, as well as poetic over scientific knowledge, which Sand celebrates in her drama, and I agree with Sara Stambaugh that Sand's drama might be subtitled "An Arch-Romantic's Re-Writing of the Faust Legend."[5]

George Sand, one of the most prolific writers of her time, composed *Seven Strings of the Lyre* in 1838 during the early months of her romance with Frédéric Chopin. More poem than play, and as far as I am aware, one of only two Faust dramas penned by a woman – Dorothy Sayer's *The Devil to Pay* represents the other – *Seven Strings of the Lyre* was never intended for production, as its lengthy speeches and lack of action clearly indicate. In her retelling of Goethe's play from a "feminine" and Romantic perspective, Sand has changed the time period from the sixteenth century to sometime around 1838, while maintaining the physical setting of a small German university town. Her closet drama is based loosely on Goethe's *Faust, Part I*, while also retaining elements of Marlowe's tragedy.

However, Sand has assembled a cast of characters both similar to and very different from those inhabiting Marlowe's and Goethe's dramas. Sand's ostensible hero is Master Albertus, a gifted and effective teacher of philosophy, the descendant of Faust and Margarete – although this would be impossible in Goethe's drama since a delusional Margarete smothers her only infant before her execution. Master Albertus, whose name recalls the thirteenth-century scholastic philosopher and theologian Albertus Magnus,[6] follows the profession of his ancestor Faust and, like his predecessors in their initial presentations, has rejected the joys of romance in his single-minded pursuit of truth.

Although the play contains no Margarete or Helen of Troy, the leading female character, named Helen, incorporates a number of the qualities of Goethe's redemptive heroine. Before the beginning of the play, Albertus has adopted as his ward the lovely Helen, the daughter of his deceased friend, the famous instrument maker Meinbaker, and has attempted without much success to tame Helen's poetic spirit to the rigors of the philosophical mind. As the play opens, Helen has blossomed into a desirable seventeen-year-old, thereby awakening an unwelcomed passion in the heart of Albertus and plunging him into the throes of a mid-life crisis. At this point, like his predecessors in Marlowe and Goethe, the philosopher begins to question his choice of profession and his rejection of earthly pleasure in his quest for the ideal. The figure of Helen of Troy haunts the Faust narrative from its conception in the *Faustbooks* to its fulfillment in Goethe's *Faust*. In Sand's adaptation, however, Helen becomes not a demonic temptress nor an abstract ideal, but simply a beautiful woman – perhaps, as suggested by Kennedy, an alter ego of Sand herself[7] – who, although bewildered by Albertus's stale books, responds to poetry and music and ultimately achieves an insight into the nature of God, a compassion for human suffering, and a knowledge of love impossible in the rational philosophy Albertus seeks to teach her.

Sand's Mephistopheles retains the traits of Goethe's Devil – malicious and conniving – and the action of the play revolves around the Devil's attempts to entrap the soul of the Faust avatar Albertus. In his temptation of Faustus, Marlowe's Devil assumes the guise of a friar, thus reflecting the anti-Catholicism of sixteenth-century England; in his temptation of Albertus, Sand's Devil masquerades as the Jew Jonathas Taer, thereby revealing the anti-Semitism of Sand's society. Mephistopheles grumbles that "the mystical pedant Albertus" gives him more pain than did the philosopher's ancestor Faust, since the rather staid philosophy teacher seems to lack the passionate instincts and pompous egotism of his predecessor. In order to seduce Albertus, Mephistopheles realizes that he must destroy a remarkable object in the philosopher's possession, a magical lyre, a legacy to Helen from her dead father, inhabited by a puissant spirit that protects both Helen and Albertus. Without the protection of the lyre, Mephistopheles hopes to defile the vulnerable Helen and arouse in the heart of Albertus a violent lust that will make him susceptible to the Devil's machinations. Fortunately, the power of the lyre and the spiritual potency of Helen hinder the Devil's schemes. Thus, in order to destroy the lyre, the Devil must enlist Albertus as his tool. In the course of his temptation, Mephistopheles convinces Albertus that the lyre is the cause of Helen's "madness," actually a kind of poetic rapture the logical philosopher cannot comprehend, and maneuvers his victim to deliberately remove all seven strings of the musical instrument.

The central character of this strange drama is not the Faust figure Albertus or his tempter Mephistopheles or even the much-desired Helen but the Spirit of the Lyre. This Spirit, imprisoned by some cruel sorcerer in the magic instrument, symbolizes the union of poetry and music, and perhaps, as Kennedy advocates, also Frédéric Chopin, since only Helen, perhaps representing George Sand, can communicate with him and fully understand his music.[8] Like Euphorion, the offspring of Helen and Faust in Goethe's drama – who, according to Goethe's own statement in his July 1827 letter to Eckermann, represents both the spirit of poetry and Lord Byron[9] – the Spirit of the Lyre may signify both an abstract concept and a historical figure. During the action of the play Helen and the Spirit of the Lyre achieve a harmony and unity; according to Kennedy, "they learn from each other and come to love one another, and together they escape from the constraints and suffering of the world into an ideal union of bliss and harmony."[10] Thus, at the denouement of the drama, even though Albertus destroys the lyre by breaking all its seven strings, the love between Helen and the Spirit of the Lyre triumphs: the Spirit of the Lyre is released from imprisonment in the musical instrument; Helen dies, united with the Spirit of the Lyre in a celestial paradise; and Albertus eludes the clutches of Mephistopheles, continuing to teach his students the avenue to knowledge and truth.

Although Sand's play retains some of the marvelous ambiguity of both Marlowe's and Goethe's dramas, consistently affirming the value of both emotion and reason, poetry and logic, in its denouement Sand's drama unequivocally exalts the "feminine" and Romantic principles celebrated both in Sand's oeuvre and in her personal life.

The Countess Cathleen

Of all the plays analyzed in this chapter, W. B. Yeats's *The Countess Cathleen*, a hauntingly beautiful drama penned by a poet who challenges Marlowe's mighty line with his resonant verse, offers the most celebratory portrait of the Faust figure. The play's effectiveness perhaps reflects Yeats's years of work on the drama, which he revised five times between 1892 and 1913. Facing this daunting plethora of possibilities, I have selected to discuss the verse version of the play in its December 1911 revival at the Abbey Theatre as constituting Yeats's ultimate vision of the drama.[11]

If George Sand's *Seven Strings of the Lyre* represents one of the few Faust plays authored by a woman, W. B. Yeats's *The Countess Cathleen* features one of the only two female Faust figures in the plays and films analyzed in this study, and this is only one of the distinctive characteristics of this unorthodox Faust drama. *The Countess Cathleen* differs markedly from the other plays discussed in this chapter, perhaps because its provenance derives from Irish folklore and fairy tale as well as from German legend.[12] Moreover, the Countess Cathleen, sui generis among Faust avatars, is like no Faust figure who ever sold his/her soul to the Devil. Unlike Marlowe's Faust who longs to "gain a Deity" or Goethe's hero who yearns to experience all aspects of life, the Countess Cathleen chooses to sacrifice her immortal soul to save the starving peasants of her village from damnation.

The setting and situation of the play reflect both the medieval and contemporary periods. Although *The Countess Cathleen* is set in Ireland in the "old times," the dearth of food and the privation suffered by the poor in the play clearly held a contemporary relevance for the revolutionary Yeats, recalling both the Great Irish Famine of 1845–49 and the more recent Famine of 1879. When the play opens, a similar famine grips the land; the crops have failed, "the very rats, / Badgers and hedgehogs seem to have died of drought, / And there was scarce a wing in the parched leaves" (1.32–34). As in Ireland in the 1840s, the peasants scavenge for food, eating anything they can scrounge, even sorrel, dock, and dandelions. Into this bleak world swoop two demons in the shape of owls with human faces to prey upon vulnerable humanity. Once inside the peasant hovels, the demons metamorphose into exotic merchants from the East, offering money for that "vapourous thing" that all humans possess, "a second self / They call immortal for a story's sake" (1.242–44). Into the huts of the starving peasants also glides the beautiful lady of the manor, the Countess Cathleen, accompanied by her adoring troubadour Aleel and her old nurse Oona, distributing her money in a desperate attempt to ward off the starvation of the poor.

All of her actions identify the Countess as an untraditional Faust figure. Returning to her castle to appraise her assets – her gold, her pastures, her forests, and her wealth – the Countess commands her Steward to sell everything she owns and return with herds of cattle and ships of meal. When informed by her Steward that peasants have stolen half a cart of green cabbage, she defends their actions, observing: "A learned theologian has laid down / That starving men may take what's necessary, / And yet be sinless" (2.375–77). The Countess's defense of the poor echoes the words of Maud Gonne, Yeats's long-time friend and love object, who, in a similar situation in 1898, advocated theft as a morally defensible solution for the starving peasants.[13] With the piteous wails of the famished peasants ringing in her ears night and day, the Countess resolves to use all her riches to provide sustenance for the poor until the time of dearth has passed, thereby preventing the peasants from selling their souls for gold simply to survive. Thus the play evolves, like Marlowe's *Doctor Faustus*, into a classic battle between good and evil, tinged, in this instance, with the more modern conflict between spirituality and commercialism.

Despite the commitment of the Countess, the manipulative demons quickly gain control of the situation, spreading a doleful rumor of cattle unsold and grain ships becalmed in the dark night, when actually the cattle have been vended for profit and the ships bearing the Countess's grain are but three days away. However, the naïve Countess and the gullible villagers fatally believe the canny devils and, frantic to survive, the starving peasants pour into the hovel occupied by the demons to trade their souls for gold. The scene of the demon merchants bartering gold for souls must invariably remind the theater historian of the episode from the Chester Cycle play in which the Antichrist opens his money bags to parody God's true love for humanity, revealing "Antichrist's most insidious tool for the capture of souls: money."[14] Into this scene of callous haggling sweeps the Countess Cathleen, presenting the two merchants with a deal they cannot resist:

a pristine soul for five hundred thousand crowns, enough, the Countess calculates, to feed the entire village until the famine passes. Moreover, she includes an additional codicil: all the souls the merchants have bought must be set free. Jubilant, the demon merchants do not blanch at the astronomical price they must pay to secure this saint with the sapphire eyes for their infernal Lord. They immediately close the deal, complete with the proverbial contract, signed this time not in blood but with a quill plucked from the cock that crowed when Peter denied Jesus thrice. Through the actions of his female hero, Yeats transforms his Faust avatar into a Christ figure, whose compassion exceeds even that of the Savior to whom she prays. For although according to Christian doctrine, Christ sacrificed his life to ransom the souls of sinful humanity, the Countess goes beyond this, offering her most valued possession, her immortal soul, to redeem the villagers from starvation and damnation.

But the sacrifice proves too great for the Countess to bear. The moment she signs the bond, her heart breaks with grief, and soon after she lies dying. But before she dies, she orders her nurse Oona to lay all the bags of the dearly bought gold in a heap and parcel them out to each according to his or her need. The passing of so great a soul fractures the fabric of the universe; both the brazen doors of hell and the pearly gates of heaven swing open and, in a scene that resonates with echoes of Goethe's *Faust*, angels and devils combat for the infinitely precious soul. Yeats's drama concludes as heaven opens to receive the soul of the saintly Countess Cathleen, where she will sit next to the Virgin Mary for all eternity. Like Goethe's masterpiece, Yeats's Faust drama ends in triumph, with the Devil bested and heaven victorious.

At least, this is my reading of the play. Not all critics view the Countess as approvingly as I do, and the diverse responses of commentators to the Countess's sacrifice mirror the fascinating ambivalence toward their heroes in the dramas of Marlowe and Goethe. Nancy Ann Watanabe speaks for the ironic perspective, associating the Countess's willing martyrdom with Faustus's hubris, asserting: "Owing to excessive pride, the Countess transforms human souls into commodities," assuming that the "more souls she redeems from the merchants ... the greater her reward in Heaven."[15] Conversely, although viewing the Countess as a noble figure, Peter Ure finds her character underdeveloped, since Yeats never grants his female hero that "struggle between self and soul, subjective and objective, in the single personality" that we associate with fully realized characters.[16] Without denying the ambiguity that permeates the play, and agreeing that the Countess never displays the soul-struggle we expect from heroic figures, I would respond that the denouement of Yeats's drama, like that of Goethe's *Faust*, appears to vindicate the Countess's sacrifice, and since no one, in either heaven or earth, censures the Countess, the audience remains convinced of her triumph.

Yet in his letters, Yeats himself seems ambivalent about his heroine. On the one hand, he praises Cathleen: "The Countess herself is a soul which is always, in all laborious and self-denying persons, selling itself into captivity and unrest that it may redeem 'God's children,' and finding the peace it has not sought because all high motives are of the substance of peace."[17] However, on another occasion, Yeats appears to question the Countess's deliberate martyrdom, relating it to excessive ardor, even fanaticism. As Yeats explains to Maud Gonne, the fiery radical to whom he dedicated the play: "he had come to interpret the life of a woman who sells her soul as a symbol of all souls that lose their peace, their fineness, in politics, serving but change."[18] Therefore, the ambivalence aroused by the play seems to engulf not only its audience but also its author.

Yeats's powerful drama exemplifies the thesis of this study, demonstrating how the Faust legend can be adapted to comment forcefully on topical issues of the period. The famine described in the play clearly bears relevance to the Irish famines of 1845–49 and 1879. Moreover, the demon merchants, seeking to take advantage of the misery of the peasants, can be seen as representing the English landlords, with the play offering a serious criticism of English exploitation of the Irish. This criticism was certainly not lost on contemporary commentators, and the first production of the play at the Abbey Theatre in 1911 provoked considerable controversy, both from critics who judged the play anti-English and those who felt that it expressed blasphemous attitudes toward the Catholic Church. Apparently, some commentators interpreted the reference to the quill plucked from the cock that crowed when Peter denied Christ thrice as a barb against the Papacy.[19] In addition, I agree with Michael McAteer that the demon merchants operate simultaneously as "supernatural presences" and as "manifestations of a historical situation in which materialism was destroying faith in supernatural reality," and everything was becoming "susceptible to the power of commerce."[20]

Finally, it is tempting to find autobiographical nuances in the play, with the Countess Cathleen offering a parallel to Maud Gonne, the ardent revolutionary to whom Yeats dedicated the play, and Aleel, her adoring troubadour who begs her not to make the fatal contract, representing her devoted poet/lover, W. B. Yeats. The Countess's echoing of Maud Gonne's defense of the starving peasants and Yeats's criticism of the fanaticism of the Countess cited above add ballast to these identifications. Peter Ure adopts this reading, commenting that in Yeats's later revisions of the play, the Countess began to look "like a heroic mask modelled from Maud Gonne's noble lineaments."[21]

Therefore, whatever the critical response to the Countess's monumental sacrifice, I would argue that Yeats's memorable play, like Sand's less impressive closet drama, comments significantly on conflicts in both his society and his personal life.

Faust and the City

Even as French novelist/playwright George Sand appropriates Goethe's *Faust, Part I* to reflect her proto-feminist, Romantic commitment, and the Irish playwright W. B. Yeats frames the Faust legend to comment on the political and economic exploitation of Ireland in his own time, so Ukrainian playwright A. V. Lunacharski, an ardent Marxist and compatriot of Lenin, adapts the controversial fifth act of Goethe's *Faust, Part II* to express his own political vision. In Faust's famous speech at the end of Act 5, the exultant magus envisions a "brave new world" of "free people" working together in a "free land" (5.11578, 11580). As discussed in Chapter 3, [22] many ideologies have sought to appropriate this speech to their cause, with Marxist critics, in particular, interpreting Faust's final utopian dream of free people in a free land working together in a collective spirit as anticipating a great classless socialist republic. In his play *Faust and the City*, Lunacharski develops this concept, expanding Faust's apotheosis of "free people in a free land" to dramatize the construction of a democratic/socialist state.

Faust and the City, a prose drama originally written in 1908 and revised in 1916,[23] and thus virtually contemporaneous with Yeats's poetic adaptation, is based loosely on the final, much-debated episode in Goethe's *Faust, Part II*, in which the hero envisions establishing a free city from land reclaimed from the ocean. The play is subtitled "A Drama for the Reader," identifying it, like Sand's *Seven Strings of the Lyre*, as a species of closet drama not intended for production, and, as far as I can ascertain, the play has never been performed.

In *Faust and the City*, Lunacharski creates a scenario in which Faust does not die at the hands of Mephistopheles but lives on to build the great city prophesied in Act 5. As the play opens, the Emperor has granted Faust suzerainty over land reclaimed from the ocean, which the entrepreneur has transformed into a thriving merchant community called Trotzburg. But the city he constructs is not the "brave new world" of "free people in a free land"; instead it is an autocracy over which Faust reigns as an absolute albeit benevolent monarch, with the Baron Mephistopheles as his hench- man. Faust remains motivated by concern for the welfare of the populace but hesitates to grant them self-government since he regards them as "children," incapable of democracy. Lunacharski's Faust has been married, widowed, and has sired two children, an arrogant son Prince Faustulus and an initially docile daughter Princess Faustina, whose names provide emblems of Faust's hubris. The simmering unrest in the community explodes when Faustulus, encouraged by the cynical Mephistopheles, attempts to kidnap and rape one of the village virgins, later killing the girl's brother when he seeks revenge (echoing Faust's slaying of Valentine in Goethe's drama). The merchants band together into a militia to chal- lenge the forces of Prince Faustulus and Mephistopheles on the battlefield; Faust's beloved daughter Faustina elopes with one of the leading rebels, the Tribune Gabriel, whose name recalls one of the archangels who battled against Lucifer in the fabled war in heaven; and a disillusioned Faust retires into seclusion with his books, leaving the forces of despotism and democ- racy to battle it out without his intervention.

Lunacharski's Mephistopheles, who lacks both the guile and the power of Goethe's Devil, attempts to defeat the rebels with an infernal force of dead knights – the autocrats of the past – but he is thwarted by the Spirit of Life, Speranza (Hope), and her army of the not-yet-born – the democrats of the future. Departing from the format of Goethe's *Faust, Part II*, in which Mephistopheles's demonic army rescues the feckless Emperor, in Lunacharski's drama, democracy conquers. Faust reconciles with his daughter and the defenders of self-government and glorying in his young grandson, another namesake, dies in a moment of rapturous happiness and self-recognition.

Initially, the relationship between Lunacharski's protagonist and antagonist appears to mirror that of Goethe's mighty opposites, juxtapos- ing Faust, the eternal striver, exulting in "life, life that desires increase" (14), with Mephistopheles, his shadow, the spirit of nothingness. And, as in Goethe's drama, Lunacharski's Devil, reveling in schadenfreude, gloats on Faust's inevitable demise and (implicitly) his damnation in words recalling Goethe's diabolic manipulator: "and you will toss and toss until you ask for real rest – and then you will be mine, Faust, – then!" (22). But, of course, as in Goethe's drama, this is not what happens, and a comparison between the Prologue and denouement of Lunacharski's play highlights the polarity between his Faust and his Mephistopheles. In the Prologue, the Devil announces his philosophy: "true Being is perfection, immobility, a sleep without dreams, a majestic repose" (3). In contrast to this glorification of inertia and immobility, at the end of the play Faust dies in a moment of ecstasy and fulfillment, celebrating life: "There is no death! There is life, so immense, beyond all surmise ... Wonderful ... Triumphant ...What strength ... what an unsurmountable, translucent, glittering, foaming wave ..." Faust concludes with a ringing phrase that recalls the dying words of Goethe's hero, "Life ... We ... Moment of happiness, abide!" (133). As Eric A. Blackall observes, Lunacharski depicts "Faust as [the] life force, with echoes of both Nietzsche and Bernard Shaw, and, correspondingly, Mephistopheles as inertia, non-striving stasis,"[24] thereby recalling the central contrast animating Goethe's drama. Inez Hedges also sees Faust as representing aspiration and, ultimately, democracy, remarking that at the play's denouement, "Faust has triumphed over Mephistopheles's nihilism in the name of the workers: 'We are the builders; you – the dust.'"[25]

However, closer scrutiny reveals that despite these surface similarities, this often engrossing drama departs notably from Goethe's script. The play, written in prose rather than verse, contains no contract, or even, as in Goethe's drama, a "gentleman's agreement." And except for a few implicit allusions in Mephistopheles's Prologue and his conversations with Faust, it has been purged of any reference to God, the Devil, heaven, or hell. Importantly, after Faust's death, the play makes no mention of salvation or damnation, although Gabriel, Faust's erstwhile opponent, assures the audience that Faust will achieve an earthly immortality, "Faust is alive in all things! He lives in us! He lives for ever!" (134). Moreover, Lunacharski's Mephistopheles, despite his ability to raise an army of infernal shades, is never identified as God's Adversary and exerts no control over Faust, or vice versa. Richard Ilgner agrees that "his [Lunacharski's] Mephisto is but a caricature of Goethe's, more or less superfluous in the new society." He proceeds by observing that "Lunacharsky's Faust dies not like Goethe's hypothesizing in the subjunctive mood about the homeostasis of the moment but thinking that that moment is now at hand."[26]

In other ways, Lunacharski's hero follows the Goethean format, like Goethe's Faust regenerating rather than degenerating during the course of the play. Moreover, the drama, tracing Faust's evolution from benevolent autocrat to committed socialist, becomes a mouthpiece for the author's Marxist views. At the same time, the drama displays striking parallels to Shakespeare's *King Lear*: both plays dramatize the story of an egocentric, benevolently autocratic monarch who abdicates his throne, is initially deserted by his beloved daughter, learns through suffering that he has failed as a ruler, is reunited with his daughter, achieves enlightenment, and dies, although Lear's death is not as joyful as that of Lunacharski's Faust. Whether or not he is entirely successful is debatable, but clearly Lunacharski has attempted to create a tragic Faust, in the mode of Marlowe and Goethe, a man of great aspiration, who makes choices, errs, suffers, and achieves awareness before his death.

Although in many ways Lunacharski's secularized adaptation lacks the central components that define the Faust legend, it does provide a prime example of the manner in which playwrights have throughout the ages appropriated the flexible Faust narrative as a forum for contemporary political and philosophical comment. Roland Boer associates Lunacharski with the God-builders, perhaps one of the most intriguing components of the socialistic-democratic movement in Russia during the first years of the twentieth century. Although Marxists and atheists, these thinkers were resolutely opposed to Stalin and sought to increase the emotional power of Marxism by drawing upon positive elements from religion, especially Christianity, thereby providing to Marxism a source of enthusiasm and emotional and ethical appeal that went beyond cold theory.[27] Boer's description of the God-builders seem particularly relevant to this play, in which Lunacharski dramatizes the fulfillment of his own idealistic Marxist vision of the construction of a democratic/socialist republic, a republic in some ways very different from the state-controlled communism of the Soviet Union. Also, in his portrait of the strong-man Faust evolving into a private citizen dedicated to the welfare of the people, Lunacharski presents a warning against the cult of personality that was to become such an important element of the Soviet revolution.

Franziska

Among all the post-Goethe plays that I have surveyed, only two feature a female Faust avatar – Yeats's *The Countess Cathleen* and Frank Wedekind's *Franziska*. I categorize both of these dramas as appropriations, since neither play, despite adopting many elements of the Faust legend for its ideological agenda, makes explicit references to the source text. But despite these similarities, these two female-dominated plays are also very different. Yeats's eloquent verse drama nostalgically evokes the past of both Irish and German myth while Wedekind's surprisingly prescient, ironic play foreshadows the future. Indeed, Philip Ward identifies Wedekind as the "godfather to that German variant of Modernism which we call Expressionism," producing a type of drama that intentionally provokes by its "effervescence of language which constantly surprises," and its "anarchic humour far ahead of its time."[28] However, in one respect, *Franziska* strongly resembles the two Faustian dramas with which it is contemporaneous: like *The Countess Cathleen* and *Faust and the City*, *Franziska* comments trenchantly on the social issues of its day. Even as *The Countess Cathleen* indicts the economic exploitation of the Irish peasants by the English and *Faust and the City* critiques the political exploitation of citizens by the monarchy, so *Franziska* exposes the social exploitation of women by the patriarchy.

 Franziska, which never enjoyed the theatrical success of *Spring Awakening* and some of Wedekind's other plays, premiered in Munich in November 1912, one year after *The Countess Cathleen* opened at the Abbey Theatre in Dublin. It was restaged in Berlin a year later in a production by the great Max Reinhardt, experienced a number of other performances in the 1920s, but disappeared from the German theater after 1930. A French translation of the play received a belated revival in Paris in 1995 and an English-language version was produced in London in 1998, but since that time the play has virtually disappeared from the stages of the world.[29]

 Like the majority of the plays discussed in this chapter, *Franziska* finds its primary inspiration in Goethe's *Faust*; in fact, as Ward contends, *Franziska*'s adventures offer an "irreverent, but affectionate parody" of that icon of German literature, in which all the elements are either exaggerated or, more often, reversed.[30] Wedekind has transformed Goethe's despairing professor, disillusioned with the sterility of academic life, into an eighteen-year old girl, bored with the limited horizons offered to women in her society. Having viewed the contentious marriage of her parents, Franziska wants no part of matrimony and longs for the life of a liberated woman. And just as Faust's attempted translation of St. John's Gospel evokes the appearance of Mephistopheles, who tempts Faust with an irresistible bargain, so Franziska's efforts to express her frustration in writing summon her secular Mephistopheles, Veit Kunz, theatrical impresario and insurance salesman extraordinaire, who climbs through Franziska's window to offer her a deal she cannot refuse. Kunz promises to grant Franziska her desideratum, in this case, freedom and the full enjoyment of life, for a period of two years, after which Franziska will agree to become Kunz's wife for life and thus his chattel and slave (1.3, p. 27). And since complete freedom and the full enjoyment of sexual pleasure were unavailable to women in the society of the time, Franziska agrees to assume the gender, if not the sex, of a man. However, although Kunz lacks the magical power to offer Franziska a sex-change, he pledges,

Pygmalion-like, to transform this young woman with no apparent vocal talent into a musical star. Obviously, the bargain Kunz proposes to Franziska falls far short of the timeless opportunities Mephistopheles promises Faust; however, the collateral demanded is also less dire. For, in anticipation of so many of the modern recreations of the Faust legend, Wedekind has stripped the narrative of its supernatural aspects, erasing all reference to a soul, a blood-signed contract, salvation, or damnation, although Kunz equates marriage with slavery, a kind of damnation.

The middle section of the play follows the Faustian format by dramatizing Franziska's adventures with her secular Mephistopheles. Clara's Wine Bar, the haunt of debauched writers and prostitutes, presents a parallel/constrast to Auerbach Tavern, the rowdy student rendezvous in Goethe's *Faust*. However, whereas the episode in Auerbach Tavern (*Faust*, 1.8) concludes triumphantly with Mephistopheles controlling the student rabble with his magical feats, the scene in Clara's Wine Bar (11) culminates in the pathetic death of a prostitute at the hands of her jealous lover. Her only crime: falling in love with the transvestite Franziska, now known as Franz.

Similarly, the Sophia episode in *Franziska* inverts the Gretchen narrative in Goethe's *Faust*. In Act III of *Franziska* the reader/spectator learns that despite her consistent maligning of marriage, Franziska has unaccountably wedded the heiress Sophia. Perhaps it is only the woman's role in marriage that Franziska finds so intolerable. At any rate, preposterously unaware of her husband's actual sex, Sophia yearns to consummate her marriage to her beloved Franz and bear his children. When Franz declines to fulfill his marital obligations, she understandably concludes that since Franz does not desire her, he must love another woman; whereas, in actuality, Franziska has become the mistress of Kunz. When Sophia's brother Dirckens discovers the secret of Franz's sex, a despairing Sophia kills herself, the second woman to die because of her love of Franz. *Franziska* thus neatly inverts Goethe's drama: in *Faust* the hero impregnates the woman he loves but does not marry, resulting in her humiliation and death; in Wedekind's appropriation, the Faust figure fails to impregnate the woman he marries but does not love, resulting in her suicide.

As Ward observes, the first two acts of *Franziska*, following the format of Goethe's *Faust, Part I*, dramatize the domestic sphere, the "'little world' of private emotions," whereas the latter acts imitate Goethe's *Faust, Part II*, transporting Franziska and her Mephistopheles to the "great world" of public affairs and art.[31] And, like her predecessors in Marlowe and Goethe, Franziska travels to the Court to entertain a royal patron, not an Emperor this time but a Duke. In Goethe's *Faust, Part II*, while at the Court of the

Emperor the titular hero descends into Hades to rescue Helen of Troy; in *Franziska,* Kunz writes and directs a mystery play in which Christ descends into hell to rescue not only the virtuous Jewish patriarchs, as in the biblical cycle play *The Harrowing of Hell,* but also selected heroes of classical lore. In an inversion of both Goethe's *Faust* and the biblical cycle play, the Faust avatar, Franziska, plays the role of Helen of Troy whereas the Mephistophelean figure, Kunz, enacts the role of Christ. Moreover, in Goethe's drama, the union of Faust and Helen symbolizes the merger of Romantic and classical, Christian and pagan; *Franziska* adds an intriguing twist whereby the Faust figure and the Helen figure, the male and female principles, combine in the person of the androgynous Franziska. However, the audience never learns how Kunz's play concludes since in the middle of the rehearsal, Franziska loses interest in the performance and runs off with her co-star, a handsome young actor who plays the role of Samson.

The last act of *Franziska* inverts the trajectory of Goethe's *Faust,* presenting the female hero alive and triumphant. Having broken her bargain with Kunz and abandoned her new lover, the actor Breitenbach, Franziska retires to her country retreat, a kind of maternal paradise, with her four-year-old baby Vietralf – the child of either Kunz or Breitenbach, we never know for certain. Totally rejecting her former lovers, she acquires a new protector, the gentle painter Karl Almer, although whether or not she will marry Almer remains problematic. Audrone B. Willeke pronounces this final scene as "an exaltation of maternal womanhood as a parallel to Goethe's apotheosis of the active male spirit";[32] however, the ironic tone dominating Wedekind's play makes such a celebratory ending unlikely.

This brings us to the central question of the play – is *Franziska* a feminist document in the contemporary meaning of the word? While admitting that the play offers "a radical critique of the prevailing social order," "which prevented women from achieving the sexual freedom long taken for granted by men and which institutionalized reproduction within the patriarchal confines of marriage," Ward concludes that "Wedekind was probably not a feminist in any sense we would recognize today," since he "subscribed to an essentialism which saw an 'unbridgeable abyss' (his phrase) between male and female 'natures.'"[33]

However, I would demur that the play consistently problematizes the essentialism that it often appears to advocate. Significantly, it is Kunz, the Mephistophelean figure, who most forcefully affirms the ineluctable laws of nature, thus rendering these sentiments suspect. On his first meeting with Franziska, for example, Kunz asserts that "the law of nature" will command her to become his wife and his vassal (1.3, p. 28), a view that he

later reaffirms (IV.4, p. 60). In her male persona, Franziska also occasionally parrots the patriarchal party line, as when Franz lectures Sophia on the
inherent differences between men and women: "But for you, / nature is
business; it is what you do;/ it shapes your destinies, as daughters, wives, /
mothers" (III.I, pp. 36–37). Yet the action of the play constantly undermines these pronouncements. Nature does not compel Franziska to marry
Kunz; instead she leaves him and runs off with another man. Also,
although she embraces the role of motherhood, we are never certain
whether or not she will dwindle into a wife. Moreover, Franziska's sexual
independence as both a man and a woman refutes her words to Sophia: no
pawn to the dictates of nature, she lives by her own rules. In addition, in
the middle of the play, Kunz, contradicting his earlier affirmation of
natural law, posits the androgyne – feminine figures of masculine severity
and male figures of feminine tenderness – as a potent symbol for world
peace and unity (IV.I, p. 53). The union (whether within or outside of
marriage) of the domineering, sometime ruthless Franziska and the tender,
protective Karl Almer, foreshadowed at the end of the play, provides an
example of this androgynous ideal. Finally, Hedges comments on
a singularly contemporary aspect of the play's treatment of gender:
"Wedekind understands gender identity as theater, and masculinity and
femininity as roles that Franziska can embrace or discard," presenting the
decision to assume one gender or another as a matter of choice.[34]

   In summary, I suggest that in its interrogation of society's restrictions on
the freedom of women, in its questioning of the double standard in sexual
activities, in its reference to the androgynous ideal, in its presentation of
gender as theater and role-playing, and, most of all, in its depiction of
a liberated woman who lives by her own rules and explodes patriarchal
stereotypes, *Franziska* not only comments on the "Woman Question" as
debated during its own time period but also anticipates many of the ideas
of first wave feminists, such as Betty Friedan, Kate Millett, and Shulamith
Firestone, ideas still very relevant today.[35] *Franziska* is thus not only very
much a play for its own time, but one for our time as well.

Mr. Faust

If Sand's *Seven Strings of the Lyre* celebrates a proto-feminist, Romantic
ethos, Yeats's *The Countess Cathleen* exalts Christian compassion,
Lunacharski's *Faust and the City* glorifies democratic revolution, and
Franziska applauds women's liberation, *Mr. Faust*, penned by Arthur
Davison Ficke, extols the Nietzschean/Shavian belief in an immanent

rather than a transcendent Deity, whereby humanity, through the power of the life force, can evolve into godhead. Although the plays by Yeats, Lunacharski, Wedekind, and Ficke are almost exactly contemporaneous, they adapt the Faust legend to affirm vastly different philosophies of life.

In his penetrating study of "Faust and Anti-Faust in Modern Drama," Douglas Cole argues that "Twentieth-century dramatists, whose recreations of the Greek myths are familiar enough, have also turned to Faust, forming him perhaps into their own image, but certainly into an image of our times." Focusing on three modern dramatists – Michel de Ghelderode, Paul Valéry, and Lawrence Durrell – Cole contends that these playwrights present a Faust who "no longer strives for the absolute," but instead "struggles to find himself."[36]Although he makes no reference to Ficke's little-known play, Cole's remarks seem particularly relevant to *Mr. Faust*, which transforms the Faustian aspiration for the transcendent into a search for personal identity.

Arthur Davison Ficke, a prominent early twentieth-century American poet, conceived *Mr. Faust*, published in 1913, primarily as a closet drama, but nine years later Ficke adapted the play for the stage. The production premiered at the Cornish Theatre in Seattle on September 22, 1921, and was later performed by the Provincetown Players in New York on January 30, 1922, after which it was published in 1922. I can find no record of performances of the play after that date. In the Prologue to the 1922 version, Ficke expresses his hope that "this is the only form in which the play will ever again be read by anyone."[37] Following the wishes of the author, I will base my discussion on the 1922 verse version of *Mr. Faust* adapted for the stage.

In *Mr. Faust*, Ficke has transferred the resilient Faust legend from sixteenth-century Germany to early twentieth-century America, transforming his hero from a closeted academic into a sophisticated young man-of-the-world, sated with the pleasures of life. Significantly, the title identifies the hero as Mr. Faust, not Doctor Faust. The exact setting of the play remains obscure, but the drama appears to take place in some large city in the United States around 1912.

Following the familiar Faust formula, the play opens with a disillusioned Faust bemoaning the emptiness of his life. In response to his oath, "Faust, you fool, you fool! The devil take you" (17), a man appears, announcing himself as the Devil, not Mephistopheles this time but Nicholas Satan himself (with a reference here to "Old Nick"). Unimpressed with his visitor, Faust speaks for most early twentieth-century audiences when he quips: "Well ... don't you think yourself / A slight anachronism?" (19).

Undeterred, Satan begins his temptation, enticing his intended victim with power and wealth: "Come with me into Wall Street . . . If you have done my bidding, you shall be / Master of the finances of the world" (24–25). However, when Faust remains indifferent to these traditional lures, Satan shifts his strategy, promising his prospective victim the ultimate gift, a paradise of perfect peace. Yet Faust still resists. Desperate to gain control over this willful young man, in a wager reminiscent of the bet between Goethe's Faust and his Mephistopheles, Satan promises Faust that if he is not fully content with the paradise the Devil designs for him, Satan will pledge to become his abject slave full-time for the rest of his life. However, if Faust is satisfied with this paradise, he will voluntarily become the Devil's assistant. Still skeptical but intrigued, Faust agrees and the bargain is finalized, minus the traditional blood-inscribed contract, and Faust and Satan set off together in search of paradise.

As in Marlowe's and Goethe's dramas, the center section of Ficke's play focuses on Satan's temptations. First, the Devil transports Faust to a faraway, torrid clime, probably India, where they meet a Holy Man, a follower of Buddha, who offers the jaded young man the eternal tranquility of Nirvana, the perfect peace resulting from the cessation of all desire. Although Faust hesitates, ultimately, the cold serenity of Nirvana can no more satisfy his fevered striving than the baits of pleasure, wealth, or power, and so he resists the Devil's temptation. Discombobulated, the Devil assumes a different tack, craftily admitting that he was only testing Faust and that since the young man has passed the test, he will now reveal to Faust the true Paradise. So the two magically materialize in a grand cathedral in the city of Faust's birth. Here Faust first meets his friend Brander, who has recently converted to Christianity, and Brander's new wife Midge (another diminutive for Margarete). At this point the Devil assumes a mock piety, explaining that the poets (presumably, Milton as well as Marlowe and Goethe) have maligned him and that instead of being the embodiment of evil, Satan actually operates as God's servant, appearing to entice humankind into evil while through his temptation actually bringing them closer to God. Although consistent with the sentiments expressed in "The Prologue in Heaven" in Goethe's *Faust*, in Ficke's drama, Satan's remonstrations are clearly half-truths intended to deceive. Nevertheless, Brander's confession of faith moves his friend, and when the two kneel together in prayer, the audience/reader begins to suspect that Ficke has written an orthodox but modernized Christian version of the ancient legend. But not so. When Brander urges his friend to repeat after him, "Not my will but Thine be done," the phrase, "Thy will," sticks in

Faust's throat. Unable to resign his own volition to another, even the Deity, Faust wildly retorts: "My Will be done, not Thy Will!" In the dramatic exchange that follows, Brander murmurs: "Father, forgive! He knows not what he does," to which Faust vigorously protests: "I know! I know! . . . There is no God but Satan, and he is death!" (52). At this point, Brander, horrified at Faust's blasphemy, seizes a heavy crucifix from the altar and strikes Faust to the ground.

As in so many of the Faust plays discussed in this chapter, the final scene witnesses Faust's *anagnorisis*. This enlightenment occurs in Faust's library where Brander comes to seek forgiveness from his dying friend. However, Brander encounters an ecstatic Faust, who has at last found the truth he has sought all his life, a faith not in Buddha nor in the traditional Christian God, but in the life force moving through nature – pulsing, whirling, but striving always toward perfection, eventually producing the superman, and this man will be God:

> . . . Thou who seemed near,
> Oh unborn man, whose soul is of my soul,
> Thou, too, shalt fight with Satan, as I fought,
> Fight, in eternal battles, with him who seeks
> To lure the soul toward darkness and toward sleep.
> But vain his victories; slowly there is born
> Light from darkness, Faust's from Satan's soul.
> This is my faith; this is my happiness;
> This is my hope of heaven; this is my God. (56)

Moreover, Faust has written a manifesto revealing his insights into the nature of both God and the Devil and the last line of the manuscript encapsulates his new creed: "Man, work thy will, and God shall come of thee" (60). After Brander leaves, Satan returns, still determined to gain domination over his willful adversary, although in this secular updating of the legend the Devil never utters the words "damnation" or "hell." Upon hearing of the manuscript, Satan proceeds to wheedle Faust, promising him a painless death in return for the damaging manifesto. But the enlightened Faust, in a master-stroke of one-upmanship, instead hands the manuscript (perhaps the play *Mr. Faust?*) to the loyal Midge, who, like Margarete in Goethe's drama, functions as a redemptive figure. Through this action Faust overcomes the Devil and dies in exaltation, epitomizing Cole's modern Faust figure who no longer seeks a transcendental absolute but finds the absolute within himself.

In the first version of *Mr. Faust* (1913), Ficke dedicates his Faust play to Goethe, Marlowe, and Lessing,[38] and the text displays the influence of all these poets. In addition, the celebration of the life force by Ficke's Faust recalls the consistent glorification of the aspiring spirit of humanity in Goethe's *Faust*. Edwin Björkman, although never referring to any of the contemporary popularizers of "the life force," describes the philosophy informing the play in the following manner: "The evolutionary conception of life is the foundation of that philosophy," in which man becomes "the foremost servant of a life-principle which asserts itself in the grain of sand as in the brain of man."[39] I would like to expand Björkman's very general observation to specifically associate the enlightenment of Ficke's Faust with Frederick Nietzsche's and George Bernard Shaw's glorification of the life force that will produce the superman. I find the influence of Shaw particularly salient here. As Richard Dietrich explains, the scientific ethos of the nineteenth century emptied the skies of God the Father while democratic leveling banished monarchs and aristocrats as objects of venera-tion, "creating a double vacuum that Nature especially abhorred." Nietzsche rushed into the vacuum, "with his call for 'the Superman,' a 'new' aristocracy based on specific qualities. Shaw then democratized Nietzsche's call, changing the call for a new elite into a call for evolving a universal 'democracy of Supermen.'" As Blackall comments: the philo-sophy affirmed in Ficke's play – like that of Nietzsche and Shaw – is a "completely humanistic gospel," representing a total secularization of the Faust legend.[40] Thus, although rarely performed and largely ignored by critics, Ficke's play reflects the philosophical questions and emerging responses of the period, offering a novel variation on the Faust legend, a drama strongly influenced by both Marlowe and Goethe, yet very much a play for its own time.

The Death of Doctor Faust: A Tragedy for the Music Hall

One of the central conflicts permeating the Faust dramas of Marlowe and Goethe is the tension between the celebratory and ironic perspectives toward the Faustian overreacher. Unlike any of the plays treated above, *The Death of Doctor Faust: A Tragedy for the Music Hall* (henceforth referred to as *The Death of Doctor Faust*) by the Belgian playwright Michel de Ghelderode adopts an unambiguously ironic perspective, deflat-ing the Faust avatar to a type of anti-hero. Cole locates the influence on the play in the "restless probing for self-identity so characteristic of the plays of Pirandello, who was then at the height of his success," and also in "the militant anti-realism of the French *avant-garde*." [41] I agree that the play consistently explodes theatrical verisimilitude, employing the alienation techniques of Luigi Pirandello and Bertolt Brecht to remind the audience that they are watching a play not experiencing reality. However, I find equally persuasive Hedges's association of Ghelderode's drama with Antonin Artaud's "Theatre of Cruelty," an impact particularly evident in the final violent episodes of the drama. [42] I also suggest an affinity between Ghelderode's play and the works of Ionesco and Beckett, although both of these playwrights were too young to influence Ghelderode directly. Yet *Death of Faust* displays many of the characteristics associated with the Theatre of the Absurd, and like all the plays written in this dramatic mode, Ghelderode's "tragedy for the music hall" expresses a deep pessimism about society and the human condition.

Ghelderode penned over sixty plays during his lifetime, writing the prose drama *The Death of Doctor Faust* in 1925[43] and premiering it at the Théâtre Art et Action on January 27, 1928. Like most of the adaptations discussed above, Ghelderode's *The Death of Doctor Faust* finds its inspiration in Goethe's *Faust*, not the relatively little-known Part II this time, but the highly popular Part I, the Margarete episode beloved by opera aficionados everywhere. But, as the oxymoronic subtitle of the play, *A Tragedy for the Music Hall*, indicates, the tone of Ghelderode's play differs dramatically from that of Goethe, and also from the dramas of Sand, Yeats, Lunacharski, and Ficke. Ghelderode's contribution to the Faustian rogues' gallery merges past and present, farce and pathos, theatrical and literary reality in an often confusing but always stimulating potpourri of burlesque and Theatre of the Absurd.

Ghelderode sets the play in Flanders, in the sixteenth and twentieth centuries simultaneously, and both Doctor Faust and the play's Mephisthophelean figure Diamotoruscant move easily between these two very different eras. When the play opens, we discover the sixteenth-century Doctor Faust fretting as he paces throughout his gloomy chamber, like his predecessors in both Marlowe's and Goethe's dramas, bored and depressed by the confinement of his scholarly life. He remains totally unaware of the modern world that unfolds around his house until he decides to leave his chamber and the sixteenth century to attend the fair.

Ghelderode situates Faust's meeting first with the Devil and later with his lover-to-be within the Tavern of the Four Seasons in the twentieth century. Here Faust first encounters Diamotoruscant, the Devil figure of the play, and later a seventeen-year-old servant girl named Marguerite, who enacts the role of Goethe's abused heroine. Giving a metatheatrical twist to Goethe's narrative, the three watch and discuss a debased music hall version of Goethe's *Faust, Part I* – recalling the truncated adaptations of Marlowe's *Doctor Faustus* so popular in Germany in the seventeenth century – performed by three second-rate actors: the Actor Faust, the Actor Devil, and the Actress Marguerite. Leaving the music hall burlesque in disgust, Faust, following the script written for him by Goethe, seduces and deserts Marguerite.

However, the differences between Goethe's and Ghelderode's scenarios overshadow their similarities. I agree with Cole that "Ghelderode's Faust is a tragic clown, without the philosophical nobility of Goethe's, and indeed with a self-defeating antipathy for the principle that is the life-blood of the Goethean Faust: the desire of the absolute." [44] Thus, instead of striving for the transcendent, Ghelderode's anti-hero seeks only to discover his own identity in a wildly confusing world. Moreover, far more callous than Goethe's hero, Ghelderode's anti-hero experiences no conflict between lust and pity in his seduction of Marguerite. Similarly, Ghelderode's more calculating Marguerite, far less naïve than Goethe's heroine, has come to the Tavern in search of a husband and encourages the elderly Faust (who, unlike Goethe's hero, does not receive the gift of juvenescence), willingly accompanying this strange man to a seedy hotel, until she discovers he has no intention of marrying her. Then, refusing to suffer in silence like Goethe's martyred innocent, this more modern Marguerite loudly denounces the elderly man who lured her to a sleazy hotel, violated her, and then abandoned her. When in desperation she throws herself under a streetcar, which mutilates her body into twenty-three pieces, the revelers at the fair, aroused to a fever pitch by a film recounting the events, demand the death of the caddish Doctor Faust. Perhaps, as Hedges posits, this intense scene, as well as the later lynching of the Actor Faust, comments on the way in which the modern mass media can incite citizens to violence.[45]

The latter acts stress the metadramatic nuances of the play as well as the protagonist's search for identity. Pursued by the increasingly irate mob, both the Actor Faust, accompanied by his mistress the Actress Marguerite, and the literary Doctor Faust bridge four centuries as they seek sanctuary in Faust's sixteenth-century study. Here, they both experience identity crises concerning the "real" Faust. Is he the theatrical persona (Actor Faust) or the literary persona (Doctor Faust), or neither, or both? (Of course, the audience/reader understands the fictional nature of both personae.) Unable to bear the stress of this identity questioning, the Actor Faust leaps into the twentieth century, only to be shot by the belligerent rabble, while the literary Faust, misled by the wily Devil, shoots himself trying to kill the phantom Actor Faust. Thus both Fausts meet their demise in Ghelderode's parodic Dance of Death.

In his music hall version of the Faust legend, Ghelderode punctures the grandeur of Goethe's drama, demeaning not only Faust, the Devil, and Margarete, but even Wagner, the apprentice to both Marlowe's and Goethe's magi, whom he transforms into the moronic Cretinus. Upon hearing of the death of his master, Cretinus begins to prance with glee around the corpse, exulting: "Dead? Is he dead? What delight! I'm his successor! Tomorrow I'll be the doctor! Hurrah!" (149). He then turns his attention to the Actress Marguerite, and enacting the role of his master begins the seduction of the trembling actress. The curtain falls to the uncontrollable laughter of Faust's cretin apprentice accompanied by Diamotoruscant's reiterated rumble "Imbecile! Imbecile! Imbecile!" (150), as the Devil stumbles away into the twentieth century.

During Ghelderode's play, Doctor Faust and Diamotoruscant exchange barbed remarks about the debased, music hall lampoon of *Faust* presented at the Tavern of the Four Seasons. But, of course, as its subtitle announces, Ghelderode's play is itself a music hall travesty of Goethe's masterpiece, in which every element has been trivialized. Christine Kiebuzińska comments on the debasement of Ghelderode's hero: "Faust has become a bad actor stuck in the eternal replaying of his solipsistic role."[46] I would add that even the Devil proves impotent, unable to significantly control events.

In addition, the drama debunks, or at least questions, the supernatural basis of the Faust legend, a skepticism revealed in the following exchange between Faust and the Devil, the only reference in the play to the fatal contract. After Faust, in desperation, deserts the hysterical Marguerite, the Devil tempts the agitated old man:

DIAMOTORUSCANT In exchange for your eternal soul I would give you youth, the gift of passions, a bit of gold, the wherewithal to begin your life again, knowing, however, what you know!

FAUST Yes!

DIAMOTORUSCANT As in the play they were giving at the Tavern of the Four Seasons?

FAUST As in the play!
[Long silence.]

DIAMOTORUSCANT My poor old fellow! [Pause] That's exactly what I dream of. I too have an eternal soul that I would willingly swap, and for less ... [Furious] It's stupid. [He turns his back.]

FAUST Devil! Devil! Have pity! My soul! Will you?

DIAMOTORUSCANT [Coming back] Are you really sure of having one? (128–29)

After this exchange, the evasive Devil drops the subject and the contract never takes place. Later, as Faust lies dying, he demands of Diamotoruscant: "Tell me! There is something urgent! Tell me, have I a soul?" To which the agnostic Devil hedges: "I don't know. You will soon know, or you will never know . . ." (148–49). In Ghelderode's revision of the Faust legend, therefore, heaven and hell, as well as salvation and damnation, all appear to be anachronisms, no longer relevant in the twentieth century. Even the Devil questions the existence of the soul.

At the same time, the play provides a sophisticated commentary on the fragility of theatrical and literary illusion. According to Kiebuzińska, "Ghelderode attempted to shatter all traces of illusion – creating drama in order to reveal the transparency of the theatrical World."[47] Cole also comments on the "Pirandello-like confusion of reality and illusion" in the play, which features "a sixteenth-century Faust who desperately wants to be a real person rather than a man playing a part, a twentieth-century actor playing Faust; two modern Marguerites – one a servant girl in costume, the other an actress in costume; and two devils: one an actor and the other a real one thought to be an actor."[48] Finally, June Schlueter identifies the personae in Ghelderode's burlesque as "Among the earliest metafictional characters in modern drama."[49] Therefore, Ghelderode's adaptation of the Faust legend not only departs markedly from the plays of Marlowe and Goethe by presenting a skeptical Devil for a skeptical era as well as an anti-hero for an anti-heroic age, but also anticipates postmodern theories of alienation and self-reflexive drama.

The Devil to Pay

Dorothy Sayers's *A Devil to Pay* might be read as a response to *Mr. Faust*, for Sayers's play disputes the principal thesis of Ficke's drama: the celebration of the perfectibility of humankind separate from a personal God. Sayers's drama is distinctive in many aspects: among all the Faust-themed dramas treated in this study, it offers the most orthodox Christian message; it conforms most closely to Marlowe's tragedy; and it ranks as one of only two dramas written by a woman.

However, the name Dorothy Sayers generally conjures thoughts of mystery, murder, and the famous private detective Lord Peter Wimsey, not recollections of Marlowe's or Goethe's famous plays. Probably most of Sayers's fans do not even know that she was an active playwright, who scripted nine plays. Her version of the Faust legend was first presented in June 1939 at the Canterbury Cathedral Festival. Following the play's enthusiastic reception in Canterbury, it moved to the Haymarket Theatre in London in August 1939, where it ran for four weeks, receiving laudable reviews and playing to full houses until the advent of World War II forced its premature closing in September. In the Preface to her play, Dorothy Sayers explains that in revising the Faust narrative for a contemporary audience she sought to "offer a new presentment of Faustus,"[50] while still maintaining the spirit of the sixteenth century and the verse form of both Marlowe's and Goethe's dramas. Commenting on the durability of the story, she affirms that "the legend of Faust remains one of the great stories of the world . . . For at the base of it lies the question of all questions: the nature of Evil and its place in the universe" (Preface, 8).

In her "new presentment of Faustus," Sayers closely follows the episodes in Marlowe's *Doctor Faustus*: Faustus's rejection of the traditional disciplines; his conjuring of Mephistopheles; his demand that the Devil be at his command; his disputations with Mephistopheles on philosophical subjects; the diabolical contract, accompanied by the heavenly caveat *Homo fuge*; his miracles at the courts of both the Pope and the Emperor; his disillusionment with his fraudulent bargain and escape into the fantasy love of Helen of Troy; and, finally, his degeneration into futility and despair. However, Sayers offers a surprise ending that provides a compromise between the denouements of Marlowe's and Goethe's dramas.

But if her storyline adheres to Marlowe's blueprint, Sayers's depiction of the leading dramatis personae differs vastly from Marlowe's portraits. Her Faustus, in particular, is her own original creation, bearing little affinity to either Marlowe's or Goethe's heroes. Indeed, Sayers's magician resembles none of his progenitors, except, at least at the beginning of the play, Yeats's Countess Cathleen. In the Preface to her play, Sayers notes that she does not feel that the "present generation of English people needs to be warned against the passionate pursuit of knowledge for its own sake"; that is not their "besetting sin." Instead she chooses for her hero a do-gooder who takes a wrong turn, an "impulsive reformer, over-sensitive to suffering" (10).

Following Marlowe's blueprint, Sayers sets her version of the Faust legend in sixteenth-century Wittenberg. Marlowe's *Doctor Faustus* opens with a Prologue identifying the tragic weakness of its eponymous hero, the classic flaw of hubris. In Sayers's treatment, Faustus's apprentice Wagner and his serving maid Lisa also chorus-like discuss the illustrious theologian/philosopher before his entrance. However, they depict an individual very different from the renowned rhetorician praised in Marlowe's play, a man distinguished not only by his learning but also by his humaneness. When

Wagner cavils at the rag-tag solicitors constantly besieging Faustus, Lisa demurs: "He is so kind . . . He can't bear to see anyone suffer" (21). When Faustus appears, we immediately see the "impulsive reformer, over-sensitive to suffering," eager to heal the pain of humankind. This Faustus, unlike Marlowe's magus, cares nothing for such toys as riches or either political or godlike power; nor, like Goethe's hero, does he seek the most intense experience of life. Rather, his stated goal is to "resolve the mystery of wickedness" (27). He has rejected the revered disciplines of the day and embraced magic because the former do not provide him with the power to eradicate the suffering plaguing humankind and thus to remake the world, a goal he hopes magic will facilitate. After the conjura-tion, although Sayers's Devil agrees to be Faustus's servant, he makes no mention of a contract with the Devil; that will come later. Dancing fiends also appear bearing platters of fruit, goblets of wine, rich apparel, and gold, which Faustus immediately bestows upon the poor, who plead for alms outside the door. At this point, it appears that Sayers's Faustus will receive all the benefits of the contract gratis, with no Devil to pay. However, while Faustus is offstage showering gold on the poor, a gloating Mephistopheles ominously calls to his ally in hell: "Lucifer, Lucifer! the bird is caught" (46).

Even as Sayers has transformed her Faustus, so her Mephistopheles diverges markedly from Marlowe's tormented fiend, bearing closer affi-nities to both the smirking charlatan of the medieval morality plays and the cynical con artist of Goethe than to Marlowe's disjunctive demon. The opening scene between Faustus and Mephistopheles exemplifies this dif-ference. Whereas, before he signs the contract, Marlowe's Devil passio-nately urges Faustus to "leave these frivolous demands" (DF, 1.3.83) and testifies to the agony of his separation from God, Sayers's demon, char-acterized by Paul R. Fetters as "a liar" and "the master of fraud, deception, and confusion,"[51] maligns the Deity, questioning both His compassion and His power: "Look at the world He made, and ask yourself what is He like that made it? . . . War, fire, famine, pestilence – is He all-good that delights in these, or all-powerful that likes them not and endures them?" (35). Seduced by the Devil's diatribe, Faustus affirms: "If God permits / Such suffering in this damnable world, He's blind, / Deaf, mad, cruel, helpless, imbecile or dead!" (45). Faustus thus accepts the fiend's view of God, and, followed by the dutiful Wagner and Lisa, he and Mephistopheles journey to Rome on the back of winged dragons.

Upon arriving in Rome, Sayers's Faustus enacts the roles of both Simon Magus and the Antichrist, distributing gold to the poor, healing the sick, and raising the dead, while also defaming God and Christ. In his confrontation with the Pope, Faustus affirms his willingness to be damned to save humanity: "I am not afraid / To suffer; for their sakes I would be damned / Willingly, so I first might do away / Suffering for ever from the pleasant earth" (67), lines that recall the compassion for the villagers expressed by Yeats's Countess Cathleen. However, Sayers's Pope, unlike Marlowe's, is not a buffoon, but a very wise man who pities Faustus and realizes that Faustus sins through love, not pride (I suspect Sayers's sympathetic treatment of the Pope reflects her own Christian beliefs). After the populace that Faustus has succored and cured turn against him, the magician, disheartened and disillusioned, considers returning to Wittenberg and to the comforting arms of Lisa, who expresses her love for him.

At this point, the beleaguered Mephistopheles, like Marlowe's Devil in a similar crisis, summons his secret weapon – Helen of Troy. Besotted with the vision of the fair Helen, Sayers's Faustus forgets all about his love for humanity, pledging to sell his soul for Helen and twenty-four years of youth. Mephistopheles has the contract ready and Faustus pierces his arm to sign the compact in blood. Ignoring the stigmatic warning, *Homo fuge*, that appears on this arm, Sayers's lust-entranced magician instead flees into the embrace of Helen, vowing: "Sweet Helen, receive my soul" (81), echoing the words of Marlowe's Faustus: "Her lips suck forth my soul" (DF, 5.1.94). However, Sayers's Helen demands more than Marlowe's succubus; she requires that before Faustus can possess her, he must deny "The bitter knowledge / Of good and evil" (77). Faustus agrees, and, like so many of his predecessors, he begins his downward spiral.

Still adhering to Marlowe's scenario, Sayers transports Faust and Mephistopheles to the Emperor's court. Here we encounter a sorcerer enormously different from either Marlowe's or Goethe's hero. Degeneration remains a constant in the Faust legend; with a few exceptions, most of the Faust figures reviewed in this book undergo some degree of moral deterioration after signing their contract with the Devil. But few fall as far as Sayers's magician. Having denied the knowledge of good and evil, in the twenty-four years since the contract, the rejuvenated Faustus has degenerated into a monster. The man "who was once so tender-hearted he would rescue the fly from the spider" (91) now revels in battle, pillage, and carnage, lusting after every attractive woman he meets (he long ago tired of Helen of Troy and cast her aside). In the tumultuous scene in the Emperor's court, Faustus displays his degradation, commanding Mephistopheles to torment the captive Pope brought bound and helpless before him. He also challenges the Emperor's pursuit of Helen of Troy.

Although he has discarded Helen himself and seeks to seduce the Empress, he refuses to allow another man to possess his former lover.

In both Marlowe's and Goethe's dramas, the hero dies at the hands of Mephistopheles; Sayers's Faust – like the Actor Faust in Ghelderode's play – is killed by the angry mob. Chaos erupts and in the melee that follows, Faustus brandishes his sword as he threatens the Emperor, whereupon the populace rise up and slay the sorcerer. The scene concludes with the good angel Azrael and the evil angel Mephistopheles struggling over Faustus's soul, much like the good and evil angels in Goethe's play. Then suddenly, to the amazement of the grasping fiend, a black dog springs out of the bag presumably holding Faustus's soul. Mephistopheles had bargained for a human soul, but in denying the knowledge of good and evil, Faustus has become brutalized into a beast.

Again deviating from the denouements of all previous Faust dramas, the final scene transitions from earth to heaven, where Mephistopheles, Azrael, Faustus, and the Judge (God?) debate issues of good and evil, freedom and slavery. In Marlowe's tragedy, before his death Faustus pleads with God to transform him into an unknowing, soulless beast. Sayers's Judge offers the sorcerer, restored to his human soul, just that choice: he may select to be a mindless beast, wandering for all time between heaven and hell,[52] or he may retain his human soul and his awareness of good and evil and go to hell with Mephistopheles to endure punishment for his sins. When Faustus passes the test, electing to preserve his human soul even if this means torment in hell, the Judge, in a Solomon-like decision that satisfies the demands of both justice and mercy, decrees that Faustus must, for a time, suffer in hell to expiate his sin; but when he has been thoroughly purged, God will claim him as His own. Here Sayers introduces into the Faust legend the concept of purgatory, turning a potential tragedy into a delayed divine comedy.

In addition to Sayers's own sincere Christian faith, *The Devil to Pay* may reflect the influence of Sayers's friends, the "Inklings" C. S. Lewis and J. R. R. Tolkien, with whom she frequently met to discuss literature and ethics. Sayers's adaptation of the Faust archetype also seems particularly relevant to the climate of the late thirties. As Suzanne Bray observes: "A man who was prepared to abandon his country's Judeo-Christian traditions and devote himself to a totalitarian master in order to provide a quick fix to the people's physical and economic sufferings had a clear message to the British people on the verge of war."[53] I would also suggest that Sayers crafts a drama that reaffirms her deeply held religious beliefs as a way of sustaining her beleaguered country at a time of national crisis, thus creating the Christian version of the Faust legend that commentators have long sought, not always too successfully, in Marlowe's *Doctor Faustus*.

My Faust

Written only a year after Sayers's *The Devil to Pay*, also at a time of national crisis, Paul Valéry's *Mon Faust* (*My Faust*) presents a very different version of the Faust legend. In its ironic presentation of its anti-hero, its interrogation of the metaphysical underpinnings of the Faust legend, and its use of alienation techniques to fracture the illusion of reality, Valéry's play recalls the "music hall tragedy" of Ghelderode. Moreover, deviating from all the adaptations discussed above, *My Faust* is primarily "a discussion play," more a philosophical debate than a viable dramatic vehicle. Explaining the play itself, Valéry admits he has sketched it in quickly "with little care for plot, action, or ultimate scope";[54] instead, his interest centers on the ideas he seeks to probe through the lengthy debates between Mephistopheles and Faust. According to Francis Fergusson, *My Faust* belongs to the genre of intellectual comedy, linking Valéry to Jean Giraudoux and George Bernard Shaw, a similarity also noted by Cole.[55] Furthermore, the playwright proposes to place Goethe's two protagonists, Faust and Mephistopheles, in his own time period,[56] where they can debate the issues current in the mid-twentieth century.

The French poet/playwright Paul Valéry wrote his prose version of the Faust legend in 1940 amid the shattering fall of France in World War II. The play actually consists of two unfinished fragments: the first, titled *Luste or the Crystal Girl*, includes the subtitle "a Comedy"; the second, titled *The Only One or the Curses of the Cosmos*, bears the subtitle "A Dramatic Fairy Tale." Rather surprisingly, these two unfinished plays have enjoyed a number of readings and performances. Valéry himself gave several readings of both plays in 1940 and 1941 at the homes of various friends, and other readings include one organized by Radio-Genéoe and presented by the Compagnie Madeleine Renaud–Jean-Louis Barrault. The two fragments have also been performed in Paris, Brussels, and Helsinki. [57] In this chapter, I will discuss only the first of these two unfinished dramas, since the second hardly qualifies as a play at all, consisting primarily of a long disputation between a figure named Faust and the symbol of solitude, the Only One, on the relationship between mind and body, flesh and spirit, while making no reference to any specific elements of the Faust legend.

Luste or the Crystal Girl derives its name from Faust's love-struck amanuensis Luste, a fetching young woman who has fallen under the spell of the learned professor for whom she takes dictation. The story, removed from sixteenth-century Germany to 1940s Europe, occurs long after Faust's bargain with Mephistopheles, although the Devil occasionally refers to it in passing, as when he quips: "After an affront like that, you can take my horns. Anyway, you'll soon be having a pair of your own, Professor (38)."[58] Throughout, the play treats damnation in a light-hearted way, as appropriate to its genre of intellectual comedy. Moreover, in this remarkably self-reflexive drama, both Mephistopheles and Faust seem acutely aware of themselves as both individual beings and as characters in a literary landscape. When Faust proposes to Mephistopheles his ambition to write a book literally to end all books, his fiendish familiar replies: "You? Aren't you satisfied with *being* a book?" (32). Earlier when asked by the wide-eyed Luste if he has really encountered the Devil, Faust jokes: "So people say. And write. And sing. Especially sing! So much has been said, written, and sung about it that I finally believed it myself" (20).

The design of the play departs markedly from all previous versions of the Faust legend. When we first meet Valéry's Faust, he is no longer the impassioned overreacher of Marlowe or the fervent aspirer of Goethe; rather he is a world-weary man who has lived too long and experienced too much. As Cole remarks: Valéry's Faust is no longer "the restless spirit poised on the brink of a boundless and inviting future, but a spirit who has already been through it all."[59] The plot, such as it is, centers around Faust's desire to write a book that will render all subsequent books unnecessary; apparently, this is the only challenge remaining to the sated magus. Since he no longer writes by hand – noting wryly, in one of the play's few explicit allusions to the fatal contract, that "The mere fact of knowing how to sign my name cost me dear once, long ago, in my old age" (54) – he will dictate this memorable book to Luste, his Crystal Girl. In a long dissertation on the dehumanization of society that has occurred while the Devil has been "sitting back in [his] lazy eternity, relying on methods dating from Year One" (36), Faust explains that in this secular age, the soul has lost its meaning and value, death its terror, vice and virtue their discrimination: "The individual is dying. He is drowning in numbers. The accumulation of human beings is effacing all distinction" (38). In addition: "Beauty is extinct. And Evil has seen better days" (41). In such a world, both God and the Devil have become anachronisms. Cole comments on the "curious reversal of the traditional pact relationship": "Faust does not seek the devil's aid so much as he wishes to teach the devil a lesson – to show him

how obsolete he is in the modern world," a world "in which people are
clever enough to damn themselves by their own devices." [60] Faust's
magnum opus will thus record "the Devil's reactions to all the exaspera-
tions which a visit to the new age cannot fail to excite in the infernal mind"
(37). Whether Faust and Mephistopheles ever co-operate to create this
memorable book, we never know, since the play remains unfinished.

On first reading, *My Faust* appears to be a modern, skeptical reworking
of the Faust legend in its many permutations, like so many of the plays
discussed in this chapter. However, Igor Stravinsky, not only
a contemporary but also a friend of the French poet/playwright, discovers
in Valéry's *My Faust* a perspective that can be called "religious," although
certainly not orthodox. Stravinsky cites Mephistopheles's cryptic evoking
of God – "No one has ever talked to me this way before. At least . . . not for
a long time" (30) – as underscoring the Devil's belief in a Deity.[61] I would
add that Faust's genuine regret at humanity's loss of faith in a soul and the
afterlife may reflect Valéry's own nostalgic yearning for a more religious age.

Therefore, although this provocative play lacks most of the accepted
characteristics of either Marlowe's or Goethe's scenarios, its relevance to
this study resides in the manner in which it exploits the Faust legend to
comment on the secular zeitgeist of the period in which it was composed,
and in its self-reflexive observations on the resilience and popularity of the
Faust legend.

An Irish Faustus: A Morality in Nine Scenes

If Wedekind's drama successfully eliminates God, the Devil, and Hell, all
of these established components of the Faust legend reappear in Lawrence
Durrell's *An Irish Faustus: A Morality in Nine Scenes.*[62] Written in 1963 and
performed at Hamburg's Deutsches Schauspielhaus in 1964, Durrell's play
was not a critical success, and, as far as I can ascertain, this was the only
performance ever given to this very different Faustian drama. For although
Durrell's play features a protagonist named Faustus and a Devil antagonist
called Mephisto, with its great ring of power and its threatening vampire
An Irish Faustus often seems closer to J. R. R. Tolkien's *Lord of the Rings*
and Bram Stoker's *Dracula* than to the traditional Faust narrative. A new
film titled *Dracula*, directed by Terence Fisher and released in Britain in
1958, had generated considerable interest, and Tolkien's *Lord of the Rings*,
published in 1954, was a phenomenal success. Perhaps the excitement
engendered by these two fantasies influenced Durrell's decision to append

them to his Faust narration. However, in my opinion – an opinion shared by most critics – in this case, the commingling of intertextual elements detracts from the effectiveness of the drama.

Like Yeats before him, Durrell cloaks his play in medieval pageantry, transferring his setting from sixteenth-century Germany to medieval Ireland, in this case, to the city of Galway in the time of Eric the Red. He follows his predecessors in limning his hero as a philosopher, teacher, healer, and thaumaturge, although this time a follower of white rather than black magic. However, unlike the heroes of Marlowe and Goethe, Durrell's Faustus bears a heavy burden: the great ring of power, transmuted from base metal into gold, bequeathed to him by his mentor Tremethius after the magician's execution for sorcery. Composed of alchemized gold, this ring cannot be burned by any earthly fire or kiln, eaten away by any acid, or ground to dust by any mill. Thus, for many years, Faustus has secreted the magic ring in a metal casket, wearing the key to the box around his neck. However, in the second scene of the play, he discovers that the metal casket is empty and the key is gone.

As in Goethe's drama, Faustus does not conjure the Devil; rather, Durrell's Mephisto simply appears in the philosopher's cabinet, this time not disguised as a Friar (as in Marlowe) or a black dog (as in Goethe) or a Jewish moneylender (as in Sand). Instead, Durrell's Devil materializes with the form and face of Faustus himself, suggesting his role as Faustus's dark doppelgänger, Mr. Hyde to Faustus's Dr. Jekyll. G. S. Fraser, viewing this phenomenon through a Jungian lens, agrees that Mephisto represents the dark side of Faustus, and the *Time Magazine* reviewer of the play concurs, caviling at the play's lack of subtlety: "Mephistopheles shows up dressed almost exactly like Faustus, indicating to the slow-witted that good and evil are close kin."[63] Although Mephisto never mentions a contract, the indoctrinated reader of Faustian literature immediately recognizes that this ostensibly jovial stranger has come to entrap Faustus's soul.

Like most of his demonic predecessors, Mephisto possesses impressive magical powers, and as part of his strategy of temptation, the Devil immediately solves the mystery of the missing ring. Among his many duties, Faustus serves as tutor to the Princess Margaret (whose name recalls Faust's doomed beloved in Goethe's drama), niece and ward of the widowed Queen Katherine, whose husband Eric the Red disappeared mysteriously twenty years before the opening of the play. Hoping to impress his precocious student, Faustus revealed the secret of the hidden ring to Margaret, who then passed on the knowledge to her tyrannical aunt, who, in turn, bullied Margaret into stealing the ring from her tutor.

Tempting Faustus with traditional visions of power, the Devil urges the philosopher to retrieve the magic object by any means possible.

However, instead of seeking power, as in Marlowe's tragedy, or personal fulfillment, as in Goethe's drama, in a scenario that finds no precedent in previous Faust narratives the magus becomes a vampire-slayer and the defender of the realm. Rushing to the palace to succor the deranged and disheveled Queen, Faust learns that the Queen, ravenous with desire, used the magic ring to conjure her vampire husband, who seized the ring before disappearing. Following the mad Queen as she flees from the palace, Faustus locates the casket of Eric the Red, retrieves the ring, and impales the vampire with a stake through his heart. Later, alone in the dark forest, Faustus suddenly finds himself surrounded by the ghosts of dead magicians, who instruct him to destroy the ring in the only way possible: he must recite the Great Formula (55). Quaking with fear, Faustus returns to his cabinet to find Mephisto lounging insouciantly in a chair before the fire, drinking wine. Upon hearing Faustus has retrieved the ring, Mephisto exults, attempting to seduce Faustus with the unlimited power he could wield through the possession of the alchemist's secret stone. But the lure of power, so intoxicating to most Faust figures, holds little appeal to Durrell's philosopher, who easily resists all Mephisto's enticements.

Rejecting the power he could achieve through possession of the ring, Faustus becomes obsessed with its destruction, vowing to recite the dreaded Great Formula and to drag Mephisto with him to hell. Ignoring Mephisto's frantic pleas, Faustus begins to intone the portentous incantation, and amid a crash of thunder, hell's mouth opens with tongues of flame. As Faustus descends into hell, the Devil desperately protests: "You are killing reason; you will reverse the wheel / Of cause and effect. Faustus desist" (66). And, indeed, Durrell's Faustus does reverse all tradition: at the end of Marlowe's tragedy, the devils haul a screaming, dismembered Faustus into hell; in Durrell's comedy, Faustus drags the cringing Devil into the fiery pit and returns, reborn, and, in the view of some critics, psychically reintegrated. According to Michael Cartwright: "When Faustus descends into hell, he takes with him a cross, the symbol, in this case, of white magic, and the gold ring, the symbol of black magic. *Both* are burned to ashes."[64]

Recalling many epic heroes but no previous Faust figures, Durrell's magus descends into hell, accomplishes his mission, and miraculously returns. His clothes have been burned to rags, his hair has turned white, but he is alive and happier than he has ever been in his life. In reward for his heroic exploits, Queen Katherine banishes the philosopher – she cannot forgive him for slaying her beloved vampire husband – but the euphoric

Faustus remains unfazed and jubilantly departs to visit his friend, the hermit Matthew, like Faustus a former apprentice to the magician Tremethius. Martin the Pardoner, who as a purveyor of false relics provides a trenchant satire of the medieval Catholic Church, accompanies Faustus on his journey to begin a new life with the hermit Matthew.

In the final scene of the play, Faustus, Martin, and Matthew join together in a fraternity devoted to the appreciation of nature, knowledge, good wine, delicious food, and great conversation. Everything seems fine until Matthew introduces the affable gentleman who will join them as the fourth player in their game of cards. Who else but Mephisto? As the four settle down to their card game, the audience is left with the queasy feeling that Faustus may not have banished his dark doppelgänger after all, adding a very Faustian touch of ambiguity to the play's denouement. Peter Christensen comments on this ambiguity: "This change of direction makes the play's ending problematic, for the audience must decide whether [or not] his decision to retire to Matthew's hermitage represents a step toward his personal enlightenment."[65]

Despite the problematic ending, *An Irish Faust* may be one of the most un-Faustian of all the plays analyzed in this chapter. Durrell creates a Faust who, unlike most of his predecessors, resists the lures and baits of Mephisto and thus never degenerates, a unique Faust who instead of being carried off to hell by the Devil, turns the tables and carries Mephisto kicking and screaming into the inferno. Critics have responded differently to Durrell's triumphant Faust. The reviewer for *Time Magazine* finds Durrell's hero too good to be true, a kind of "boy scout Faust."[66] Cartwright identifies him as the comic hero who emerges from the fiery pit integrated and complete.[67] Cole shares my view that Durrell's hero is totally un-Faustian, a type of anti-Faust: "he bears none of the marks of the vigorous man in search of new boundaries and new experiences. He is rather a safe, calm, contemplative sort who becomes even calmer and more contemplative after his courageous journey to hell. His spirit is not restless but restful; though he is neither complacent nor slothful, he would probably be damned by Goethe's God for lack of *Streben*."[68] Nevertheless, whether or not he was successful, Durrell has attempted to depict a genuinely heroic, triumphant Faust, thereby reversing the twentieth-century trend toward ironizing the Faust figure.

Temptation

Temptation depicts a very different Faust figure in a very different society. *Temptation* holds the distinction of being one of the few plays analyzed in this chapter that does not acknowledge the Faust legend in its title and does not feature a supernatural Mephistophelean figure, although the name of the protagonist, Foustka, clearly alludes to the legendary magus. Moreover, with its absurdist tone, its anti-naturalistic techniques, and its ironic undercutting of its anti-hero, Havel's play resembles the Faust dramas of Ghelderode and Valéry more than those of Marlowe and Goethe. Nevertheless, *Temptation* offers a palimpsest for the Faust story, particularly Goethe's epic drama, modernized to comment on the conflicts of its own historical period.

Like so many of the plays analyzed in this chapter, *Temptation* by Czech playwright, politician, and later President of Czechoslovakia, Václav Havel (written in 1985, translated in 1989),[69] undertakes an expansion and revision of Goethe's epic drama. As Ehrhard Bahr observes, names in this play resonate with the influence of Goethe: Havel's Faust figure, Henry Foustka, recalls Goethe's hero Heinrich rather than the John or Johann or Johannes Faust or Faustus of Marlowe and the *Faustbooks*; Marketa, the innocent young woman whom Foustka destroys, suggests Goethe's Margarete, seduced and abandoned by Faust.[70] According to the legend that has grown up around the play, Havel mysteriously received unsolicited copies of two Faust narratives while in prison – those by Goethe and Thomas Mann.[71] Although this account makes no mention of Marlowe's *Doctor Faustus*, I would argue that the influence of Marlowe looms large. These three Faust narratives, I contend, inspired the creation of Havel's own modern Faust play.

The Communist regime in Czechoslovakia routinely banned Havel's plays during the years between 1969 and 1989, although his dramas were frequently performed abroad. *Temptation* premiered at the Akademietheater in Austria in 1986, received its British premiere at the Royal Shakespeare Company in Stratford-upon-Avon in 1987, and enjoyed its United States premiere on the East Coast at the Public Theatre in New York City in May 1989 and on the West Coast at the Mark Taper Forum in Los Angeles in July–August 1989. Finally, it belatedly premiered in Czechoslovakia on October 27, 1990.[72]

Written in prose and set in an unnamed metropolis dominated by an Institute dedicated to combating the "irrational impulses" of humanity, *Temptation* depicts a totalitarian society that rejects everything metaphysical and tolerates no ideology but a brand of atheistic science. As the autocratic Director of the Institute explains to his Deputy: the state must be vigilant in combating "irrational attitudes cropping up primarily among a particular segment of the younger generation" and including "an entire spectrum of mystical prejudices, superstitions, obscure doctrines, and practices disseminated by certain charlatans, psychopaths, and intelligent people" (13). Joan Erben comments on the empty generalizations and double-speak characteristic of this corrupt society, arguing that the language of the play – its overblown rhetoric, meaningless generalizations, and banal clichés – mirrors the absurd society where nothing ever appears to get done and where the scientists fritter away their time in vacuous meetings. Marketa Goetz-Stankiewicz agrees, identifying the linguistic acrobatics the characters in Havel's play employ to obfuscate truth and manipulate individuals.[73]

Havel depicts Doctor Foustka, like his predecessors in Marlowe and Goethe, as an adept in the sanctioned discipline(s) of his society. Also, like both Marlowe's and Goethe's protagonists, Havel's hero chafes against the limitations imposed by this narrow authorized ideology and seeks forbidden knowledge, in this case, knowledge of the metaphysical world and of God. In pursuit of this knowledge, like Marlowe's hero, he immerses himself in occult books and experiments with black magic, employing the familiar medieval paraphernalia of incantations and circles in an attempt to conjure the Devil. When a wizened cripple called Fistula mysteriously materializes at his door, the audience assumes this grotesque dwarf, who bears many of the stigmata of the traditional Devil – including the limp and the sulfurous odor – to be a demon. Here, as so often in this play, names prove significant. The Internet Surname Database explains that there are two possible meanings for the name Faustus. The first and most common derives from Latin, meaning "fortunate" or "auspicious." The second comes from the German, meaning "fist," often a nickname for a strong-willed, angry person. The similarity in the names Fistula and Foustka implies that the Devil figure may be the dark alter ego of the respected scientist.

Following Marlowe's script, Fistula "tempts" Doctor Foustka to make a number of disastrous errors that lead to his degeneration and ultimate denunciation and disgrace. First, as confirmation of his prowess, Fistula promises to cause Marketa, the secretary at the Institute, to fall in love with Foustka, although the scientist, unlike Goethe's Faust with Margarete, insists he has no interest in Marketa; after all, he is involved in a passionate love affair with Vilma, a colleague at the Institute. However, despite his hesitation, the following evening at the office party, which Bahr posits as a parallel to the Garden scene in Goethe's *Faust*,[74] Foustka causes Marketa to fall desperately in love with him, dazzling the impressionable young women with his metaphysical and philosophical theories, even as, in

Goethe's play, Faust mesmerizes Margarete with his brilliance. Also, like Goethe's Margarete, Marketa remains faithful to Foustka throughout all his travails. When, the morning after the office party, the Director vehemently denounces Foustka, Marketa vigorously defends him, and in retaliation for her loyalty the Director first fires her and later places her in a psychiatric ward, while Foustka does nothing to aid her. At the end of the play, we view the distraught Marketa in a white gown, singing mad ditties that recall the crazed songs of both Shakespeare's Ophelia and Goethe's Margarete. Like Goethe's Faust with Margarete, Foustka seduces the inexperienced Marketa (albeit intellectually, not physically), and ultimately destroys her. Later, prodded by his tempter, Foustka accuses his mistress Vilma of revealing his subversive activities to the Director and drives her into the arms of another man.

The climax of the play occurs at a garden party, envisioned as a type of "Walpurgis Night," in which the Director reveals that the real stool pigeon is not Foustka's mistress Vilma, but Fistula, who, far from being an emissary of Satan (at least not literally), has been operating throughout as a spy for the state. The Director, significantly garbed in the traditional costume of the Devil, denounces Foustka as a traitor, and in the chaotic denouement, Foustka's cape ignites and the play literally explodes in fire and brimstone. However, before his immolation, Foustka, in a moment of *anagnorisis*, expresses the central message of the play. In response to the Director's accusation that Foustka has stigmatized science as the source of all evil, the eminent scientist passionately retorts:

> I want to accuse the pride of that intolerant, all-powerful, and self-serving power that uses the sciences merely as a handy weapon for shooting down anything that threatens it, that is, anything that doesn't derive its authority from this power or that is related to an authority deriving its power elsewhere. (100)

I endorse the reading of Bahr who posits an additional level of meaning to the play, insisting that Havel's *Temptation* is concerned not only with political ideologies but also with existential issues such as personal integrity and liability for one's actions. According to Bahr: "Foustka shifts his 'own responsibility ... to a place outside of [his] own ego,' in this case onto Fistula, the devil of the play, in order to ease his own conscience by means of 'transference,' as modern psychology calls it, or 'projection.'"[75] Even at the play's denouement, Foustka refuses to accept accountability for the insanity of Marketa, the alienation of Vilma, or his own destruction. In this way, he mirrors his predecessors, Marlowe's Faustus and Goethe's Faust.

Of course, Faustus does have one brief moment of recognition in his final soliloquy when, after blaming the stars and his parents for his fall, he proclaims: "No, Faustus, curse thyself"; but then, almost immediately, he transfers the guilt to the Devil, lamenting: "Curse Lucifer, / That hath deprived thee of the joys of heaven" (DF, 5.4.14–15). Except for this one flicker of awareness, throughout most of the play Marlowe's hero fails to accept responsibility for his actions, consistently shifting the blame to Mephistopheles, even as Foustka transfers his guilt to Fistula. Although Goethe's development of this theme remains more nuanced, arguably his Faust also frequently delegates to Mephistopheles many important enter-prises (such as the removal of Baucis and Philemon) that he should super-vise himself, thus transferring to his infernal familiar both the responsibility and the guilt associated with these endeavors. I would thus contend that the theme of personal responsibility adumbrated in the Faust plays of Marlowe and Goethe finds full expression in Havel's modern reworking of the Faust legend, which emerges not only as an indictment of totalitarianism but also as a ringing affirmation of personal integrity and commitment as the only effective means of combating despotism.

As the above summary indicates, Havel's contemporary Faust play dis-plays many salient similarities to Marlowe's tragedy. However, Havel's drama also deviates strikingly from the traditional Faust blueprint. Although Havel's protagonist certainly deteriorates ethically after meeting Fistula, Havel's play contains no contract, no reference to the bartering of souls, no mention of salvation or damnation, and no Devil; in fact, Fistula turns out to be a secret agent of the state – no demon at all. But perhaps that is the point. Rather than questioning God or Providence or the nature of the universe, the play becomes an indictment of despotism and censor-ship in which the tyrannical state symbolically replaces hell, the manip-ulative Director with his cadre of conniving secret agents and ubiquitous messengers symbolizes the Devil incarnate, and denunciation by the state, a fate suffered by Doctor Foustka, symbolizes the ultimate damnation. Jayne Blanchard of the *Washington Times* concurs, asserting that Václav Havel's adaptation of the Faust legend "suggests repression and the regula-tion of ideas" – not a demonic tempter – "are the real mortal enemies of humanity."[76] *Faust and the City* remodels the Faust format to extol the joys of the socialist state as Lunacharski envisioned them. *Temptation*, written some seventy years later, presents a very different image of socialism, depicting it not as a kind of utopia of free men working together in a common cause, but as a repressive government, that saps all creativity and drives its citizens to seek solace in a pact with the Devil. Both plays

appropriate the Faust legend in the service of the political views of
a particular author at a particular moment in history.

Faustus

David Mamet scripted the first Faust play of the new millennium (2004),
and a dark play it is, yet, at the same time, strangely compelling.[77] Mamet's
Faustus premiered at San Francisco Magic Theatre in 2004 to mixed
reviews, and this often puzzling, always challenging play has never shared
the theatrical success enjoyed by so many of Mamet's dramas.

Mamet's haunting play merges the traditional with the innovative.
Although, as the title indicates, Marlowe's influence dominates, as in so
many of the plays analyzed in this chapter Mamet has remodeled
Marlowe's wrenching tragedy for a contemporary audience, adopting the
ironic perspective and the anti-realistic tone so characteristic of twentieth-
and twenty-first-century drama. However, in one aspect, Mamet departs
from the modernist format, retaining the God-centered ideology associated with earlier versions of the Faust legend. Like Goethe's *Faust*,
Yeats's *The Countess Cathleen*, and Sayers's *The Devil to Pay*, the denouement of the play includes a vision of heaven, in this case, problematizing
issues of salvation and damnation. Finally, although Mamet wrote his
contemporary version of the Faust legend in prose, a number of critics
have commented on the rather archaic eloquence of the dialogue. Suzanne
Weiss characterizes the language as very poetic, "almost Shakespearean, in
contrast to the man-in-the-street vernacular that marks most of his
[Mamet's] other work." [78]

As part of his modernization of Marlowe's tragedy, Mamet depicts his
hero not only as a successful academician but also as a married man with
a devoted wife and an adoring son. It soon becomes clear, however, that
Faustus neglects both his loving wife and his worshiping yet ailing son in
his monomaniacal dedication to his scholarship. Significantly, neither
member of Faustus's family possesses a name, identified in the play only
as "Wife" and "Boy," thereby emphasizing their position as appurtenances
to Faustus's life. For Mamet's Faustus soon emerges not only as the
archetypical overreacher but also as the supreme narcissist.

Faust's narcissism becomes evident in the opening scene of the play as
the Wife prepares for a party to celebrate the Boy's birthday, a festivity in
which Faustus shows only a passing interest. But the Boy, unwell and
unhappy, desperate for a smidgen of his neglectful father's attention, has
written a poignant poem in honor of his absentee parent. On this very

same day, Faustus has completed his magnum opus, his life's work, which he believes will ensure him lasting fame. When Faustus's friend Fabian (who, notably, does have a name) arrives for the birthday celebration, Faustus, heady with triumph, tells his companion of his great accomplishment, debunking God and all things metaphysical, boasting that his magnum opus has reduced all knowledge to a mathematical equation, which allows him to predict the future and unveil the "secret engine of the world." In response to Faustus's bravado, a mysterious character named Magus, bearing a suitcase emblazoned with a devil's hand, intrudes into the potentially explosive atmosphere, explaining that he is a magician hired to entertain the Boy at his birthday fest. Only later does the audience realize that Faustus through his blasphemy has summoned the Devil.

As in Marlowe's tragedy, Faustus and the Magus/Devil become involved in a long disputation, this time on the nature of magic and the metaphysical. Throughout this debate, the Wife continues to intrude, sometimes accompanied by the Friend, sometimes alone, urging Faustus to come to the ailing son who so eagerly awaits him. As Faustus brushes her off with continual excuses and the disputation continues unabated, both the Wife and the Friend become more intense and insistent. In response, Magus's prestidigitations, employed to amuse and distract the philosopher, become more bizarre. As Dennis Harvey perceptively remarks: "In a different production, his [Faustus's] umpteen callous responses, forever delaying parental duty for one more 'moment,' might qualify as a running gag."[79] But, in Mamet's drama, the recurrent appearances of the increasingly desperate Wife contribute to the rising tension of the scene until, at last, we hear the cries of the Boy. As Faustus at last prepares to attend to his sick son, Magus, like Marlowe's Mephistopheles desperate to distract Faustus, plays his trump card. He questions the validity of Faustus's magnum opus, asserting (hypothetically) that the philosopher's great, comprehensive work may contain a fatal flaw, the most damning flaw that can mar an academic manuscript: plagiarism. In a moment of conflict – a struggle between familial duty and personal ambition – Faustus wagers the life of his wife and son on the authenticity of the work. But the Devil, a trickster and con man par excellence, has another card up his sleeve: he has purloined the Boy's moving poem and substituted this tribute for the final page of Faustus's manuscript. Therefore, the manuscript that Faustus holds in his hand does not solely represent the philosopher's work and he loses the wager on a technicality.

Reality dissolves and Faustus finds himself in a world of gray desolation and ruined buildings. Encountering his former friend Fabian – now an old, old man, blind and crippled – he learns that many, many years have passed as if in a moment. The Boy died of grief at his abandonment by his father, who never came to succor him. After much anguish at the loss of both husband and son, the Wife took her own life, a mortal sin in both the Christian and Jewish faiths. As a result, the innocent Boy has gone to heaven, the suicidal Wife to hell. Like Marlowe's Faustus, mesmerized by his disputations with the Devil, Mamet's anti-hero has unwittingly allowed time to fly by, causing the two people closest to him to die of grief at his desertion. Upon hearing the results of his negligence, Faustus, temporally seized with remorse, begs Magus to permit him to atone for his indifference, to make everything as it was before his fatal wager, but the Devil remains adamant. However, finally succumbing to Faustus's pleading, Magus allows the grieving husband/father to see both his suffering wife in the underworld and his beatific son in heaven. Neither recognizes him, even as he had failed to recognize his obligations to them on earth. Nevertheless, the Boy kindly agrees to plead for him to the Almighty on this propitious day, the Day of Atonement. When the Boy fails to remember his father, Faustus seeks to prod his son's memory by showing him the poem of tribute the Boy had written so long ago. At first, Magus refuses to relinquish the poem, but, after much protestation, the Devil finally agrees to give Faustus the purloined tribute.

Then something unexpected occurs. Reveling in his victory over Magus, Faustus suddenly seems oblivious to salvation and damnation, instead gloating that he has wrenched from his adversary the licence to see heaven and hell and walk free. As the bell begins to toll signaling the end of the time of audience and the closing of the gates of heaven, Faustus, in the throes of egomania, again forgets all about his wife and son, exulting that he has found "the Secret Engine of the World" and that he has "become as God" (102). The gates of heaven clang shut and Faustus is damned! Or is he? Reflecting a characteristic Faustian ambiguity, the ending of the play remains enigmatic, and we are never sure whether Faustus is damned or saved.

Weiss has remarked on Mamet's merging in the play of Christian and Judaic traditions.[80] Weiss contends that Mamet maintains many of the Christian elements of the story while also adding a Jewish veneer, particularly notable in the references to the closing of the gates, "a deliberate echo of the Day of Atonement Yom Kippur liturgy."[81] Yet whether one stresses its Christian or Judaic provenance, I would insist that Mamet's *Faustus*, unlike so many of the secular adaptations discussed in this chapter, remains a strikingly religious play.

In its merging of the traditional and the modern, the drama retains many of the conventional ingredients of the Faust story: the overreaching hero, the diabolical tempter, the soul struggle – this time not between faith and despair, as in Marlowe's tragedy, or inertia and striving, as in Goethe's drama, but essentially between love of oneself and love of others. However, in modernizing the play for a contemporary audience, Mamet, like so many adapters of the Faust legend, has also made important alterations: he substitutes a wager for the blood-signed contract of Marlowe's tragedy, recalling the wager in Goethe's drama; his Faustus does not degenerate or regenerate as do most Faust avatars but remains the same self-centered academic from the beginning to the end of the play; finally, Mamet diminishes and simplifies his protagonist. For Mamet's Faustus, banal in his egotism, lacks the glorious rhetoric of Marlowe's hero, the expanding vision of Goethe's, and the multivalent complexity of both. One can also see Mamet's characteristic touch in his concern for familial relationships, for in his *Faustus* he creates a monumentally dysfunctional family. Mamet's *Faustus* may not represent a play for all seasons, but it is very much a Faust drama for our contemporary disillusioned, anti-heroic age.

Wittenberg

While much more affirmative than Mamet's pessimistic play, David Davalos's *Wittenberg*, with its dramatization of Faustus's search for identity and its ironic, interrogative tone, demonstrates many of the characteristics of the adaptations analyzed above.[82] Written in 2008, *Wittenberg* is a learned, often philosophical yet always hilarious "tragical-comical-historical" mélange of fact and fiction, in which the University of Wittenberg's three most famous luminaries – Martin Luther, Doctor Faustus, and Prince Hamlet – magically co-exist at this famous citadel of interrogation and revolution. Like Valéry's unfinished Faust adaptation, although much more dramatically effective, *Wittenberg* is a play about ideas, a type of intellectual comedy in the manner of Giraudoux and Shaw. The play enjoyed its world premiere at the Arden Theatre in Philadelphia in 2008 and has since been performed in 27 theaters all over the country, including the Pearl Theatre in New York City in 2011.[83]

The action of the play occurs just before Martin Luther, Doctor Faustus, and Prince Hamlet emerge from relative obscurity to change the course of both history and literature, before Luther incites the Protestant Reformation, before Doctor Faustus barters his soul to the Devil, and before Hamlet returns to cleanse the rotten state of Denmark. In the University of Wittenberg, each occupies a position appropriate to his role in history or drama. The monk Martin Luther teaches theology. The polymath Faustus – PhD, MD, LLD, DD – serves a dual role, as

University Physician, tending to the physical health of the students, and as Professor of Philosophy, Socrates-like provoking them to question everything. The student-prince Hamlet, the most famous of Wittenberg's alums, vacillates through the role of the indecisive undergraduate who cannot decide on his major. In what Eric Grode terms a "daft campus comedy," replete with Shakespearean puns (Faustus's office number is 2B), [84] these three formidable intellects wittily debate issues of God and the Devil, truth and dogma, faith and works, and being and non-being in a pastiche of quotations from Luther's writings and Marlowe's and Shakespeare's most famous plays. Here, also, Luther and Faustus spar to persuade their favorite student Hamlet to embrace their chosen discipline or, as Grode cleverly describes their efforts, "Dueling Mentors Bedevil a Dithering Young Dane."[85]

Among this troika of wits, Davalos grants Faustus center stage, depicting the eminent scholar as the play's alpha skeptic and also something of a heroic figure. Faustus encourages Hamlet to interrogate all certainties, causing the young Dane to ponder: "To believe or not to believe" (46). Faustus also goads Luther to mount his society-changing challenge to the Catholic Church. Indeed, it is Faustus in his role as physician who prescribes Luther a daily writing assignment as an antidote against depression and then purloins the Monk's 95 theses and surreptitiously nails them to the church door, thus serving as catalyst to the Protestant Reformation.

The play becomes most riveting when the dithering Prince is offstage and the two mighty opposites, with diametrically opposed views of life, clash in exciting debate. Luther exhorts his colleague: "Save your soul, John!" Equally passionate, Faustus admonishes his friend: "Free your mind, Martin!" (17). Of course, as most students of literature know, Faustus does not save his soul, although, as all students of history can affirm, Luther does free his mind and orchestrates a rebellion that reverberates throughout Europe.

To complicate matters still further, Goethe's "eternal feminine" is represented by two characters appropriately named Gretchen and Helen, both of whom interact with the star of the show, Doctor Faustus.

Critics reviewing the play have relished the voluminous references to both *Doctor Faustus* and *Hamlet* and the equally hilarious homages to Goethe, as well as the allusions to Freud, Sartre, Kierkegaard, the film *2001*, and even Timothy Leary. Moreover, the play functions as a kind of prequel to both *Doctor Faustus* and *Hamlet*, foreshadowing much of the action of both Marlowe's and Shakespeare's most famous plays; in fact, the play is first and foremost a witty initiate parody of Marlowe's and Shakespeare's most popular tragedies. However, although this fascinating tour de force presents a number of rich insights into both *Doctor Faustus* and *Hamlet*, as well as Luther's revolutionary theories, like *Temptation*, it includes no Devil figure, no contract, and no supernatural underpinnings, and thus, like many of the other plays in this chapter, deviates markedly from the traditional blueprint of the Faust narrative as introduced by the *Faustbooks* and Marlowe.

It thus may seem ironic that I should conclude this chapter with this most un-Faustian of Faust plays. However, like all of the dramas discussed in this chapter, this one adapts the Faust legend to comment on contemporaneous concepts. Early in the play, Doctor Faustus affirms the skeptical, questioning attitude that guides his actions throughout the play:

> Choose carefully. Read, question, discuss, explore, test, doubt, defy convention ... Above all, think for yourself. Granted, about those things which we cannot think, we must believe. But about those things which we cannot believe, we must think. (13)

On other occasions, Faustus debunks the importance of the Church and even of metaphysical reality, urging Hamlet: "Be your own god ... For without you, there would be no god at all" (50). Moreover, Faustus's consistent references to the importance of choice – as he proclaims on one occasion: "You are what you choose" (10) and on another: "I choose, therefore I am" (53) – associate him with existential thought, and his allusions to "the leap beyond" (46) reveal the particular influence of Søren Kierkegaard. Toward the end of the play, Faustus, having questioned everything, suffered much, survived his rejection by Helen – not Helen of Troy this time but a beautiful ex-nun whom Faustus loves – and achieved a kind of *anagnorisis*, gives full expression to his existential philosophy of life:

> Do we go on, or do we give up? And when we choose to be, we must really choose to *be*. It is not enough to simply exist, helpless as a slave to the will of others. We must master ourselves so that we may master all. (46)

Ultimately, therefore, the drama extolls both the existentialism of the mid-twentieth century and the skepticism and interrogative mode so central to postmodernist thought, a skepticism and interrogative mode associated with Wittenberg's three most celebrated rebels: Martin Luther, Hamlet, and, most prominent in this dramatic context, Doctor Faustus.

Summary

As this chapter has attempted to demonstrate, despite their wide diversity of setting, action, and characters, the majority of twentieth- and twenty-first-century dramatic adaptations and appropriations of the Faust legend reflect the philosophical trends of the centuries in which they were written, displaying a movement from the heroic to the ironic, from the spiritual to the secular, and from aspiration for transcendence to search for personal identity. There are, of course, exceptions: *The Countess Cathleen, The Devil to Pay,* and, more recently, Mamet's *Faustus* affirm a spiritual rather than a secular vision, and in *An Irish Faustus,* Durrell challenges the anti-heroic ethos of his era in his attempt to depict a heroic Faust figure. But whatever their philosophical or aesthetic differences, all of these adaptations and appropriations – to a greater or lesser degree – hold up a mirror to the zeitgeist of their times and sometimes also to the personalities of the authors who created them.

CHAPTER 5

Cinematic Fausts

In this chapter I shall treat both cinematic adaptations and appropriations of the Faust legend. As discussed in the Prologue, I will employ the term adaptations to refer to films that make explicit reference to the Faust legend (indeed, all but one of these adaptations is titled *Faustus* or *Faust*), that base the narrative events of the film, however loosely, on either Marlowe's or Goethe's script, and that feature the central dramatis personae of these plays, particularly Faust and Mephistopheles. Conversely, filmic appropriations make no explicit reference to the Faust legend and generally do not follow the narrative structure of either Marlowe's or Goethe's dramas, while, at the same time, incorporating many of the central ingredients of the Faust tradition without explicitly acknowledging their debt to this legend.

A few words should be said about one marked difference in the dramatic and cinematic adaptations/appropriations of the Faust legend. The majority of the plays analyzed follow the modernist trend toward ironizing and secularizing the Faust legend; conversely, although some of the films deflate whereas others celebrate their hero, the majority of the cinematic recreations retain the supernatural aspects of the legend, although the treatment of both God and the Devil differs enormously, depending on the time in which the film was produced and the vision of its creators.

English-Language Cinematic Adaptations of the Faust Legend

The Tragical History of Doctor Faustus

I appropriately begin my discussion of cinematic treatments of the Faust legend with the Nevill Coghill/Richard Burton film, the only cinematic adaptation of Marlowe's *Doctor Faustus* that I have discovered and a film that exemplifies the thesis of this study, skillfully adapting the source text to reflect the zeitgeist of the 1960s. This cinematic version of Marlowe's play, originally a stage production performed by the Oxford University Dramatic Society in 1966, was revised for the screen in 1967 by Nevill Coghill, and directed by Coghill and Richard Burton with Burton assuming the titular role.[1] Seeking to appeal to a 1960s audience caught in the throes of the "sexual revolution," the film shifts its emphasis from power to lust, designating lechery rather than pride as Faustus's mortal sin.

The early portion of the Coghill/Burton *Faustus* adheres fairly closely to the language and action of Marlowe's original text. However, as Jennifer Yirinec demonstrates in her definitive article on the adaptation, the film also introduces several significant additions that stress the centrality of lust as Faustus's *hamartia*.[2] Wrestling with his soul in a battle between apostasy and faith as he gazes into the hollow eye sockets of a skull, Faustus sees a harem of beautiful, naked women. In addition, Valdes and Cornelius, borrowing from Goethe, tempt Faustus to necromancy by showing him an apparition of Helen of Troy in a crystal ball.[3] Later, in the contract scene, when God's warning causes Faustus to hesitate, Mephistopheles conjures something to delight the mind of his wavering victim, not the gold and rich apparel of Marlowe's script but a second vision of Helen of Troy. This figure, played throughout the film by Burton's wife, the glamorous Elizabeth Taylor, haunts the film, reappearing in multiple incarnations: Helen of Troy, a grotesque devil wife, Diana, and Alexander the Great's Paramour. Following the signing of the bond, in Marlowe's text Faustus first requests knowledge of hell, and only after satisfying his curiosity does he entreat Mephistopheles for a wife. In the Coghill/Burton version, while Mephistopheles explains the nature of hell, an image of Helen of Troy suddenly appears before Faustus's eyes and the magus immediately forgets all about hell, demanding that his demon familiar give him a wife to assuage his wanton and lascivious desires (DF, 2.1.143–45). As in Marlowe's text, the Devil refuses, offering instead a demonic substitute and courtesans innumerable, none of whom holds great appeal for Burton's Faustus, who has just seen a vision of Helen of Troy, although, ironically, Elizabeth Taylor doubles as both the devil wife and Helen.

Marlowe's treatment of the Seven Deadly Sins episode has traditionally presented a challenge for directors. This masque, a staple of moralities and thus accessible to an early modern audience, often seems quaint and anachronistic to modern spectators, with its homey portrayal of these familiar transgressions. Coghill addresses this challenge by rewriting this section, interpolating the most famous lines from Marlowe's other plays into the dialogue, thus creating a more histrionic version of the deadly sins. The film replaces Pride, which traditionally holds priority in the hierarchy of sins, with Lechery, who guides Faustus into a bucolic paradise peopled with lissome young male and female acrobats, leaping and gamboling in a Garden of Delight, while instead of intoning the rather trite bromides from *Doctor Faustus*, Lechery recites from Gaveston's sensuous soliloquy in Marlowe's *Edward II*.[4] At the close of his soliloquy, Gaveston makes reference to the Actaeon myth in which the most infamous Peeping Tom of Greek lore, in punishment for spying on the goddess Diana while bathing, is transformed into a hart, whereupon Elizabeth Taylor appears in the guise of the goddess Diana, thereby foreshadowing Faustus's later destruction through the malign influence of another Diana figure, Helen of Troy.[5] Faustus also encounters Avarice, embodied as a man incarcerated in a cage counting his bags of gold, who filches the most famous line from Marlowe's *The Jew of Malta* to explain that he represents "infinite riches in a little room" (*JM*, 1.1.3). Later Faustus confronts Pride, a powerful general flanked by his two sons Wrath and Envy, who inflames ambition with the ringing phrases of Marlowe's archetypical overreacher Tamburlaine the Great: "Is it not passing brave to be a king / And pass in triumph through Persepolis?" (*Tam I*, 1.5.53–54). The pastiche of quotations from Marlowe's other plays concludes with Faustus echoing Tamburlaine's dying request, the epitome of hubris: "Give me a map, then, let me see how much / Is left for me to conquer all the world" (*Tam II*, 5.3.123–24). Gluttony and Sloth are left on the cutting-room floor.

Coghill severely truncates the center section of the play, omitting the episodes with the Duke of Anholt, the Horse-Courser, and the clowns, while retaining the scenes with the Emperor and the Pope. What remains of the middle section is a pallid scene with the Emperor, highlighting the mute but beautiful Elizabeth Taylor as the Paramour of Alexander the Great, plus Faustus's slapstick encounter with the Pope, stripped of all political ramifications.

The climax of Marlowe's drama focuses on Faustus's conflict between repentance and despair, catalyzed by the Old Man, a kindly neighbor who pleads with Faustus to reject the Devil and turn to God. In response to the Old Man's admonition, the tormented magician struggles to repent, but Mephistopheles's threat to dismember him cows him into subservience, and desperate to find some distraction from his angst, Faustus entreats Mephistopheles to give him the lovely Helen of Troy as his paramour. However, in Marlowe's tragedy, Helen serves not as the cause of Faustus's damnation, but rather as a palliative to soothe his despair. Conversely, in the Coghill/Burton recreation, Faustus becomes obsessed with Helen from his first view of her in the crystal orb and this fixation continues throughout the

Figure 5.1 Elizabeth Taylor and Richard Burton in a scene from the 1967 movie, *The Tragical History of Doctor Faustus,* directed by Nevill Coghill and Richard Burton. Photograph by Bettmann Collection/Getty Images.

film. The episode with the Old Man, who delivers not a passionate exhortation but an abridged, muted homily, seems more like an incidental episode than the climactic moment in the film. Burton's Faustus does experience a momentary conflict but almost immediately returns to his original obsession, entreating Mephistopheles to grant him Helen of Troy as his paramour. Wooing the fabled beauty with some of the most glorious language Marlowe ever wrote, Burton's Faustus seems genuinely besotted with Helen, even though he must realize she is a succubus (see Figure 5.1).

In the treatment of the Faustus/Helen amour, the Coghill/Burton film dramatizes the thesis of W. W. Greg, who first argued that the term "spirit" in Marlowe's play always equals "devil" and that in coupling with a demon, Faustus commits the unpardonable sin of demoniality, or "bodily intercourse with demons," and thus is irredeemably damned.[6] Coghill adds a scene not included in Marlowe's play in which after having intercourse with Helen, Faustus glances into a mirror and sees that his reflection has disappeared, further validating Greg's assumption that the succubus Helen has sucked forth Faustus's soul and led him to damnation.[7] The grisly denouement of the Coghill/Burton film further reinforces this interpretation. In the last hour of his life, Burton's Faustus futilely strives to repent, but when he fails in his attempt to leap up to God, sadistic, gloating demons pull him down to a fiery hell, most prominent among them an exultant green-hued Helen.

In his adaptation of *Doctor Faustus* for the screen, Coghill makes a number of striking alterations to accommodate Marlowe's play to a 1960s cinematic audience. These include the omission of the clown comedy, a type of physically rowdy, verbally obscure humor no longer accessible to modern audiences; unfortunately, in eliminating the clowns, the film also sacrifices the deflative counterpoint stressing the similarity between the aspiring Faustus and the low-life buffoons.[8] Coghill also drastically abridges the center section of the play, excising a number of rather banal episodes, but, in so doing, he also eradicates the carefully constructed pattern of social and intellectual decline accentuating Faustus's progressive degeneration after making the contract. [9] Finally, Coghill reimagines the Faustian bargain, shifting Faustus's motivation from the search for either power or knowledge to lust for Helen of Troy, a radical change appropriate to the sexual revolution consuming the society of the 1960s. Significantly, the Burton/Coghill film was released the year of the famous "summer of love."[10] Also, the tabloid scandal surrounding the archetypical celebrity couple Richard Burton and Elizabeth Taylor adds a special piquancy to the Coghill/Burton topos of a soul badly lost for love (or lust). As Bevington observes, "One can hardly imagine a more apt fable for this disillusioning era in the wake of the assassinations of the Kennedys and of Martin Luther King, the escalating and often violent conflict over the Vietnam war, and so much more."[11] Thus, Coghill has crafted an unheroic, sex-obsessed film for an anti-heroic, sex-obsessed era. He has created a *Doctor Faustus* not for all time but for a particular audience in a particular age.

Foreign-Language Cinematic Adaptations of the Faust Legend

F. W. Murnau's Faust

Reinterpreting Goethe's drama rather than Marlowe's tragedy, F. W. Murnau's silent film offers a much more sympathetic portrait of the Faustian overreacher. From Christopher Marlowe to David Mamet, an ambivalent perspective toward the aspiring hero has been the hallmark of

Faustian drama. The majority of modern dramatic adaptations tend to view the overreaching hero from an ironic although often sympathetic perspective. This same ambivalent perspective pervades the film versions of the legend, both adaptations and appropriations. Perhaps the most celebratory of all the Faust films discussed in this chapter is F. W. Murnau's 1926 silent German film *Faust*.[12] Because this celebratory tone frequently lapses into sentimentality, Murnau's adaptation is also one of the most controversial, although, paradoxically, one of the most influential of Faust films.

Murnau's memorable motion picture has aroused widely divergent responses from film critics: Herman Weinberg lauds the film as "a great fresco painted with lights and shadows," displaying an "exultant flight of the cinema spirit"; conversely, C. A. Lejeune condemns the film as flaunting "all the tinsel and bombast of a world circus," while Siegfried Kracauer judges "the metaphysical conflict between good and evil" to be "thoroughly vulgarized." Although the majority of critics recognize Murnau's cinematic skill and innovative techniques, many fault the director for deviating so markedly from Goethe's masterpiece, the most revered icon of German literature, whereas others cavil at the blatant sentimentality pervading the film. Philip Kemp speaks for critical consensus when he praises Murnau's pictorial genius, while admitting that occasionally the film "lurches into kitsch," as in the often mawkish love scenes between Faust and Gretchen.[13]

Channeling both Goethe's sweeping vision as well as Marlowe's wrenching tragedy, the film opens in heaven, dramatizing a Manichean confrontation between good and evil, in this case between the Devil Mephisto, shrouded in black, and the Archangel of the Lord, attired in shining white (an agon more reminiscent of the contests between the Good and Evil Angels in Marlowe's tragedy than of the wager between God and the Devil in Goethe's drama). Murnau's Mephisto, more hubristic than Goethe's Devil, defies God, declaring, "The earth is mine," to which the Archangel replies, "The earth and all within it belongs to God." When the Archangel asks Mephisto if he knows Faust, the swaggering demon confidently boasts: "A wager. I will wrest Faust's soul away from God." Assured of Faust's virtue, the Archangel rashly counters: "If you can destroy the divine in Faust, the earth will be thine." Confidently, Mephisto responds: "No one can resist evil, you can count on that."

Following the confrontation in heaven, the scene shifts to earth with the evil Mephisto shadowing the world with his vast dark wings, like some malignant bird of prey (see Figure 5.2). Covered by this murky penumbra, a circus performer falls dead; the diagnosis – the deadly plague! The film

Figure 5.2 Devil of an Actor. Emil Jennings plays the winged Mephistopheles in the 1926 silent film *Faust*, directed by F. W. Murnau. Photograph by John Kobal Foundation/Getty Images.

cuts to the venerable philosopher Faust, who spends night and day search-ing for a cure for the plague. Unlike Marlowe's and Goethe's heroes, Murnau's Faust is initially motivated not by a narcissistic desire for power, wealth, or knowledge or by a yearning for the fullest experience of life, but, like the Faust figures of W. B. Yeats and Dorothy Sayers, by a desire to save humanity. Unable to cure the plague and enraged at his impotence, Faustus burns all his books of knowledge, including his Bible, and in desperation turns to his necromantic tomes. Then, mimicking Marlowe's magus, Murnau's Faust conjures the Devil, in this case journey-ing to a crossroads with a lifeless tree etched against a sepia sky, where he inscribes the traditional circle and invokes the Spirit of Darkness.

The plot of the film mingles the traditions of Marlowe and Goethe with many of Murnau's own innovations. Mephisto offers Faust the proverbial contract signed in blood; however, the wily Devil adds an enticing, almost irresistible twist not found in any previous treatments of the legend: "Try it. Just one trial day. Then when the hourglass has run out, you will be free." So Faust signs his name in blood, but with the understanding that the contract will be valid for only one day, naïvely vowing: "I will do good in the Devil's name." After making his pact with the Devil, Faust proceeds to heal the sick by the laying on of hands, recalling the miracles of both Simon Magus and the Antichrist. Yet, suspicious of his power, the superstitious villagers turn upon him and attempt to stone him to death, and only the intervention of Mephisto shields Faust from the fusillade of stones.

Following Goethe's hero, in despair Murnau's Faust attempts to commit suicide, but Mephisto restrains him, showing his victim the image of his rejuvenated self in a mirror, promising him youth, virility, and pleasure. Forgetting the dying populace for whom he had earlier risked his soul, Faust pleads: "Give me youth!" So Mephisto casts Faust into a deep sleep from which he awakens as a young and handsome man. In an episode that finds no analogy in previous versions of the Faust legend, Mephisto, now transformed into a dapper gallant, takes Faustus on a bizarre journey to the court of the Duchess of Parma, the most beautiful woman in Italy (perhaps a stand-in for Helen of Troy). Here, as the sand runs through the hourglass, Faust seduces the Duchess while Mephisto slays her bridegroom. When Mephisto threatens to turn Faust back into his senescent self, the magus, desperate for pleasure, finalizes a permanent bargain, and the erstwhile philosopher/physician/theologian, like so many Faust figures before him, indulges in a bacchanal of hedonistic pleasure. However, again like so many of his predecessors, Faust soon becomes disillusioned with the rewards of his contract and demands to go home to his small German village.

At this point, Murnau's film returns to Goethe's script, with occasional deviations. Faust encounters the pristine maiden Gretchen entering a church; smitten, he demands of his demonic enabler: "I must have her!" Mephisto places a gold necklace in Gretchen's jewelry box, which the young woman suspects comes from the young gallant she met at the church. Unwilling to confide in her puritanical mother, Gretchen shares the information with her risqué Aunt Martha. Thus Faust and Mephisto follow Gretchen to her aunt's home, and while Faust woos the young woman, his infernal companion amuses Aunt Martha with flattering words and golden gifts. As in Goethe's drama, Faust easily wins the love of the chaste and innocent maiden. In the meantime, the pseudo-romance of the flirtatious Aunt Martha and the malicious Mephisto provides a comic counterpoint to the tragic love affair of Faust and Gretchen. Later, Mephisto urges Faust: "Go to her, I will keep the brother away." Then, as the eager lover climbs through Gretchen's window, the double-dealing Devil hurries to the tavern to inform Gretchen's brother of the "debauchery" of his beautiful sister, suggesting that if Valentine hurries he might apprehend Gretchen's lover leaving her room.

Murnau makes two significant changes in the tragic events following this consummation that absolve Faust of culpability in the deaths of Gretchen's mother and brother. In Goethe's play, the complicity of Faust in the murder of Gretchen's mother remains problematic (does he suspect that the sleeping draught that he gives the mother is poisoned?); Murnau's film deletes the poisoned draught and thus all ambiguity. Instead, the malevolent Mephisto raises a wind that awakens Gretchen's mother, and when the concerned parent rushes to Gretchen's room to find her daughter in the arms of a strange man, she melodramatically dies of shock. Moreover, in Goethe's drama, Faust slays Gretchen's brother, albeit in self-defense, whereas, in Murnau's adaptation, Valentine is stabbed in the back by Mephisto. In a final act of deceit, the Devil runs through the street calling "Murder," and, as the deputies arrive, Faust is forced to flee and desert Gretchen.

The latter section of the film poignantly dramatizes the suffering of Gretchen, only narrated in Goethe's drama. Convicted of the sin of fornication, rejected by all, even Aunt Martha, Gretchen stands in the stocks, ridiculed by the jeers of the coarse peasants of the village. Finally released, she returns home to an empty house, bereft of mother and brother, the collateral damages of her transgression. Here the wretched outcast lives alone and bears a child, the fruit of her one night of love. Deserted by everyone, freezing, hungry, Gretchen struggles through a snowstorm to find help for her child, only to be spurned by the "devout" Christians of the village. In a delusion bred of hunger and cold, Gretchen hallucinates that she has placed her child in a warm cradle when actually she has buried the infant in the snow. Guards arrive and seize the delusional but innocent young woman, calling her a murderess.

The denouement of Murnau's film further exonerates his Faust figure. On a high mountain with Mephisto, the magus has a premonition of Gretchen's suffering and commands his infernal familiar to aid him in her rescue. Even as Faust and Mephisto race through the night air on their demonic steeds, the villagers prepare the pyre to burn Gretchen. Seeing the pyre, Faust curses: "If only I had not wished for youth. Damn, damn the illusion of youth, which caused all this misery!" Reveling in schadenfreude, the Devil gloats: "You have cursed youth yourself! And I must do whatever you wish." Therefore, as Faust desperately rushes to rescue Gretchen,

Mephisto transforms him back into a feeble old man, too infirm to save the woman he has wronged. However, Murnau's Faust, much more caring than Goethe's hero, does not desert his beloved but instead staggers into the flames to die with her. As he embraces the doomed maiden, Faust transforms again into the handsome young lover to whom Gretchen gave her heart. Murnau's adaptation, like Goethe's drama, ends in triumph as the heavens open, but this time to receive not one but two saved souls. The film closes with the final image of the white-winged Archangel denying the black-winged fallen Angel entry into heaven. And the spectators realize that not only Faust and Gretchen but the entire world is redeemed by love.

Murnau's silent film masterpiece casts a long shadow over subsequent Faust films, not only the German and European versions but also English-language appropriations. Echoes of Murnau's *Faust* emerge everywhere in the films treated in this chapter. The transmutation from old age to youth in *The Beauty of the Devil* and *Damn Yankees* probably derives not only from Goethe but also from Murnau. The limited trial bargain dangled before Joe Hardy in *Damn Yankees* probably finds its provenance in the one-day trial offered by Murnau's Mephisto. The momentous stakes God hazards in his poker game with the Devil in *Oh, God! You Devil* probably originates in the dangerous wager made between the Archangel and Mephisto in Murnau's film. Finally, the indelible image of the lonely crossroads with its lifeless tree etched against a sepia sky where Robert Johnson bargains with the Devil in *Crossroads* offers an hommage to Murnau's memorable conjuration scene.

Murnau's *Faust* was produced in 1926, and the film's melodramatic acting and rather heavy-handed morality might seem anachronistic to the more cinematically sophisticated, secular audience of the new millennium. However, a number of critics have commented on the film's innovations in the treatment of dark and light and also on the pervasive painterly quality of many of the scenes, which recall the masterpieces of Rembrandt, Dürer, Vermeer, and Caravaggio.[14] Furthermore, the vivid chiaroscuro characteristic of Murnau's mise-en-scène endows the film with an evocative beauty, strangely appropriate to this fable of good versus evil. Yet, with its overt moralizing, the film has undoubtedly stripped the Faust story of its intriguing ambiguity, a central feature of both Marlowe's and Goethe's dramas, reducing Mephisto to a stereotypical Devil, complete with horns and tail. Moreover, it completely ameliorates Faust, thereby creating a much less callous, but also less interesting hero than his often egotistical predecessor. But what Murnau loses in complexity, he gains in forcefulness, investing the story with the simplicity of a morality play and the power of a fable – one of society's most cherished fables, redemption through love.

The Beauty of the Devil

René Clair's French-language, lavishly mounted, bittersweet tragicomedy, *The Beauty of the Devil*, filmed in 1950, combines the celebratory and ironic perspectives toward the Faust legend. The film shifts the setting from sixteenth- to nineteenth-century Germany, interweaving the motifs of the Faust narrative with amusing topical references while filtering everything through the prism of Clair's Gallic wit and elegance.[15] The film also adds some interesting innovations: as Hedges suggests, the film introduces the motif of masquerade, as the elderly Faust assumes the body of the youthful Henri, and vice versa.[16] It also includes a highly irregular contract and a magic mirror that foretells the future. Finally, Clair creates one of the most sympathetic Devils in the Faustian rogues' gallery of deceptive demons.

The hero of the movie, Professor Henri Faust, disheveled and somewhat befuddled with a long white beard and arthritic gait, is an eminent alchemist who among other aspirations has been striving to transmute sand into gold, an endeavor never undertaken by any previous Faust avatar. Like Goethe's hero, Clair's Faust does not conjure the Devil; rather, returning to his cluttered study at the beginning of the film, he discovers a strange guest, an unusually handsome young rapscallion with hair curled to resemble horns, who reveals himself to be none other than Mephistopheles. However, although tempted by the Devil with the usual lures – youth, wealth, and fame – this Faust, unlike most of his predecessors, refuses to sign the traditional contract. Stymied, Mephistopheles makes Faust an unusual offer, one that finds no precedent in the other Faust plays or films I have surveyed: he will grant Faust youth and pleasure without penalty while promising not to mention the diabolical contract unless the Professor himself initiates the topic. So the two make an agreement of sorts and change shapes. Mephistopheles appropriates the aging, arthritic body of Professor Faust and Faust transforms into the young, virile form initially assumed by Mephistopheles.

Freed from the burdens of age, like his predecessor in Goethe's drama, a jubilant Faust determines to sample all the pleasures of life he has never enjoyed. He stumbles on a troop of itinerant players and meets a beautiful, dark-haired gypsy girl, appropriately named Marguerite, and, immediately smitten, runs away with the company of thespians. However, Faust's valet, having spied the young man in his master's home rummaging through the drawers for money, denounces the interloper to the police, who apprehend Faust and charge him with theft and homicide. At the very last minute, as Faust's conviction looms, Mephistopheles appears in the form of Professor Faust to exonerate the young man, now known simply as Henri.

Realizing he cannot bully Faust into making a bargain, Mephistopheles tries a new strategy, suggesting that the two of them co-operate sans contract. So the Devil and the alchemist, who has apparently forgotten Marguerite, begin to work together and with their combined efforts achieve the alchemist's dream of transforming sand into gold. Faust becomes rich and famous and, like many other Faust figures, enjoys a lifestyle never before imagined, eating only the finest food and drinking only the choicest wines. Knighted by the grateful Prince, Faust becomes Chevalier Henri and Mephistopheles and Faust dine and dance with royalty, honored and esteemed by all. Faust also enjoys an affair with the lovely blonde Princess, wife of the rather dull-witted Prince. It appears that Faust has obtained all his wishes gratis. At this point, Mephistopheles intervenes and transports Faust back to his days of poverty, dismissing the Chevalier's memories of wealth and fame as only a dream. Desperate to regain these markers of success, Faust at last surrenders to the Devil, echoing Marlowe's doomed hero as he slashes his palm to draw blood to sign the fatal contract.

Reinstated into his old life, like Murnau's hero and many other Faust incarnations, Henri soon becomes sated with the wealth, fame, and power that earlier so delighted him. Aware that Mephistopheles possesses the power of precognition, and ignoring all the Devil's remonstrations, Faust commands his fiendish familiar to show him the future. Standing before an enchanted mirror, Faust views the dark saga of the days to come, a dreary narrative of progressive degradation, recalling the downward trajectory of Marlowe's Faustus. Having already committed adultery, within the next year, Faust will become an accomplice in the murder of the Prince, who will be poisoned by the magus's demonic enabler, even as Margarete's mother was poisoned by Goethe's Mephistopheles. Soon, however, Faust will develop a roving eye and the jealous Princess will become a burden rather than a pleasure, so Mephistopheles will dispatch her as well, allowing Faust the freedom to woo all of the women of the court. Bored with pursuing women, Faust will seize political power, degenerating from an absolute monarch into a ruthless dictator. Having designed a submarine, a flying machine, and a steam engine, Faust will invent the atomic bomb and wreak havoc on all the countries that oppose him. Finally, when his

contract becomes due, the despot will be carried screaming off to hell by
a triumphant Mephistopheles. Thus the once sage philosopher/alchemist
will become first an adulterer, then a murderer, then a libertine, then
a tyrant, and finally a mass killer.

Upon beholding his destiny under the tutelage of Mephistopheles, Faust
falls into despair and flees the court to return to his first love, Marguerite.
Mephistopheles follows, and intrigued at the opportunity of corrupting
such a pristine soul, attempts to seduce Marguerite with the traditional
enticements of youth, wealth, and love. However, like the saintly Justina in
the legend of St. Cyprian, Marguerite proves impervious to the lures of the
Devil. In retaliation, Mephistopheles causes all of the gold in the kingdom
to miraculously dissolve into sand, surreptitiously spreading the rumor that
this disaster has been initiated by the witch Marguerite. The innocent
Marguerite is convicted and imprisoned, with a howling crowd demanding
she be burned at the stake, as in Murnau's film, and Faust, who tries to
rescue her, is apprehended as well. Before Marguerite's execution,
Mephistopheles tries again to secure the young woman's signature on the
contract; producing Faust's blood-signed bond, he insists that only if
Marguerite signs the contract can the two lovers be united in the afterlife,
albeit in hell rather than in heaven. Unfazed, the plucky Marguerite – like
Goethe's heroine, the redemptive figure in the film – snatches the paper
and throws it out the barred window where it falls into the hands of the
throng of angry citizens, who immediately demand the death of the real
witch, Professor Faust (really, of course, the Devil assuming the shape of
the venerable professor). Praying to Lucifer to be released from his borrowed body, which can, of course, suffer pain, Mephistopheles grabs the
bond and leaps to his death as the contract explodes in a cloud of smoke.
Faust, who has hurried to the prison to rescue Marguerite, glances at the
wound on his hand, and seeing that the gash has healed, realizes that at last
he is free. The final scene of the film shows Faust and Marguerite, having
rejoined the traveling players, preparing to live happily ever after.

Although revising the central episode of Goethe's *Faust, Part I*, Clair's
film draws equally from Marlowe's tragedy. Yet, while incorporating most
of the familiar elements of the Faust legend, Clair's adaptation brings an
unexpected hopefulness to this timeless narrative. Clair's irrepressibly
innocent Faust exudes a Gallic charm and his Mephistopheles – canny
yet bumbling, sinister yet impish – arouses both humor and compassion.
Yet Clair leavens his buoyant optimism with a dash of Voltairean cynicism
as he satirizes the corruption of the courtiers and the superstition of the
peasants. Mephistopheles expresses this Voltairean skepticism as he prays

to escape his human body: "Lucifer, help! Hell is less cruel than man!" The film also contains trenchant political satire. In a bit of forgivable anachronism, David Sterritt relates Faust's alchemist enterprise of manufacturing money out of sand to the bitcoin speculation or credit-default swapping of our own time. More relevantly, he suggests that Faust's plans to devote his vast technological wizardry to producing the atomic bomb would have held a frightening resonance for the world of the 1950s, still reeling from the shock of Hiroshima and Nagasaki.[17] Ultimately, Clair's Faust learns the Voltairean lesson that wealth, power, and fame cannot bring happiness, but instead of tending his own garden, he runs off with a troupe of players and the woman he loves.

I suggest that with its mixture of wry cynicism and exuberant optimism, René Clair's *The Beauty of the Devil* has adapted the Faust narrative to mirror the mood of post-World War II Europe in the early 1950s.

Jan Švankmajer's Faust

A much darker film, created in a different country in a different time period, Jan Švankmajer's surreal, Kafkaesque *Faust* depicts the protagonist as marionette, manipulated by forces that he does not understand and over which he has no control. The film reflects the trends dominant in modern dramatic adaptations of the legend: the ironic perspective, the reduction of the hero to an Everyman figure, the metatheatrical nuances. Švankmajer's 1994 Czech nightmare also blends live action with stop motion, marionettes, and animation, while drawing on numerous different sources of the venerable legend, not only Marlowe's and Goethe's dramas but also Gounod's opera and the Czech Puppet Play.[18]

Švankmajer's film opens with a weary Czech Everyman emerging from a dingy subway in Prague to receive a map from two nondescript figures standing on the street corner. Compelled by some unknown force, the Everyman figure follows the route outlined on the map to a dilapidated theater. Entering the battered door, the nameless hero finds himself in a phantasmagoric world of furtive black cats, weird Bosch-like creatures scuttling to and fro, alchemists' alembics, and a clay homunculus bearing his own face that ages before his eyes from infant to adult to old man to grinning skull. Moving into the dressing room, the Everyman figure proceeds to dress himself in the costume of Faust, complete with magician's robe, wig, false beard, even make-up. In this case, clothes do proclaim the man, and once he has attired himself in the regalia of Faust, the nameless hero becomes the role he plays. He at last finds his voice and speaks the first words in the film, but they are not his own words; rather they are lines recited from the tattered manuscript of Goethe's *Faust* he discovers among the theatrical paraphernalia littering the dressing room. He also acquires a name, alternatively Faustus or Faust, and henceforth all the dialogue of the film consists of a collage: the mighty lines of Marlowe and the heroic verse of Goethe alternating with snippets from Gounod's opera and the banal doggerel from the Czech Puppet Play. The film dramatizes two very different realms: the gray, mundane world outside the theater, where nameless men and women perform their quotidian tasks, and the fantastic world of bizarre images and vibrant chiaroscuro inside the theater, which recreates the Faust legend in multiple permutations.

In Švankmajer's play within a play – or, more accurately, play within a film – Faust struggles to regain his volition as he is pulled back and forth between these two realms. Briefly escaping into the drab cinéma vérité world outside the enchanted theater, the newly minted Faust discovers a briefcase containing all the accoutrements of the magician and, irresistibly drawn back into the magic theater, he begins to conjure, but not before marionette versions of Marlowe's Good and Evil Angels emerge to caution or goad Faust to either salvation or damnation. Finally, amid surreal images of fire, lightning, and shooting arrows, Mephistopheles at last materializes as a clay replica of Faust himself, and both Faust and his demonic alter ego recite by rote the exact words from Marlowe's conjuration scene (DF, 1.3). Also, as in Marlowe's play, clowns – this time, not human jesters but marionettes – burlesque the actions of both Faust and Mephistopheles.

Throughout the film, the action shifts abruptly back and forth from the chaotic wizardry of the theater to the dreary reality of the café outside. Yet, even here, cinéma vérité and fantasy blend: several times the devil marionette flees from the theater into the street and puppet heads frequently roll ominously up and down the cobblestone paths. Also, an old man with a human foot protruding from a rolled newspaper is relentlessly stalked by a black dog, barking raucously, until in desperation the old man throws the amputated limb into the river. Another time, briefly escaping from the theater, Faust spies the menacing men who handed him the map at the subway station skulking behind the serving tables, where they conjure a geyser of wine to spout from Faust's table, thereby linking them with Mephistopheles who performs a similar miracle in Auerbach's Tavern in Goethe's *Faust*.

Every time Faust attempts to escape from the world of fantasy into the world of reality, he is inevitably dragged back to the theater, where unknown hands force him again to don the magician's costume. In a sequence that mimics familiar dream experiences, the confused Faust finds himself performing the titular role in Gounod's operatic adaptation before an applauding audience. In the midst of one of Faust's soaring arias, Mephistopheles appears in the prompter's box and the two, forgetting the opera and the audience, begin immediately to recite almost verbatim the contract scene from Marlowe's tragedy (DF, 2.1). However, the actual contract scene, with its pierced arm, its bloody quill, and its sanguinary signature, is performed not by the human Faust but by marionette replicas of Faust and Mephistopheles. Or so we think until after the signing of the contract, when the marionette Faust tears off his visor to reveal the human Faust beneath the marionette's mask. We then realize that Faust, in signing the contract, has become a puppet. Throughout, Faust alternates from marionette to human and back to marionette, participating in a number of ludicrous episodes derived from the Czech Puppet Plays. Finally, disgusted with the triviality of these escapades, the human Faust seeks to repent, and, as in Marlowe's tragedy, Mephistopheles conjures Helen of Troy, this time a marionette, to lure his victim to damnation. In one of the most incongruous scenes in the film, the human Faust makes love to a marionette Helen.

Time, like everything else in this film, appears fluid and dreamlike, and suddenly Faust's twenty-four years are over and the contract due. In Švankmajer's shocking addition to the Faust narrative, Faust flees from the nightmare theater only to be hit and killed by a red car driven by no one. The old man who earlier had discarded the amputated limb scoops up Faust's shattered foot and wraps it in a newspaper (recalling Faustus's dismembered limbs in Marlowe's tragedy), as the two sinister messengers from hell lurk nearby, smirking with pleasure. Earlier, as Faust fled from the theater, he collided with another Czech Everyman entering the dilapidated building clutching a map, and so the entire scenario will be replayed.

In many ways, despite its surreal potpourri of cinematic styles, Švankmajer's film remains true to the traditional Faustian blueprint as developed in the *Faustbooks* and Marlowe's tragedy. However, the merging of human figures with marionettes links all of the dramatis personae to puppets, thus calling into question Faustus's free will, such a central element of the Faust legend. Perhaps because of its bold experiments in cinematic style or because of its fascinating fusion of Faustian traditions, Ian Christie praises Švankmajer's film as "the most notable modern Faust on film."[19] Moreover, as Caryn Jones notes in her review, "A Passive Faust Goes to the Devil Slowly," in addition to its cinematic pyrotechnics and

innovative medley of blank verse, rhyme, and doggerel, the film offers
salient observations on the dilemmas of our dissonant and disordered
contemporary society. Jones posits that "Faustus has passively accepted
capitalism as easily as he used to swallow totalitarianism"; in Švankmajer's
own words: "Faust is manipulated like a puppet."[20] Michael Wilmington,
in his film review in the *Chicago Tribune*, offers a similar interpretation,
asserting: "This film is about the ways the devil claims his due in capitalism
and communism alike."[21] Hedges expands this interpretation: "When
Faust becomes a puppet, Švankmajer tries to show him as a manipulated
character in the contemporary world . . . The presentation of Faust, on the
one hand, as a marionette, and on the other, as a disorientated modern
citizen, corresponds to the filmmaker's deep pessimism concerning the
future of humankind in the post-Cold War world."[22]

Alexander Sokurov's Faust

Like Švankmajer's film, Russian auteur Alexander Sokurov's bizarre 2011
German-language *Faust* [23] offers a bleak, postmodern reinterpretation of
the Faust narrative, epitomizing the ironic perspective dominating modern
versions of the legend whereby all the dramatis personae are deflated and
the supernatural aspects of the source text minimized. Yet, whereas
Švankmajer's adaptation draws inspiration from a kaleidoscope of
Faustian traditions, Sokurov's film is primarily a recreation of Goethe's
Faust, Part I. Sokurov's film depicts a dark, gritty world of poverty, filth,
thievery, and suffering. Although the Russian director has transferred the
setting from sixteenth- to nineteenth-century Germany, the film seems to
exist in an earlier, more benighted period of human history. Also,
Sokurov's weird camera angles and distorted, hallucinatory images reflect
a world askew and out of joint. According to Sokurov, *Faust* completes the
auteur's "tetralogy of power," which includes three films centering on
infamous political leaders of the early twentieth century – Hitler
(*Moloch*, 1999), Lenin (*Tauros*, 2001), and Hirohito (*The Sun*, 2005) –
although the connection of *Faust* to these three historical films is not
immediately apparent.[24]

   Initially, the film appears to bear little relationship to Goethe's drama,
although recalling Goethe's Prologue, it does open with a view of the
heavens. However, the camera almost immediately sweeps to earth, a bleak
apocalyptic landscape of jutting cliffs and barren plains, shifting quickly to
focus first on a bloody penis, then on a doctor covered with blood and
grime manipulating the sanguinary organs of a cadaver, perhaps in search

of its soul. We soon learn that Faust, although an adept in the four accepted disciplines of the age, unlike his more celebrated predecessors, lives in penury, having sacrificed everything to his dogged pursuit of truth. When we first meet Faust, he is penniless, harassed by creditors, weary, and literally starving. Unlike Marlowe's Faust, Sokurov's hero does not seek out the Devil, nor does the Prince of Darkness pursue him, as in Goethe's drama. Rather, in desperation, Faust turns to a moneylender – a sinister, shuffling old man named Mauricius Müeller – hoping to obtain enough money for a decent meal. However, the moneylender refuses to take Faust's most marketable possession, his ring, insinuating that he seeks something far more valuable from his prospective client. After leaving the moneylender, Sokurov's despairing Faust, like Goethe's hero, decides to take his own life. But Sokurov's truth-seeker is deterred from suicide not, as in Goethe, by an Easter hymn celebrating Christ's resurrection, but by the appearance of the grotesque moneylender, who hobbles into Faust's disordered flat to return the ring Faust had left with him by mistake. When Mauricius swigs down the hemlock intended for Faust and does not die, the spectator begins to suspect that this superannuated old man represents a very unlikely Devil. Mauricius later explains that his name means "the dark one."

However, at his debut, Mauricius makes no mention of a bargain or a soul. Instead, he escorts Faust on a journey, a kind of bizarre parade of the seven deadly sins. Waiting for Mauricius while the moneylender blasphemously defecates inside a church, Faust meets a few of the moneylender's "clients," some of whom seem *envious* of Faust's apparent familiarity with the evil one. Moreover, one of Mauricius's "clients" insists that he believes in Satan but not God, asserting that evil exists in the world but not good, a phrase that could serve as a mantra for the entire film. Later, Faust experiences *lust* when he views a group of voluptuous women washing clothes and bathing in a grotto, among them the nubile Margarete/Gretchen. Next, he becomes involved in a deadly barroom brawl, in which the *wrathful*, roistering soldiers in a tavern attack the decrepit moneylender, who refuses to pay his bar bill. In the nick of time, Mauricius performs his sole magical trick in the film, jamming a large fork into the brick wall from which spurts fountains of wine, an echo of Mephistopheles's miracle in Auerbach's Tavern in Goethe's *Faust*. After performing this magic trick, Mauricius thrusts the fork into Faust's hand and in the melee that follows, as the *gluttonous* revelers rush to fill their glasses with wine, Faust unwittingly slays Gretchen's brother Valentine, as he does in Goethe's drama, albeit under very different circumstances.

Racked with guilt, Faust insists that Mauricius recompense Valentine's family for their loss and to obtain the necessary gold the two descend into the moneylender's lair, a dark pit where Mauricius *avariciously* hoards his ill-gotten gains.

At this point, the film at last introduces Goethe's script but with many variations. Still burning with lust despite his guilt, Faust signs a contract agreeing to sell his soul in return for one night alone with Gretchen. When his pen runs dry, Mauricius pierces Faust's hand with a quill and his victim signs the bond in blood. Later, Faust attends the funeral of the man he has slain, meets and woos Gretchen, and after conspiring with his demonic henchman to poison Gretchen's mother with a herbal tea, seduces the most willing young woman. But immediately after the seduction, as in Goethe's text, Mauricius spirits Faust away, since the formerly respected Professor is now implicated in two murders, that of Gretchen's brother and her mother.

The denouement of the film departs dramatically from the scenarios of both Marlowe and Goethe. Arriving on the same bleak purgatorial land- scape that opened the film, Faust angrily confronts the man who has tempted him to lechery and murder, demanding: "What will happen to the girl?" When Mauricius cavalierly replies: "She will be imprisoned, most likely," and totally ignores Faust's insistence that they rescue Gretchen, something snaps. The enraged Faust tears up the contract and hurls one giant rock after another at the old man, crying: "This is for Margarete," "This is for her mother," until he has totally buried his devilish companion in a mountain of boulders. Mauricius's last whimpering words echo in the silence: "Who will guide you out of here?" In the distance, a flash of light appears and Margarete's voice is heard asking: "Where are you going?" In response, Faust begins to run madly across the isolated terrain, frantically crying: "Over there, farther and farther." With this cry still ringing in the air, the film ends.

In true postmodernist fashion, Sokurov's film diminishes all its char- acters. In the moneylender Mauricius, Sokurov creates the most sniveling, shuffling Devil in the entire repertoire of demonic tempters, described by film critic Ian Christie as an "extraordinary prancing, epicene creation" and by Tony Rayns as "a jovial grotesque straight out of Bosch or Bruegel."[25] Rob White also comments on the grotesque deformity of Sokurov's "knavish Mephistopheles."[26] In many ways, Mauricius, with his deformed body and fetid odor, resembles the misshapen Fistula in Havel's *Temptation*. Moreover, this creepy demon appears to have minimal super- natural powers. His only magical moment occurs in the tavern when he causes the bricks to bleed wine; otherwise, he relies on bribery, cajolery, and poison to accomplish his mischief. Similarly, the film strips the other characters of their dignity. Wagner, the humorous, albeit indefatigably loyal commentator of Marlowe's tragedy, has been transformed into a parody of Goethe's Wagner, a frenzied rival of Faust, maniacally obsessed by a desire to create the homunculus. Gretchen, although ripe and fetching, lacks the purity and sincerity of Goethe's pious innocent. She flirts with Faust at her brother's funeral, although she knows that Faust has slain him. Gretchen's mother, ostensibly a strict guardian of Gretchen's virtue, avidly accepts gold from Mauricius, and one suspects that she is one of the moneylender's "clients." Gretchen's brother Valentine dies not in defense of Gretchen's honor but in a barroom brawl. More importantly, Sokurov portrays a much deflated Faust, possibly the most dour, charmless Faust figure on screen, totally divested of the grandeur Goethe bestows upon his striving overreacher. He depicts a Faust totally motivated by lust, who suffers no conflict in his pursuit of Gretchen, a Faust unequivocally complicit in the murder of Gretchen's mother, a Faust who deserts Gretchen without remonstration. Christie labels Sokurov's Faust "a bold opportunist" and Tony Rayns judges him a "driven and somewhat sadistic materialist."[27]

However, Sokurov's film does maintain one of the central characteristics of the Faust story: the fusion of the comic and the serious. Yet, Marlowe's tragedy relegates most of the hijinks to the clowns and Goethe's drama demarcates the comic and the sublime. Conversely, Sokurov's *Faust* intermingles moments of slapstick and near tragedy, with Mauricius portraying one of the most buffoonish Devils in the history of Faust films, mimicking the comic treatment of the Vice in the moralities. Moreover, with their constant bickering, accompanied by shoving, rough-housing, even biting, Faust and Mauricius often resemble the Marx brothers rather than two of the most famous antagonists in mythic lore.

Finally, the ending of the film, although sharing the ambiguity that critics have discovered in Marlowe's and Goethe's texts, in other respects departs decisively from both of their scripts. Faust's slaying of Mauricius by burying him beneath boulders seems to imply that Faust ultimately escapes from the Devil and the contract, but we are left wondering, can it really be this easy to destroy evil in the world? Or has the evil of Mauricius been transferred to Faust? In addition, the presence of a dazzling light and a female voice, offering the sole luminous moment in this crepuscular film, could foreshadow Faust's salvation through the love of Margarete, as in Goethe's drama. But we never know. I tend to agree with Rayns, who takes a darker view of the film's conclusion, suggesting that when we last see Faust "striking out across Nietzschean wastes in defiance of an off-screen deity," "liberated by acts of violence – a murder, a stoning, and the taking of a woman who has best reason to hate him . . . the harsh landscape becomes new territory for him to conquer, and not a sign of his ruination," or, I would add, his redemption. If so, then Sokurov has totally reversed Goethe's transcendent denouement: he "comes to bury Goethe, not to praise him."[28] According to Graham Fuller, Sokurov has linked his protagonist with the other failed dictators in his "tetralogy of power," insisting that his Faust "walks off to become a tyrant, a political oligarch."[29]

This enigmatic film, with its fusion of comedy and tragedy and its problematic, ambiguous ending, provides a genuinely postmodern version of the ancient legend, presenting a sometimes frightening, sometimes absurd hero for a frightening, anti-heroic age.

Cinematic Appropriations of the Faust Legend

The Devil and Daniel Webster

The influence of *The Devil and Daniel Webster* on English-language Faust films can scarcely be overstated. The film owes an enormous debt to Marlowe: the diabolical contract signed in blood; the conniving, comic devil, although of a more rustic variety than usual; the infernal siren who distracts the hero from repentance; and the ethical disintegration of the protagonist. In addition, from Goethe the film inherits the redemptive female and the surprise happy ending, and from the numerous modern stage adaptations, the diminution of the hero to an ordinary citizen. However, this memorable film also adds a number of innovations to the Faust scenario: the iconic vow to the Devil; the juxtaposition of the redemptive female and the femme fatale; the savior figure, who intervenes to rescue the protagonist from the Devil at the eleventh hour. These additions pervade the other English-language films discussed in this chapter.

The Devil and Daniel Webster began life in 1936 as a short story penned by Stephen Vincent Benét, developed into an opera in 1937, and in 1941 was translated into a film bearing the title *All That Money Can Buy*, directed by William Dieterle (who played the role of Gretchen's brother Valentine in Murnau's *Faust*)[30] with a screenplay by Benét. The quandary over the film's title reveals a great deal about the social climate of the 1940s: producers feared that the term "Devil" in the title might arouse disapproval in the Bible Belt south, whereas the name Daniel Webster, recalling the famous nineteenth-century US statesman and senator, identified the film as a "period piece," a hard sell in the 1940s. Ultimately, the producers decided to take the risk and return to the original title. Unfortunately, their concern appears to have been well-founded since this splendid film was not a financial success in 1941, [31] although it has since become recognized as the Ur-English-language Faust film.

The film Americanizes the Faust legend, setting the action in Cross Corners, New Hampshire, 1841, while reminding the audience that this could happen anytime, anywhere. For his twentieth-century Faust, Benét selects not an eminent philosopher/physician/theologian, but an ordinary farmer in New Hampshire, who has had bad luck all his life. Perhaps his name, Jabez Stone, reflects the rocky path he has traveled. Not dreams of power, knowledge, or experience, but practical reality motivates this Faust figure, whose bad luck reaches its climax one Sunday morning as Jabez, his wife Mary, and his mother Ma Stone prepare to go to church. An overdue mortgage hovers; hard times make cash spare; Jabez has even secretly purloined his wife's butter money. All hell breaks loose when the family dog injures the prize pig Jabez plans to give to old Miser Stevens in lieu of the overdue mortgage. Then, when a big bag of seed Jabez had reserved as a back-up for the unpaid mortgage splits and spills on the ground, the exasperated farmer utters the vow that will resonate throughout so many English-language Faust films: "I vow it's enough to make a man want to sell his soul to the devil! And I would, too, for two cents!" In one of the film's most memorable moments, Jabez opens his clenched fist to find two big copper pennies ominously nestled in his palm. Then from a dark penumbra emerges the Devil figure, Mr. Scratch, who introduces himself with an incendiary calling card and a diabolical chuckle, offering Jabez the money and success that has always eluded him. So Scratch and Jabez go into the barn where Scratch uncovers a pile of Hessian gold hidden beneath a loose plank – recalling the Antichrist of the medieval biblical plays, who often bribes his victims with bags of gold. As the Devil and his "client" prepare to strike their bargain, Scratch produces the traditional contract. When Jabez demurs at the inflated price demanded, Scratch cavalierly brushes aside all objections: "A soul – a soul is nothing. Can you see it, smell it, touch it? This soul – your soul – is nothing against seven whole years of good luck!" A slick con man, Scratch gets Jabez cheap, granting him a measly seven years rather than the traditional twenty-four; but then in reputation and accomplishment Jabez Stone hardly rivals Doctor Faustus. So after a prick of his finger, Jabez signs the contract in blood. In another vivid cinematic moment, as he departs, Scratch deeply sears the contract due date into the bark of an oak tree with his cigar. The compact finalized, Jabez gets rich, buys a big house, and degenerates from an honest, caring neighbor and devoted husband into an exploiter of his fellow farmers and an unfaithful spouse.

Like Marlowe's hero, Jabez runs the gamut of the seven deadly sins. First, he falls prey to *avarice*; no matter how much money he accumulates, he must have more and more and more. When a hailstorm devastates all of his neighbors' crops, leaving only Jabez's fields miraculously unscathed, Jabez pretends to aid his neighbors while actually luring them into draconian contracts, squeezing them more ruthlessly than did his former persecutor, Miser Stevens. Avarice leads to *wrath*. Jabez catches a hungry neighbor fishing from a pond on his land, and, like the bully he has become, fires a pistol as the interloper scampers away. And, as in Marlowe's tragedy, *lechery* looms large among Jabez's sins. The temptress, a seductive demon-woman named Belle D (Devil? Damned?), bearing a letter of reference from Scratch himself, mysteriously appears as the child's nursemaid the night that Jabez's son Daniel (named after the famous senator) is born. Filled with joy at the birth of his son and remorse for his past deeds, Jabez teeters on the edge of contrition, and, like Marlowe's Mephistopheles, Scratch quickly dispatches a female temptress to distract the hero from thoughts of repentance. Moreover, for an American audience of the 1940s, Belle's enticing French accent would immediately establish her problematic morality. In addition, Jabez indulges in the sins of *gluttony* and *sloth*. The industrious farmer, who earlier expressed his love for seed and soil, hires others to work his fields, while he squanders his precious time and money drinking, gambling, and fox hunting on the Sabbath. Finally, Jabez commits the sin of *pride*, flaunting his wealth by building a huge house and establishing Belle as the mistress of his mansion, dressing in fancy clothes, and ignoring his former friends, his disapproving mother, and his patient but unassuming wife.

As in Marlowe's tragedy, the time of reckoning finally arrives. Swollen with self-conceit, Jabez throws a huge house party to celebrate his new mansion and invites everyone of status, including his friend Daniel Webster. To Jabez's chagrin, no one attends the grand affair except a wraithlike Miser Stevens (who, like Jabez, is a "client" of Mr. Scratch) and a horde of lost souls from "over the mountains." Webster does finally arrive and pleads with Jabez to tear up the penalizing contracts he has made with his neighbors. However, blinded by avarice, Jabez refuses, blaming everything on his long-suffering wife whom he orders out of the house.

Thus, Webster, Mary, and little Daniel depart, leaving Jabez alone in the eerie mansion with only Mr. Scratch, Belle, and the pack of hungry shades for company. During a ghoulish danse macabre, the malicious Belle literally dances Miser Stevens to death, and hearing a poignant shriek from a moth handily captured by Scratch in a kerchief, Jabez realizes to his horror that the crying insect represents Stevens's soul. Too late, Jabez, like Marlowe's Faustus before him, realizes that the soul is not a trifle after all.

The denouement departs radically from all previous Faustian scripts, introducing the savior figure who rescues the hero from the Devil. With the seven years up and the payment of the bond due, Scratch offers to grant his victim a reprieve if he will hand over his son as a surrogate sacrifice. This proposition shocks Jabez back to reality. Adamantly refusing this blackmail, he realizes for the first time how much he loves both his son and his wife. Springing on his horse, Jabez gallops frantically after Webster, Mary, and little Daniel, throwing himself on the mercy of his former friend and his forbearing wife. The Patient Griselda Mary never wavers in her devotion to her profligate husband, and Webster, a fabled defender of the underdog, generously agrees to plead Jabez's case with the Devil, vowing: "I'd fight 10,000 devils to save a New Hampshire man."

What follows finds no precedent in any previous recreation of the Faust legend. Jabez and Webster return to the fatal barn to meet the Devil, with the typical sexism of the 1940s banishing Mary. When the Devil arrives, Webster and Scratch begin negotiations for the soul of Jabez Stone. Having exhausted all of his legal expertise, Webster evokes the Constitution and the Bill of Rights: "You shall not have this man! A man isn't property! Mr. Stone is an American citizen and no American citizen can be forced into the service of a foreign Prince." Scratch vehemently denies the title of a foreign Prince, explaining in lines trenchant with irony: "When the first wrong was done to the first Indian, I was there. When the first slaver put out for the Congo, I stood on the deck . . . To tell the truth, Mr. Webster, though I don't like to boast of it, my name is older in this country than yours." Again appealing to the Constitution, Webster insists on a trial by jury: "Let it be any court you choose, so it is an American judge and an American jury! Let it be the quick or the dead; I'll abide the issue." He then adds with a touch of bravado: "If I can't win this case with a jury, you will have me, too. If two New Hampshire men aren't a match for the Devil, we might as well give this country back to the Indians." Scratch takes the great orator at his word, and Webster agrees to defend Jabez Stone before a jury of the damned, a motley crew of notorious American renegades including the most demonized traitor in American history, the Revolutionary War general who betrayed George Washington, Benedict Arnold. Webster's eloquent defense celebrates the dominant discourse of twentieth-century America, the belief in the dignity of the free, autonomous individual, a dignity surviving even the sulfurous fires of hell. As Hedges suggests, Webster's defense may also be read as "a statement of faith in the idea of a unique American destiny that places it above the rest of the world."[32] Thus with his stirring rhetoric Webster moves even the damned to compassion; the dominant ideology of the time prevails; the jury finds for the defendant; and the Devil is bested.

Compared to the overreachers of Marlowe and Goethe, Jabez Stone represents a much reduced Faust figure, and his desire for financial success seems considerably more mundane than the lofty aspirations of his predecessors. Perhaps the focus on wealth in Benét's version reflects the centrality of the almighty dollar in the American mythology, a centrality still relevant today but even more crucial in 1941 to an America still in the throes of the Great Depression. Nevertheless, in our own time of recent recession and unemployment, of con artists, Ponzi schemes, and foreclosures, Jabez's willingness to make a bad deal with the Devil still has an uncomfortable resonance, as does the film's demonization of the financial world of bankers and moneylenders.

If *The Devil and Daniel Webster* follows modernist trends by deflating its hero to an Everyman figure, the superman qualities associated with the legend have been displaced from the victim, Jabez Stone, to the rescuer, Daniel Webster, historically a renowned US senator and fabled champion of the working man. According to legend, this American folk hero possessed a number of the mythic powers, such as the control of nature, for which sorcerers traditionally bartered their souls, as well as the rhetorical skill associated with Marlowe's Faustus. This eloquent wonder-worker thus takes the titan role normally played by the Faust figure. He even displays Faustian ambition, aspiring to be President of the United States. However, the Devil thwarts this ambition because Webster proves to be that rare individual, an honest politician. In one scene, while Webster pens a persuasive address defending the rights of the embattled farmers, Scratch whispers in his ear that if he delivers the speech, he will never be President of the United States.

Like almost all the post-Goethe treatments of the Faust legend, *The Devil and Daniel Webster* redeems its protagonist at the eleventh hour, and, as in Goethe's drama, a devoted woman plays a principal role in his salvation. As Thomas Cooksey remarks: "Central, especially to the early

American contribution to the tradition, is the addition of a wife to the Faust figure."[33] Jabez's wife Mary assumes the role of the faithful, loving woman played by Gretchen in Goethe's *Faust*, soliciting Daniel Webster to save her husband and acting as the Good Angel to Belle's Evil one.

The Devil and Daniel Webster domesticates not only the Faust figure but also his infernal tempter to the milieu of rural America. The name Old Scratch appears to have been a commonplace nickname for the Devil in pre-Civil War America,[34] the same name employed by Washington Irving in "The Devil and Tom Walker," published approximately 100 years before Benét's short story.[35] Although Benét's coaxing, cagey Devil lacks the complexity of Marlowe's tormented demon and the sophistication of Goethe's urbane fiend, he brilliantly mimics the Devil of the biblical plays and the Vice of the moralities. An uncanny combination of the homespun and the menacing, like his baleful ancestor the morality Vice, Scratch is both entertainingly comic and scary as hell, and he steals the film even as he steals carrots, peach pie, and immortal souls. Mr. Scratch establishes the template for all of the Devils in the twentieth- and twenty-first-century cinematic appropriations that I will examine in this chapter (in Figure 5.3 see Walter Huston in his brilliant portrayal as the conniving Mr. Scratch).

Like all the Faustian plays and films treated in this study, *The Devil and Daniel Webster* comments on the social issues of its time, in this case 1941, a period of depression and financial struggle. Moreover, although owing much to the moralities, *The Devil and Daniel Webster* focuses on the political conflict with the issues of good and evil clearly delineated along political lines: evil is equated with predatory capitalism and good with the honest but exploited worker. Interestingly, the Devil on the medieval stage was also frequently associated with socially privileged individuals. Cox cites an instance in the biblical drama, the N-Town *Passion Play I*, in which "the devil is dressed and behaves like an arrogant courtier," and he argues that in the pre-Reformation secular moralities, the Devils are often used to satirize the social abuses that were perpetrated almost exclusively by members of the upper class,[36] as we see in *The Devil and Daniel Webster*. More specifically, the social context of the film details the clash between the corporate landowner and the farmer and between the moneylender and the small businessman, with the loan-shark Scratch, armed with contracts, paralleling the film's bankers, fortified with similar legal paraphernalia. Robert Singer supports this interpretation, observing that the film "contextualizes the sociopolitical crises of the Depression and World War II with the genre conventions of Dieterle's noir stylistics, thus demonstrating the polymorphic quality of the Faust legend."[37] At the end of the play, the

Figure 5.3 Walter Huston plays Mr. Scratch in the 1941 film, *The Devil and Daniel Webster*, directed by William Dieterle. Photograph by John Springer Collection/Corbis Historical/Getty Images.

jury nullifies Jabez's deed with the Devil and the exonerated defendant gratefully tears up the punitive agreements he has made with his neighbors. Thus, at least in this extremely patriotic fable of the 1940s, the jury of American citizens, even though dead and damned, sides with the individual against the establishment and America is not allowed to go to the Devil.

Alias Nick Beal

In 1949, eight years after *The Devil and Daniel Webster*, Hollywood adapted the Faust legend to the mode of cinema noir in a film titled *Alias Nick Beal*, directed by John Farrow and written by Jonathan Latimer and Mindre Lord.[38] Although replete with stereotyped characters and predictable situations, of more historical interest than entertainment value, this minor effort showcases the central aspects of the Faust rubric as first codified by Marlowe and later developed by Benét. These features, which will be replayed in American and British cinema throughout the following six decades, include the following: the fatal vow, "I would sell my soul to the Devil for . . ."; the suave, demonic confidence-man; the diabolic contract; the Madonna/temptress binary; the degeneration of the Faust figure; Faustus's rescue by a savior figure; and, departing from Marlowe but following Goethe and Benét, the last-minute salvation of the protagonist. Moreover, the film's hero, Joseph Foster, whose initials replicate those of Johannes Faustus, like his predecessors in Marlowe and Goethe but unlike so many twentieth- and twenty-first-century Faust avatars, is not an ordinary Everyman but an exceptional individual, in this case, that rare commodity, an honest lawyer. He is also a self-made man, the champion of the common people, and the befriender of wayward boys. Foster represents the ideal of 1940s America, even as Marlowe's Faustus – adept in philoso-phy, medicine, law, and divinity – embodies the ideal of Renaissance England.

The film takes place in the 1940s in an unidentified state somewhere in the United States, everywhere and nowhere. As the film opens, Foster, the state prosecutor, has embarked on a crusade to convict one of the state's most notorious racketeers and rid his community of the gangsters who intimidate and bully the "little people," but vital evidence necessary for conviction has been destroyed. In frustration, Foster utters the fatal oath, "I'd give my soul to nail him." As in *The Devil and Daniel Webster* and numerous subsequent versions of the legend, the Devil promptly appears, this time in the form of a note from an unknown source promising, "If you want to nail Hanson, meet me at the China Coast Café."

As Hedges aptly observes: "The China Coast Café, where he [Foster] is to meet the sender, is a quintessential noir hangout on the waterfront, complete with a neon sign, a foggy atmosphere, and the whistles of off-shore boats."[39] In this gloomy, claustrophobic setting, reminiscent of a dozen film noir "gin joints," Foster encounters Nick Beal – Agent (whose name conflates "Old Nick" and "Beelzebub"), a slick, sophisticated con man totally lacking the humor traditionally associated with human-ity's tempter. However, Nick soon reveals himself as a canny manipulator of human beings, like his predecessor the Vice in the moralities. Intuiting the fatal weakness hidden in all individuals, Nick immediately recognizes that Foster's *hamartia* derives from his idealism: he desires to be Governor, drive out the racketeers, eliminate corruption, and transform his state into a caring, safe community. Understanding the nature of his victim, Nick does not offer Foster power, knowledge, or wealth; instead, he promises him a chance to become Governor and fulfill his idealistic dreams. Nor does Satan's emissary initially mention a contract. Rather, Nick Beal produces the evidence from Hanson's accounts that Foster believed was destroyed, and Foster, accepting the dangerous proposition that the meritorious end, convicting Hanson, justifies the dubious means, seizing evidence without a warrant, embarks on a series of compromises that almost destroys him.

Also deviating from the traditional Faustian rubric, Foster's corruption begins before rather than after the contract. First, Foster confiscates evidence without a warrant. Next he accepts $25,000 from Nick, whom he recognizes as a devious operator, to help finance his campaign for Governor. Sinking deeper into ethical equivocation, he pays off a blackmailer, Hanson's bookkeeper, who threatens to reveal his theft of the evidence. Finally, in order to be elected Governor, he allows Nick, now his right-hand man, to make a deal with the biggest crook in the state, thus undermining his goal of cleansing the community of racketeers, while ignoring Nick's other shady machinations, such as extortion and bribery. Even as his professional ethics deteriorate, so his personal morals degenerate. He becomes estranged from his loyal wife Martha (echoes of Goethe's Margarete) – the moral center of the movie, who tries to stem his ethical devolution – and begins an affair with Donna Allan, the blonde temptress enlisted by Beal to hasten Foster's debasement. Therefore, even without a contract, Foster sells his soul for easy success and sordid sex, becoming an unfaithful husband and an ethically tarnished politician.

The film develops the Madonna/temptress dichotomy introduced in *The Devil and Daniel Webster*, a dichotomy that will become a staple of English-language Faust films. As in Marlowe's *Doctor Faustus*, when the Devil fears the loss of his victim, he enlists reinforcements in the form of a beautiful vamp, in this case Donna Allan, whom he hopes will play the Evil Angel to Martha's Good one. Donna re-enacts the roles of Helen of Troy and Belle, with this difference: Donna is not herself a damned soul or succubus, only an appealing, down-on-her-luck blonde manipulated by Nick Beal and recruited to seduce Foster. Moreover, departing from the Faust template and anticipating Lola in *Damn Yankees*, Donna falls in love with her prey and warns him against Nick, although too late to prevent Foster's fall.

The identity of Nick Beal remains murky throughout most of the film. When Reverend Garfield, Foster's friend and spiritual guide, expresses his suspicions concerning Nick's infernal heritage, Foster scoffs: "This is the twentieth century. No one has believed in such things since the days of the Salem Witch trials." Even when Nick presents the contract, its significance remains unclear. Nick has surreptitiously arranged to frame Foster for the murder of Hanson's bookkeeper, the blackmailer Henry Finch, and to prevent his indictment, Foster agrees to sign a compact promising to appoint Nick to the position of Keeper of the State Seal. The contract states that if Foster fails to make this appointment, he will accompany Nick to the Island of Almas Pardidus, which Foster only later learns means "The Island of Lost Souls." Desperate to escape prosecution for murder, Foster signs the contract, not in blood this time but with a strong, clear signature.

Ultimately, Foster achieves self-knowledge, realizing that no end, however meritorious, can justify the shoddy means he has employed to achieve the Governorship. In his inauguration speech, Foster admits his guilt, resigns as Governor, and names his impeccably honest Lieutenant Governor as his successor, thereby maneuvering through the traditional steps of repentance: contrition, confession, and amendment. Of course, since he has resigned as Governor, he cannot appoint Nick as Keeper of the State Seal; thus in abdicating the Governorship, he forfeits his soul, or so he thinks. However, persuaded by Reverend Garfield of the invalidity of the contract, Foster tries to return to his wife residing at the Garfield residence, only to find that the cabby driving his escape car is none other than Nick Beal.

The denouement of the film reprises the conclusion of *The Devil and Daniel Webster*. Nick drives Foster to the China Coast Café, and in this portentous locale, Reverend Garfield (taking the role of Daniel Webster) and Martha (re-enacting the devoted wife Mary) confront the Devil and his victim for the climactic battle for Foster's soul. Assuming the role of savior, Reverend Garfield casts the demonic pact to the floor, throwing the Bible on top of it. The Bible thus trumps the contract, even as, according to Christian doctrine, Christ's sacrifice trumped the Devil, and Foster is saved from the Prince of Darkness, not as in Benét's film by the eloquence of man, but by the holy word of God. Unwilling to touch the sacerdotal book even to secure his contract, yet furious at being "cheated" out of his prize, Nick acknowledges his ancestry in a double allusion to the medieval drama and Marlowe's *Doctor Faustus*: "You've jockeyed me into a kind of morality play … It's always been bell and candle and that worn out book of yours."[40] Nick Beal's final lines also recall the poignant regret expressed by Marlowe's passionate fiend: "In every one there is a seed of destruction, a fatal weakness. You know that now, Foster. You're lucky, luckier than I was when I fell. But that was a long time ago."

Despite its adherence to many of the traditional elements associated with the Faust legend, *Alias Nick Beal* totally lacks the thrilling ambiguity so central to the Faustian ethos, as well as the provocative mingling of the comic and the serious. This film, written and produced a long time ago, with its often strident moralistic value system, its rather wooden acting, and its dated dialogue, to a new millennium audience might seem rather quaint, as distant in time as the Fall of Lucifer referred to by the Devil. Nevertheless, like so many Faust movies, this film tells us a great deal about the time in which it was made: its concern for corruption in politics (as big an issue today as it was in the 1940s); its clearly demarcated system of right and wrong (still endorsed by some but often considered naïve in this age of relativity); its Hays Office prudery (Joseph and Donna never even kiss, although the film makes it patent that they are having an affair); and its Bible Belt faith (which still has its fervent, albeit dwindling following). *Alias Nick Beal* owes a good deal to Marlowe and even more to Benét, but its greatest debt is to the zeitgeist of its time.

Damn Yankees

If *The Devil and Daniel Webster* indicts America's valorization of wealth and success as the ultimate good, *Damn Yankees* spoofs another American weakness – its national obsession with sports. Originally a 1955 hit musical, directed by George Abbott and Stanley Donen, *Damn Yankees* was translated by the same crew into an equally successful film in 1958.[41] Humor has always been an integral part of the Faust legend, as well as of the moralities that partially inspired it, but despite the sometimes comic treatment of evil in *The Devil and Daniel Webster*, the film, like its dramatic antecedents, remains basically a serious examination of exploitation and freedom, damnation and salvation. Conversely, *Damn Yankees* is always tongue-in-cheek and never takes itself too seriously, as indicated by the humorous profanity of its title. Moreover, *Damn Yankees* adds a provocative innovation to the Faustian scenario: a hero who fervently desires not knowledge, power, sexual pleasure, or money, but a winning team for the Washington Senators, and is willing to sell his soul to achieve this goal.

Set in Washington, DC in the 1950s, this satirical musical features another Faust as Everyman, this time a real estate agent and fanatical baseball partisan named Joe Boyd. Joe has a good marriage and a loving wife, but he feels something lacking in his life. In his youth, Joe secretly dreamed of being a professional baseball player, and he has sequestered his old spiked shoes and baseball glove in his closet for twenty-five years. Also, as his wife Meg (shades of Goethe's Margarete) complains, during half the year she endures the role of a baseball widow, amusing herself with girlfriends while Joe sits mesmerized in front of the television watching his favorite team suffer defeat after defeat after defeat.

The film opens on one such evening in 1958 when the particularly dismal showing of the Senators leads Joe to utter the iconic vow: "One long ballhitter, that's what we need. I'd sell my soul to the Devil for one long ballhitter." This blasphemous cue summons Applegate, a fast-talking infernal entrepreneur, whose name reminds the audience of the Devil's mischief as a gatecrasher in the Garden of Eden. Like Devils before him, Applegate tempts Joe with his secret yearnings: Joe will regain his youth (echoes here of Goethe), become the greatest baseball star in history, and the Washington Senators will win the pennant. However, unlike Marlowe's Faustus, given twenty-four years of pleasure, Joe will receive a scant eight months before Applegate seizes his soul. When Joe asks: "What happens after I stop being a baseball player?" the Devil replies dryly: "Well, of course, that's fairly well known." When Joe hesitates, Applegate coaxes: "I have chosen you, the most dedicated partisan of the noble Washington Senators, to be the hero who leads them out of the wilderness to the championship." The combined lures of youth, victory for his team, and the Moses analogy prove irresistible. Joe falls.

The rest of the film provides standard Faustian fare but always with a twist and a chuckle. Applegate insists on a contract but accepts a double handshake in lieu of the standard bloody signature, which he rejects as too "phony." Joe, a shrewd real estate salesman, makes a commitment but with an escape clause, allowing him until midnight on September 24 to change his mind. True to his word, Applegate transforms Joe into an athletic young man, as handsome as Tab Hunter, and Joe leaves his wife and home to embark on a more heroic life. Again, true to his word, Applegate arranges an audition with the crusty manager of the Washington Senators, a trial run that not surprisingly proves spectacularly successful: Joe hits ball after ball after ball out of the park and is hired on the spot. So, Joe joins the team – a cadre of good-natured players with more dedication than ability, as they flaunt in the rollicking song, "You Gotta Have Heart" – and becomes a star with a coterie of adoring fans, while the Senators embark on a winning streak that puts them into competition for the coveted pennant. Yet, unlike many of his predecessors who initially exult in the fruits of their contracts, even from the beginning fame leaves Joe unfulfilled, as he yearns for his wife and home. Finally, Joe seeks to rent a room from Meg, who fails to recognize her rejuvenated husband. Despite her loneliness, Meg remains steadfast in her belief that her husband will return; however, her friends encourage her to take in a boarder as an antidote to depression, so Joe finds a haven near his wife in his old study.

Fearful that Joe will exercise his escape clause, like Marlowe's Mephistopheles and other of his fiendish antecedents, Applegate recruits reinforcements in the form of an irresistible siren, Lola, temptress extraordinaire, to seduce Joe and make him forget his wife, for, as Applegate grouses: "Wives! They cause me more trouble than the Methodist church!" In one of the most memorable musical sequences of the film, Lola, masquerading as Miss West Indies, strips to her working clothes – slinky black leotard, black lace fishnet stockings, stiletto heels – seeking to tantalize Joe with the sultry number, "Whatever Lola Wants, Lola Gets." However, in this case, Lola does not get what she wants, and the unassailable Joe goes home to his wife.[42] Names usually resonate morality play fashion in Faust narratives, and the name Joe Hardy probably suggests both his Everyman role and his spiritual invulnerability, although "hardy" may also refer to Joe's prowess on the baseball diamond.

A typically wily Devil figure, Applegate is not so easily foiled. Livid at Joe's perfidy and Lola's failure, the Devil hatches a plot designed to prevent Joe from reneging on his contract, spreading the rumor that Joe Hardy may be an alias for the notorious Slinky McCoy, a corrupt minor league player who threw a game in Mexico City and has been on the lam ever since. Since no one in Hannibal, Missouri remembers a Joe Hardy, the baseball commission subpoenas Joe to appear to defend himself. Things look bad for Joe until the trusting Meg and her supportive friends, hoping to exonerate her boarder, appear as material witnesses, perjuring themselves by claiming to be childhood friends of Joe Hardy in Hannibal. All of this occurs on the evening of September 24. The witching hour comes and goes as prosecutors grill Joe and listen to the evidence of his defenders, and rather than be transformed to his original shape by the Devil in the presence of his wife and her friends, Joe relinquishes his chance for escape and the cunning Applegate wins Joe's soul. The clock strikes twelve and Joe realizes he is damned.

With no Daniel Webster or Reverend Garfield to act as savior, things look bleak for Joe. Thus, "two lost souls on the highway of life," Joe and Lola bond in their misery and spend the night before the big championship game commiserating together in a torrid nightclub amid contorted Boschean dancers; yet, despite one chaste kiss, even damned and hopeless, Joe remains true to his wife Meg. Yet, unbeknown to Joe, Applegate does not intend to keep his promise and allow the Senators to win the pennant in the championship play-off the next day. Instead, the Devil, true to form, has conceived a sneaky, malignant plan. The fans of the Washington Senators have doggedly supported their losing team through many dismal seasons. Now, exploiting the success of their star, Applegate has churned the hopes of these fans into a frenzy of expectation that he plans to crush at the most suspenseful moment of the championship game with the hated New York Yankees. Since this game will be played on September 25, the day after Applegate has taken possession of Joe's soul, Applegate will force the star to throw the game, hoping to galvanize a reaction equal to the national despair that followed the stock market crash of 1929.

However, things do not turn out as Applegate has planned. As in *Alias Nick Beal*, the temptress has fallen in love with her intended victim, and Lola, determined to save Joe, slips four sleeping pills into Applegate's glass of Demon Rum the night before the game. The next day, Applegate sleeps through most of the big game, only awakening at the last minute to discover that the game is nearly over. Furious, after vindictively metamorphosing Lola back into her crone-like former self, Applegate rushes to the stadium just as the game enters its final ninth inning. The Senators lead 1 to 0; the Yankees are at bat; the batter leans into a fast pitch and sends a towering fly ball deep into Joe Hardy's territory as Joe runs farther into the outfield for an easy catch and a third out, thereby sewing up the pennant for the Washington Senators. But as Joe lopes backward, Applegate changes the buff, big-league hero back into the paunchy real estate agent (echoes of Murnau's Faust). Amazingly, the middle-aged couch potato snags the catch and the Senators become the American League champions. Joe Boyd has heart!

The Washington Senators have won the pennant, but Joe's soul remains in jeopardy. Amid the jubilant chaos as euphoric fans surge onto the baseball field, Joe Boyd flees to the refuge of his wife Meg, pleading for her forgiveness. True to her Patient Griselda prototype, Meg welcomes her husband back, no questions asked. Clearly for Meg Boyd, as for Mary Stone, love is never having to say one is sorry. As Meg cuddles her husband's head, crooning softly, Applegate materializes to claim the soul he has contractually won. Invisible to all but Joe, Applegate tempts his lost prize with grandiose rewards, including youth, Lola, and even a victory for the Senators in the World Series. However, this time Joe turns a deaf ear to fame while literally embracing domestic bliss, and true love conquers all.

Damn Yankees cleverly parodies both the moralities and the Faust legend. Applegate, cast in the mold of the comic Vice, revels in his villainy: "Enjoy it Joe," he smirks, "I do." He also relishes tricks; magically lighting his cigarette, he quips: "I'm handy with fire." Ironically, this modern Vice, straight out of the six-hundred-year-old morality play tradition, rebukes the siren Lola: "Your methods are too old-fashioned," even though Applegate's gesture and language establish him throughout the film as simultaneously the most contemporary and the most old-fashioned of demons.

Similarly, Lola, substituting for Helen of Troy, provides a hilarious burlesque of one of the most durable stereotypes in literature and film, woman as temptress. Lola, like Belle, is a lost soul, originally the ugliest woman in Providence, Rhode Island, who bartered her spiritual salvation for earthly beauty. However, in her complexity, Lola represents a departure from the Faust legend which typically marginalizes both Madonnas and temptresses.

Ultimately, Joe Hardy is redeemed, partially by his own incorruptible innocence and partially by the love of two women: one good and one bad. The final scene of the film enacts a *psychomachia* recalling the moralities, as Love or Mercy (represented by the devoted Meg) and the Vice (embodied in the apoplectic Applegate) vie for the soul of the penitent Everyman/ Faust/Joe Boyd. This scene also recalls the struggles of the Good and Evil Angels for the soul of Marlowe's Faustus as well as the final conflict between the cherubic angels and the sinister devils in Goethe's drama. However, in this revision of the Faust legend/morality play, evil does not have a chance: the values of 1950s America prevail as Joe chooses domestic happiness over fame, and, as in so many of the Faust plays and films following Goethe, love bests the Devil.

Damn Yankees, despite its humor, offers more than a clever spoof of the Faust tradition and the moralities; it also employs these traditions to craft a trenchant satire of the mania for sports in the United States, an obsession the country shares with much of the world. In addition, at least according to Andrew Bush, *Damn Yankees*, written approximately ten years after World War II, is not only a satire of the American sports obsession but also a celebration of America's strength and innocence. As Bush explains: "In this Americanization of the Faust theme, Joe's strength was represented as a concomitant of his innocence," and the temptress whom he resists is not only Lola, but something beyond her, "a vision of the corrupting force of knowledge, sophistication, and high culture, in a word, of Europe, of which *Faust* itself was the ready examplar."[43] Thus, in this very American Faust fable, Joe's innocence combined with Meg's love resists the temptations of Lola and the Devil to foil all Applegate's machination.

Marlowe's Faustus learns (too late) to burn his necromantic books; Goethe's Faust discovers (before his death) that to live free means to eschew the prop of magic; Jabez Stone acknowledges (before the end) that money does not bring happiness; Joseph Foster recognizes (at the eleventh hour) that no end, however meritorious, can justify compromise and corruption; and Joe Boyd finally realizes (just in time) that there is something in life more important than baseball.

Bedazzled

As discussed above, Marlowe's *Doctor Faustus* boasts an unusual ancestry, the unlikely offspring of classical tragedy and medieval jest book. Some of the progeny of this strange marriage have stressed the comic elements of the drama, others the tragic or epic aspects. In *Damn Yankees*, George Abbott and Stanley Donen attempt to create a Faustian potpourri of the humorous and the homiletic, and perhaps encouraged by his success in this 1950s musical, Donen, aided by screenwriters Peter Cook and Dudley Moore, who also starred in the film, essayed a more farcical treatment of the Faust legend in the 1967 film *Bedazzled* (whose title suggests "bedeviled").[44] Like William Mountfort's *Harlequin Faust*, which focuses on the gallimaufry and buffoonery of the center section of *Doctor Faustus, Bedazzled* strips the Faust legend of its tragic frame and retains only its jest book tomfoolery, albeit repackaged in a more sophisticated parcel. At the same time, the film ironizes the Faust narrative, deflating the Faustian hero, the demonic tempter, and the entire metaphysical apparatus associated with the legend. As appropriate to the iconoclastic 1960s, this irreverent parody of the Faust legend turns all tradition topsy-turvy.

First, the film belittles its hero Stanley Moon, who epitomizes an anti-Faust for an anti-heroic age. Instead of an eminent scholar like Marlowe's and Goethe's overachievers, Stanley is a diminutive, short-order cook at a fast food restaurant appropriately named Whimpy's Burgers. While tossing burgers, Stanley moons over the statuesque waitress named Margaret (more echoes of Goethe's Margarete), who works at the same eatery and barely knows that he exists. Although Marlowe's Faustus demands a wife from Mephistopheles and Goethe's Faust lusts to seduce Margarete, sexual desire remains an appurtenance to these original diabolical pacts, not their cause. Indeed, Stanley appears to be the first man willing to sell his soul to the Devil for love of a woman since the fourth-century servant of Senator Proterius of Caesarea reputedly engaged Satan's aid in winning his master's comely daughter in marriage.[45] Despairing of achieving his desideratum, the love of Margaret, Stanley laments: "I've got a boring job, no money, no prospects, no girlfriend." Goaded by despair,

Stanley, imitating Goethe's hero, seeks to end his life but proves unable even to pull off a successful suicide. Enter the Devil, unaccountably named George Spiggot, an anti-Mephistopheles for a skeptical age. Sporting a red cloak and black suit and equipped with the traditional contract, George initially appears the stereotypical tempter. Interrupting Stanley's abortive hanging, George offers Stanley an unusual deal: seven remains the magic number, but instead of the seven years of good luck granted Jabez Stone, Stanley will receive seven wishes in return for his soul. When Stanley hesitates, George echoes Mr. Scratch: "All I want from you is something you don't even know you have – your soul," later adding, "You see, a soul's rather like your appendix: totally expendable." So Stanley signs the contract in blood with the understanding that in return he will receive seven wishes; if anything goes wrong, he can always terminate the wish by blowing a raspberry.

Even as the film diminishes its Faust figure, so it also deflates his tempter. We soon realize that George's self-assured, poised persona is only a façade, and that, like his dupe Stanley, he is a loser, who spends his time obsessed with the pettifoggery of evil: loosing pigeons to defecate on the bald heads of hatless passersby, releasing wasps to torment lolling flower children, ringing wrong numbers in the middle of the night, and, in general, playing puerile jokes on vulnerable people. Like Stanley, George has a boring job, no friends (except the Seven Deadly Sins), and no prospects. Stanley longs for Margaret; George, recalling the passionate yearning of Marlowe's Mephistopheles, hankers to return to his role as God's favorite angel. Finally, the film depicts a much more contemporary love-object for its diminished Faust. Street-smart and poised, totally unlike the naïve peasant girl seduced by Goethe's Faust, Margaret presents an anti-Margarete for a less romantic age.

Therefore, despite the inclusion of the diabolic contract and the ambivalent Devil – part Vice, part angel manqué – the film departs strikingly from the dramas of Marlowe and Goethe. However, it does retain, and indeed exaggerates to the point of burlesque, one aspect of Marlowe's play: the disparity between aspiration and achievement. Certainly, Stanley, the anti-Faust, never achieves the *summum bonum* for which he sells his soul, the love of Margaret. Although George promises Stanley seven wishes, Stanley fails to be specific enough when voicing his request, and the crafty Devil always finds a loophole, fulfilling the letter but not the spirit of the wishes so that the result of each wish turns out to be the very opposite of Stanley's desire. George transforms Stanley into an intellectual, an industrialist, a pop star, and, through a slip of the tongue, a fly on the wall. Finally, wishing for a loving relationship with Margaret in a serene and holy environment, Stanley (who forgot to specify his sex) ends up as a nun cocooned with Margaret in a convent. Between each vacuous episode in which the cagey Devil fools the obtuse hero, the film interweaves a witty colloquy between George and Stanley on the banality of evil and the impossibility of free will.

Ultimately, after tricking Stanley out of all seven wishes, the Devil makes an atypical decision, without precedent in Faustian literature. For centuries, we learn, the Devil and God have engaged in a competition for souls with the understanding that the first to secure one hundred billion souls will win the bout. This contest for souls draws loosely on the Book of Job but also perhaps on the opening debate in Heaven in Goethe's *Faust*. George hopes that after the competition has been resolved, he can reconcile with God and return to his status as God's favorite angel. The same day that George gulls Stanley into wasting his last wish, the Devil also hits the one hundred billion mark, and to celebrate his victory he commits an act of undiabolical clemency: for the first time in the history of the Faust legend, the Devil returns a contract to a client. So Stanley goes free and George proceeds to heaven, pushing past St. Peter, boasting that he has not only won the contest with God but has also committed one good deed. However, clearly not wishing to reinstate George/Satan/Lucifer, God, following the example of his cunning adversary, finds a loophole: according to St. Peter, George has failed the entrance exams since he committed his single act of kindness not for unselfish purposes but for personal advancement. At the conclusion of the movie, therefore, both Stanley and George resume their original occupations: Stanley, the boring job of flipping burgers, George, the tedious task of bedeviling humankind. However, Stanley, at least, has learned his lesson and remains content to be himself and to pursue Margaret in his own hopeless way, while the Devil wallows in his infernal discontent.

In the end, the trickster is tricked and God plays the same joke on the Devil that George has played on Stanley throughout the movie. Therefore, behind the apparently silly façade of the film lurks an un-Faustian nihilism, more akin to Voltaire's *Candide* than to either Marlowe's or Goethe's Faust dramas. *Bedazzled* was produced in 1967 during the heyday of the Theatre of the Absurd – Tom Stoppard's anti-*Hamlet* play, *Rosencrantz and Guildenstern Are Dead*, debuted on the London stage the same year – and the universe of *Bedazzled* mirrors an absurd universe in which all bargains are frauds and both God and the Devil are charlatans. If Murnau's *Faust* presents the most celebratory film version of the Faust legend,

Bedazzled may well offer the most deflative. Appropriately, the film concludes with the diabolical laughter of God.

Oh, God! You Devil

Cinematically, the 1980s ushered in a devilishly auspicious decade for the
Faust legend. Between 1984 and 1987, three different English-language
films feature Faust avatars bartering their souls to the Prince of Darkness,
and despite their very different personalities, these three Faust figures share
the same goal: musical stardom. The shift in desideratum from financial
success (*The Devil and Daniel Webster*), political power (*Alias Nick Beal*),
or sports celebrity (*Damn Yankees*) to rock stardom tells us something
about the value system of the 1980s.

  The first of these films celebrating musical celebrity, *Oh, God! You Devil*,
produced in 1984 and directed by Paul Bogart, offers a response to the
nihilism of *Bedazzled*, endorsing a world view as sentimental and affirmative as *Bedazzled*'s perspective is skeptical and pessimistic.[46] *Oh, God! You
Devil* is the third movie in the *Oh, God!* series, and a number of movie
reviewers have praised it as the best of the three, although some also found
the plot convoluted and the body-switching (reminiscent of *The Beauty of
the Devil*) confusing. Like so many of the English-language movies treated
in this chapter, the film serves as a palimpsest for *The Devil and Daniel
Webster* with its Everyman hero, its iconic vow, its redemptive wife, and,
particularly, its climactic contest, not a trial by jury this time but a poker
game with God himself taking the role of savior. It also adds an intriguing
twist: God and the Devil are portrayed by the same actor, George Burns.
Yet, the film also manifests the salient influence of *Damn Yankees* in its
Devil figure, its hero, and its tongue-in-cheek tone. The Devil, Harry
O. Tophet, whose sartorial elegance – red jacket with white pants, red
vest and red bow tie with black tux – contrasts sharply with God's
proletarian dress, recalls the similar attire of the debonair Applegate, and
Tophet's gusto for racial tension, pestilence, and plague parrots
Applegates's equally comic craving for the "bad old days" of calamity
and devastation. Additionally, Bobby's longing for his wife after his brief
fling with promiscuity re-enacts Joe Hardy's unswerving devotion to Meg.
Despite the supernatural aid rendered Bobby, the love for a good woman
provides a key element in his redemption, evoking one of the central motifs
of both *Damn Yankees* and Goethe's *Faust*. Finally, this film dramatizes the
search for identity and the motif of masquerade so characteristic of works
based on the Faust legend.

Although the story reveals most of the stigmata of the Faust legend, particularly as reimagined in the two immensely influential films, *The Devil and Daniel Webster* and *Damn Yankees, Oh, God! You Devil* often varies the script with surprising innovations. The Prologue, which establishes the setting as New York, 1960, opens not with the disillusioned hero invoking the Devil but with a distraught father calling on God to cure his feverish son. A shabby figure, dressed in a bill cap, dark jacket, khaki trousers, and tennis shoes appears in the street outside, checking his address book. As the film later reveals, the desperate man has invoked not the Devil, like the traditional Faust figure, but his powerful antithesis, God. Many critics have commented on the absence of God from Marlowe's *Doctor Faustus* and, indeed, from Faust adaptations and appropriations generally, for despite the Devil's literal presence in most of these plays and films, God invariably must act through His surrogates. Conversely, in this feel-good film, God moves from the wings and seizes center stage.

However, when the film takes us fast-forward twenty-four years to Los Angeles, 1984, the narrative returns to the traditional Faustian script. The feverish little boy has developed into a deeply frustrated Faust figure cast in the mold of Joe Boyd, a musician manqué/house husband, who does the laundry, buys the groceries, and cooks, supported both financially and emotionally by his devoted wife Wendy, while he strives futilely to fulfill his dreams of becoming a song writer. One day, struggling to succeed but battered by rejections, Bobby Shelton echoes Jabez Stone's famous vow: "I'd sell my soul to the Devil to make it in this business." Of course, the Devil, alias Harry O. Tophet, arrives promptly on cue. Here, as so often in Faust adaptations and appropriations, names prove significant. In the Old Testament, the word "Tophet," which originally referred to a place near Jerusalem dedicated to the horrible rites of human sacrifice, came to be associated with hell, thus providing an appropriate name for a Mephistophelean tempter. Living in an electronic age, Tophet, unlike previous tempters, does not telepathically hear Bobby's vow, but accesses it electronically on his car computer, which keeps him updated on current and potential clients. Later, encountering Bobby in the office of a musical promoter where Bobby and his agent await an appointment, Tophet offers Bobby a tempting proposition, promising to fulfill all of his dreams – stardom, gold records, the cover of *Time Magazine*, everything – if Bobby will sign a contract with him. He even proposes a trial period to test the validity of the contract (reminiscent of both Murnau's *Faust* and *Damn Yankees*), but he makes no mention of a soul or salvation or damnation. Frantic to get a break, Bobby dumps his longtime agent and agrees to sign the seven-year contract, but only on a "trial basis"; however, as he signs the fatal deed, his signature miraculously transforms into that of the rock star Billy Wayne, another of Tophet's recruits. Since Tophet now controls the lives of both young men, he simply switches their physical personae: in a body-switching that recalls *The Beauty of the Devil*, Bobby assumes the body and identity of the famous rock star Billy Wayne, and Billy takes Bobby's body and role as struggling musician and husband to Wendy. But although Billy will believe himself to be Bobby, Bobby will retain his own memories in Billy Wayne's body. For the first time fully realizing Tophet's identity, Bobby gasps, "Good God!" "Think again," Tophet wryly quips. Too late, Bobby realizes to his horror that he has gained fame and fortune at the stratospheric price not only of his soul but also of his identity.

Like most Faust figures before him, Bobby initially relishes the fruits of his contract: the thunderous applause; the adulation of screaming fans; the luscious groupies filling his bed, often in duos or trios; his face on the cover of *Time*; his private helicopter; his gorgeous twenty-four-room mountain-top mansion. However, Bobby soon becomes disillusioned with his bar-gain. After a brief five months of chaotic stardom, Bobby has had enough and longs for his former life. On the night of his sixth wedding anniversary, he returns to his favorite restaurant, where he encounters his wife with Billy Wayne, the ersatz Bobby Shelton, and, after a little quick math, realizes that Wendy is pregnant with his, not Billy's child. Feeling helpless and trapped, like his father before him, he desperately turns to God.

When Marlowe's Faustus calls on Christ, Lucifer appears instead. Bobby is more fortunate. In a Las Vegas hotel, Bobby pages "the Lord," who, blending modern technology with Old Testament miracle, answers the telephone, while providing a rainbow outside the window as an imprima-tur of his authenticity. In Marlowe's *Doctor Faustus*, shrouded as it is in ambiguity, we are never sure about the binding nature of the contract or the ubiquitous possibility of repentance. However, in *Oh, God! You Devil* the rules are clear: Bobby has made a contract with the Devil; thus, God cannot grant him a reprieve. So, like many Faust figures before him, Bobby falls into despair and attempts suicide.

The climax of the film reprises the trial scene in *The Devil and Daniel Webster*, but with a difference. In this pivotal moment, God challenges the Devil to a poker game with the soul of Bobby Shelton as the stake. According to the rubric approved by both adversaries, Bobby should belong to Tophet since he has signed the fatal contract; however, the Devil has reneged on his initial promise to grant Bobby a trial period. Therefore, the validity of the contract lies in a gray area, and God suggests a modern version of the trial by ordeal to decide the contract's legitimacy – not a medieval joust this time but a more contemporary contest, a poker game. Because each of the puissant adversaries possesses the power to control the cards, they decide to play "straight" and let the luckiest player win. If God wins, Bobby Shelton will be released from the contract and the Devil will be prohibited from meddling with any of the millions of souls protected by God, even if they call on God's Adversary; if the Devil wins, Bobby Shelton's soul will be forfeit and the Devil will have free rein to tempt all souls, even those watched over by God. With the stakes so high, the Devil folds. Then, when the two adversaries reveal their hands, Tophet realizes that God has been bluffing; He has nothing but divine chutzpah and a busted flush.

While God and the Devil engage in the monumental poker game, Bobby falls into despair, taking a massive overdose of drugs, and the body of Billy Wayne, containing the soul of Bobby Shelton, lies dying on Wayne's dressing room floor. However, when God wins the game and the wager, Bobby Shelton, having regained both his physical identity and his freedom, rises from the dead corpse of Billy Wayne, whose soul is presumably carried off to hell by Tophet. But before Bobby returns to his wife, God appears to him in the Las Vegas nightclub where Billy Wayne, alias Bobby Shelton, was performing. During their meeting, God explains that He has been protecting Bobby ever since answering his father's prayer and that He won Bobby's freedom from the Devil in a poker game. Nevertheless, the film denies its audience a fairytale ending. God, a no-nonsense Deity, never promises Bobby fame or fortune; he simply instructs Bobby to go home to his wife and be a loving father and husband. Thus, Bobby, like Joe Boyd, returns home, embraces his wife, and tells her he loves her.

The film's epilogue, occurring five years later, mirrors the prologue, showing a concerned Bobby sitting at the bedside of his very ill young daughter. Feeling his daughter's feverish brow, he utters a simple prayer, then croons the same ditty that his father sang to him thirty years before, a refrain from the movie *Guys and Dolls* beginning, "I have a horse right here, / His name is Paul Revere," a refrain underscoring both the upbeat tone and the gambling motif in both *Guys and Dolls* and *Oh, God! You Devil.* However, this time, the voice of God joins the refrain, "Can Do, Can Do," and we know that all is well and that not only the horse named Paul Revere but also Bobby and his daughter will survive and prosper.

Despite its similarity to many film versions of the Faust legend, in other ways *Oh, God! You Devil* deviates markedly from previous Faust reincarnations, particularly in its treatment of God. The presentation of an urbane, delightfully wicked Devil vanquished by an avuncular, proletarian God, who cares for his flock and even makes house calls, renders *Oh, God! You Devil* the most optimistic, feel-good version of the Faust legend yet to be immortalized in film.

Crossroads

In *The Devil and Daniel Webster*, the great orator stands before a jury of the damned, pleading for a second chance for his client: "It is the eternal right of every man to raise his fist against his fate. When he does, he is at a crossroads. You took the wrong turn and so did Jabez Stone." *Crossroads* reprises *The Devil and Daniel Webster* to dramatize the tale of another man who raised his fist against his fate, took a wrong turn, stood trial by a jury of the damned, and was redeemed by the melodic eloquence of his friend.

The opening shot of *Crossroads* also offers an hommage to Murnau's German adaptation: a young black man carrying a guitar, waiting at a bleak, lonely crossroads, a single leafless tree etched against a sepia sky. The camera then cuts to a recording studio where the fabled guitarist Robert Johnson, the greatest of all Mississippi bluesmen, who, according to blues legend, "traveled to a country crossroads [in Fulton Point] to sell his soul to the devil in exchange for masterful musical abilities," plays his heart out as he makes blues history. Blues legend insists that Johnson's records, "Cross Road Blues," "Me and the Devil Blues," and "Hellhound on My Trail," suggest such a pact, and when he died a violent death, presumably by poison, legend attributed this to the Devil claiming his soul.[47]

Appearing in 1986 and set in the United States in the same period, *Crossroads*, directed by Walter Hill with a screenplay by John Fusco, adapts the Faust motif to the blues culture of the 1980s.[48.] In Willie Brown, a.k.a. Blind Dog Fulton (a sobriquet derived from both Willie's thick glasses and his connection with Fulton Point, Mississippi), the film presents an unlikely Faust incarnation. When he was seventeen years old, Willie Brown met an emissary of the mysterious Legbone – alias Lucifer, Satan, Mephistopheles – at the Fulton Point Crossroads and signed the traditional pact with the Devil, bartering his immortal soul to become the greatest blues harmonica player of all times.

However, the true star of the film is not the Faust figure but his savior, a brilliant seventeen-year-old musical prodigy named Eugene Martone, studying classical guitar at Juilliard but obsessed with the blues. Eugene, like Goethe's hero, struggles with the "two souls" at war within his breast, in this case, his love for classical music and his passion for the blues. His desire to be a "blues man" drives him to seek the lost song from Johnson's famed recording of "Cross Road Blues" as his entry into the elite world of the blues.[49] In his quest to discover the lost record, Eugene helps Willie Brown, the last person to see Robert Johnson alive, escape from a Harlem state penitentiary hospital ward, and, in return, Willie Brown agrees to teach Eugene Johnson's lost song. Sprung from his hospital jail, Blind Dog Fulton and the guitar virtuoso, to whom Brown gives the moniker Lightning Boy Eugene, embark on an odyssey down Highway 61 from Memphis to New Orleans, the "royal road" of the blues.[50] Since *Crossroads* is a bildungsroman as well as a Faust recreation, physical travel becomes a metaphor for maturation, with Eugene simultaneously journeying into the Deep South and into adulthood. The film dramatizes two quests: an elderly blues man travels to the South to save his soul; an aspiring young blues man with dazzling technical skill but little heart treks to the South to find his soul. Fortunately, in this upbeat movie, both quests will be successful.

En route, Lightning Boy and Blind Dog join up with a tough but tender teenager called Frances, and the unlikely trio – an octogenarian fugitive, a seventeen-year-old musical prodigy, and a teenage runaway – "hobo" together, sharing a number of picaresque adventures. They confront a predatory motel manager with rape on his mind, thwarting his lust and stealing his car. They are arrested, robbed by the police, and released. Scrounging to survive, the three travelers pick pockets, brandish guns, and get into fights. More importantly, Lightning Boy enjoys a brief but poignant love affair with Frances, climaxing in his *rite de passage* into manhood in a hayloft. Finally, he makes his triumphant debut as a blues guitarist before a crowd of cheering fans in an African-American dive in Mississippi. Thus, in a dark hayloft and a black "juke joint," Eugene finds the heart needed to make him a genuine blues man. However, on the rainy morning following Eugene's great success, Frances secretly slips away, and in the weepy aftermath Eugene learns that no lost song exists. First Eugene loses his love; then he loses his dream; the road to maturation is clearly not for sissies.

The denouement of the film reintroduces the Faust topos. Although he has lost his girl and his song, Eugene has other challenges to face, including the little problem of a lost soul. So, ultimately, the two pilgrims arrive at the Crossroads to bargain with the Devil, not his viceroy this time but the sinister Legbone himself. Willie Brown, echoing Faust figures from the *Faustbooks* to *The Devil and Daniel Webster* and beyond, tries to weasel out of his bargain, denouncing the contract as a fraud and thus invalid. However, always the opportunist, the Devil refuses to void the contract until more valuable collateral is proffered, wheedling Lightning Boy to participate in a winner-take-all musical contest in which he will be pitted against a guitar wizard, a Mick Jagger look-alike named Jack Butler, now dead and damned. If Lightning Boy wins the contest, Blind Dog will be released from his contract; if the jury of damned revelers grant Butler their applause, Legbone (recalling Scratch in *Daniel Webster*) will gain the souls of both Lightning Boy and Blind Dog. Young and full of bravado, Lightning Boy agrees to stick by his friend, and immediately Legbone and his prospective victims find themselves magically transported to a chaotic black Mississippi blues bar, peopled with frenzied dancers and gyrating musicians. One wonders, "Is this hell?"

The final scene of the film recalls the trial scene in *The Devil and Daniel Webster* as the contest begins and the guitar gladiators joust for souls. Predictably, the seventeen-year-old wunderkind overcomes his formidable opponent, but not, as expected, with the riffs of the blues, but, surprisingly, with the chords of Mozart, or, to be more precise, with Paganini's variation on a theme from Mozart (Caprice No. 5). Thus the combined genius of two musical prodigies – Wolfgang Amadeus Mozart and Lightning Boy Eugene – vanquishes not only Jack Butler but the Devil himself, and Willie Brown receives a second chance. The movie concludes with Lightning Boy and Blind Dog at the Crossroads ready to light out to other territory and together take Chicago by storm.

The film, a palimpsest of classical myth, German legend, American literature, and modern movies, resonates with literary and cinematic allusions. The contest between rival musicians playing for stratospheric stakes finds its provenance in Greek myth, in which the satyr Marsyas challenged the god Apollo to a musical bout, the satyr's flute against the god's lyre. In addition, Lightning Boy's plummet into the hell of an anarchic blues nightclub echoes the descent into Hades of the mythical musician Orpheus. For just as the strings of Orpheus's harp so charmed the King and Queen of Hades that they allowed the harpist to retrieve his beloved Eurydice and ascend to earth (as long as he never glanced behind him), Lightning Boy so enthralls the nightclub revelers with his riffs and chords that the Devil permits him to rescue his venerable sidekick Blind Dog and depart. However, unlike the ill-fated Orpheus, Lightning Boy sets his sights on the future and never looks back. Moreover, the symbiotic relationship between an older man and a younger one in which each learns from the other provides a staple of current cinema, including such films as the 1984 movie *The Karate Kid* and the popular *Star Wars* trilogy of the late 1970s and early 1980s.[51] Lastly, the picaresque journey to Mississippi in which a good-hearted white naïf attempts to liberate an elderly black man from imprisonment recalls one of the great bildungsroman tales of American literature, the journey down the Mississippi by Huckleberry Finn and his black friend Jim. Significantly, Huck, like Eugene, is willing to risk damnation in hell to save his friend.

However, despite its debt to Greek mythology, contemporary cinema, and Mark Twain, *Crossroads* remains first and foremost a Faust fable, with the most important ingredients of the legend intact. Moreover, the Ur-text for the film is clearly Benét's version of the Faust legend to which the title *Crossroads* offers an hommage, a debt the Devil's lieutenant acknowledges when he quips that Legbone has changed his name to "Scratch." Both *The Devil and Daniel Webster* and *Crossroads* filter the Faust fable through the lens of American folklore; both affirm the traditional values of courage, loyalty, and male bonding; and both end happily with the Faust figure escaping by the skin of his teeth.

Comparing these two American films to Marlowe's and Goethe's dramas reveals something about the shift in value systems from sixteenth- and nineteenth-century England and Germany to America in the 1940s and 1980s. Both Marlowe's and Goethe's heroes – eminent scholars and seekers after truth, knowledge, and experience of the world – epitomize the ideal man of the Renaissance and the Post-Enlightenment. Conversely, Daniel Webster – the orator and statesman who moves the jury of the damned with the eloquence of his rhetoric – represents the role model for 1940s America. Finally, Lightning Boy Eugene – the virtuoso guitarist who captivates the jury of damned revelers with the enchantment of his music – embodies the icon of 1980s America. Music has replaced learning and language, and the rock, blues, or jazz musician has supplanted the scholar and statesman as the new royalty, a change reflected in the popular designation "rock star" as a metaphor for eminence in any field. Ultimately, Goethe's Faust, Jabez Stone, and Blind Dog Fulton all cheat the Devil of his due in the spirit and lexicon of their respective times.

With its taut plotting and rich intertextuality, in my opinion, *Crossroads* ranks as the most provocative appropriation of the Faust legend in the American cinema since *The Devil and Daniel Webster*, to which it owes so much. It is also a triumphant celebration of "American cultural hybridization,"[52] revealed in Eugene's blending of classical and rock in his victorious musical contest, in the reconciliation of the races and the generations in the friendship of Eugene and Willie, and in the melding of classical myth, German legend, American literature, and contemporary cinema into a singularly successful appropriation of the Faust legend. Also, *Crossroads* offers the cinematic world its first and, as far as I can discover, only African-American Faust.

Angel Heart

The third appropriation of the Faust legend in which the protagonist sells his soul for musical stardom appeared the following year (1987). This film, titled *Angel Heart*, presents a far more somber vision of the world than the images created in *Oh God! You Devil* or *Crossroads*. Alan Parker, who wrote and directed *Angel Heart*, based on the novel *Falling Angel* by William Hjortsberg, was strongly influenced by the chaotic culture of the 1980s – one of the most violent decades in US history, when homicide rates ballooned while murder and mayhem stalked the streets as well as the media screens.[53] Parker thus transforms the Faust legend into a detective story/slasher flick/film noir.[54] Singer postulates that throughout the decades the Faust topos has been "redesigned within the film aesthetic to fit the mold of two popular film genres, the romance and horror."[55] *Angel Heart*, wallowing in the lurid sex and graphic gore that have become the signature of late twentieth-century cinema, certainly belongs within the horror genre.

Angel Heart, set in New York in 1955, begins like a typical detective yarn with Faustian overtones. A mysterious magnate called Louis Cyphre (suggestive of Lucifer) hires a down-at-the-heel private detective with the allusive name of Harold Angel (nicknamed Harry Angel) to locate the famous big band crooner Johnny Favorite. When Cyphre explains that Johnny Favorite made an agreement promising certain collateral that he failed to deliver, all devotees of the Faust story would immediately suspect the nature of this compact. Sleuthing the tracks of Johnny Favorite leads Harry Angel into the Deep South, this time to sweltering Louisiana, where every footprint he discovers swims in blood. Angel's investigations all explode into mutilation and murder, as every witness he interrogates suffers a grisly death. As Angel maneuvers between these scenes of butchery, he uncovers a fragmented and elusive portrait of the sinister crooner Johnny Favorite. Tormented by surreal dreams of satanic orgies and recurring bloodbaths, and prompted to the truth by Ethan Krusemark, Angel reluctantly begins to realize his own complicity in these gruesome slayings, ultimately acknowledging himself as the unknown killer whom he seeks, both Harry Angel and Johnny Favorite, in a sense, both the Good and Evil Angel of his own Faustian nightmare.

At this point, the film reintroduces the Faustian scenario. Recalling the Faustian musicians of *Oh, God! You Devil* and *Crossroads*, the singer Johnny Favorite, Harry Angel's alter ego, sold his soul to the Devil many years earlier in return for musical stardom. As the time for his payment came due, Favorite, like so many Faust figures before him, attempted to escape the inevitable consequences of his bargain, in this instance, employing an arcane rite of soul transference. With the help of his fiancée Margaret Krusemark and her father Ethan, Favorite kidnapped an innocent soldier named Harry Angel from Times Square, killed him, sliced him open, ate his still-beating heart, and took his identity. However, before completing the soul transference, Favorite was drafted and seriously injured in World War II, which resulted in a complete facial reconstruction and amnesia. In 1945, Margaret and Ethan Krusemark rescued Favorite, still in a state of amnesia, from the hospital, took him to the very spot in Times Square where they had earlier kidnapped the unknown soldier, and released him amid the jubilant D-Day celebration. When Favorite's memory finally returned, he had submerged his real self beneath the psyche of Harry Angel, adopting both Angel's identity and his memories. However, like his ultimate role model, Dr. Jekyll, Angel proves unable to control his evil persona, his Mr. Hyde, who periodically emerges and commits atrocities of which his better self remains unaware. Even as Angel doggedly pursues information about Johnny Favorite, his dark doppelgänger savagely murders and dismembers anyone who might reveal his true identity.

At last, confronting Louis Cyphre, Angel accepts the shattering truth: the name of his employer translates as Lucifer, and the serial killer he seeks is actually himself. At this moment of revelation, Cyphre makes a direct reference to Marlowe and Goethe, explaining that he selected the name Louis Cyphre because "Mephistopheles is such a mouthful in Manhattan." Later, Cyphre triumphantly boasts: "Your soul is mine!" Denied the last-minute salvation granted Goethe's Faust and the flawed Faustian heroes of so many plays and films, Johnny Favorite remains one of the few Faust figures since Marlowe's doomed hero to pay the ultimate penalty for his contract.

Angel Heart depicts a maimed and mutilated world, fallen into sleaze and squalor as well as vice, a world devoid of divine intervention or human decency. Not only is God absent from the film, but religion has degenerated into choral hysteria, and scenes of religious frenzy – the charismatic paroxysms of a black revival meeting, the febrile chaos of a voodoo ritual, and the catatonic paralysis of entranced proselytes – frame this story of demonic possession, black magic, murder, dismemberment, and cannibalism. Scenes of unrelated violence also punctuate the savagery of the film's action – boxing matches, cockfights, brutal chases. As Louis Cyphre cynically explains in lines still relevant today, "There's just enough religion in the world to make people hate each other but not enough to make them love each other." Nevertheless, if God remains absent from the world of *Angel Heart*, the Devil continues to be very much present, and Louis Cyphre offers us one of the most sinister demons in the rogues' gallery of satanic tempters, a menacing fiend whose malice remains unleavened by the comedy typically associated with the Faust legend.

Like *Crossroads*, *Angel Heart* draws much of its macabre power from its intertextuality. Despite its cinema noir ambience and its updated Faustian goals, the film resonates with echoes of literary works both preceding and succeeding the Faust legend. The story of a detective searching for a maniacal slasher only to find he is himself the ripper bears affinities to the Theban King in Sophocles's *Oedipus Rex*, who seeks to uncover the impostume infecting his country only to learn that he is himself the murderous cause of that plague. As the comic-book philosopher Pogo admits, "We have met the enemy and it is us." Also, Harry Angel, alias Johnny Favorite, like Oedipus, involuntarily violates the most universal of taboos, although he commits incest not with his mother Jocasta but with his daughter Epiphany. On another level, the nightmare tale of a dual personality, one persona admirable and sympathetic, the other depraved and corrupt, draws on the terrifying story of *Dr. Jekyll and Mr. Hyde*.

As in the black mass celebrated in the film, everything in this fallen world becomes inverted and the characters' names function emblematically (as in the moralities) to stress this reversal. Ultimately, Harold Angel (suggesting Herald Angel) acts as a harbinger not of a divine but of an infernal incarnation, a servant not of God but of Lucifer (Louis Cyphre). Angel's former fiancée Margaret Krusemark (an anti-Margarete figure whose surname means "Mark of the Cross") suffers a type of mock crucifixion. Finally, Epiphany (defined as "a revelatory manifestation of a divine being"[56]), sex partner of Angel and mother of the Devil's child, suggests a demonic Madonna. A similar linguistic inversion of the sacred and the profane characterizes both the moralities and Marlowe's *Doctor Faustus*. These linguistic inversions coupled with literary reverberations add power and terror to this modern Faust fable, making it the satanic story critics have searched in vain to find in Marlowe's tragedy.

In America, the 1980s was an era of sharp partisan divide, increasing inequality, and burgeoning crime. For some – primarily the most prosperous – the decade offered economic growth and a realization of the American dream. Others, reeling from two major economic downturns (the 1982 recession and the stock market plummet of 1987), stagnating wages, and escalating violence on the streets, experienced the despair and alienation of the American dream transformed into the American nightmare.[57] Thus in 1984 this decade would present the most upbeat, feel-good movie in the entire Faustian cinematic repertoire (*Oh, God! You Devil*), while three years later in 1987, it would produce the most violent and sordid of all Faust films (*Angel Heart*). Like today in the US, the 1980s was the best of times and the worst of times, and this cultural chasm is reflected in the very different Faust films created during this period.

Bedazzled *II*

The original *Bedazzled*, despite its skilled acting and witty repartee, never achieved box-office success, a bit too cynical perhaps even for the iconoclastic 1960s. In 2000, Hollywood decided to try again, maintaining essentially the same storyline while updating the film to the new millennium. As appropriate to the more sanguine mood of the pre-9/11 millennium, director and screenwriter Harold Ramis, together with screenwriters Larry Gelbart and Peter Tolan, awards the film a happy ending and a more hopeful view of the universe.[58] The three screenwriters also modernize their hero from a depressed short-order cook to a friendless geek. Finally, in recognition of the increasing prominence of women in positions of power, they promote the traditional gorgeous temptress from Satan's Girl Friday to the role of head honcho, the Princess of Darkness herself.

The storyline closely follows the earlier script written by Peter Cook and Dudley Moore, selecting for the Faust figure a born loser, this time named Elliot Richards, who has a hopeless crush on a co-worker named Alison who doesn't even know he exists. Mimicking *Bedazzled* I, Richards signs a contract with the Devil and receives seven wishes, but no matter what he stipulates, the crafty Devil always finds ways to thwart his desires. Fortunately, Elliot has a pager he can use to escape from the disastrous results of his unsuccessful wishes. In using five of his six wishes, Elliot runs through a gauntlet of clichés: the rich, powerful man married to Alison in the form of a Colombian drug lord despised by his wife; the sensitive guy in touch with his feelings, who becomes so cloyingly romantic that the sated Alison runs off with a macho beach bum; the gigantic basketball star with a pea-sized brain and a minuscule penis; the suave, articulate, handsome writer, who wins the love of Alison but then turns out to be gay. Finally, realizing that none of his wishes will bring him happiness, Elliot decides to dedicate himself to saving the world and wishes to be President of the United States, only to find himself transformed into Abraham Lincoln at the Ford Theatre. Elliot fortunately hits his pager just as John Wilkes Booth springs forward shouting, "*Sic semper tyrannis.*" Totally disillusioned, in his final request Elliot simply wishes that Alison will have a happy life. This singular, absolutely altruistic act nullifies the entire contract, and Elliot escapes, the first victim in 6,000 years to give away a wish to someone else.

As in *Bedazzled* I, the Devil reveals a love/hate relationship with her victim, and the pathetic Elliot, parroting Stanley Moon from the earlier film, sheepishly admits that his temptress/tormenter, devilishly beautiful in fashionable, form-fitting, red or black ensembles, is the best friend he has ever had. Also, in between Elliot's disastrous magical excursions, like her infernal predecessor in *Bedazzled* I, the Princess of Darkness consistently engages in minor, and not so minor, mischief – jinxing parking meters so that drivers will receive unjustified tickets, creating traffic havoc by switching green and red traffic lights, exacerbating patients' health problems by substituting M&Ms for medication on the hospital trays – while all the time grousing about the disadvantages of the job she has been doomed to perform for eternity.

However, before she allows Elliot to leave, expressing a bit of worldly wisdom as old as Marlowe's Mephistopheles, the glamorous Devil teaches Elliot that heaven and hell dwell within, [59] and Elliot accepts the rather trite bromide that success and failure reside within the individual and cannot be achieved by the wave of a magic wand or the signing of a contract. So Elliot stands up to his badgering colleagues, musters the courage to speak to Alison, only to discover that she is involved with someone else, and then unexpectedly meets Nicole, a beautiful woman miraculously resembling Alison, who just happens to be moving in next door and just happens to be unattached. So, the film concludes on a happy-ever-after note, and as Elliot and Nicole stroll arm in arm, we spot the Devil, for the first time in the film dressed all in white rather than in her characteristic black or red, playing chess with an angel figure introduced earlier in the film, and we wonder: "Who is the good angel, and who the evil?"

Despite a few intriguing innovations, stripped of the trenchantly witty badinage of Stanley Moon and George Spiggot, as well as the provocative conceit of an absurdist universe, *Bedazzled* redux turns out to be a rather bland rewrite of the original, just another feel-good, self-help, sentimental comedy. But it does introduce one startling addition, the alluring female malign/benign Devil. However, although the stage has produced at least two female Faust figures and the screen has relished its first female Devil, the cinema still awaits its first female Faust.

Epilogue

The Faust Legend in Drama and Film

Returning to the question posed in the first page of this study: What do men and women most desire? For what would they be willing to barter their immortal souls? As I hope this study has convincingly argued, the answer to this question depends not only on the personalities of the individuals but also on the values and mores of their societies. In the sixteenth century, in the fevered excitement of England's expanding dominance on the world stage, Marlowe's Renaissance Faustus sells his soul primarily for power and for its ancillary benefits, wealth and fame. Two centuries later, in the post-Enlightenment era in Germany, Goethe's Faust bargains his most precious commodity for enhanced experience and knowledge of the world. Many years later, in the depression-oppressed United States, Jabez Stone trades his soul for money, and in the twentieth century, when romance ruled the box office around the world, several Faust figures sell their souls for love. In addition, throughout drama and film, Faust avatars have bartered their souls for political sovereignty, sports celebrity, and rock stardom; some few have even offered their souls to save humanity. Thus, to cite the brilliant Czech film auteur Jan Švankmajer, in a quotation that could serve as a motto for this book, "Each age makes its own pact with the devil."[1]

As noted in the Prologue of this book, when I first began this project, I was astonished at the number of dramatic adaptations of the Faust legend that I discovered, most of them virtually unknown even to the student of drama. These plays represent a polyglot of languages (Czech, English, French, German, and Russian), many dramatic modes (comedy, drama, tragedy, epic, romance, Theatre of the Absurd), and numerous historical periods (ranging from George Sand's lyrical 1838 feminist appropriation, *Seven Strings of the Lyre*, to David Davalos's witty 2008 parody,

Wittenberg). Not surprisingly, these plays also display both salient similarities and marked disparities.

Yet despite their wide diversity, the plays (as opposed to the films) analyzed in this study demonstrate a number of significant trends. First and foremost, these plays reveal the predominant influence of Goethe. Only four of the dramas, all English-language plays – Dorothy Sayers's *The Devil to Pay*, Lawrence Durrell's *An Irish Faustus*, David Mamet's *Faustus*, and David Davalos's *Wittenberg* – are primarily indebted to Marlowe's tragedy, although a number of these works commingle the very different Faustian legacies inherited from Marlowe and Goethe. Nevertheless, one element introduced by Marlowe appears in the majority of the plays examined: the ubiquitous blood-signed contract with the Devil.

Second, the majority of the plays reviewed secularize the Faust legend; only four plays – W. B. Yeats's *The Countess Cathleen*, Sayers's *The Devil to Pay*, Durrell's *An Irish Faustus*, and Mamet's *Faustus* – retain the metaphysical foundation underpinning the Faust tradition. The other plays either erase all explicit reference to heaven and hell, salvation and damnation, or, like Ghelderode's skeptical Devil in *The Death of Doctor Faustus*, question the existence of these supernatural realities.

Finally, as would be expected, many of these plays meld the influence of Marlowe and Goethe with that of contemporaneous writers and literary movements. Moreover, political events, economic upheavals, and philosophical developments combine with literary inspirations to mold these various permutations of the Faust legend.

The films examined in this study also represent a wide array of languages (Czech, English, French, German, and Russian), multiple cinematic genres (drama, comedy, farce, musical, romance, animation, horror film), and numerous time periods (ranging from F. W. Murnau's 1926 silent German movie to Alexander Sokurov's surreal 2011 Russian adaptation).

As I continued to work on this project, I was amazed at the striking difference between the foreign-language and English-language films that I encountered. All of the foreign-language films that I surveyed reveal an explicit debt to the Faust tradition, and, like the plays discussed above, all show the marked influence of Goethe, although these cinematic adaptations also retain certain Marlovian elements. In addition, all of the foreign-language films treated in this study feature a protagonist named Faust, an antagonist filling the role of Mephistopheles, and a female love interest called either Gretchen/Margarete or Helen. Conversely, of the English-language films analyzed, only one explicitly dramatizes the Faust narrative, in this case, Marlowe's *Doctor Faustus*. All of the other films, although deeply influenced by the Faustian blueprint – as derived more often from Marlowe than from Goethe – never explicitly acknowledge this debt. However, one Goethean element remains pervasive in both the plays and films analyzed: the appearance of a female character named either Helen or, more often, Margarete, frequently in a modified form such as Margaret, Martha, Marketa, Meg, or Midge, perhaps a tribute to the popularity of the Faust/Margarete tragedy immortalized in operas throughout the world.

Box-office considerations might explain the lack of explicit reference to the Faust theme in English-language movies as compared to the overt allusion to the Faust legend in foreign-language films and plays. Unfortunately, in today's culture, the theater has become a largely elitist art form, whereas films dominate popular culture entertainment. Films thus seek a wider audience than do stage plays and box-office concerns become a more critical factor. The prestige of Goethe in Europe might ensure the success of a film bearing the title of his greatest work; however, in the United States, overt reference to this classic, or to Marlowe's, might spell box-office poison at the movie house. Thus film producers might choose to follow the example of two seminal (and highly successful) Faust films, *The Devil and Daniel Webster* and *Damn Yankees*, which appropriate the central elements of the Faust narrative without explicit reference to the legend itself.

As observed above and as might be expected in our skeptical age, the majority of the plays discussed tend to secularize the Faust legend. However, surprisingly, without exception, the films reviewed in this chapter – both adaptations and appropriations – retain the supernatural foundation of the legend with overt references to God, the Devil, heaven, and hell. However, the depiction of God and the Devil differs remarkably in the various films. In many of the films God is notably absent (especially Švankmajer's *Faust*, Sokurov's *Faust*, *Alias Nick Beal*, and *Angel Heart*), or even treated satirically (*Bedazzled* I), or ambiguously (*Bedazzled* II). In others, God must work through human proxies (Daniel Webster, Reverend Garfield, Lightning Boy Eugene). One film even portrays a benevolent and caring Deity (*Oh, God! You Devil*). Similarly, some of the films depict the Devil in a humorous manner (*Damn Yankees, Oh, God! You Devil*) or even sympathetically (*The Beauty of the Devil, Bedazzled* I and II), whereas others limn the Prince of Darkness as sinister and terrifying (Murnau's *Faust, Alias Nick Beal, Angel Heart*). The treatment of both God and the Devil conforms to the vision of the director and screenwriter as well as the values and mores of the country and time period in which a particular film was produced.

In addition to the Faust tradition, the majority of the plays explored in this study derive inspiration from the literary conventions of their time. Conversely, almost all of the films show the overwhelming influence of the medieval moralities, an impact revealed in the humorous treatment of evil, the emblematic function of names, and, most of all, the ubiquitous battle of good and evil for the soul of the Faust figure, a battle animating almost all the films examined but notably absent from a number of the Faust plays discussed in this study. I speculate that the predominance of the morality motif in English-language cinematic appropriations may be due to the enormous influence of two American film classics: *The Devil and Daniel Webster* and *Damn Yankees.*

Yet cinematic revisions of the Faust narrative, like the theatrical ones, are fashioned by a confluence of forces: other successful Faust films, literary movements, cinematic innovations, historical events, political controversies, and the value systems and conventions of the time and place that created them.

The Durability of the Faust Legend

The Faustian Bargain: In her death, even more than in her life, Princess Diana has become a global celebrity. But what forces create such fame?

The Economist, September 4, 1997

Many Republican members of Congress have made a Faustian bargain with Donald Trump.

David Brooks, "The Republican Fausts," *New York Times*, January 31, 2017

How did Ryan's Faustian bargain with Trump work out?

Jennifer Rubin, *Washington Post*, May 2, 2017

And that in a nutshell is the Faustian bargain Republicans have made with a President whom the world now knows cannot be trusted with sensitive information, who coddles dictators, who has gone to war with the national security establishment and whose legion of financial conflicts of interest ensure that the best interests of the nation finish a distant second to his own.

John Micek, "Faustian Bargain with Trump," *Jackson Sun*, May 18, 2017

Faust made a better bargain than the vice-president [Mike Pence] did.
Frank Bruni, "Sorry Mike Pence, You're Damned," *New York Times*,
August 9, 2017

Jack Knox is right about the Prime Minister's [Trudeau's] miscalcula-
tion. Faustian bargains seldom work out well.
Janet Baudlas, "Trudeau Made a Faustian Bargain,"
Times Colonist, April 10, 2018

Who is offering Israel this Faustian bargain?
Mosche Arens, "Faustian Bargain," *Haaretz*, May 23, 2018

The surprising election in 2016 of a highly untraditional candidate to the
position of President of the United States generated a plethora of allusions
to the Faust legend in US newspapers, of which some of the above
quotations offer a typical sample. However, the citations from *The
Economist* (British), *The Times Colonist* (Canadian), and *Haaretz* (Israeli)
demonstrate that references to Faust, and particularly to the Faustian
bargain, are not limited to US newspapers or to discussions of President
Trump. The casualness of all of these references, without preamble or
explanation, supports my assertions concerning the relevance and familiarity of the Faust topos in our Western society.

What is the reason for the durability and pervasiveness of this legend?
Surely, behind this riveting narrative lies a deeper meaning, for all of us
cherish secret yearnings and seemingly unattainable aspirations. And
although few of us will encounter the Devil in the privy, as did Martin
Luther, or come face to face with the Prince of Darkness, as do so many
Faust figures, many of us, at least once in our lives, will be tempted
metaphorically to sell our souls for some deeply desired goal. How we
resolve the temptation to make our own personal pact with the Devil will
define our identity. This, I suggest, is the true significance of the Faust
legend for all of us, both in the past, in the present, and in the future.

Notes

Prologue

1. Inez Hedges notes most of these contemporary adapters of the Faust legend in her valuable analysis of cinematic treatments of the Faust legend. See Hedges, *Framing Faust: Twentieth-Century Cultural Struggles* (Carbondale: Southern Illinois University Press, 2005), 4.
2. Noted by David Bevington and Eric Rasmussen, "Introduction" to DF, 4.
3. Throughout this study, I have adapted the accepted spelling of the name "Mephistopheles," except when discussing the Devil in the English and German *Faustbooks*, whose name is always spelled "Mephostophiles."
4. See Linda Hutcheon, *A Theory of Adaptation* (London: Routledge, 2006), 8.
5. *Ibid.*, 174.
6. Julie Sanders, *Adaptation and Appropriation* (London: Routledge, 2006), 24, 35.
7. For a comprehensive survey of the critical literature on appropriation and adaptation, see Christy Desmet and Suyata Lyengar, "Adaptation, appropriation, or what you will," *Shakespeare*, 11/1 (February, 2015): 10–19.
8. Sanders, *Adaptation and Appropriation*, 35–36.

Chapter 1 The Background of the Faust Legend

1. King James VI and I, *Daemonologie*, a facsimile edition, (Amsterdam: Da Capo Press, 1969; 1st edn. 1597), 8. I have modernized the spelling.
2. SOED defines the term as follows: "A member of the ancient Persian priestly caste. Hence, one skilled in Oriental magic and astrology, an ancient magician or sorcerer" (1187).
3. All biblical quotations are from *The 1560 Geneva New Testament*, ed. David L. Brown and William H. Noah (Murfreesboro, TN: Avalon Press, 2005). I have modernized the spelling throughout.
4. SFT, 10.
5. *Acts of the Holy Apostles Peter and Paul*, in SFT, 29–41; see also Elizabeth M. Butler, *Myth of the Magus* (Cambridge University Press, 1948), 73–83.

6. For a discussion of the similarities in the legends of Simon Magus and Faustus, see Beatrice Daw Brown, "Marlowe, Faustus, and Simon Magus," *PMLA*, 54 (1939): 82–121. See also Neil Brough, *New Perspectives of Faust: Studies in the Origins and Philosophy of the Faust Theme in the Dramas of Marlowe and Goethe* (New York: Peter Lang, 1994), 42–43; and Bevington and Rasmussen, "Introduction" to *Doctor Faustus*, 7–8.

7. "Cyprian of Antioch," in *The Golden Legend or Lives of the Saints as Englished by William Caxton*, in SFT, 41–58; Butler, *Myth of the Magus*, 87–94.

8. *Golden Legend*, SFT, 76.

9. "A Miracle of the Virgin Mary Concerning Theophilus the Penitent," in SFT, 60–75.

10. SFT, 76 n.10.

11. John Bakeless, *The Tragicall History of Christopher Marlowe*, vol. 1 (Hamden, CT: Archon, 1964), 285–86; Henry Ansgar Kelly, *The Devil, Demonology, and Witchcraft: The Development of Christian Beliefs in Evil Spirits* (1968; repr. New York: Doubleday, 1974), 50.

12. Butler, *Myth of the Magus*, 94.

13. Brown, "Marlowe, Faustus, and Simon Magus," 99.

14. *Ibid.*, 100.

15. Michael Kelley, *Flamboyant Drama: A Study of The Castle of Perseverance, Mankind, and Wisdom* (Carbondale: Southern Illinois University Press, 1979), 24, warns that we should use the term "drama" cautiously in discussing moralities since the figures in these plays are "rooted in exposition, not imitation." However, I agree with Andrea Louise Young, *Vision and Audience in Medieval Drama: A Study of the Castle of Perseverance* (London: Routledge, 2015), 7, who argues that both the biblical cycle plays and the moralities employ mimesis, and thus can be considered "dramas" in the traditional sense.

16. David Bevington, *From Mankind to Marlowe: Growth of Structure in the Popular Drama of Tudor England* (Cambridge, MA: Harvard University Press, 1963), 9.

17. *Ibid.*, 10.

18. Dorothy Castle, *The Diabolical Game to Win Man's Soul: A Rhetorical and Structural Approach to Mankind* (New York: Peter Lang, 1990), 30.

19. Murray Roston, *Biblical Drama in England* (Evanston, IL: Northwestern University Press, 1968), 24.

20. *Ibid.*, 27.

21. See Clifford Davidson, *Visualizing the Moral Life: Medieval Iconography and the Macro Morality Plays* (New York: AMC Press, 1989), 26.

22. For a full discussion of these issues, E. K. Chambers, *The Mediaeval Stage*, vol. II (Oxford: Clarendon Press, 1903), 68–148; O. B. Hardison, *Christian Rite*

and Christian Drama in the Middle Ages (Baltimore, MD: Johns Hopkins University Press, 1966), 4–18; V. A. Kolve, *The Play Called Corpus Christi* (Stanford University Press, 1966), 134–44; John D. Cox, *The Devil and the Sacred in English Drama, 1350–1642* (Cambridge University Press, 2000), 5–12.

23. Cox, *The Devil and the Sacred*, 31–32.

24. Citations to *The Coming of the Antichrist* are from David Mills (ed.), *The Chester Mystery Cycle: A New Edition with Modernized Spelling* (East Lansing, MI: Colleagues Press, 1992). All subsequent citations will be included within the text. For a comprehensive study of the significance of the Antichrist figure in the drama of the medieval period, see John Parker, *The Aesthetics of Antichrist* (Ithaca, NY: Cornell University Press, 2007).

25. Marlowe, *Doctor Faustus,* ed. Bevington and Rasmussen. All citations to *Doctor Faustus* in this study will be to the A-text of this edition unless otherwise noted and will be included within the text.

26. Bernard Spivack, *Shakespeare and the Allegory of Evil* (New York: Columbia University Press, 1958), 132.

27. *Ibid.,* 132.

28. *Ibid.,* 151.

29. *Ibid.,* 186.

30. Davidson, *Visualizing the Moral Life*, 36.

31. Frank Baron, *Doctor Faustus from History to Legend* (Munich: Wilhelm Fink Verlag, 1978), 15; Ian Watt, *Myths of Modern Individualism: Faust, Don Quixote, Don Juan, Robinson Crusoe* (Cambridge University Press, 1996), 3 n.1, 8.

32. Noted by Bevington and Rasmussen, "Introduction" to *Doctor Faustus*, 4.

33. Baron, *From History to Legend*, 12. See also H. G. Haile, "Introduction" to H. G. Haile (ed.), *The History of Doctor Johann Faustus* (Urbana: University of Illinois Press, 1965), 5–7. For a comprehensive compilation of references to the historical Faust, see SFT, 81–126. See also Watt, *Myths of Modern Individualism,* 3–16.

34. For a discussion of the controversy surrounding the different names of Faustus, see Philip Brockbank, *Marlowe: Dr Faustus* (London: Edward Arnold, 1962), 12; SFT, 82; Baron, *From History to Legend,* 32–33; and Brough, *New Perspectives on Faust,* 17–18.

35. "Letter of Johannes Tritheim to Johannes Virdung," in SFT, 83, 85. For discussion of the various titles assumed by Faustus, see Brough, *New Perspectives on Faust,* 17–18. See also Brown, "Marlowe, Faustus, and Simon Magus," 88, who contends that the terms *junior* and *second* suggest that "Sabellicus assumed the name of Faustus in imitation of some earlier magus who had borne it," positing that this earlier magician was probably Simon Magus.

36. "Letter of Johannes Tritheim to Johannes Virdung," in SFT, 86.

37. "Letter of Conrad Mutianus Rufus to Heinrich Urbanus," in SFT, 87–88.

38. "From The Account Book of the Bishop of Bamberg, 1519–1520," in SFT, 88–89.
39. "From The Records of the City of Ingolstadt," in SFT, 90.
40. "Entry in the Records of the City Council of Nuremberg, May 10, 1532," in SFT, 90.
41. "Letter of Joachim Camerarius to Daniel Stibar," in SFT, 92.
42. "From the Christlich Bedencken of Augustin Lercheimer," in SFT, 119–20.
43. "From the Journal of Kilian Lieb, July 1528," in SFT, 89.
44. "From the Waldeck Chronicle," in SFT, 91.
45. "From the Tischreden of Martin Luther," in SFT, 93.
46. "From the Explicationes Melanchthoniae, Part II" and "From the Locorum Communium Collectanea of Johannes Manlius," both in SFT, 99, 101.
47. "From the Sermones Convivales of Johannes Gast," in SFT, 96–98.
48. "From the Explicationes Melanchthoniae, Part IV," in SFT, 99–100.
49. "From the Sermones Convivales of Johannes Gast" and "From the Locorum Communium Collectanea of Johannes Manlius," both in SFT, 98, 102.
50. "From the De Praestigis Daemonum of Johannes Wier" and "From the Christlich Bedencken of Augustin Lercheimer," both in SFT, 105–07, 119–21.
51. Baron, "Georg Lukàcs on the Origin of the Faust Legend," in Peter Boemer and Sidney Johnson (eds.), *Faust through Four Centuries: Retrospect and Analysis* (Tübingen: Max Niemeyer Verlag, 1989), 18–23; and Watt, *Myths of Modern Individualism*, 17.
52. Michael H. Keefer, "Right Eye and Left Heel: Ideological Origins of the Legend of Faustus," *Mosaic*, 22 (1989): 83–84.
53. SFT, 129. See also Gareth Roberts's argument for a parallel between the life of Agrippa and that of Marlowe's Faustus, in "Necromantic Books: Christopher Marlowe, *Doctor Faustus*, and Agrippa of Nettesheim," in Darryll Grantley and Peter Roberts (eds.), *Christopher Marlowe and English Renaissance Culture* (Aldershot: Scolar Press, 1996), 148–71. Andrew Duxfield also sees a strong parallel between Marlowe's Faustus and Hermes Trismegistus: see "Doctor Faustus and Renaissance Hermeticism," in Sara Munson Deats (ed.), *Doctor Faustus: A Critical Guide* (London: Continuum, 2010), 96–110.
54. Haile, "Introduction" to *History of Doctor Johann Faustus*, 6–7.
55. *Ibid.*, 8.
56. William Rose, "Introduction" to William Rose (ed.), *The Historie of the Damnable Life and Deserved Death of Doctor John Faustus* (University of Notre Dame Press, 1963), 30; Haile, "Introduction" to *History of Doctor Johann Faustus*, 12; SFT, 129.
57. Haile, "Introduction" to *History of Doctor Johann Faustus*, 11–13, argues that his translation of the Wolfenbüttel Manuscript is probably as close as we shall ever get to knowing how the *German Faustbook* looked when it was first written.

58. Haile, "Introduction" to *History of Doctor Johann Faustus*, 13. For more information on the first edition of the *German Faustbook*, see Rose, "Introduction" to *Historie of the Damnable Life*, 23–25.

59. For a full discussion of this controversy, see Brough, *New Perspectives of Faust*, 38–39. See also Haile, "Introduction" to *History of Doctor Johann Faustus*, 7–16; and Rose, "Introduction" to *Historie of the Damnable Life*, 23–41.

60. Elizabeth M. Butler, *The Fortunes of Faust* (Cambridge University Press, 1952), 11.

61. Rose, "Introduction" to *Historie of the Damnable Life*, 26–28, esp. 27.

62. Wolff, *Faust und Luther: Ein Beitrag zur Entstehung der Faustdichtung* (Halle: Verlag von Max Niemeyer, 1912), 52–61.

63. Here I am supporting the argument of Rose, "Introduction" to *The Historie of the Damnable Life*, 28–29.

64. All references to the *English Faustbook* will be to John Henry Jones (ed.), *The English Faust Book: A Critical Edition Based on the Text of 1592* (Cambridge University Press, 1994); all citations will henceforth be included within the text of this chapter. For Jones's discussion of the identity of P. F., see his "Introduction" to *English Faust Book*, 29–34.

65. Fortunately, the version of the EFB on which I am relying was edited by John Henry Jones, who earlier translated large portions of the GFB into English. In his critical edition of the EFB, he presents the portions representing the original GFB in regular type, distinguishing P. F.'s additions by placing them in bold type, while also identifying all of P. F.'s deletions to the GFB in endnotes. Thus the motivated reader can clearly recognize and evaluate all the additions and omissions P. F. has made to the German original.

66. For a fuller discussion of this issue, see Chapter 2 below, *Doctor Faustus*, endnotes 1, 2, and 3. See also Jones's persuasive argument for 1588 as the date of the publication of the first edition of the EFB, in his "Introduction" to *English Faust Book*, 52–72.

67. Rose, "Introduction" to *Historie of the Damnable Life*, 44; Jones, "Introduction" to *English Faust Book*, 18.

68. For discussion of these multiple sources, see Brough, *New Perspectives of Faust*, 39.

69. Jones, "Introduction" to William Empson, *Faustus and the Censor: The English Faustbook and Marlowe's Doctor Faustus* (Oxford: Basil Blackwell, 1987), 18.

70. For a discussion of Origen's "universalist" theory, see Kelly, *Devil, Demonology, and Witchcraft*, 33–35; and Diarmaid MacCulloch, *Christianity: The First Three Thousand Years* (New York: Viking, 2010), 153. Intriguingly, this unorthodox theory appears to be tentatively affirmed by Mephostophiles, although not necessarily by the author of the GFB or EFB.

71. Jones, "Introduction" to *Faustus and the Censor*, 24, suggests that Faustus's putative raising of Alexander and his Paramour to entertain the Emperor may

find its origin in the story of Trithemius raising Mary of Burgundy before the Emperor Maximilian.
72. *Ibid.*, 25–26.
73. See Butler, *Myth of the Magus*, 78.
74. Erich Kahler, "Doctor Faustus from Adam to Sartre," *Comparative Drama*, 1/ 2 (1967): 75–92 (at 83).
75. Jones, "Introduction" to *English Faust Book*, 12.
76. Jones comments on these changes from the GFB to the EFB in his "Postscript" to *Faustus and the Censor*, 203–05. He develops his interpretation of Mephostophiles more fully in his "Introduction" to *English Faust Book*, 19–21.
77. Empson, *Faustus and the Censor*, 81–84; and Jones, Introduction to *English Faust Book*, 19.
78. For a list of these illustrious magi, see Butler, *Myth of the Magus*, who allots a chapter to all the magi listed above plus many others.

Chapter 2 Marlowe's *Doctor Faustus*

1. Bruce Brandt, "The Critical Backstory," in Deats (ed.), *Doctor Faustus: A Critical Guide*, 17–40 (at 21).
2. Cited by David Bevington, "The Performance History," in Deats (ed.), *Doctor Faustus: A Critical Guide*, 41–71 (at 41).
3. For a fuller discussion of the problem of dating the play, see Brandt, "Critical Backstory," 21–22; and Bevington and Rasmussen, "Introduction" to *Doctor Faustus*, 1–3. For a persuasive defense of an early date for the *English Faustbook*, see Jones, "Introduction" to *English Faust Book*, 54–72. See also R. J. Fehrenbach, "A Pre-1592 English Faust Book and the Date of Marlowe's *Doctor Faustus*," *Library*, 2 (2001): 327–35. My thanks to Laurie Maguire for alerting me to this significant reference.
4. Michael J. Warren, "*Doctor Faustus:* The Old Man and the Text," *English Literary Renaissance*, 11 (1981): 111–47; Leah S. Marcus, "Textual Indeterminacy and Ideological Difference: The Case of *Doctor Faustus*," *Renaissance Drama*, n.s. 20 (1989): 1–29.
5. For an extremely comprehensive comparison of the two texts, see Bevington and Rasmussen, "Introduction" to *Doctor Faustus*, 62–70, 72–77. Bevington and Rasmussen speak for many contemporary editors when they state, "Because the B-text incorporates a thorough if intermittent reworking of concept and language, it deserves to be treated as a text by itself. All the evidence adduced here, on the other hand, points to the A-text as closer in most ways to the original work of Marlowe and his collaborator ... Both texts of *Doctor Faustus* continue to deserve our divided attention" (77).

6. W. W. Greg, "The Damnation of Faustus," *Modern Language Review*, 41/2 (1946): 97–107 (at 99).

7. G. K. Hunter, "Five-Act Structure in 'Doctor Faustus,'" *Tulane Drama Review*, 8/4 (Summer 1964): 77–91.

8. In my opinion, the most detailed explication of the parodic function of the farcical clown sequences is offered by Robert Ornstein, "The Comic Synthesis in *Doctor Faustus*," *English Literary History*, 22 (1955): 165–72.

9. Goethe's response to Marlowe's play is cited by Otto Heller, *Faust and Faustus: A Study of Goethe's Relationship to Marlowe* (New York: Cooper Square, 1972), 16.

10. For a fuller analysis of the possible candidates for Marlowe's collaborator, see Brandt, "Critical Backstory," 23; and Bevington and Rasmussen, "Introduction" to *Doctor Faustus*, 70–72.

11. See John D. Jump, "Introduction" to Christopher Marlowe, *Doctor Faustus*, ed. John D. Jump, Revels Plays (London: Methuen, 1962), xxxix. For a fuller discussion of the changes from the German original that identify the EFB as Marlowe's source, see Jump, xxxviii–xxxix. My discussion of the EFB will be based on the edition by Jones and all citations to this work will be included within the text of this chapter.

12. Bevington, "Performance History," 43. My brief discussion of the staging of Marlowe's tragedy is much indebted to Bevington's comprehensive performance history.

13. Joel B. Altman, *The Tudor Play of Mind: Rhetorical Inquiry and the Development of Elizabethan Drama* (Berkeley: University of California Press, 1978), 321–88.

14. Una Ellis-Fermor, *The Frontiers of Drama* (London: Methuen, 1964; 1st edn. 1945), 142; George Santayana, *Three Philosophical Poets: Lucretius, Dante, and Goethe* (New York: Doubleday, 1938; 1st edn. 1910), 135; and Leo Kirschbaum, "Marlowe's *Faustus*: A Reconsideration," *Review of English Studies*, 19/75 (1943): 225–41 (at 229).

15. Robert A. Logan, *Shakespeare's Marlowe: The Influence of Christopher Marlowe on Shakespeare's Artistry* (Aldershot: Ashgate, 2007), 84, 134. Logan further develops these ideas in his most recent book, *Shakespeare, Antony and Cleopatra, and the Nature of Fame* (Kalamazoo, MI: Medieval Institute Publications, 2018), 162. Other critics who agree that *Doctor Faustus* represents an interrogative drama in which the contradictory discourses balance precariously and are never resolved include the following: Altman, *Tudor Play of Mind*, 321–88; Lawrence Danson, "Christopher Marlowe: The Questioner," *English Literary Renaissance*, 12 (1982): 3–29; Jonathan Dollimore, *Radical Tragedy: Religion, Ideology, and Power in the Drama of Shakespeare and his Contemporaries* (Durham, NC:

Duke University Press, 1984), 109–19; Carol Leventen Duane, "Marlowe's Mixed Messages: A Model for Shakespeare?" *Medieval and Renaissance Drama in England*, 3 (1986): 51–67 (at 51); Bevington, "Marlowe and God," *Explorations in Renaissance Culture*, 17 (1991): 1–38; James Shapiro, *Rival Playwrights: Marlowe, Jonson, Shakespeare* (New York: Columbia University Press, 1991), 96; Deats, "Marlowe's Interrogative Drama: *Dido, Tamburlaine, Faustus*, and *Edward II*," in Deats and Robert A. Logan (eds.), *Marlowe's Empery: Expanding His Critical Contexts* (Newark: University of Delaware Press, 2002), 107–32 (at 117–20); Ruth Lunney, *Marlowe and the Popular Tradition* (Manchester University Press, 2002), 124–57; and Thomas Healy, "*Doctor Faustus*," in Patrick Cheney (ed.), *The Cambridge Companion to Christopher Marlowe* (Cambridge University Press, 2004), 174–92.

16. For two comparisons between source and play, see Douglas Cole, *Suffering and Evil in the Plays of Christopher Marlowe* (Princeton University Press, 1962), 191–243; and Deats, "*Doctor Faustus*: From Chapbook to Tragedy," *Essays in Literature*, 3 (1976): 3–16.

17. A. W. Ward (ed.), *Old English Drama: Select Plays* (Oxford: Clarendon Press, 1892), 137–38. For a reproduction and discussion of the sumptuary laws of the period, see Paul L. Hughes and James F. Larkin (eds.), *Tudor Royal Proclamations*, 3 vols. (New Haven, CT: Yale University Press, 1969), vols. II and III, #464, #493, #494, #496, #542, #601, #697, #786, #787.

18. For a description of the war fever infecting England at this time, see Leah S. Marcus, "Epilogue: Marlowe *in tempore belli*," in Sara Munson Deats, Lagretta Tallent Lenker, and Merry G. Perry (eds.), *War and Words: Horror and Heroism in the Literature of Warfare* (New York: Lexington Books, 2004), 295–316; Robert A. Logan, "Violence, Terrorism, and War," in *Ibid.*, 65–81 (at 78); and Sara Munson Deats, "Mars or Gorgon? Tamburlaine and Henry V," *Marlowe Studies: An Annual*, 1 (2011): 99–124 (at 103).

19. R. W. Dent, "Ramist Faustus or Ramist Marlowe?" *Neuphilologische Mitteilungen*, 73 (1972): 63–74 (at 64); Ward, *Old English Drama*, 130, was the first editor to identify this misquotation.

20. See Pierre de La Primaudaye, *The French Academie*, (London, 1605), i.4, quoted by Brockbank, *Marlowe: Doctor Faustus*, 31.

21. Dent, "Ramist Faustus," 64; Jump, "Introduction" to *Doctor Faustus*, 7 n.12.

22. Jump, "Introduction" to *Doctor Faustus*, 7 n.13.

23. On the presence of this biblical verse in *Homily on the Misery of Mankind*, see Tom Rutter, *The Cambridge Introduction to Christopher Marlowe* (Cambridge University Press, 2012), 48. See also *The Book of Common Prayer* (London, 1965) and *The Thirty-Nine Articles of the Church of England* (London: Printed in

Powles Church Yard by Richard Jugg and John Cawood, 1563), unpaginated. The language has been modernized.

24. All biblical citations are from *The 1560 Geneva New Testament*.

25. Critics who have focused on Faustus's failure to "sound the depths" of what he will profess include the following: Joseph T. McCullen, "*Dr. Faustus* and Renaissance Learning," *Modern Language Review*, 51 (1956): 6–16; Joseph Westlund, "The Orthodox Christian Framework of Marlowe's *Faustus*," *Studies in English Literature 1500–1900*, 3 (1963): 191–205; A. L. French, "The Philosophy of *Dr. Faustus*," *Essays in Criticism*, 20 (1970): 123–42; Dent, "Ramist Faustus"; Richard Waswo, "Damnation, Protestant Style: Macbeth, Faustus, and Christian Tragedy," *Journal of Medieval and Renaissance Studies*, 4 (1974): 63–99; James A. Reynolds, "Faustus' Flawed Learning," *English Studies*, 57 (1976): 329–36; A. N. Okerlund, "The Intellectual Folly of Dr. Faustus," *Studies in Philology*, 74 (1977): 258–78; R.W. Ingram, "'Pride in learning goeth before a fall': Dr. Faustus' Opening Soliloquy," *Mosaic*, 13/1 (Fall 1979): 73–80; Danson, "Questioner," 17–24; Phoebe S. Spinard, "The Dilettante Lie in *Doctor Faustus*," *Texas Studies in Literature and Language*, 24 (1982): 243–54; David Riggs, *The World of Christopher Marlowe* (New York: Henry Holt, 2005), 239–44; and Rutter, *Cambridge Introduction to Christopher Marlowe*, 48.

26. Thomas Becon, *Works*, 626–28, cited in Kocher, *Christopher Marlowe: A Study of his Thought, Learning, and Character* (Chapel Hill: University of North Carolina Press, 1946), 106–07; Susan Snyder, "The Left Hand of God: Despair in the Medieval and Renaissance Tradition," *Studies in the Renaissance*, 12 (1965): 18–59 (at 30–32).

27. See Greg, "Damnation of Faustus"; and T. W. Craik, "Faustus' Damnation Reconsidered," *Renaissance Drama*, n.s. 2 (1969): 189–96. For an illuminating explanation of the power traditionally associated with spirits in general and the limitations identified with devils in particular, see Robert Hunter West, *The Invisible World: A Study of Pneumatology in Elizabethan Drama* (New York: Octagon, 1969; 1st edn. 1939), 24–25.

28. Cole, *Suffering and Evil*, 192–231.

29. For the harrowing description of Faustus's dilacerated body, see the B-text of DF, 5.3.1–19.

30. For an account of Faustus's escapades in the Grand Turk's harem, see EFB, 139–41; for his dalliance with the seven fair women, see EFB, 171.

31. For authoritative discussions of the controversy, see Francis R. Johnson, "Marlowe's 'Imperial Heaven,'" *English Literary History*, 12 (1945): 35–44, and "Marlowe's Astronomy and Renaissance Skepticism," *English Literary History* 13 (1946): 241–54; and Kocher, *Christopher Marlowe*, 214–40.

32. Helen Gardner, "Milton's 'Satan' and the Theme of Damnation in Elizabethan Tragedy," *English Studies*, 1 (1948): 46–66 (at 53).

33. In the B-text, in Act 3, scenes 1 and 2, Faustus and Mephistopheles rescue Bruno, the rival Pope, from the de facto Pope in Rome and later transport him to the Emperor. In the A-text, Faustus and his demonic enabler are content to harass the Pope with foolish pranks.

34. Hunter, "Five-Act Structure," offers the most detailed analysis of Faustus's descent down the ladder of early modern professions; Gardner, "Milton's 'Satan,'" further compares Faustus's downward trajectory to that of Macbeth, Beatrice-Joanna, and Milton's Satan.

35. See Ornstein, "Comic Synthesis." See also Bevington's analysis of the parodic representation of the Seven Deadly Sins in the farcical sub-plot ("Marlowe and God," 7–8). Bevington also defends the farcical scenes as an integral part of the morality tradition from which *Doctor Faustus* evolved: see *From Mankind to Marlowe*, 252–57.

36. Ellis-Fermor, *Frontiers of Drama*, 141; Harry Levin, *Christopher Marlowe: The Overreacher* (Boston, Beacon Press, 1962; 1st edn. 1952), 133; Nicholas Brooke, "The Moral Tragedy of *Doctor Faustus*," *Cambridge Journal*, 5 (1952): 662–87; Irving Ribner, "Introduction" to *Christopher Marlowe, The Complete Plays*, ed. Irving Ribner (New York: Odyssey Press, 1963), xxxix.

37. Kirschbaum, "Reconsideration"; Lily Bess Campbell, "Doctor Faustus: A Case of Conscience," *PMLA*, 67 (1952): 219–39; Westlund, "Orthodox Christian Framework"; Cole, *Suffering and Evil*.

38. See James Smith, "Marlowe's *Dr. Faustus*," *Scrutiny*, 8/1 (1939–40): 48–49; Greg, "Damnation of Faustus"; Craik, "Faustus' Damnation Reconsidered"; and Kiessling, "Doctor Faustus and the Sin of Demoniality," *Studies in English Literature 1500–1900*, 15 (1975): 205–11. See Bevington's summary of this controversy ("Marlowe and God," 8–9). For a brief but provocative discussion of the role of Helen of Troy in Marlowe's play, see Laurie Maguire, *Helen of Troy: From Homer to Hollywood* (Oxford: Wiley-Blackwell, 2009), 150–54.

39. See Ariel Sachs, "The Religious Despair of Doctor Faustus," *Journal of English and German Philology*, 63 (1964): 625–47, esp. 644; Wilbur Sanders, *The Dramatist and the Received Idea: Studies in the Plays of Marlowe and Shakespeare* (Cambridge University Press, 1968), chaps. 11 and 12; John Stachniewski, *The Persecutory Imagination: English Puritanism and the Literature of Religious Despair* (Oxford: Clarendon Press, 1991), 292–331; A. D. Nuttall, *The Alternative Trinity: Gnostic Heresy in Marlowe, Milton, and Blake* (Oxford: Clarendon Press, 1998), 30.

40. Origen, *De Principiis*, 3, 2,4, quoted in Kelly, *Devil, Demonology, and Witchcraft*, 38–39.

41. Pierre de La Primaudaye, *The French Academie*, 11.27, 167. I have modernized the spelling of all works cited in this section.

42. Heinrich Kramer and James Sprenger, *The Malleus Maleficarum of Heinrich Kramer and James Sprenger*, trans. Montague Summers (New York: Dover, 1971; 1st edn. 1569), Part I, Ques. 5, p. 32.

43. John Calvin, *The Institution of the Christian Religion*, trans. Thomas Norton (Glasgow: Printed by John Bryce and Archibald M'Lean, junior, for Alexander Irving, 1762), Book I, chap. 14, p. 64. I have modernized the spelling.

44. See M. C. Bradbrook, *Themes and Conventions of Elizabethan Tragedy* (Cambridge University Press, 1935), 143; Greg, "Damnation of Faustus," 103–04; Levin, *Christopher Marlowe: The Overreacher*, 131; Elmer Edgar Stoll, "The Objectivity of the Ghosts in Shakespeare," *PMLA*, 22/2 (1907): 202–33 (at 232 n.2); West, *Invisible World*, 104; Campbell, "A Case of Conscience," 233; and Smith, "Marlowe's *Dr. Faustus*," 38, 47.

45. G. A. Lester (ed.), *Three Late Medieval Morality Plays: Mankind, Everyman, Mundus et Infans*, New Mermaids (London: A & C Black, 1981).

46. See St. Thomas Aquinas, *Summa theologica*, vol. xx, trans. fathers of the English Dominican Province (London: Encyclopedia Britannica, 1952), Part II, Ques. 6, Art. I, p. 414; and Richard Hooker, *Laws of Ecclesiastical Polity*, in *The Works of Richard Hooker*, vol. II, ed. John Keble (New York: Burt Franklin Press, 1888), Part 42, pp. 588–90.

47. See Waswo, "Damnation, Protestant Style," 86; and Nuttall, *Alternative Trinity*, 45. See also Lester (ed.), *Mankind*, 32. For a discussion of Faustus's pervasive inversion of scripture, see Sara Munson Deats, "Biblical Allusion in Marlowe's *Doctor Faustus*," *Medievalia et Humanistica*, n.s. 10 (1981): 203–16.

48. See particularly Max Bluestone, "*Libido Speculandi*: Doctrine and Dramaturgy in Contemporary Interpretations of Marlowe's *Doctor Faustus*," in Norman Rabkin (ed.), *Reinterpretations of Elizabethan Drama* (New York: Columbia University Press, 1969), 33–88.

49. SOED, 377; Bluestone discusses the ambiguity involved in the reference to the "conspiring heavens," in "*Libido Speculandi*," 73.

50. Cox, *The Devil and the Sacred*, 116–17.

51. Kocher, *Christopher Marlowe*, 118.

52. Bluestone, "*Libido Speculandi*," 65–75, esp. 66.

53. See Westlund, "Orthodox Christian Framework," 203–04, and Marcus, "Textual Indeterminacy."

54. Kristen Poole, "*Dr. Faustus* and Reformation Theology," in Garrett A. Sullivan, Jr., Patrick Cheney, and Andrew Hadfield (eds.), *Early Modern English Drama: A Critical Companion* (Oxford University Press, 2006), 96–107 (at 101).

55. *Thirty-Nine Articles of the Church of England*, unpaginated.

56. Hooker, *Laws of Ecclesiastical Polity*, Part 42, 588–90.

57. See Calvin, *Institution of the Christian Religion*, Book 1, chap. 18, p. 95.
58. Kocher, *Christopher Marlowe*, 111–12; Campbell supports this reading of these lines, in "Case of Conscience," 235.
59. See Pauline Honderich, "John Calvin and Doctor Faustus," *Modern Language Review*, 68 (1973): 1–13. See also Poole, "*Dr. Faustus* and Reformation Theology"; Nuttall, *Alternative Trinity*, 41–70; Clifford Davidson, "Doctor Faustus of Wittenberg," *Studies in Philology*, 59 (1962), 514–23; Angus Fletcher, "*Doctor Faustus* and the Lutheran Aesthetic," *English Literary Renaissance*, 35 (2005): 187–209; and Barbara Parker, "'Cursed Necromancy': Marlowe's *Faustus* as Anti-Catholic Satire," *Marlowe Studies*, 1 (2011): 59–77.
60. Empson, *Faustus and the Censor*, 46–47.
61. See Logan, *Shakespeare's Marlowe*, 201.
62. Emily Bartels also discusses Faustus's interiority and compares him to Hamlet: see *Spectacles of Strangeness: Imperialism, Alienation, and Marlowe* (Philadelphia: University of Pennsylvania Press, 1993), 115–17. In addition, Lunney recognizes Faustus as the "first of the new 'debatable' characters" emerging in the late 1580s and early 1590s and also associates him with the indecisive Hamlet, in *Marlowe and the Popular Tradition*, 131–32.
63. Sherman Hawkins, "The Education of Faustus," *Studies in English Literature 1500–1900*, 6 (1966): 193–209, finds the unity of the play's central episodes in an enactment by both Faustus and his adversaries of all the seven deadly sins. Bevington also discusses the way in which Faustus embodies all of the seven deadly sins ("Marlowe and God," 7). On the "sin against the Holy Ghost," see Campbell, "Case of Conscience," 221.
64. See MacCulloch, *Christianity*, on Origen, 153, and on Isaac, 250. Kelly examines Origen's "universalist" theory, its provenance, and its implications, in *Devil, Demonology, and Witchcraft*, 34–35. For a discussion of St. Paul's affirmation that all created beings would ultimately be brought within the scope of God's redemption, see Kelly, 22–23.
65. E. Gordon Rupp and Philip S. Watson (ed. and trans.), *Luther and Erasmus: Free Will and Salvation* (Philadelphia: Westminster Press, 1969), 41.
66. Patrick Cheney, *Marlowe's Counterfeit Profession: Ovid, Spenser, Counter-Nationhood* (University of Toronto Press, 1997), 190–220, esp. 213. Sara Munson Deats also interprets Faustus as a type of the playwright with magic as a metaphor for the drama: see "'Mark this show': Magic and Theater in Marlowe's *Doctor Faustus*," in Sara Munson Deats and Robert A. Logan (eds.), *Placing the Plays of Christopher Marlowe* (Aldershot: Ashgate, 2008), 13–24. Other critics who have sympathetically likened Faustus to the artist or the playwright include Alvin B. Kernan, *The Playwright as Magician: Shakespeare's Image of the Poet in the English Public Theatre* (New Haven, CT: Yale University Press, 1979), 157; Altman, *Tudor Play of Mind*, 321–88;

Barbara Howard Traister, *Heavenly Necromancy: The Magician in English Renaissance Drama* (Columbia: University of Missouri Press, 1984), 89–107; John Mebane, *Renaissance Magic and the Return of the Golden Age* (Lincoln: University of Nebraska Press, 1989), 113–36; Darryll Grantley, "'What means this show?': Theatricalism, Camp and Subversion in *Doctor Faustus* and *The Jew of Malta*," in Grantley and Roberts (eds.), *Christopher Marlowe and English Renaissance Culture*, 224–38; Huston Diehl, *Staging Reform, Reforming the Stage: Protestantism and Popular Theatre in Early Modern England* (Ithaca, NY: Cornell University Press, 1997), 67–81; Ian McAdam, *The Irony of Identity: Self and Imagination in the Drama of Christopher Marlowe* (Newark: University of Delaware Press, 1999), 112–45; Healy, "*Doctor Faustus*," 186–89.

67. Alison Findlay, *A Feminist Perspective on Renaissance Drama* (Oxford: Blackwell, 1999), 14–25. For a fuller discussion of contemporary critical approaches to *Doctor Faustus*, see Sara Munson Deats, "*Doctor Faustus*," in Sara Munson Deats and Robert A. Logan (eds.), *Christopher Marlowe at 450* (Farnham: Ashgate, 2015), 71–100 (at 89–91).

68. Fletcher, "*Doctor Faustus* and the Lutheran Aesthetic," 204.

69. Jane K. Brown, "The Prosperous Wonder Worker: Faust in the Renaissance," in Boemer and Johnson (eds.), *Faust through Four Centuries*, 53–64 (at 55).

70. Bevington, "Marlowe and God," 17.

71. The allusion is to the "couzening picture, which one way / Shows like a crow, another like a swan," from George Chapman's *All Fools*, 1.1.47, quoted in Ernest B. Gilman, *The Curious Perspective: Literary and Pictorial Wit in the Seventeenth Century* (New Haven, CT: Yale University Press, 1978), 36.

72. See Diehl's perceptive discussion of Marlowe's simultaneous enchantment and disenchantment, *Staging Reform, Reforming the Stage*, 73–81.

Chapter 3 Goethe's *Faust*

1. Charles Mountfort, *The Life and Death of Doctor Faustus: Made into a Farce* (London: printed and sold by E. Whitelock near Stationers' Hall, 1697).

2. *Ibid.*, 6.

3. On Faustus's last jig as a kind of dance of death, see Christa Knellwolf King, *Faustus and the Promises of the New Science, c.1580–1730* (Farnham: Ashgate, 2008), 170, and, for a discussion of the ironic undercutting of the Faust legend in Mountfort's play, 166–71.

4. Bevington, "Performance History," 46.

5. For an insightful discussion of the subversive nature of the harlequinades, see King, *Promises of the New Science*, 166–81.

6. Bevington, "Performance History," 46; for a valuable examination of the early performance history of Marlowe's play, see 41–46.

7. For a comprehensive discussion of the corrupt German versions and the puppet plays based (loosely) on Marlowe's play, see SFT, 239–51.

8. *Ibid.*, 243–51.

9. *Ibid.*, 241.

10. See David Luke, "Introduction" to FI-L, xiv. Goethe's response to Marlowe's play is cited by Heller, *Faust and Faustus*, 16.

11. Martin Swales, "The Character and Characterization of Faust," in Paul Bishop (ed.), *A Companion to Goethe's Faust, Parts I and II* (Rochester, NY: Camden House, 2001), 28–55 (at 30).

12. Heller, *Faust and Faustus*, 11–49.

13. Paul Bishop, "Introduction" to Bishop (ed.), *Companion to Goethe's Faust*, xv.

14. *Ibid.*, xv–xviii; Stuart Atkins, *Goethe's Faust: A Literary Analysis* (Cambridge, MA: Harvard University Press, 1964), 1–2; Cyrus Hamlin, "The Composition of *Faust*," in F-AH, 505–13 (at 505–07).

15. Jane K. Brown, *Faust: Theater of the World* (New York: Twayne, 1992), 3–6.

16. See Hans Schulte, "Introduction" to Hans Schulte, John Noyes, and Pia Kleber (eds.), *Goethe's Faust: Theatre of Modernity* (Cambridge University Press, 2011), 8; see also Ulrich Gaier, "Schwankende Gestalten: Virtuality in Goethe's *Faust*," in Schulte, Noyes, and Kleber (eds.), *Theatre of Modernity*, 54.

17. For a discussion of the performance history of Goethe's *Faust* until the 1960s, see Luke, "Introduction" to FI-L, xlvii–xlix.

18. I wish to thank Martina Maria Sam for the information she provided me personally on the original production of Goethe's *Faust* at the Goetheanum. For detailed information on productions of Goethe's *Faust* at the Goetheanum, see Martina Maria Sam, *Rudolf Steiners Faust-Rezeption: Interpretationen und Imaginationen als Vorbereitung der Welturaufführung des gesamten Goetheschen Faust 1938* (Basel: Schwabe Verlag, 2011). David G. John also describes the 2004 production of *Faust* at the Goetheanum, which took only eighteen hours to perform, in "The Complete *Faust* on Stage: Peter Stein and the Goetheanum," in Lorna Fitzsimmons (ed.), *Goethe's Faust and Cultural Memory* (Bethlehem, PA: Lehigh University Press, 2012), 107–28 (at 107, 124).

19. See the interview with Peter Stein, "Directing *Faust*: An Interview," in Schulte, Noyes, and Kleber (eds.), *Theatre of Modernity*, 267–79. See also Dirk Pilz, "A Contradictory Whole: Peter Stein stages *Faust*," in Schulte, Noyes, and Kleber (eds.), *Theatre of Modernity*, 280–92; and John, "Complete *Faust* on Stage," 123.

20. See Pilz, "Contradictory Whole," 291.

21. See SFT, 273. For a German version of the scene published in Lessing's "Seventeenth Letter" and also the "Berlin Scenario," composed at about the same time but not published until after Lessing's death, see SFT, 274–79.

22. Gotthold Ephraim Lessing, *Werke*, ed. Herbert G. Göpfert, 8 vols. (Munich: Carl Hanser Verlag, 1970–79), vol. 11, 780, cited in Jeffrey Barnouw, "Faust and the Ethos of Technology," in Jane K. Brown, Meredith Lee, and Thomas P. Saine, with Paul Hernadi and Cyrus Hamlin (eds.), *Interpreting Goethe's Faust Today* (Columbia, SC: Camden House, 1994), 29–42 (at 33). For a discussion of both Lessing's "Seventeenth Letter" and his "Berlin Scenario," see Klaus L. Berghahn, "Georg Johann Heinrich Faust: The Myth and its History," in Reinhold Grimm and Jost Hermand (eds.), *Our Faust? Roots and Ramifications of a Modern German Myth* (Madison: University of Wisconsin Press, 1987), 3–21 (at 11–13).

23. Jaroslav Pelikan, "Faust as Doctor of Theology," in Goethe, *Faust*, ed. Hamlin, 586–97 (at 594); Franziska Schöfsler, "Progress and Restorative Utopia in *Faust II* and *Wilhelm Meisters Wanderjahre*," in Bishop (ed.), *Companion to Goethe's Faust*, 169–93 (at 182).

24. All quotations from Goethe's *Faust, Part I*, unless otherwise indicated, are taken from the translation by David Luke (F1-L). All quotations from Goethe's *Faust, Part II* are also taken from Luke's translation (F2-L). All citations from both Part I and Part II are included within the text.

25. Butler, *Fortunes of Faust*, 136; Hamlin, "Interpretive Notes," in Goethe, *Faust*, ed. Hamlin, 476; Luke, "Explanatory Notes" to F1-L, 166 n. 89; Jane K. Brown, "Faust," in Lesley Sharp (ed.), *The Cambridge Companion to Goethe* (Cambridge University Press, 2002), 84–100 (at 88); see also Brown, *Theater of the World*, 23.

26. See Alfred Hoelzel, *The Paradoxical Quest: A Study of Faustian Vicissitudes* (New York: Peter Lang, 1988), 86–87; and Hamlin, "Interpretive Notes," 348. See also Brown, "Faust," 88.

27. Ritchie Robertson, "Literary Techniques and Aesthetic Texture in *Faust*," in Bishop (ed.), *Companion to Goethe's Faust*, 1–27, esp. 12.

28. On the significance of Satan's name, see Kelly, *Devil, Demonology, and Witchcraft*, 13. The name "Satan" derives from the Hebrew for "adversary" and from the French verb "to oppose" (SOED).

29. Swales, "Character and Characterization," 38.

30. Heller, *Faust and Faustus*, 34.

31. Hamlin, "Interpretive Notes," 13 n. 4.

32. Hamlin, "Interpretive Notes," 354.

33. Brown, *Theater of the World*, 41–44; Charles E. Passage, "Introduction" to F-P, xli; Jeffrey Burton Russell, *Mephistopheles: The Devil in the Modern World* (Ithaca, NY: Cornell University Press, 1986), 159; Osman Durrani, "The Character and Qualities of Mephistopheles," in Bishop (ed.), *Companion to Goethe's Faust*, 76–94 (at 80); Peter-André Alt, "Mephisto's Principles: On the Construction of Evil in Goethe's *Faust I*," *Modern*

Language Review, 106/1 (2011): 149–63 (at 152); Dieter Borchmeyer, "Mephisto or the Spirit of Laughter," trans. Lene Heilmann, in Simon Richter and Richard Block (eds.), *Goethe's Ghosts: Reading and the Persistence of Literature* (Rochester, NY: Camden House, 2013), 111–25 (at 113).

34. See Bishop, "Introduction" to *A Companion to Faust*, xxiv.
35. Atkins, *Literary Analysis*, 40.
36. Brown, *Theater of the World*, 36; Durrani, "Character and Qualities," 81; Hellmut Ammerlahn, "From Haunting Visions to Revealing (Self-) Reflections: The Goethean Hero between Subject and Object," in Richter and Block (eds.), *Goethe's Ghosts*, 97–110 (at 101).
37. For a fascinating treatment of the image of Helen of Troy in literature, see Maguire, *Helen of Troy*.
38. See Marilyn French, *Shakespeare's Division of Experience* (New York: Ballantine, 1981), 13. Significantly, French divides the "feminine principle" into the "in-law feminine principle" and the "out-law feminine principle." It is the "in-law feminine principle" which is significant in Goethe's *Faust*.
39. See Sara Munson Deats, *Sex, Gender, and Desire in the Plays of Christopher Marlowe* (Newark: University of Delaware Press, 1997), 202–24, esp. 204 and 223–24.
40. Hoelzel, *Paradoxical Quest*, 98–102.
41. For discussions of the various political appropriations of the play, see Alberto Destro, "The Guilty Hero, or the Tragic Salvation of Faust," in Bishop (ed.), *Companion to Goethe's Faust*, 56–75 (at 56); Swales, "Character and Characterization," 48; and Schöfsler, "Progress and Restorative Utopia," 184. See the following summaries of critical exegeses on the play: Stuart Atkins, "Survey of the Faust Theme," in Goethe, *Faust*, ed. Hamlin, 573–85 (at 582–84); Hoelzel, *Paradoxical Quest*, 98–102; Pelikan, "Faust as Doctor of Theology," 586–87; Hans Rudolf Vaget, "The Ethics of Faust's Last Action," in Goethe, *Faust*, ed. Hamlin, 704–14 (at 704–07); and John R. Williams, "The Problem of the Mothers," in Bishop (ed.), *Companion to Goethe's Faust*, 122–43 (at 123–26).
42. Passage, "Introduction" to *f-p*, xcii; Marshall Berman, "Faust as Developer," in Goethe, *Faust*, ed. Hamlin, 715–27 (at 17–18); Heller, *Faust and Faustus*, 47; Berman, "Faust as Developer," 722; Atkins, "Survey of the Faust Theme," 581.
43. Hamlin, "Interpretive Notes," 461; Vaget, "Ethics of Faust's Last Action," 715, 713.
44. See Atkins, a most sympathetic interpreter of Faust and his actions, *Literary Analysis*, 81 (see also 79–80).
45. In discussing the provenance of the Gretchen episode, Luke makes reference to Goethe's own romance with a simple country girl, Friederike Brion, whom the playwright cruelly abandoned. However, Luke posits as a more probable stimulus the trial and execution for infanticide of Susanna Margaretha

Brandt, whose prison stood only 200 yards from Goethe's house in Frankfurt. This deplorable historical episode offers striking parallels to Goethe's drama. Susanna, a simple country girl whose brother was a soldier, claimed to have been seduced by a traveling goldsmith with the help of a drug and at the prompting of the Devil, and killed her infant child to avoid public disgrace. For a discussion of the possible influence of these biographical incidents, see Luke, "Introduction" to FI-L, xviii.

46. Franco Moretti expresses this view in "Goethe's *Faust* as Modern Epic," in Goethe, *Faust*, ed. Hamlin, 611–33 (at 617).

47. Hamlin, "Interpretive Notes," 376; Brown, *Theater of the World*, 66.

48. Jane K. Brown discusses the differences in the mimetic and non-mimetic dramatic modes, in *Goethe's Faust: The German Tragedy* (Ithaca, NY: Cornell University Press, 1986), 19–25. Richard T. Gray also analyzes the tension between the empathetic, illusionist qualities and the mediated emblematic qualities of the play: see "Shipwreck with Spectators: Ideologies of Observation in Goethe's *Faust*, Part II," in Richter and Block (eds.), *Goethe's Ghosts*, 126–48 (at 133–34).

49. Brown, *Theater of the World*, 80, 72; Hamlin, "Interpretive Notes," 441. See also Anthony Phelan, "The Classical and the Medieval in *Faust II*," in Bishop (ed.), *Companion to Goethe's Faust*, 143–67; and Atkins, *Literary Analysis*, 142.

50. See Williams, "Problem of the Mothers," 123–31 (esp. 123), for a survey of critical responses to "the Mothers." For a discussion of the phallic imagery throughout the drama, see Robert Tobin, "Faust's Membership in Male Society: Prometheus and Ganymede as Models," in Brown *et al.* (eds.), *Interpreting Goethe's Faust Today*, 17–28.

51. For a discussion of the significance of the Walpurgis Night sequence, see Hamlin, "Interpretive Notes," 183–84.

52. Luke, "Introduction" to FI-L, xlii.

53. Robertson, "Literary Techniques," 14. For other perceptive analyses of Goethe's use of diverse poetic styles in the Helena sequence, see Hamlin, "Interpretive Notes," 440–46; and Phelan, "Classical and Medieval," 161–66.

54. Luke, "Introduction" to *f2-l*, xlvi.

55. Brown, *Theater of the World*, 78–79.

56. "Letter to Eckermann, December 20th, 1829," trans. in Hamlin, "Interpretive Notes," 542.

57. Luke, "Introduction" to *f2-l*, xli.

58. "Letter to Eckermann, July 5, 1827" and "Conversation with Eckermann, December 20, 1829," trans. in Hamlin, "Interpretive Notes," 536 n.9, 542.

59. Brown, *Theater of the World*, 73.

60. For a discussion of Faust as a pioneer of modern technology and Goethe's ambivalence toward his hero, see Barnouw, "Ethics of Technology."

61. Hamlin, "Interpretive Notes," 454–55.
62. Leading advocates of this ironic reading, in addition to Hamlin, include Vaget, "Ethics of Faust's Last Action," 709; Swales, "Character and Characterization," 47; and Destro, "Guilty Hero," 59–60, 70.
63. Hamlin, "Interpretive Notes," 455.
64. Butler, *Fortunes of Faust*, 260–61. Other commentators expressing this point of view include Virgil Nemoianu, "Absorbing Modernization: The Dilemmas of Progress in the Novels of Walter Scott and in *Faust II*," in Brown *et al.* (eds.), *Interpreting Goethe's Faust Today*, 1–16 (at 6); and Moretti, "Modern Epic," 616–17.
65. Berman, "Faust as Developer," 724, 720. Scholars endorsing this perspective include Atkins, *Literary Analysis*, 250–55.
66. Critics who see Faust as gaining a tragic *anagnorisis* in this speech include Butler, *Fortunes of Faust*, 264; Atkins, *Literary Analysis*, 251; Luke, "Introduction" to *f2-l*, lxvii.
67. For an ironic interpretation of this speech, see Hamlin, "Interpretive Notes," 477–78.
68. For the celebratory reading, see Berman, "Faust as Developer," 720–24. Ironic commentators include Vaget, "Ethics of Faust's Last Action," 715, 713; and Destro, "Guilty Hero."
69. Hoelzel, *Paradoxical Quest*, 108–15, esp. 108, 111. See also Luke, who defines "Lemurs" as "the restless ghosts of the dead," in his Index to *f2-l*, 296.
70. Butler, *Fortunes of Faust*, 262.
71. Cf. Luke's translation (*f2-l*, 223) to those of Arndt (*f-ah*, 329) and Passage (*f-p*, 393).
72. Cf. the translation by Luke (*f2-l*, 224), which follows Luther's translation of Christ's last words on the cross, to those of Arndt (*f-ah*, 329), and Passage (*f-p*, 394), both of which adopt the more familiar translation from the King James Bible.
73. Brown depicts *Faust* as a dialectical drama that will be interpreted differently depending on the perspective from which it is viewed (*Theater of the World*, 33, 99).
74. "Letter to Eckermann, June 6th, 1831," trans. in Goethe, *Faust*, ed. Hamlin, 546.
75. Ellis Dye, "Figurations of the Feminine in Goethe's *Faust*," in Bishop (ed.), *Companion to Goethe's Faust*, 95–121 (at 117). For other insightful discussions of the tension between the masculine and feminine principles in *Faust*, see Gail K. Hart, "Das Ewig-Weibliche nasführet dich: Feminine Leadership in Goethe's *Faust* and Sacher-Masoch's *Venus*," in Brown *et al.* (eds.), *Interpreting Goethe's Faust Today*, 112–22; Christoph E. Schweitzer, "Gretchen and the Feminine in Goethe's *Faust*," in Brown *et al.* (eds.),

Interpreting Goethe's Faust Today, 133–41; and Patricia Anne Simpson in "Gretchen's Ghosts: Goethe, Adorno, and the Literature of Refuge," in Richter and Block (eds.), *Goethe's Ghosts*, 168–85. For an iconoclastic reading of the symbolism of the "eternal feminine" in the drama, see Hamlin, "Tracking the Eternal-Feminine in Goethe's *Faust II*," in Brown *et al.* (eds.), *Interpreting Goethe's Faust Today*, 142–57. Applying a feminist approach to *Faust Part I* and *II*, Barbara Becker-Cantarino, "Goethe and Gender," in Sharp (ed.), *Cambridge Companion to Goethe*, 179–92 (at 190), concludes that the drama is a "patriarchal text with a well-defined gender dichotomy."

76. Both Arndt and Passage translate this phrase (12110) as the "Eternal Feminine"; cf. Luke, (*f2-l*, 239), Arndt (*f-ah*, 344), and Passage (*f-p*, 413). Passage relates Goethe's "Eternal Feminine" to "the perfection of Love in Dante's final lines in the *Paradiso*, 'the Love that moves the sun and other stars,'" 413 n. 23.

Chapter 4 Post-Goethe Dramatic Versions of the Faust Legend

1. For a survey of the critical literature on appropriation and adaptation, see Desmet and Lyengar, "Adaptation, Appropriation."
2. See Hamlin, "Interpretive Notes," 454–55.
3. For a discussion of these traditional gender binaries, see Mary Vetterling-Braggin (ed.), "Introduction" to *"Femininity," "Masculinity," and "Androgyny"* (Totowa, NJ: Rowman & Littlefield, 1982), 6; and Hélène Cixous and Catherine Clement, "Sorties: Out and Out: Attacks/Ways Out/Forays," in *The Newly Born Woman*, trans. Betsy Wing (Minneapolis: University of Minnesota Press, 1986), 63–134 (at 63, 65). See also Deats's feminist reading of Marlowe's plays, *Sex, Gender, and Desire*, 71.
4. For a discussion of Sand's play in relation to "the two cultures" of C. P. Snow and F. R. Leavis, as well as the theory of gynesis advocated by Alice A. Jardine, see George A. Kennedy, "Introduction" to George Sand, *A Woman's Version of the Faust Legend: The Seven Strings of the Lyre*, trans. and ed. George A. Kennedy (Chapel Hill: University of North Carolina Press, 1989), 21–22. All citations to the play will be to this edition and will be included within the text.
5. Sara Stambaugh, "Review of *A Woman's Version of the Faust Legend: The Seven Strings of the Lyre*," *Victorian Review*, 16/1 (Summer 1990): 83–85 (at 83).
6. Kennedy, "Introduction" to *Seven Strings of the Lyre*, 13.
7. *Ibid.*, 12.
8. *Ibid.*, 12.
9. See above, Chapter 3, note 58.

10. See Kennedy, "Introduction" to *Seven Strings of the Lyre*, 12.

11. For a comprehensive discussion of all the variant versions of the play, see W. B. Yeats, *The Countess Cathleen: Manuscript Materials*, ed. Michael J. Sidnell and Wayne K. Chapman (Ithaca, NY: Cornell University Press, 1999). All citations to the play will be to this edition and will be included in the text.

12. Yeats found the story of the play while collecting material for his *Fairy and Folk Tales of the Irish Peasantry*. The Irish story appears to have been adapted from a French narrative titled "Les merchands d'âmes" by Léo Lépès; see Sidnell and Chapman, "Introduction" to *Countess Cathleen, Manuscript Materials*, xxxvii. For a full discussion of the provenance of the play, see *Ibid.*, xxxvii–xxxviii.

13. See Sidnell and Chapman, "Introduction" to *Countess Cathleen*, xl.

14. *Coming of the Antichrist*, ll. 215–45. See also Parker, *Aesthetics of Antichrist*, 92. For information on the first edition of *The Chester Cycle* edited by Thomas Wright for the New Shakespeare Society in 1843 and 1847, see *Chester Mystery Cycle*, xxxi. Since the first edition of the full Chester Cycle had been published for the New Shakespeare Society in 1843 and 1847, Yeats, a voracious reader, might well have been familiar with this particular biblical cycle; however, without specific reference, we cannot be certain of any direct influence.

15. Nancy Ann Watanabe, "Yeats's Merlin-Faust Design in *The Countess Cathleen*," in Charlotte Spivack (ed.), *Merlin Versus Faust: Contending Archetypes in Western Culture* (Lewiston, NY: Edwin Mellen Press, 1992), 139–59 (at 149).

16. Peter Ure, "The Evolution of Yeats's *The Countess Cathleen*," *Modern Language Review*, 57 (1962), 12–24 (at 22).

17. *The Letters of W. B. Yeats*, ed. Allan Wade (New York: Macmillan, 1955), 319, cited in Watanabe, "Merlin-Faust Design," 148.

18. Cited by Joseph M. Hone, *W. B. Yeats 1865–1939* (New York: Macmillan, 1943), 92.

19. Ure, "Evolution of *Countess Cathleen*," 23–24.

20. Michael McAteer, *Yeats and the European Drama* (Cambridge University Press, 2010), 26.

21. Ure, "Evolution of *Countess Cathleen*," 18.

22. For a survey of ideological appropriations of Faust's great speech in Act 5 for political purposes, see Chapter 3, n.41.

23. *Three Plays of A. V. Lunacharski*, trans. L. A. Magnus and K. Walker (London: George Routledge & Sons, 1923). All references to *Faust and the City* will be taken from this edition and included in the text of this chapter.

24. See Eric A. Blackall, "What the devil?!—Twentieth-Century Fausts," in Boemer and Johnson (eds.), *Faust through Four Centuries*, 197–212 (at 202).

25. Hedges, *Framing Faust*, 78.
26. Richard Ilgner, "Goethe's 'Geist, der stets verneint' and Its Emergence in the Faust Works of Odoevvsky, Lunacharsky, and Bulgakov," *Germano-Slavica: A Canadian Journal of Germanic and Slavic Comparative Studies*, 2 (1977): 169–80 (at 176–77).
27. Roland Boer, "Utopia, Religion and the God-Builders: From Anatoly Lunacharsky to Ernest Block," in Ligia Tomoiaga, Minodorä Barbul, and Ramona Demarcsek (eds.), *From Francis Bacon to William Golding: Utopias and Dystopias of Today and of Yore* (Newcastle: Cambridge Scholars, 2012), 2–20 (at 1).
28. Philip Ward, "Introduction" to Frank Wedekind, *Franziska*, trans. Philip Ward, adapted Eleanor Brown (London: Oberon, 1998), 7. All citations from the play will be to this edition and will be included in the text of this chapter.
29. For a performance history of *Franziska*, see Ward, "Introduction" to *Franziska*, 8.
30. *Ibid.*, 9. My discussion of *Franziska* is deeply indebted to Ward's informative "Introduction" (see 9–12).
31. *Ibid.*, 9.
32. Audrone B. Willeke, "Frank Wedekind and the 'Frauenfrage,'" *Monatshefte*, 72/1 (1980): 26–38 (at 34).
33. Ward, "Introduction" to *Franziska*, 11.
34. Hedges, *Framing Faust*, 105.
35. For a discussion of the first and second waves of feminism, see Hester Eisenstein, *Contemporary Feminist Thought* (Boston: G. K. Hall, 1983).
36. See Cole, "Faust and Anti-Faust in Modern Drama," *Drama Survey*, 5 (1966): 39–52 (at 39).
37. See Ficke's "Introductory Note" to the 1922 version of *Mr. Faust: An Entirely New Version, Reconstructed for Stage Production* (New York: Frank Shay, 1922). Subsequent citations will be this version and will be included within the text.
38. Dedication to *Mr. Faust*, by Arthur Davison Ficke (Norwood, MA: Plimpson Press, 1913).
39. Edwin Björkman, "Introduction" to *Mr. Faust* (New York: M. Kennedy, 1913), vii–viii.
40. Richard Dietrich, *Bernard Shaw's Novels: Portraits of the Artist as Man and Superman* (Gainesville: University Press of Florida, 1996), 73 (for a particularly lucid explanation of Shaw's concept of the "Superman," see 73–76). See also Blackall, "What the devil?!," 203. For Nietzsche's theory of the "Superman," or the "overman," see Walter Kaufmann, "Editor's Note" to *Thus Spoke Zurathustra*, in *The Portable Nietzsche*, ed. and trans. Walter Kaufmann (New York: Viking, 1968), 115–16.

41. Cole, "Faust and Anti-Faust," 39.

42. Hedges, *Framing Faust*, 125.

43. See *The Death of Doctor Faust*, in Michel de Ghelderode, *Seven Plays*, trans. George Hauger, vol. II (New York: Hill & Wang, 1950). Subsequent references will be to this edition and will be included within the text.

44. Cole, "Faust and Anti-Faust," 42.

45. Hedges, *Framing Faust*, 126.

46. Christine Kiebuzińska, "Witkacy and Ghelderode: Goethe's *Faust* Transformed into a Grotesque Cabaret," *Polish Journal of Aesthetics*, 31 (2013): 207–20 (at 209).

47. *Ibid.*, 214.

48. Cole, "Faust and Anti-Faust," 40.

49. June Schlueter, *Metafictional Characters in Modern Drama* (New York: Columbia University Press, 1979), 14.

50. Dorothy Sayers, "Preface" to *The Devil to Pay* (New York: Harcourt, Brace, 1939), 10. Subsequent references to the Preface and the play will be to this edition and will be included within the text.

51. Paul R. Fetters, "Dorothy Sayers and the Wiles of the Wicked One as Observed in her Contribution to the Faustus Legend, *The Devil to Pay*," *Inklings Forever*, 5 (2006), unpaginated.

52. Animal behaviorists and psychologists today accept the view that animals are far more than the unknowing, mindless brutes described in Sayers's play; however, the attitude expressed by the Judge was widely accepted in the 1930s, when the play was first performed.

53. Suzanne Bray, "Temptations for the Time in the Mystical Rewritings of British Christian Authors 1933–1945," in Suzanne Bray, Adrienne E. Gavin, and Peter Merchant (eds.),*Re-Embroidering the Robe: Faith, Myth and Literary Creation since 1850* (Newcastle: Cambridge Scholars, 2008), 127–43 (at 133).

54. See Francis Fergusson, "The Theater of Paul Valéry," in Paul Valéry, *Plays*, trans. David Paul and Robert Fitzgerald (New York: Pantheon, 1960), vii–xix (at xvi).

55. *Ibid.*, xviii; see also Cole, "Faust and Anti-Faust," 45.

56. Fergusson, "Theater of Paul Valéry," xvi.

57. In addition to the readings mentioned above, *Mon Faust (My Faust)* was given a single performance at the Théâtre Rochefort in Paris in July 29, 1946, and was later performed in Brussels and Helsinki in 1947 and 1952, respectively. More recently it has been performed at several theaters in Paris: the Théâtre de l'Œuvre in 1962, The Théâtre des Célestins in 1964, the Théâtre de la Michodière in 1971, the Théâtre du Rond-Point in 1987, and the Théâtre de Carouge in 2014. https://fr.wikipedia.org/wiki/Mon_Faust.

58. *My Faust*, in Valéry, *Plays*, 38. All subsequent references will be to this edition and will be included within the text.

59. Cole, "Faust and Anti-Faust," 45.
60. *Ibid.*, 46.
61. Igor Stravinsky, "Valéry: A Memoir," in Valéry, *Plays*, xxiv.
62. Lawrence Durrell, *An Irish Faustus: A Morality in Nine Scenes* (New York: E. P. Dutton, 1964), 37. All subsequent references will be to this edition of the play and will be included within the text.
63. "Goethe Go Home," *Time Magazine*, Friday, January 3, 1964, 56. For a discussion of the Jungian elements in the play, see G. S. Fraser, *Lawrence Durrell: A Critical Study* (New York: E. P. Dutton, 1968), 115–16.
64. Michael Cartwright, "The Playwright as Miracle Worker: *An Irish Faustus*," *Deus Loci: The Lawrence Durrell Newsletter*, 3/4 (1980): 3–12 (at 8).
65. Peter G. Christensen, "Lawrence Durrell's Plays: A Reevaluation," in Frank Kersnowski (ed.), *Into the Labyrinth: Essays on the Art of Lawrence Durrell* (Ann Arbor, MI: UMI Research Press, 1989), 73–85 (at 77).
66. "Goethe Go Home," 56.
67. Cartwright, "Playwright as Miracle Worker," 9.
68. Cole, "Faust and Anti-Faust," 51.
69. All references to the play will be to Václav Havel, *Temptation*, trans. Marie Winn (New York: Grove Press, 1989), and will be included within the text.
70. Ehrhard Bahr, "Václav Havel's Faust Drama *Temptation* (1985): Or, The Challenge of Influence," *Goethe Yearbook*, 7 (1994): 194–209 (at 195). My interpretation of the play is much indebted to this illuminating article.
71. See Marketa Goetz-Stankiewicz, "Variations of Temptation – Václav Havel's Politics of Language," in Marketa Goetz-Stankiewicz and Phyllis Carey (eds.), *Critical Essays on Václav Havel* (New York: G. K. Hall, 1999), 228–42 (at 230).
72. See the performance history of the play in Bahr, "Havel's *Temptation*," 195.
73. See Joan Erben, "The Spirit from Below: A Theoretical Approach to Václav Havel's *Temptation*," *European Studies Journal*, 15 (1998): 10–19; and Goetz-Stankiewicz, "Variations of Temptation," 234–39.
74. Bahr, "Havel's *Temptation*," 201. Bahr also associates the final costume party with Goethe's Walpurgis Night.
75. *Ibid.*, 201.
76. Jayne Blanchard, "Václav Havel's *Temptation*," *Washington Times*, October 15, 2008.
77. All references to the play are to David Mamet, *Faustus* (New York: Vintage, 2004), and will be included in the text.
78. Suzanne Weiss, "*Dr. Faustus* – David Mamet," *Culture Vulture*, March 3, 2004, http://culturevulture.net/theater/dr-faustus-david-mamet.
79. See Dennis Harvey, "Review: 'Dr. Faustus,'" *Variety*, March 9, 2004, variety.com/2004/legit/reviews/dr-faustus-1200534615.
80. See Weiss, "*Dr. Faustus* – David Mamet Review."

81. *Ibid.*
82. See David Davalos, *Wittenberg* (New York: Dramatist Play Service, 2010). All quotations of the play will be from this edition and will be included within the text.
83. *Wittenberg* has also been produced in London, Bristol, Berlin, Vancouver, and Melbourne. See www.daviddavalos.com/production-history.html.
84. I take both the felicitous phrase "daft campus comedy" and the reference to the pun on Faustus's office from the review by Eric Grode, "Dueling Mentors Bedevil a Dithering Young Dane," *New York Times*, March 30, 2011. For two other perceptive reviews of the play, see Robert Hurwitt, "Wittenberg Review: A Pop Culture Hamlet Primer," *SFGate*, April 24, 2014; and Ronni Reich, "'Wittenberg' Review: Hamlet and Faustus as 'bros with big ideas,'" *Star-Ledger*, September 16, 2014.
85. Grode, "Dueling Mentors."

Chapter 5 Cinematic Fausts

1. See the Tyburn Entertainment DVD of Nevill Coghill and Richard Burton's *The Tragical History of Doctor Faustus*. All quotations will be from this DVD.
2. See Jennifer Yirinec, "Re-envisioning the Faust Legend: Christopher Marlowe's *The Tragical History of Doctor Faustus* and Richard Burton and Nevill Coghill's *Doctor Faustus*," *Literature/Film Quarterly*, 41 (2013): 67–76.
3. In Goethe's *Faust, Part I*, in "The Witch's Kitchen," Mephistopheles shows Faust a vision of a beautiful woman that haunts him throughout the play (9.2429–41).
4. *Edward II* (1.1.49–70), in Christopher Marlowe, *Doctor Faustus and Other Plays*, ed. David Bevington and Eric Rasmussen (Oxford University Press, 1995).
5. See Yirinec's discussion of the significance of the Actaeon/Diana pantomime in "Re-envisioning the Faust Legend," 72.
6. Greg, "Damnation of Faustus." For a full discussion of Greg's thesis and the scholarly refutations of it, see Chapter 2 above, 55–56 and 60.
7. Yirinec examines the ramifications of the "mirror scene," in "Re-envisioning the Faust Legend," 73.
8. For an exploration of the relationship of the comic sub-plot to the tragic action of Marlowe's play, see Ornstein, "Comic Synthesis."
9. For an analysis of this downward trajectory, see Hunter, "Five-Act Structure."
10. Yirinec relates the Burton/Coghill film to the summer of love in "Re-envisioning the Faust Legend," 73.
11. See Bevington, "Performance History," 5.
12. See the Kino Restored Deluxe Edition of F. W. Murnau's *Faust*. All quotations from this film will be from this DVD.

13. Philip Kemp quotes Weinberg, Lejeune, and Kracauer in his review, "*Faust*" in *Sight and Sound*, 24/9 (September 2014): 112.

14. For Hedges's valuable discussion of the pictorial quality of Murnau's *Faust*, see *Framing Faust*, 35–40.

15. See the Cohen Film Collection DVD of René Clair's *The Beauty of the Devil*. All quotations from this film will be from this DVD.

16. Hedges, *Framing Faust*, 189.

17. Sterritt, "'I Married a Witch' and 'The Beauty of the Devil,'" *Cineaste* 39.2 (Spring, 2014): 50–52 (at 52).

18. See the Kino DVD of Jan Švankmajer's *Faust*. All quotations from this film will be from this DVD.

19. Ian Christie, "Faust and Furious," *Sight and Sound*, 21 (2011): 38–40 (at 38).

20. Jones, "A Passive Faust Goes to the Devil Slowly," *New York Times*, October 26, 1994.

21. Michael Wilmington, "Svankmajer's 'Faust': A Nightmare Not Easily Forgotten," *Chicago Tribune*, February 24, 1995.

22. Hedges, *Framing Faust*, 183.

23. See the Kino Lober DVD of Sokurov's *Faust*. All quotations from this film will be from this DVD.

24. For the background of Sokurov's *Faust*, see Christie, "Faust and Furious," 39.

25. Christie, "Faust and Furious," 39; Tony Rayns, "*Faust*," *Sight and Sound*, 22/6 (June 2012): 53.

26. Rob White, "Fiendish," *Film Quarterly*, 65.2 (Winter, 2011): 77.

27. Christie, "Faust and Furious," 39; Rayns, "*Faust*."

28. Rayns, "*Faust*."

29. Graham Fuller, "Devil's Pact: Goethe's Morality Tale Revisited," *Modern Picture*, 25 (2013): 57.

30. Noted by Hedges, *Framing Faust*, 164.

31. I am indebted in this discussion to the information provided by film historian Bruce Eder and bibliographer Steven C. Smith in the Commentary on the Criterion Collection DVD of *The Devil and Daniel Webster*. All quotations from this film will be from this DVD.

32. Hedges, *Framing Faust*, 165–66.

33. See Thomas Cooksey, "'Talk not of a wife': *The Devil and Daniel Webster, A Cabin in the Sky*, and *Damn Yankees* – American Contributions to the Faust Myth," *Journal of Popular Film and Television*, 27 (1999): 18–27 (at 20).

34. "Old Scratch," *American Heritage Dictionary of the English Language*, 4th edn. (Boston: Houghton Mifflin, 2000).

35. Washington Irving, "*The Devil and Tom Walker*" (Woodstock, VT: R & A Colton, 1830).

36. Cox, *The Devil and the Sacred*, 61–62.
37. Robert Singer, "One Against All: The New England Past and Present Responsibilities in *The Devil and Daniel Webster*," *Literature-Film Quarterly* 22 (1994): 265–71 (at 271).
38. See the Loving the Classics DVD of John Farrow's *Alias Nick Beal*. All quotations from this film will be from this DVD.
39. Hedges, *Framing Faust*, 160.
40. For the relevant lines from Marlowe's *Doctor Faustus*, see DF, 3.1.84.
41. See the Warner Bros. Entertainment DVD of George Abbot's and Stanley Donen's *Damn Yankees*.
42. Cooksey comments on the binary between the temptress Lola and the devoted wife Meg who, like Gretchen in Goethe's *Faust* and Mary in *The Devil and Daniel Webster*, acts as Joe's savior figure. See "Talk not of a Wife," 23.
43. Andrew Bush, "Remembering *Faust* in Argentina," in Fitzsimmons (ed.), *Goethe's Faust and Cultural Memory*, 91–106 (at 91).
44. See the Twentieth Century Fox Film Corporation and Stanley Donen Enterprises DVD of Stanley Donen's *Bedazzled*.
45. For a discussion of this pact, see Ingrid H. Shafer, "'The Phenomenon of Faust': The Faust Challenge: Science as Diabolic or Divine," *Zygon: Journal of Religion and Science*, 40/4 (December 2005): 891–915 (at 899).
46. See the Warner Bros. Entertainment DVD of Paul Bogart's *Oh, God! You Devil*.
47. For a discussion of the legends that have grown up around the great blues guitarist Robert Johnson, see Matt Copeland and Chris Goering, "Blues You Can Use: Teaching the Faust Theme through Music, Literature, and Film," *Journal of Adolescent and Adult Literacy*, 46 (2003): 436–41 (at 437).
48. See the Columbia Pictures DVD of Walter Hill's *Crossroads*.
49. The film is constructed around the myth – more fiction than fact – that Johnson wrote thirty songs for the album containing "Cross Road Blues," but recorded only twenty-nine. In actuality, "Cross Road Blues" was first recorded in 1936 as a single on the then standard 78 rpm record and never appears to have been part of an album, at least during Johnson's life.
50. I owe the designation of Highway 61 as "the royal road of the blues" to Hedges, *Framing Faust*, 176.
51. For a discussion of the influence of *The Karate Kid* on *Crossroads*, see Roger Ebert, "*Crossroads*," *Sun Times*, March 14, 1986. Also pertinent here is the relationship between Obi-Wan Kenobi and Luke Skywalker in *A New Hope, The Empire Strikes Back, The Return of the Jedi*, all part of the *Star Wars* saga.
52. I borrow the term "American cultural hybridization" from Hedges, *Framing Faust*, 177.

53. According to information gathered by the Disaster Center, homicide rates in the US soared in the 1980s and 1990s. Indeed, although most US citizens are shocked by the levels of violence prevalent today, homicide rates and other forms of violent crime have actually fallen significantly since their zenith in the 1980s and 1990s. For more information, see www.disastercenter.com/crime/uscrime.htm.
54. See the Lionsgate Home Entertainment DVD of Alan Parker's *Angel Heart*.
55. See Robert Singer, "The Merlin/Faust Archetypes in *Excalibur* and *Angel Street*," in Spivack (ed.), *Merlin Versus Faust*, 95–113 (at 97).
56. *The American Heritage Dictionary of the English Language*, New College Edition, ed. William Morris (Boston: Houghton Mifflin, 1981).
57. Singer, "Merlin/Faust Archetypes," 103, discusses *Angel Heart* as visualizing the despair and alienation of the American nightmare.
58. See the Dolby Digital DVD of Harold Ramis's *Bedazzled*.
59. See the relevant lines spoken by Mephistopheles in Marlowe's *Doctor Faustus*:

> Hell hath no limits, nor is circumscribed
> In one self place, for where we are is hell,
> And where hell is, there must we ever be.   (DF, 2.1.124–26)

Epilogue

1. See the film review by Jones, "Passive Faust."

Bibliography

Abbot, George, and Stanley Donen (dirs.). *Damn Yankees*. Film. 1955.

Alt, Peter-Andre. "Mephisto's Principles: On the Construction of Evil in Goethe's *Faust I*." *Modern Language Review*, 106/1 (2011): 149–63.

Altman, Joel B. *The Tudor Play of Mind: Rhetorical Inquiry and the Development of Elizabethan Drama*. Berkeley: University of California Press, 1978.

The American Heritage Dictionary of the English Language, ed. William Morris. New College Edition. Boston: Houghton Mifflin, 1981.

The American Heritage Dictionary of the English Language. 4th edn. Boston: Houghton Mifflin, 2000.

Ammerlahn, Hellmut. "From Haunting Visions to Revealing (Self-) Reflections: The Goethean Hero between Subject and Object." In Richter and Block (eds.), *Goethe's Ghosts*, 97–110.

Aquinas, Thomas. *Summa theologica*, trans. fathers of the English Dominican Province. Vol. xx. London: Encyclopedia Britannica, 1952.

Atkins, Stuart. *Goethe's Faust: A Literary Analysis*. Cambridge, MA: Harvard University Press, 1964.

"Survey of the Faust Theme." In Goethe, *Faust*, ed. Hamlin, 573–85.

Bahr, Ehrhard. "Václav Havel's Faust Drama *Temptation* (1985): Or, The Challenge of Influence." *Goethe Yearbook*, 7 (1994): 194–209.

Bakeless, John. *The Tragicall History of Christopher Marlowe*, vol. 1. Hamden, CT: Archon, 1964.

Barnouw, Jeffrey. "Faust and the Ethos of Technology." In Brown *et al.* (eds.), *Interpreting Goethe's Faust Today*, 29–42.

Baron, Frank. *Doctor Faustus from History to Legend*. Munich: Wilhelm Fink Verlag, 1978.

"Georg Lukàcs on the Origin of the Faust Legend." In Boemer and Johnson (eds.), *Faust through Four Centuries*, 13–26.

Bartels, Emily. *Spectacles of Strangeness: Imperialism, Alienation, and Marlowe*. Philadelphia: University of Pennsylvania Press, 1993.

Becker-Cantarino, Barbara. "Goethe and Gender." In Lesley Sharp (ed.), *The Cambridge Companion to Goethe*, 179–92. Cambridge University Press, 2002.

Berghahn, Klaus L. "Georg Johann Heinrich Faust: The Myth and its History." In Reinhold Grimm and Jost Hermand (eds.), *Our Faust? Roots and Ramifications* of a Modern German Myth, 3–21. Madison: University of Wisconsin Press, 1987.

Bergson, Henri. *Creative Evolution*, trans. Arthur Mitchell. Mineola, NY: Dover, 1998.

Berman, Marshall. "Faust as Developer." In Goethe, *Faust*, ed. Hamlin, 715–27.

Bevington, David. *From Mankind to Marlowe: Growth of Structure in the Popular Drama of Tudor England*. Cambridge, MA: Harvard University Press, 1963.

"Marlowe and God." *Explorations in Renaissance Culture*, 17 (1991): 1–38.

"The Performance History." In Deats (ed.), *Doctor Faustus: A Critical Guide*, 41–71.

Bevington, David, and Eric Rasmussen. "Introduction" to Marlowe, *Doctor Faustus*, ed. Bevington and Rasmussen.

Bishop, Paul. "Introduction" to Bishop (ed.), *Companion to Goethe's Faust*.

(ed.). *A Companion to Goethe's Faust, Parts I and II*. Rochester, NY: Camden House, 2001.

Björkman, Edwin. "Introduction" to Ficke, *Mr. Faust*.

Blackall, Eric A. "What the devil?—Twentieth-Century Fausts." In Boemer and Johnson (eds.), *Faust through Four Centuries*, 197–212.

Blanchard, Jayne. "Václav Havel's Temptation." Washington Times, October 15, 2008.

Bluestone, Max. "*Libido Speculandi*: Doctrine and Dramaturgy in Contemporary Interpretations of Marlowe's *Doctor Faustus*." In Norman Rabkin (ed.), *Reinterpretations of Elizabethan Drama*, 33–88. New York: Columbia University Press, 1969.

Boemer, Peter, and Sidney Johnson (eds.). *Faust through Four Centuries: Retrospect and Analysis*. Tübingen: Max Niemeyer Verlag, 1989.

Boer, Roland. "Utopia, Religion and the God-Builders from Anatoly Lunacharsky to Ernest Block." In Ligia Tomoiaga, Minodorä Barbul, and Ramona Demarcsek (eds.), *From Francis Bacon to William Golding: Utopias and Dystopias of Today and of Yore*, 2–20. Newcastle: Cambridge Scholars, 2012.

Bogart, Paul (dir.). *Oh, God! You Devil*. Film. 1984.

The Book of Common Prayer. London: 1965.

Borchmeyer, Dieter. "Mephisto or the Spirit of Laughter," trans. Lene Heilmann. In Richter and Block (eds.), *Goethe's Ghosts*, 111–25.

Bradbrook, M. C. *Themes and Conventions of Elizabethan Tragedy*. Cambridge University Press, 1935.

Brandt, Bruce. "The Critical Backstory." In Deats (ed.), *Doctor Faustus: A Critical Guide*, 17–40.

Bray, Suzanne. "Temptations for the Time in the Mystical Rewritings of British Christian Authors 1933–1945." In Suzanne Bray, Adrienne E. Gavin, and Peter Merchant (eds.), *Re-Embroidering the Robe: Faith, Myth and Literary Creation since 1850*, 127–43. Newcastle: Cambridge Scholars, 2008.

Brockbank, Philip. *Marlowe: Dr Faustus*. London: Edward Arnold, 1962.

Brooke, Nicholas. "The Moral Tragedy of *Doctor Faustus*." *Cambridge Journal*, 5 (1952): 662–87.

Brough, Neil. *New Perspectives of Faust: Studies in the Origins and Philosophy of the Faust Theme in the Dramas of Marlowe and Goethe*. New York: Peter Lang, 1994.

Brown, Beatrice Daw. "Marlowe, Faustus, and Simon Magus." *PMLA*, 54 (1939): 82–121.

Brown, Jane K. "Faust." In Lesley Sharp (ed.), *The Cambridge Companion to Goethe*. 84–100. Cambridge University Press, 2002.

Faust: Theater of the World. New York: Twayne, 1992.

Goethe's Faust: The German Tragedy. Ithaca, NY: Cornell University Press, 1986.

"The Prosperous Wonder Worker: Faust in the Renaissance." In Boemer and Johnson (eds.), *Faust through Four Centuries*, 53–64.

Brown, Jane K., Meredith Lee, Thomas P. Saine, Paul Hernadi, and Cyrus Hamlin (eds.). *Interpreting Goethe's Faust Today*. Columbia, SC: Camden House, 1994.

Bush, Andrew. "Remembering *Faust* in Argentina." In Lorna Fitzsimmons (ed.), *Goethe's Faust and Cultural Memory*, 91–106. Bethlehem, PA: Lehigh University Press, 2012.

Butler, Elizabeth M. *The Fortunes of Faust*. Cambridge University Press, 1952.

Myth of the Magus. Cambridge University Press, 1948.

Calvin, John. *The Institution of the Christian Religion*, trans. Thomas Norton. Glasgow: Printed by John Bryce and Archibald M'Lean, junior, for Alexander Irving, 1762.

Campbell, Lily Bess. "Doctor Faustus: A Case of Conscience." *PMLA*, 67 (1952): 219–39.

Cartwright, Michael. "The Playwright as Miracle Worker: *An Irish Faustus*." *Deus Loci: The Lawrence Durrell Newsletter*, 3/4 (1980): 3–12.

Castle, Dorothy. *The Diabolical Game to Win Man's Soul: A Rhetorical and Structural Approach to Mankind*. New York: Peter Lang, 1990.

Chambers, E. K. *The Mediaeval Stage*, vol. II. Oxford: Clarendon Press, 1903.

Cheney, Patrick. *Marlowe's Counterfeit Profession: Ovid, Spenser, Counter-Nationhood*. University of Toronto Press, 1997.

Christensen, Peter G. "Lawrence Durrell's Plays: A Reevaluation." In Frank Kersnowski (ed.), *Into the Labyrinth: Essays on the Art of Lawrence Durrell*, 73–85. Ann Arbor, MI: UMI Research Press, 1989.

Christie, Ian. "Faust and Furious." *Sight and Sound*, 21 (2011): 38–40.

Cixous, Hélène, and Catherine Clément. "Sorties: Out and Out: Attacks/Ways Out/Forays." In Cixous and Clément, *The Newly Born Woman*, trans. Betsy Wing, 63–134. Minneapolis: University of Minnesota Press, 1986.

Clair, René (dir.). *The Beauty of the Devil*. Film. 1950.

Coghill, Nevill, and Richard Burton (dirs.). *The Tragical History of Doctor Faustus*. Film. 1967.

Cole, Douglas. "Faust and Anti-Faust in Modern Drama." *Drama Survey*, 5 (1966): 39–52.

Suffering and Evil in the Plays of Christopher Marlowe. Princeton University Press, 1962.

Cooksey, Thomas. "'Talk not of a wife': *The Devil and Daniel Webster, A Cabin in the Sky*, and *Damn Yankees* – American Contributions to the Faust Myth." *Journal of Popular Film and Television*, 27 (1999): 18–27.

Copeland, Matt, and Chris Goering. "Blues You Can Use: Teaching the Faust Theme through Music, Literature, and Film." *Journal of Adolescent and Adult Literacy*, 46 (2003): 436–41.

Cox, John D. *The Devil and the Sacred in English Drama, 1350–1642*. Cambridge University Press, 2000.

Craik, T. W. "Faustus' Damnation Reconsidered." *Renaissance Drama*, n.s. 2 (1969): 189–96.

Danson, Lawrence. "Christopher Marlowe: The Questioner." *English Literary Renaissance*, 12 (1982): 3–29.

Davalos, David. *Playwrite*. www.daviddavalos.com/production-history.html. *Wittenberg*. New York: Dramatist Play Service, 2010.

Davidson, Clifford. "Doctor Faustus of Wittenberg." *Studies in Philology*, 59 (1962): 514–23.

Visualizing the Moral Life: Medieval Iconography and the Macro Morality Plays. New York: AMC Press, 1989.

Deats, Sara Munson. "Biblical Allusion in Marlowe's *Doctor Faustus*." *Medievalia et Humanistica*, n.s. 10 (1981): 203–16.

"*Doctor Faustus*." In Sara Munson Deats and Robert A. Logan (eds.), *Christopher Marlowe at 450*, 71–100. Farnham: Ashgate, 2015.

"*Doctor Faustus:* From Chapbook to Tragedy." Essays in Literature, 3 (1976): 3–16.

"'Mark this show': Magic and Theater in Marlowe's *Doctor Faustus*." In Sara Munson Deats and Robert A. Logan (eds.), *Placing the Plays of Christopher Marlowe*, 13–24. Aldershot: Ashgate, 2008.

"Marlowe's Interrogative Drama: *Dido, Tamburlaine, Faustus*, and *Edward II*." In Sara Munson Deats and Robert A. Logan (eds.), *Marlowe's Empery: Expanding His Critical Contexts*, 107–32. Newark: University of Delaware Press, 2002.

"Mars or Gorgon? Tamburlaine and Henry V." *Marlowe Studies: An Annual*, 1 (2011): 99–124.

Sex, Gender, and Desire in the Plays of Christopher Marlowe. Newark: University of Delaware Press, 1997.

(ed.). *Doctor Faustus: A Critical Guide*. London: Continuum, 2010.

Dent, R. W. "Ramist Faustus or Ramist Marlowe?" *Neuphilologische Mitteilungen*, 73 (1972): 63–74.

Desmet, Christy, and Sujata Lyengar. "Adaptation, Appropriation, or What You Will." *Shakespeare*, 11/1 (February 2015): 10–19.

Destro, Alberto. "The Guilty Hero, or the Tragic Salvation of Faust." In Bishop (ed.), *Companion to Goethe's Faust*, 56–75.

Diehl, Huston. *Staging Reform, Reforming the Stage: Protestantism and Popular Theatre in Early Modern England*. Ithaca, NY: Cornell University Press, 1997.

Dieterle, William (dir.). *The Devil and Daniel Webster*. Film. 1941.

Dietrich, Richard. *Bernard Shaw's Novels: Portraits of the Artist as Man and Superman*. Gainesville: University Press of Florida, 1996.

Dollimore, Jonathan. *Radical Tragedy: Religion, Ideology, and Power in the Drama of Shakespeare and his Contemporaries*. Durham, NC: Duke University Press, 1984.

Donen, Stanley (dir.). *Bedazzled*. Film. 1967.

Duane, Carol Leventen. "Marlowe's Mixed Messages: A Model for Shakespeare?" *Medieval and Renaissance Drama in England*, 3 (1986): 51–67.

Durrani, Osman. "The Character and Qualities of Mephistopheles." In Bishop (ed.), *Companion to Goethe's Faust*, 76–94.

Durrell, Lawrence. *An Irish Faustus: A Morality in Nine Scenes*. New York: E. P. Dutton, 1964.

Duxfield, Andrew. "Doctor Faustus and Renaissance Hermeticism." In Deats (ed.), *Doctor Faustus: A Critical Guide*, 96–110.

Dye, Ellis. "Figurations of the Feminine in Goethe's *Faust*." In Bishop (ed.), *Companion to Goethe's Faust*, 95–121.

Ebert, Roger. "Crossroads." *Sun Times*, March 14, 1986.

Eder, Bruce, and Steven C. Smith. "Commentary" to *The Devil and Daniel Webster*, dir. William Dieterle. Criterion Collection DVD.

Eisenstein, Hester. *Contemporary Feminist Thought*. Boston: G. K. Hall, 1983.

Ellis-Fermor, Una. *The Frontiers of Drama*. London: Methuen, 1964 (1st edn. 1945).

Empson, William. *Faustus and the Censor: The English Faust-book and Marlowe's Doctor Faustus*. Oxford: Basil Blackwell, 1987.

Erben, Joan. "The Spirit from Below: A Theoretical Approach to Václav Havel's *Temptation*." *European Studies Journal*, 15 (1998): 10–19.

Farrow, John (dir.). *Alias Nick Beal*. Film. 1949.

Fehrenbach, R. J. "A Pre-1592 English Faust Book and the Date of Marlowe's *Doctor Faustus*." *Library*, 2 (2001): 327–35.

Fergusson, Francis. "The Theater of Paul Valéry." In Paul Valéry, *Plays*, trans. David Paul and Robert Fitzgerald, vii–xix. New York: Pantheon, 1960.

Fetters, Paul R. "Dorothy Sayers and the Wiles of the Wicked One as Observed in her Contribution to the Faustus Legend, *The Devil to Pay*." *Inklings Forever*, 5 (2006), unpaginated.

Ficke, Arthur Davison. *Mr. Faust*. Norwood, MA: Plimpson Press, 1913.
   Mr. Faust: An Entirely New Version, Reconstructed for Stage Production. New York: Frank Shay, 1922.

Findlay, Alison. *A Feminist Perspective on Renaissance Drama*. Oxford: Blackwell, 1999.

Fletcher, Angus. "*Doctor Faustus* and the Lutheran Aesthetic." *English Literary Renaissance*, 35 (2005): 187–209.

Fraser, G. S. *Lawrence Durrell: A Critical Study*. New York: E. P. Dutton, 1968.

French, A. L. "The Philosophy of *Dr. Faustus*." *Essays in Criticism*, 20 (1970): 123–42.

French, Marilyn. *Shakespeare's Division of Experience.* New York: Ballantine, 1981.

Fuller, Graham. "Devil's Pact: Goethe's Morality Tale Revisited." *Modern Picture,* 25 (2013): 57.

Gaier, Ulrich. "Schwankende Gestalten: Virtuality in Goethe's *Faust.*" In Schulte, Noyes, and Kleber (eds.), *Theatre of Modernity,* 54–67.

Gardner, Helen. "Milton's 'Satan' and the Theme of Damnation in Elizabethan Tragedy." *English Studies,* 1 (1948): 46–66.

The 1560 Geneva New Testament. ed. David L. Brown and William H. Noah. Murfreesboro, TN: Avalon Press, 2005.

Ghelderode, Michel de. *The Death of Doctor Faust,* in Michel de Ghelderode, *Seven Plays,* trans. George Hauger, vol. 11. New York: Hill & Wang, 1950.

Gilman, Ernest B. *The Curious Perspective: Literary and Pictorial Wit in the Seventeenth Century.* New Haven, CT: Yale University Press, 1978.

Goethe, Johann Wolfgang von. *Faust, Part I & II,* ed. and trans. Charles E. Passage. Indianapolis: Bobbs-Merrill, 1965.

Faust. Part One, trans. David Luke. Oxford University Press, 2008 (1st edn. 1987).

Faust. Part Two, trans. David Luke. Oxford University Press, 1998 (1st edn. 1984).

Faust: A Tragedy, trans. Walter Arndt, ed. Cyrus Hamlin. 2nd edn. New York: W. W. Norton, 2001 (1st edn. 1976).

Goetz-Stankiewicz, Marketa. "Variations of Temptation – Václav Havel's Politics of Language." In Marketa Goetz-Stankiewicz and Phyllis Carey (eds.), *Critical Essays on Václav Havel,* 228–42. New York: G. K. Hall, 1999.

Grantley, Darryll. "'What means this Show?': Theatricalism, Camp, and Subversion in *Doctor Faustus* and *The Jew of Malta.*" In Darryll Grantley and Peter Roberts (eds.), *Christopher Marlowe and English Renaissance Culture,* 224–38. Aldershot: Scolar Press, 1996.

Gray, Richard T. "Shipwreck with Spectators: Ideologies of Observation in Goethe's *Faust,* Part II." In Richter and Block (eds.), *Goethe's Ghosts,* 126–48.

Greg, W. W. "The Damnation of Faustus." *Modern Language Review,* 41/2 (1946): 97–107.

Grode, Eric. "Dueling Mentors Bedevil a Dithering Young Dane." New York Times, March 30, 2011.

Haile, H. G. "Introduction" to H. G. Haile (ed.), *The History of Doctor Johann Faustus.* Urbana: University of Illinois Press, 1965.

Hamlin, Cyrus. "The Composition of *Faust.*" In Goethe, *Faust,* ed. Hamlin, 505–13.

"Interpretive Notes." In Goethe, *Faust,* ed. Hamlin, 345–492.

"Tracking the Eternal-Feminine in Goethe's *Faust II.*" In Brown et al. (eds.), *Interpreting Goethe's Faust Today,* 142–57.

Hardison, O. B. *Christian Rite and Christian Drama in the Middle Ages.* Baltimore, MD: Johns Hopkins University Press, 1965.

Hart, Gail K. "Das Ewig-Weibliche nasführet dich: Feminine Leadership in Goethe's *Faust* and Sacher-Masoch's *Venus.*" In Brown et al. (eds.), *Interpreting Goethe's Faust Today,* 112–22.

Harvey, Dennis. "Review: 'Dr. Faustus.'" *Variety*, March 9, 2004, variety.com/2 004/legit/reviews/dr-faustus-1200534615.

Havel, Václav. *Temptation*, trans. Marie Winn. New York: Grove Press, 1989.

Hawkins, Sherman. "The Education of Faustus." *Studies in English Literature 1500–1900*, 6 (1966): 193–209.

Healy, Thomas. "*Doctor Faustus*." In Patrick Cheney (ed.), *The Cambridge Companion to Christopher Marlowe*, 174–92. Cambridge University Press, 2004.

Hedges, Inez. *Framing Faust: Twentieth-Century Cultural Struggles*. Carbondale: Southern Illinois University Press, 2005.

Heller, Otto. *Faust and Faustus: A Study of Goethe's Relationship to Marlowe*. New York: Cooper Square, 1972.

Hill, Walter (dir.). *Crossroads*. Film. 1986.

Hoelzel, Alfred. *The Paradoxical Quest: A Study of Faustian Vicissitudes*. New York: Peter Lang, 1988.

Honderich, Pauline. "John Calvin and Doctor Faustus." *Modern Language Review*, 68 (1973): 1–13.

Hone, Joseph M. *W. B. Yeats 1865–1939*. New York: Macmillan, 1943.

Hooker, Richard. *Laws of Ecclesiastical Polity*, in *The Works of Richard Hooker*, ed. John Keble, vol. 11. New York: Burt Franklin Press, 1888.

Hughes, Paul L., and James F. Larkin (eds.). *Royal Tudor Proclamations*. 3 vols. New Haven, CT: Yale University Press, 1964–69.

Hunter, G. K. "Five-Act Structure in 'Doctor Faustus.'" *Tulane Drama Review*, 8/ 4 (1964): 77–91.

Hurwitt, Robert. "Wittenberg Review: A Pop Culture Hamlet Primer." SFGate, April 24, 2014.

Hutcheon, Linda. *A Theory of Adaptation*. London: Routledge, 2006.

Ilgner, Richard. "Goethe's 'Geist, der stets vemeint' and its Emergence in the Faust Works of Odoevvsky, Lunacharsky, and Bulgakov." *Germano-Slavica: A Canadian Journal of Germanic and Slavic Comparative Studies*, 2 (1977): 169–80.

Ingram, R. W. "'Pride in learning goeth before a fall': Dr. Faustus' Opening Soliloquy." *Mosaic*, 13/1 (Fall 1979): 73–80.

Irving, Washington. *The Devil and Tom Walker*. Woodstock, VT: R & A Colton, 1830.

James VI and I (King). *Daemonologie*. A facsimile edn. Amsterdam: Da Capo Press, 1969 (1st edn. 1597.)

John, David G. "The Complete *Faust* on Stage: Peter Stein and the Goetheanum." In Lorna Fitzsimmons (ed.), *Goethe's Faust and Cultural Memory*, 107–28. Bethlehem, PA: Lehigh University Press, 2012.

Johnson, Francis R. "Marlowe's Astronomy and Renaissance Skepticism." *English Literary History*, 13 (1946): 241–54.

"Marlowe's 'Imperiall Heaven.'" *English Literary History*, 12 (1945): 35–44.

Jones, Caryn. "A Passive Faust Goes to the Devil Slowly." *New York Times*, October 26, 1994.

Jones, John Henry (ed.). *The English Faust Book: A Critical Edition Based on the Text of 1592*. Cambridge University Press, 1994.

"Introduction" and "Postscript" to Empson, *Faustus and the Censor*.

Jump, John D. "Introduction" to Christopher Marlowe, *Doctor Faustus*. ed. John D. Jump. Revels Plays. London: Methuen, 1962.

Kahler, Erich. "Doctor Faustus from Adam to Sartre." *Comparative Drama*, 1/2 (1967): 75–92.

Kaufmann, Walter. "Editor's Note" to *Thus Spoke Zarathustra*. In *The Portable Nietzsche*, ed. and trans. Walter Kaufmann, 115–90. New York: Viking, 1968.

Keefer, Michael H. "Right Eye and Left Heel: Ideological Origins of the Legend of Faustus." *Mosaic*, 22 (1989): 83–84.

Kelley, Michael. *Flamboyant Drama: A Study of The Castle of Perseverance, Mankind, and Wisdom*. Carbondale: Southern Illinois University Press, 1979.

Kelly, Henry Ansgar. *The Devil, Demonology, and Witchcraft: The Development of Christian Beliefs in Evil Spirits*. New York: Doubleday, 1974 (1st edn. 1968).

Kemp, Philip. Review of "Faust." *Sight and Sound*, 24/9 (September 2014): 112.

Kennedy, George A. "Introduction" to Sand, *Seven Strings of the Lyre*.

Kernan, Alvin B. *The Playwright as Magician: Shakespeare's Image of the Poet in the English Public Theatre*. New Haven, CT: Yale University Press, 1979.

Kiebuzińska, Christine. "Witkacy and Ghelderode: Goethe's *Faust* Transformed into a Grotesque Cabaret." *Polish Journal of Aesthetics*, 31 (2013): 207–20.

Kiessling, Nicolas. "Doctor Faustus and the Sin of Demoniality." *Studies in English Literature 1500–1900*, 15 (1975): 205–11.

King, Christa Knellwolf. *Faustus and the Promises of the New Science, c. 1580–1730*. Farnham: Ashgate, 2008.

Kirschbaum, Leo. "Marlowe's *Faustus*: A Reconsideration," *Review of English Studies*, 19/75 (1943): 225–41.

Kocher, Paul. *Christopher Marlowe: A Study of His Thought, Learning, and Character*. Chapel Hill: University of North Carolina Press, 1946.

Kolve, V. A. *The Play Called Corpus Christi*. Stanford University Press, 1966.

Kramer, Heinrich, and James Sprenger. *The Malleus Maleficarum of Heinrich Kramer and James Sprenger*, trans. Montague Summers, vol. 1. New York: Dover, 1971.

La Primaudaye, Pierre de, *The French Academie*. London, 1605.

Lessing, Gotthold Ephraim. "Seventeenth Letter on Literature" and "Berlin Scenario." In SFT, 274–79. New York: Octagon, 1966.

Werke, ed. Herbert G. Göpfert. 8 vols. Munich: Carl Hanser Verlag, 1970–79.

Lester, G. A. (ed.), *Three Late Medieval Morality Plays: Mankind, Everyman, Mundus et Infans*. New Mermaids. London: A & C Black, 1981.

Levin, Harry. *Christopher Marlowe: The Overreacher*. Boston: Beacon Press, 1962 (1st edn. 1952).

Logan, Robert A. *Shakespeare, Antony and Cleopatra, and the Nature of Fame*. Kalamazoo, MI: Medieval Institute Publications, 2018.

Shakespeare's Marlowe: The Influence of Christopher Marlowe on Shakespeare's Artistry. Aldershot: Ashgate, 2007.

"Violence, Terrorism, and War." In Sara Munson Deats, Lagretta Tallent Lenker, and Merry G. Perry (eds.), *War and Words: Horror and Heroism in the Literature of Warfare*, 65–81. New York: Lexington, 2004.

Lunacharski, A. V. *Three Plays of A. V. Lunacharski*, trans. Leonard Arthur Magnus and Karl Walker. London: George Routledge & Sons, 1923.

Lunney, Ruth. *Marlowe and the Popular Tradition*. Manchester University Press, 2002.

MacCulloch, Diarmaid. *Christianity: The First Three Thousand Years*. New York: Viking, 2010.

Maguire, Laurie. *Helen of Troy: From Homer to Hollywood*. Oxford: Wiley-Blackwell, 2009.

Mamet, David. *Faustus*. New York: Vintage, 2004.

Marcus, Leah S. "Epilogue: Marlowe *in tempore belli*." In Sara Munson Deats, Lagretta Tallent Lenker, and Merry G. Perry (eds.), *War and Words: Horror and Heroism in the Literature of Warfare*, 295–316. New York: Lexington, 2004.

"Textual Indeterminacy and Ideological Difference: The Case of *Doctor Faustus*." *Renaissance Drama*, n.s. 20 (1989): 1–29.

Marlowe, Christopher. *Doctor Faustus: The A- and B-Texts (1604, 1616)*, ed. David Bevington and Eric Rasmussen. Manchester University Press, 1993.

Doctor Faustus and Other Plays, ed. David Bevington and Eric Rasmussen. Oxford University Press, 1995.

McAdam, Ian. *The Irony of Identity: Self and Imagination in the Drama of Christopher Marlowe*. Newark: University of Delaware Press, 1999.

McAteer, Michael. *Yeats and the European Drama*. Cambridge University Press, 2010.

McCullen, Joseph T. "*Dr. Faustus* and Renaissance Learning." *Modern Language Review*, 51 (1956): 6–16.

Mebane, John. *Renaissance Magic and the Return of the Golden Age*. Lincoln: University of Nebraska Press, 1989.

Mills, David (ed.). *The Chester Mystery Cycle: A New Edition with Modernised Spelling*. East Lansing, MI: Colleagues Press, 1992.

Moretti, Franco. "Goethe's *Faust* as a Modern Epic." In Goethe, *Faust*, ed. Hamlin, 611–33.

Mountfort, William. *The Life and Death of Doctor Faustus: Made into a Farce*. London: Printed and sold by E. Whitelock near Stationers' Hall, 1697.

Murnau, F. W. (dir.). *Faust*. Film. 1926.

Nemoianu, Virgil. "Absorbing Modernization: The Dilemmas of Progress in the Novels of Walter Scott and in *Faust II*." In Brown *et al.* (eds.), *Interpreting Goethe's Faust Today*, 1–16.

Nuttall, A. D. *The Alternative Trinity: Gnostic Heresy in Marlowe, Milton, and Blake*. Oxford: Clarendon Press, 1998.

Okerlund, A. N. "The Intellectual Folly of Dr. Faustus." *Studies in Philology*, 74 (1977): 258–78.

Ornstein, Robert. "The Comic Synthesis in *Doctor Faustus*." *English Literary History*, 22 (1955): 165–72.

Palmer, Philip Mason, and Robert Pattison More. *The Sources of the Faust Tradition: From Simon Magus to Lessing*. New York: Octagon, 1966.

Parker, Alan. *Angel Heart*. Film. 1987.

Parker, Barbara. "'Cursed Necromancy': Marlowe's *Faustus* as Anti-Catholic Satire." *Marlowe Studies*, 1 (2011): 59–77.

Parker, John. *The Aesthetics of Antichrist*. Ithaca, NY: Cornell University Press, 2007.

Pelikan, Jaroslav. "Faust as Doctor of Theology." In Goethe, *Faust*, ed. Hamlin, 586–97.

Phelan, Anthony. "The Classical and the Medieval in *Faust II*." In Bishop (ed.), *Companion to Goethe's Faust*, 143–67.

Pilz, Dirk. "A Contradictory Whole: Peter Stein stages *Faust*." In Schulte, Noyes, and Kleber (eds.), *Theatre of Modernity*, 280–92.

Poole, Kristin. "*Dr. Faustus* and Reformation Theology." In Garrett Sullivan, Jr., Patrick Cheney, and Andrew Hadfield (eds.), *Early Modern English Drama: A Critical Companion*, 96–107. Oxford University Press, 2006.

Ramis, Harold. *Bedazzled*. Film. 2000.

Rayns, Tony. "*Faust*." *Sight and Sound*, 22/6 (2012): 53.

Reich, Ronni. "'Wittenberg' Review: Hamlet and Faustus as Bros with Big Ideas." *Star-Ledger*, September 16, 2014.

Reynolds, James A. "Faustus' Flawed Learning." *English Studies*, 57 (1976): 329–36.

Ribner, Irving. "Introduction" to Christopher Marlowe, *The Complete Plays*, ed. Irving Ribner. New York: Odyssey Press, 1963.

Richter, Simon, and Richard Block (eds.), *Goethe's Ghosts: Reading and the Persistence of Literature*. New York: Camden House, 2013.

Riggs, David. *The World of Christopher Marlowe*. New York: Henry Holt, 2005.

Roberts, Gareth. "Necromantic Books: Christopher Marlowe, *Doctor Faustus*, and Agrippa of Nettesheim." In Darryll Grantley and Peter Roberts (eds.), *Christopher Marlowe and English Renaissance Culture*, 148–71. Aldershot: Scolar Press, 1996.

Robertson, Ritchie. "Literary Techniques and Aesthetic Texture in *Faust*." In Bishop (ed.), *Companion to Goethe's Faust*, 1–27.

Rose, William. "Introduction" to William Rose (ed.), *The Historie of the Damnable Life and Deserved Death of Doctor John Faustus*. University of Notre Dame Press, 1963.

Roston, Murray. *Biblical Drama in England*. Evanston, IL: Northwestern University Press, 1968.

Rupp, E. Gordon and Philip S. Watson (ed. and trans.). *Luther and Erasmus: Free Will and Salvation*. Philadelphia: Westminster Press, 1969.

Russell, Jeffrey Burton. *Mephistopheles: The Devil in the Modern World*. Ithaca, NY: Cornell University Press, 1986.

Rutter, Tom. *The Cambridge Introduction to Christopher Marlowe*. Cambridge University Press, 2012.

Sachs, Ariel. "The Religious Despair of Doctor Faustus." *Journal of English and German Philology*, 63 (1964): 625–47.

Sam, Martina Maria. *Rudolf Steiners Faust-Rezeption: Interpretationen und Imaginationen als Vorbereitung der Welturaufführung des gesamten Goetheschen Faust 1938.* Basel: Schwabe Verlag, 2011.

Sand, George. *A Woman's Version of the Faust Legend: The Seven Strings of the Lyre,* trans. and ed. George A. Kennedy. Chapel Hill: University of North Carolina Press, 1989.

Sanders, Julie. *Adaptation and Appropriation.* London: Routledge, 2006.

Sanders, Wilbur. *The Dramatist and the Received Idea: Studies in the Plays of Marlowe and Shakespeare.* Cambridge University Press, 1968.

Santayana, George. *Three Philosophical Poets: Lucretius, Dante, and Goethe.* New York: Doubleday, 1938 (1st edn. 1910.)

Sayers, Dorothy. *The Devil to Pay.* New York: Harcourt, Brace, 1939.

Schlueter, June. *Metafictional Characters in Modern Drama.* New York: Columbia University Press, 1977.

Schöfsler, Franziska. "Progress and Restorative Utopia in *Faust II* and *Wilhelm Meisters Wanderjahre.*" In Bishop (ed.), *Companion to Goethe's Faust,* 169–93.

Schulte, Hans. "Introduction" to Schulte, Noyes, and Kleber (eds.), *Theatre of Modernity.* Cambridge University Press, 2011.

Schulte, Hans, John Noyes, and Pia Kleber (eds.), *Goethe's Faust: Theatre of Modernity.* Cambridge University Press, 2011.

Schweitzer, Christoph E. "Gretchen and the Feminine in Goethe's *Faust.*" In Brown *et al.* (eds.), *Interpreting Goethe's Faust Today,* 133–41.

Shafer, Ingrid H. "'The Phenomenon of Faust': The Faust Challenge: Science as Diabolic or Divine." *Zygon: Journal of Religion and Science,* 40/4 (December 2005): 891–915.

Shapiro, James. *Rival Playwrights: Marlowe, Jonson, Shakespeare.* New York: Columbia University Press, 1991.

The Shorter Oxford English Dictionary, rev. and ed. C. T. Onions. Oxford: Clarendon Press, 1968.

Sidnell, Michael J., and Wayne K. Chapman, "Introduction" to W. B. Yeats, *The Countess Cathleen: Manuscript Materials,* ed. Michael J. Sidnell and Wayne K. Chapman. Ithaca, NY: Cornell University Press, 1999.

Simpson, Patricia Anne. "Gretchen's Ghosts: Goethe, Adorno, and the Literature of Refuge." In Richter and Block (eds.), *Goethe's Ghosts,* 168–85.

Singer, Robert. "The Merlin/Faust Archetypes in Excalibur and Angel Street," in Charlotte Spivack (ed.), *Merlin Versus Faust: Contending Archetypes in Western Culture,* 95–113. Lewiston, NY: Edwin Mellen Press, 1992.

"One Against All: The New England Past and Present Responsibilities in *The Devil and Daniel Webster.*" *Literature/Film Quarterly,* 22 (1994): 265–71.

Smith, James. "Marlowe's *Dr. Faustus.*" *Scrutiny,* 8/1 (1939–40): 48–49.

Snyder, Susan. "The Left Hand of God: Despair in the Medieval and Renaissance Tradition." *Studies in the Renaissance,* 12 (1965): 18–59.

Sokurov, Alexander. *Faust.* Film. 2011.

Spinard, Phoebe S. "The Dilettante Lie in *Doctor Faustus.*" *Texas Studies in Literature and Language,* 24 (1982): 243–54.

Spivack, Bernard. *Shakespeare and the Allegory of Evil.* New York: Columbia University Press, 1958.

Stachniewski, John. *The Persecutory Imagination: English Puritanism and the Literature of Religious Despair.* Oxford University Press, 1991.

Stambaugh, Sara. "Review of *A Woman's Version of the Faust Legend: The Seven Strings of the Lyre.*" *Victorian Review,* 16/1 (1990): 83–85.

Stein, Peter. "Directing *Faust*: An Interview." In Schulte, Noyes, and Kleber (eds.), *Theatre of Modernity,* 267–79. Cambridge University Press, 2011.

Sterritt, David. "'I Married a Witch' and 'The Beauty of the Devil.'" *Cineaste,* 39/2 (2014): 50–52.

Stoll, Elmer Edgar. "The Objectivity of the Ghosts in Shakspere." *PMLA,* 22/2 (1907): 201–33.

Stravinsky, Igor. "Valéry: A Memoir." In Paul Valéry, *Plays,* trans. David Paul and Robert Fitzgerald, xx–xxv. New York: Pantheon, 1960.

Švankmajer, Jan (dir.). *Faust.* Film. 2003.

Swales, Martin. "The Character and Characterization of Faust." In Bishop (ed.), *Companion to Goethe's Faust,* 28–55.

'Theater Abroad: Goethe Go Home.' *Time Magazine,* 83/1 (January 3 1964): 56.

The Thirty-Nine Articles of the Church of England. London: Printed in Powles Church Yard by Richard Jugg and John Cawood, 1563.

Tobin, Robert. "Faust's Membership in Male Society: Prometheus and Ganymede as Models." In Brown *et al.* (eds.), *Interpreting Goethe's Faust Today,* 17–28.

Traister, Barbara Howard. *Heavenly Necromancy: The Magician in English Renaissance Drama.* Columbia: University of Missouri Press, 1984.

Ure, Peter. "The Evolution of Yeats's *The Countess Cathleen,*" *Modern Language Review,* 57 (1962): 12–24.

Vaget, Hans Rudolf. "The Ethics of Faust's Last Action." In Goethe, *Faust,* ed. Hamlin, 704–14.

Vetterling-Braggin, Mary (ed.). *"Femininity," "Masculinity," and "Androgyny": A Modern Philosophical Discussion.* Totowa, NJ: Rowman & Littlefield, 1982.

Ward, A. W. (ed.). *Old English Drama: Select Plays.* Oxford: Clarendon Press, 1892.

Ward, Philip. "Introduction" to Frank Wedekind, *Franziska,* trans. Philip Ward. Adapted by Eleanor Brown. London: Oberon, 1998.

Warren, Michael J. "*Doctor Faustus:* The Old Man and the Text." *English Literary Renaissance,* 11 (1981): 111–47.

Waswo, Richard. "Damnation, Protestant Style: Macbeth, Faustus, and Christian Tragedy." *Journal of Medieval and Renaissance Studies,* 4 (1974): 63–99.

Watanabe, Nancy. "Yeats's Merlin-Faust Design in *The Countess Cathleen.*" In Charlotte Spivack (ed.), *Merlin Versus Faust: Contending Archetypes in Western Culture,* 139–59. Lewiston, NY: Edwin Mellen Press, 1992.

Watt, Ian. *Myths of Modern Individualism: Faust, Don Quixote, Don Juan, Robinson Crusoe.* Cambridge University Press, 1996.

Weiss, Suzanne. "Dr. Faustus – David Mamet." Culture Vulture, March 3, 2004, http://culturevulture.net/theater/dr-faustus-david-mamet.

West, Robert Hunter. *The Invisible World: A Study in Pneumatology in Elizabethan Drama*. New York: Octagon, 1969 (1st edn. 1939).

Westlund, Joseph. "The Orthodox Christian Framework of Marlowe's *Faustus*." *Studies in English Literature 1500–1900*, 3 (1963): 191–205.

White, Rob. "Fiendish." *Film Quarterly*, 65/2 (2011): 7.

Willeke, Audrone B. "Frank Wedekind and the 'Frauenfrage.'" *Monatshefte*, 72/1 (1980): 26–38.

Williams, John R. "The Problem of the Mothers." In Bishop (ed.), *Companion to Goethe's Faust*, 122–43.

Wilmington, Michael. "Svankmajer's 'Faust': A Nightmare Not Easily Forgotten." *Chicago Tribune*, February 24, 1995.

Wolff, Eugen. *Faust und Luther: Ein Beitrag zur Entstehung der Faustdichtung*. Halle: Max Niemeyer Verlag, 1912.

Yeats, W. B. *The Countess Cathleen: Manuscript Materials*, ed. Michael J. Sidnell and Wayne K. Chapman. Ithaca, NY: Cornell University Press, 1999.

The Letters of W. B. Yeats, ed. Allan Wade. New York: Macmillan, 1955.

Yirinec, Jennifer. "Re-envisioning the Faust Legend: Christopher Marlowe's *The Tragical History of Doctor Faustus* and Richard Burton and Nevill Coghill's *Doctor Faustus*." *Literature/Film Quarterly*, 41 (2013): 67–77.

Young, Andrea Louise. *Vision and Audience in Medieval Drama: A Study of the Castle of Perseverance*. London: Routledge, 2015.

Index

257